AF674262

NO STRINGS ATTACHED?

India's Policies and Foreign Aid

1947–1966

Centre de Sciences Humaines (Centre for Social Sciences and Humanities): Created in New Delhi in 1989 the CSH, is part of network of research centres of the French Ministry of Foreign Affairs. The Centre's research work is primarily oriented towards the study of issues concerning the contemporary dynamics of development in India and South Asia. The activities of the Centre are focused on four main themes, namely: Economic growth and sustainable development, International and regional relations, Institutional structures and political constructions of identity and Urban dynamics.

(Centre de Sciences Humaines, 2, Aurangzeb Road, New Delhi 110011, India, Tel: (91 11) 23 01 62 59/23 01 41 73, Fax: (91 11) 23 01 84 80, E-mail: public@csh-delhi.com, Website: http://www.csh-delhi.com)

Institut Français de Pondichéry (French Institute of Pondicherry): Created in 1955, the IFP is a multidisciplinary research and advanced educational institute. Major research works are focusing on Sanskrit and Tamil languages and literatures—in close collaboration with the *Ecole Française d'Extrême-Orient*—ecosystems, biodiversity and sustainability, dynamics of population and socio-economic development.

(Institut Français de Pondichéry, 11, Saint Louis Street, P.B. 33 Pondicherry 605 001, Tel: (91 413) 23 34 170/23 34 168, Telex: 469224 FRAN-In, Fax: (91 413) 23 39 534, E-mail: ifpdir@ifpindia.org, Website: http://www.ifpindia.org.)

NO STRINGS ATTACHED?

India's Policies and Foreign Aid
1947–1966

GILLES BOQUÉRAT

MANOHAR

CENTRE DE SCIENCES HUMAINES
2003

First published 2003

© Gilles Boquérat, 2003

All rights reserved. No part of this publication may be reproduced or transmitted, in any form or by any means, without prior permission of the author and the publisher

ISBN 81–7304–513–5

Published by

Ajay Kumar Jain for
Manohar Publishers & Distributors
4753/23 Ansari Road, Daryaganj
New Delhi 110 002

Typeset at

Digigrafics
New Delhi 110 049

Printed at

Lordson Publishers Pvt Ltd
Delhi 110 007

Contents

PART IV
INDIA AT THE CROSSROADS OF AID (1961-1966)

Preface

THE CORE OF THIS BOOK is a doctoral thesis submitted to the Paris I-Sorbonne University in 1991, before the formal dismantling of the USSR. The new international configuration which emerged during the last decade could lead one to question the topicality of a study dealing with non-alignment and the confrontation between the two power blocs of the Cold War. The world has indeed changed, revered concepts have become outdated, if not been discarded, and new partnerships have emerged. Yet, one has to go back to the 'Nehruvian years' if only to make a correct appraisal of the magnitude of the changes and assess the significance of the end of the Cold War for India and on its margin for policy manoeuvre. Today's perceptions of those years tend to be sometimes disconnected from their historical context. What brought me also to revise the original text is the opening of American, British, and French diplomatic records covering the last part of this study. I have also made use of the most recently released collections of documents and memoirs.

I would like to especially acknowledge the following institutions which have helped in the preparation of this study: the *Centre de Sciences Humaines*, New Delhi; the School of International Studies, Jawaharlal Nehru University; the Nehru Memorial Library & Museum; the library of the Indian Council of World Affairs; the *Bibliothèque de Documentation Internationale Contemporaine*; the *Archives du Quai d'Orsay,* Paris; the Public Record Office, London; and the French Ministry of Foreign Affairs whose financial support allowed me to spend some unforgettable years in India. Last but not the least, I would like to thank Fabienne, Simon and Hugo for their comforting presence and spare a thought for Clément, whom we miss very much.

New Delhi GILLES BOQUÉRAT
May 2003

Introduction

As a general rule, when a state decides to give aid to another state, it does not do so for purely altruistic reasons, independent of all political, strategic, or economic considerations. Among the motives of donor countries could be the strengthening of a military alliance, obtaining diplomatic support, ensuring the supply of raw materials, penetrating into foreign markets, or, more generally, influencing the political developments or the economic orientations of the aid recipient country. Even food aid is not devoid of ulterior motives of a political nature nor is it above hard bargaining by both sides. Aid is a means to obtain from the receiving country a change of policies or merely their continuance; it can assume forms that are clearly evident or which may be more subtle and not easily perceptible, their range extending from outright denial, to reductions or delays in its granting, to modifications in the terms of the aid agreement.

Whether economic or military, aid is all the more likely to be utilized to bring to bear on the political decisions of the recipient country when, as in the case that we are concerned with, the donor states are two superpowers with differing political, economic, and social systems, and which, moreover, have embarked on a Cold War in which each seeks to rally to its cause the largest number of countries. Among these, India, on account of its size, its geopolitical importance in a continent engaged in the decolonization process, and its human and natural resources, could have hardly been ignored by the American and Soviet governments. But, while in the context of a bipolarized world, it was imperative for India's development not to set aside foreign aid and capital, the country asserted its refusal to align itself with either one of the rival camps and, professed to be particularly disapproving of any encroachment on its sovereignty. It is, therefore, interesting to see how India endeavoured to conciliate two apparently antinomic acknowledged facts: the safeguard of political independence, on the one hand, and an evolving situation of economic dependence *vis-à-vis* the aid-giving countries, on the other hand. The focus of this study is the interaction between political choices and economic contingencies.

In the relations maintained by India with the United States or the Soviet Union, aid could, therefore, not be considered solely in its aspect of assistance to an underdeveloped country whose comparative advantages could be discussed with reference to purely economic criteria. Indian leaders were abundantly aware of the political or economic 'strings' attached to foreign aid programmes. Nehru once confided 'It is true that whenever a country depends upon another for aid, a certain obligation comes in and a certain involuntary dependence.'[1] To avoid this risk, the Indian government considered foreign aid, in the wake of independence, with caution. Since recourse to it appeared inevitable, it was hoped that it would be resorted to within limits. But it was precisely the reverse that happened. Food shortages, balance of payments deficits, ambitious industrialization projects, all these resulted in the increasingly large place that foreign aid came to occupy in the process of economic development.

By foreign aid, we mean all transfers of financial resources or know-how from a state or an international organization to another state, or even to its private sector, on terms that are more favourable for the receiving country than the normal conditions prevailing in the world capital and labour markets. It excludes, apart from private investments, short-term repayable loans, particularly those of the IMF. Foreign private capital could, nevertheless, enter into our picture to the extent that for the donor country it could potentially compete with public aid as a source of funding. It needs to be recalled that only grants constitute full-fledged aid, while loans are only partially subsidies, the importance of these varying according to the rate of interest, the length of the maturity period, and the grace period, or again, according to the currency in which the loan is to be repaid. The fact that the loan is linked to its source, that is to say, the requirement that the goods and services have to be procured from the donor country at prices sometimes above the prevailing international market price, can also reduce the real value of the aid.

This study covers the period from the Independence of the country in August 1947 to the Tashkent Conference of January 1966 whose object was to bring some stability in the subcontinent in the wake of the second India-Pakistan war. These years have been chosen for several reasons. The first is that the sudden death of Prime Minister

Lal Bahadur Shastri at the end of this conference, nineteen months after he took office, and the accession to power of Indira Gandhi as his successor, laid the final seal on the Nehru era. This chapter in the history of post-colonial India was dominated by the personality of Jawaharlal Nehru, who was from Independence till his death on 27 May 1964, not only the Prime Minister but also the Minister of External Affairs as well as the chairman of the Planning Commission. The second reason is that this period covers the first three five year plans—from 1951 to 1966—which are often treated as being distinct from the subsequent plans; this is because first, there was a chronological break after these plans following a deep economic crisis (the Fourth Plan only started in 1969); second, because during these fifteen years, an essential stage was crossed in the definition of a development strategy which was intended to be the erection of a self-reliant economic structure. The third and last reason which determined the choice of the Tashkent Conference as the point at which this study concludes is that this event came to confirm the growing role played by the Soviet Union in the affairs of the subcontinent, a region from which it had been completely absent in the early 1950s.

The subject of American and Soviet aid to India has been dealt with in various works, whether published in India, in the Anglo-American world or in the Soviet Union. But the aid factor has often been diluted in overall studies of bilateral relations with the USA and the USSR or seen from the angle of the economic assistance to Third World Countries at large. Few works have drawn a parallel between these two sources of aid in the specific case of India, and even fewer have covered both economic aid and military assistance in their analyses. The present study also emphasizes reactions on the Indian side, not just of the government but also those of the press and the business circles, to the foreign aid determinants of the aid-giving countries. Since the issue here is to determine whether a direct relationship may have existed between certain political decisions and the imperative necessity for taking recourse to foreign aid, we have also focused on development plans and programmes and on the hazards of the economic situation which had a direct bearing on the capacity of the donor states to exert pressure.

This study is divided into four parts or sections and follows a chronological sequence. The first section is primarily devoted to the study of the evolution of policy in the economic field and in foreign relations in the immediate post-Independence period. Since India had to obtain foreign aid in response to an economic necessity to achieve its development targets, it is necessary to begin by outlining the economic structure in India at the end of the 1940s. This involves an investigation of the role assigned to the state in designing and evolving the strategy of industrialization and the place assigned within it to foreign funding (Chapter 1). We then examine the economic justifications for resorting to aid, as well as the political risks that such a step might involve (Chapter 2). The first part concludes with an analysis of the reasons, internal as well as external, which led India to opt for a foreign policy whose main characteristic was a refusal to recognize the logic of military blocs at a point of time when this bipolar division of the world crystallized (Chapter 3).

The second part covers the period 1947-55. It is dominated by India's ambivalent attitude *vis-à-vis* the American aid policy, since there was no question then of the Indian government counting on any Soviet aid whatsoever. It may be noted that before the Second World War, Indo-American relations were minimal and Indo-Soviet relations were non-existent, as Great Britain had always sought to protect its colony from the supposedly competitive powers. Chapter 4 examines the arguments presented by Moscow to justify its hostility towards the Indian government despite the fact that the latter expressed its readiness to develop friendly relations with a country which had, in a certain way, fascinated Indian nationalists during their struggle for independence. In the light of the attitude adopted by the Roosevelt administration during the war and by the Truman administration after the war, Indian leaders considered with some misgiving the possibility of having to rely, should the need arise, on US capital, whether public or private; as it was clear to the Indians that there was sometimes little in common between the ideals that were professed and their practice (Chapter 5).

Very soon after Independence Indians and Americans discovered that their views differed considerably. To the Americans, obsession with the containment of communism and their determination to promote a liberal model of development, requiring notably the opening up of India to foreign investments, the Indian government responded by professing its adherence to non-alignment, its intention to establish a mixed economy, and expressed its reservations over the role of foreign private capital. It was readily accepted in India that it was these differences which explained the lack of eagerness of the United States to give financial assistance to it (Chapter 6). China, Korea, Kashmir: all these subjects of discord were uppermost in the mind of the US Congress, when during the first half of 1951, it debated its response to the request from India for food aid (Chapter 7). The first American programme of aid to India was to begin in 1952, the year which also witnessed the drawing up of the First Five-Year Plan. What reasons led the United States to conclude that the granting of such aid was necessary, even though New Delhi was adopting, in the mid-1950s, an increasingly critical attitude towards its policy of military alliances in Asia? This question is considered in Chapter 8.

The third part, covering the period 1955-61, opens with the willingness of the Soviet Union to compete with the West in extending economic aid to the non-communist world. This shift in policy was in line with a process of political advances or overtures being made to Asian countries headed by the national bourgeoisie, replacing the earlier antagonizing two-camps theory. What reasons motivated Moscow to take a particular interest in a rapprochement with India? This question is considered in Chapter 9. Washington could obviously not remain indifferent in the face of the challenge thrown by the Soviets, at a time, moreover, when India had another challenge to face, that of an ambitious Second Five-Year Plan (Chapter 10). The success of this plan was soon compromised by a serious foreign exchange crisis which led Indian Ministers and officials to set aside their aversion seeking aid and to approach Washington for help. The American response is dealt with in Chapter 11. Chapter 12 examines the widening of the industrial cooperation between India and the USSR to new sectors during the second half of the 1950s, and the role that the consolidation of the bonds between these two countries may have played in the deteriorating Sino-Soviet relations.

The fourth part, covering the period 1961-6, focuses on India's growing dependence on foreign aid during its Third Five-Year Plan. Chapter 13 looks at Indo-US relations following the election of John F. Kennedy who had shown keen interest in India's development as a response to the challenge posed by the model of growth proposed by China. Chapter 14 analyses the India-China war of 1962, India's decision to seek military aid, and the doubts which subsequently emerged regarding the purity of non-alignment. In the mid-1960s, the Indian economy had become heavily dependent on foreign aid to finance its development plans and even to procure supplies of much-needed food grains. In such a situation, it became increasingly difficult for Indian leaders to oppose the conditions fixed by the donor states (Chapter 15). Chapter 16 assesses the respective importance of the American and Soviet aid programmes on India's development. The conclusion returns to the examination of the objectives which had guided the United States and the USSR in their assistance to India and questions whether it impinged on its policies.

NOTE

1. 5 June 1952. J.L. Nehru, *Letters to Chief Ministers*, vol. 3, p. 5.

PART I

An Assertive Nationalism

CHAPTER 1

The Conception of Development

WHEN INDIA achieved Independence in 1947, the country displayed many of the ills that characterize economic underdevelopment. The economy was largely dependent on agriculture which was insufficiently productive to satisfy the needs of a population increasing by around five million per annum. The country had a relatively low level of industrialization and suffered from chronic unemployment and underemployment. Endemic poverty and poor health conditions resulted in an average life expectancy of thirty-two years. The decennial census of 1951 revealed widespread illiteracy; only one person out of six could read and write. The Partition of the subcontinent had contributed to the weakening of the economic infrastructure by severing the complementarity that had existed between what thereafter became Pakistan and India. Moreover, it was necessary to solve the thorny legal and administrative problems involved in the integration of 554 states into the Indian Union, when these did not degenerate into an armed conflict with Pakistan over the question of Kashmir. The newly independent country also had to grapple with the human tragedies resulting from the communal bloodshed which accompanied Partition and the distressing problem of the rehabilitation of refugees which followed it. By 1951, 7.5 million people had migrated to India from East and West Pakistan.

In 1947, three-quarters of the population depended on agriculture for its livelihood; agriculture also accounted for half the national income.[1] Nevertheless, domestic production remained notoriously insufficient and it became necessary in that year to import more than 2 million tons of food grains. Malnutrition and underfeeding were estimated to be prevalent in about 30 per cent of the population.[2] The Bengal famine, which cost some 3 million lives in 1943, was still fresh in people's memories. A study conducted on the period

1891-1947 has shown that the growth in agricultural production of 0.37 per cent—incidentally benefiting more non-food crops than food crops—was clearly below the rate of population increase, which grew at an annual average rate of 0.67 per cent.[3] The disparity between these two parameters sharpened from the 1920s onwards when the demographic growth rate accelerated.

The lack of land reforms, population pressure, and archaic methods of exploitation are all factors which explain the low yields, as also the high degree of susceptibility to climatic hazards. Before Independence, only 24 per cent of the cultivated land was irrigated in undivided India. With Partition, this figure fell to 19 per cent due to the fact that all the well-irrigated lands in Sind and West Punjab went to Pakistan.[4] While harbouring 82 per cent of the population of pre-Partition times, the new state of India could count on only 68 per cent of the rice and 65 per cent of the wheat produced earlier in British India. Following the creation of Pakistan, India's food deficit increased by nearly one million tons, in addition to the deficit of 1.39 million tons caused by the separation of Burma in 1937. The growing recourse to the import of food grains, which went up from 1 million tons in 1935 to 2.9 million tons in 1948 and then to 3.8 million tons in 1949, was barely enough to maintain the fragile balance between supply and demand, which could be endangered from one year to the next by natural calamities. A rationing system had been introduced in 1943, and by December 1947, 148 million people were receiving food rations from governmental agencies either under statutory rationing or through controlled distribution.[5]

Partition had negative repercussions on Indian industry and on the textile sector in particular. It had been written that, while 98 per cent of the cotton mills and all the jute mills were situated in India, 81 per cent of the jute fibre and 40 per cent of the raw cotton came before Independence from areas which became part of Pakistan. Despite these handicaps, the fact remained that following Partition, the large majority of mineral resources and industries were found in Indian territory. Thus, while India lost some small enterprises, it kept 91 per cent of the large industrial establishments.[6] For all that, the share of the secondary sector (mines, industrial establishments, and small enterprises) in the economy represented for the year 1948-9 just 17.1 per cent of the national income. As for modern industry alone—industrial establishments—it provided an occupation to barely 2 per cent of the working population and its share in the national income was only 6.3 per cent.[7] Consumer goods industries were then dominant, representing 80 per cent of the value of the total production of manufactured goods, leaving the smallest share to heavy industry. According to those who drew up the First Five-Year Plan, the output of consumer goods industries, such as textiles, sugar, and salt, was considered relatively satisfactory to meet the existing low level of demand. Conversely, the production of capital and producer goods was considered as being quite inadequate, unable even to satisfy what were rather modest requirements. The production of iron and steel was barely sufficient to meet even 50 per cent of the demand, and it was the same case in the field of heavy chemicals. The energy sector was insufficiently developed. As for the manufacture of machine tools, it was at a rudimentary stage; only the needs of the textile industry began to witness the beginnings of a growth.[8]

Nevertheless, India did have an industrial base at the time of Independence, a good part of which had been built with Indian capital, an achievement which many countries then freeing themselves from colonial rule could envy. National capital had come to encroach more and more on the space occupied by British capital, which was found above all in activities related to exports, leaving the major part of the domestic market to Indian industrialists. It is estimated that in 1948 the share of foreign enterprises in the total industrial production was around 25 per cent.[9]

The Second World War had given a fillip to Indian industry. The shelling of factories in Britain, the entry of Japan into the war, the dislocation of maritime traffic, all these factors forced the Allies to turn towards India to ensure supplies meant for their forces fighting in the military operation zones in the Middle East and the Far East. The industries which had experienced a significant development during the interwar period, such as iron and steel, cotton textiles, paper, cement and coal, operated to full capacity while other sectors, such as light machinery, chemicals and pharmaceuticals, received a substantial impetus. New branches of industrial activity emerged (automobiles, railway equipment, shipbuilding, bicycles, etc.), laying the foundation for the diversification of the industrial sector, which, nevertheless, remained fragile due to the absence of an adequate heavy industry.

The government resolved to respond to the problem of under-development with a deliberate decision to opt for a programme of industrialization in which the state would play a crucial role. André Malraux recalled Nehru saying: 'Nothing since the discovery of non-violence has struck me as forcibly as the development of Soviet Central Asia. And perhaps Europeans do not realize that in Asia today, industrialization is as powerful a myth as Independence was. . . .'[10] For India, rapid industrialization was as much an instrument of modernity and development as a vehicle of national independence and growing assertiveness on the international scene. In 1944, Nehru noted:

> In the context of the modern world no country can be politically and economically independent, even within the framework of international interdependence, unless it is highly industrialized and has developed its power resources to the utmost. Nor can it achieve or maintain high standards of living and liquidate poverty without the aid of modern technology in almost every sphere of life. An industrially backward country will continually upset the world equilibrium and encourage the aggressive tendencies of more developed countries. Even if it retains its political independence, this will be nominal only, and economic control will tend to pass to others.

One had, therefore, to conclude from this assessment that 'an attempt to build up a country's economy largely on the basis of cottage and small-scale industries is doomed to failure. It will not solve the basic problems of the country or maintain freedom, nor will it fit in with the world framework, except as a colonial appendage.'[11] The Gandhian approach, advocating a voluntary limitation of wants and an economy centred around village communities having as much autonomy as possible and based to a limited extent on mechanization, was soon set aside. A development approach of this kind appeared retrograde, as was underlined by the economist Sukhamoy Chakravarty:

> Gandhi and his disciples looked more like moralizing old men than like people who could be expected to change the direction of society. Thus the modernizing school under Nehru won the day as their 'scientism' seemed more compatible with the ideological priorities involved in building up a post-colonial nation-state, although some vestigial traces of the alternative approach remain in the attitude to certain very small-scale industries such as hand-spinning.[12]

Greater emphasis was laid on a state-controlled inward-looking model of industrialization. Apart from the danger of foreign interests exerting their hold over a *laissez-faire* economy, the latter appeared also incompatible with the economic and social objectives that the government was setting for itself, e.g. the creation of an independent economic structure, the gradual reduction of poverty and unemployment, the promotion of equality of opportunities with special attention being given to the uplift of the most deprived among its citizens, a balanced development of all regions, and the prevention of monopolies. The socialization of the economy was a long-held watchword since it was already implied in the resolution of the All India Congress Committee voted in 1929 which specified that 'in order to remove poverty and misery of the Indian people and to ameliorate the conditions of the masses, it is essential to make revolutionary changes in the present economic and social structure of society and to remove gross inequalities'.[13]

There was a wide consensus that in order to optimize the vast human and natural resources of the country to oversee development, and to fulfil the objectives of economic policy, a planned economy was a necessity. The principle of central planning fixing the overall orientations of economic activity gained momentum in the early 1930s, and was retained in 1938 by the Indian National Congress (INC) with the creation of the National Planning Committee headed by Jawaharlal Nehru; this body brought together politicians of all ideological hues and representatives of large industrial and financial groups.[14] During the war, several plans were drawn up, and one of the first acts of the interim government was to set up in October 1946 an Advisory Planning Board entrusted with setting out the objectives, the priorities, and the future machinery of planning. While the formulation of the First Five-Year Plan had to be adjourned for a time on account of the economic crisis that the country experienced during the first three years that followed Independence, it became a priority soon as the situation was favourable. In March 1950, the Planning Commission saw the light of day, with the prime minister as chairman.

To strengthen the means of intervention and of participation of the state in the development process, a nationalization policy had to be adopted. As early as 1931, the AICC, meeting in Bombay, had stipulated that 'the State must own or control key and basic industries and services, mineral resources, railways, waterways, shipping and other means of public transport'.[15] In November 1947, the AICC renewed this commitment, while simultaneously enlarging it, and expressed the view that 'new undertakings in defense, key and public utility industries should be started under public ownership' as well as those which are in the nature of monopolies. In respect of private undertakings already existing in these fields, the process of transfer to public ownership should start after a preparatory period of five years. As regards what remained in the private sector, it would be subjected to 'all such regulations and controls as are needed for the realization of the objective of national policy in the matter of industrial development'.[16]

Till Independence, business circles had not expressed any conflicting views over the necessity for the state to exercise in the interests of the community a considerable measure of intervention and control. They had drawn up the 'Bombay Plan' in 1944, ratified by the Federation of Indian Chambers of Commerce and Industry (FICCI). The purpose of the plan was to transform a predominantly agricultural economy into a more balanced one. The eight co-signatories included the most reputed figures in industrial and financial circles: Jehangir Ratanji Dadabhoy Tata, Ghanashyamdas Birla, Purushottamdas Thakurdas, Kasturbhai Lalbhai, Shri Ram, Ardeshir Dalal, A.D. Shroff, and John Matthai. Some of them had already been members of the National Planning Committee. The objective of this ambitious plan, estimated at Rs. 100 billion spread over a period of fifteen years, was to treble the per capita income at the end of the period—or to double it if allowance was made for the increase of population in the meantime—by banking on an increase of agricultural production by 130 per cent and of industry by 500 per cent, this sector accounting at the end of the plan for 35 per cent of the national income. As long as a satisfactory level of overall industrial development was not achieved, the planners accepted that the country would, for a time, be at the mercy of foreign countries and that, to shorten this period of dependence, it was essential to give priority to basic industries in order to accelerate the development process. Of the investments provided in this plan, 45 per cent were allocated to industry as against only 12 per cent to agriculture. It was acknowledged that 'no economic development of the kind proposed by us would be feasible except on the basis of a central directing authority and further that, in the initial stages of the plan, rigorous measures of State control would be required to prevent an inequitable distribution of the financial burdens involved in it'.[17] While the idea of public ownership of the means of production was less well received, business circles agreed that the state should take charge of those sectors important to public welfare or security and those which required heavy initial investments and whose cost-effectiveness was low, with returns coming in only in the long run.

Once Independence had been achieved, these same circles constantly expressed views much less in favour of state control, not to speak of state ownership when private capital was forthcoming for an enterprise, thus obtaining from the government in end 1947 a decontrol of prices. They also asked for assurances over the safeguard and freedom of action of the private sector by threatening a slowdown on investments. The private sector then constituted more than nine-tenths of the production and of the employment in the industrial sector. To have their points of view heard within the Nehru cabinet, industrialists could count on the support of some Ministers, the foremost being the Deputy Prime Minister and Home Minister, Vallabhbhai Patel, leader of the dominant right wing within the Congress, and the first two finance ministers, Shanmukham Chetty and John Matthai.[18] These business circles were all the more in a position to get their voices heard as the economy was in a state of stagnation and the social situation was explosive. With the stoppage of orders linked to the war and the resumption of imports, the post-war period witnessed a decline in production in most industries. This was true for textiles, jute, steel, and cement whose production in 1946 was below the level reached during the war. Numerous factories had to close down, increasing unemployment. Moreover, the industrial equipment used intensively during the war to satisfy demand and which had not subsequently been replaced with imported machines, had deteriorated or become obsolete. The general index of industrial production which was 120 in 1945—the reference year being 1937—fell to 109 in 1946.[19] Concomitant with the decline in production, and with controls being lifted on the price of food grains and sugar in December 1947, then of cotton and cloth the following month, galloping inflation set in. So much so that the government had to restore the price controls on these products during the second half of 1948 to curb their increase which had reached 30 per cent within a few months. While prices skyrocketed, salaries fell, thus fuelling popular discontent. The deteriorating social climate was reflected in the number of work stoppages and of work days lost, which reached figures in 1946 and 1947 never equalled during the rest of the period under study.[20] The government got down to the task of defusing the crisis of confidence that had set in between the state and the employers and underlined the urgency of boosting production so as to fight unemployment and inflation, preferring to put off to a less troubled time its programme of nationalization. Nehru explained this in February 1948 to the Constituent Assembly:

> Production comes first, and I am prepared to say that everything that we do should be judged from the point of view of production first of all. If nationalization adds to production, we shall have nationalization at every step. If it does not, let us see how to bring it about in order not to impede production. That is the essential thing.[21]

On 6 April 1948, the first industrial policy resolution was formulated. The state reserved to itself the exclusive monopoly on the arms and ammunition industries and on the railways, which it already had, and on the nuclear industry which had yet to be set up. In six other key sectors—coal, iron and steel, aircraft manufacture, shipbuilding, telegraph and wireless apparatus, and mineral resources—the state would have the exclusive responsibility of setting up new enterprises except wherever, in the national interest, it felt it preferable to secure the cooperation of private enterprise. A guarantee was given to those enterprises which already existed in these fields that they would not be nationalized for the next 10 years (the five-year period recommended by the AICC had not been retained), a period at the end of which their status would be reconsidered and fair compensation given in the event of nationalization. The rest of the industrial field was left open to private initiative; however, 18 sectors of activity were considered of special importance for the state to assume the right to regulate and control them. Among these were the automobile, machine tools, heavy chemicals, fertilizers, non-ferrous metals, textiles, salt, cement, sugar, and paper industries.

Business circles, which had feared a more drastic programme of nationalization, were rather favourably inclined towards the industrial policy resolution. Nehru displayed a willingness to be even more reassuring by declaring, during a FICCI meeting in March 1949, that 'we said, even in regard to certain basic and key industries, that we would not touch them for at least ten years, may be more. It did not mean that we would necessarily touch them immediately after the ten years period'.[22] The government, in fact, had then neither the financial nor the physical resources to assume the burden of the transfer to the public sector of a large number of private enterprises and preferred to concentrate its energies on building infrastructure, particularly in the hydroelectric field, and on the creation of new units of production in the public sector rather than in acquiring those that already existed. This choice was confirmed in the First Five Year Plan, in which it was stated that 'the nationalization of existing enterprises has, in our view, only a low priority, especially as most of the purposes of such a transfer of ownership can be served by judicious regulation'.[23]

A mixed economy was seen to be progressively coming into place whose 'commanding heights' would be controlled by the state and which would accord preferential treatment to the public sector. Controls over the private sector were to be exercised through a complex system of licenses, supported by legal enactments. Such Acts included the Industries (Development and Regulation) Act of 1951, whose scope, to begin with, was selective but, over the years, it expanded to cover an ever increasing number of industries, or again the Foreign Exchange Regulations Act and the Import and Export (Control) Act of 1947. This system obliged the private enterprises to obtain permission from government agencies to conduct their operations; these permissions related to the nature of the goods produced, the level of production, the location of the industrial units, the amount of foreign exchange granted for the import of equipment, the prescription of conditions of work and wages for labour, and even the sale prices. While these controls imposed a rigid framework within which private enterprises could function, they derived, in exchange the benefit of a domestic market relatively well protected both from internal competition through the system of permission to produce and from foreign competition through control over imports and over direct investments.

Considering the shortfall in Indian investment, the government turned somewhat timorously towards foreign private capital. There was a legitimate suspicion against foreign private investment in view of the political angle it had acquired in the past. Indians could not forget that the first Britons who had come and settled in India had been merchants and businessmen. When India came under the direct rule of the British crown in 1858, British power had already dominated the country for a century under cover of the East India Company. In his *Glimpses of World History*, published in 1933, Nehru, referring to the control exercised by the United States over

South America through its investments and its financial institutions, warned those who might think that once political colonial domination was over, there would be no more interference in the freedom of the country; he noted, 'but that is not so obvious, as we can see politically free countries entirely under the thumb of others because of economic domination'.[24]

Post-colonial India was determined to eliminate the conditions suitable for the emergence of new 'East India companies'. During the war industrialists had suggested that the accumulated sterling balances could be utilized to repatriate British investments in India. The report of the sub-committee on industrial finance of the National Planning Committee, chaired by A.D. Shroff, recommended that 'foreign capital, at present invested in any of the essential industries, or for the exploitation of the mineral, forest, or other forms of natural wealth, should be taken over by the State as soon as possible'.[25] Right from the turn of the century, the Indian bourgeoisie had realized that without an end to British imperialism in all its forms, it was not only economic development but also the very survival of Indian capitalism which would be endangered. The Swadeshi movement reflected this concern, and Indian business generously financed the nationalist movement. Anger over the scars of colonization and resentment of the privileged treatment from which British interests had profited led the Indian bourgeoisie to ask the government to restrict foreign investments, but with some reservations. They did not always oppose the incentives given to foreign investments, so long as these were likened to concessions to the private sector in general; at the same time Indian industrialists opposed any measure which threw them into competition against the superior financial resources and technical know-how of the big foreign corporations, which they regarded as being in all likelihood patently unfair to them. The attitude towards foreign assistance was to be more neutral, although some were reluctant to an aid package which would lead to widening the scope of the public sector in the economy.

In a report released in January 1947, the Advisory Planning Board reflected the generally hostile attitude of business circles by criticizing the intrusion of foreign firms not only in the field of key and basic industries, but also in those of consumer goods. It was considered preferable to import those consumer goods which could not yet be produced locally rather than to authorize their production by foreign companies which, once entrenched, would later become difficult to dislodge. The industrial panels consulted by the board were then of the unanimous view that the necessary capital needed for development would be amply found within the country itself and that foreign capital would not be required for direct investments in industries. Foreign participation would be acceptable only in the form of a technical input in highly specialized industries whose control of the management could be temporarily entrusted to foreign hands. But even in such cases, the effective control of the enterprise was to remain in Indian hands and the training of Indian personnel meant to finally take the place of the foreign technicians was to be a *sine qua* non condition.[26] It was also expected that sooner rather than later the investments made in the centres of excellence in higher education would pay off, and the country could depend upon its own indigenously trained scientists, managers, and engineers.

The government refused to oppose in principle foreign direct investment but it did subject it to many restraints. When a motion was submitted to the Legislative Assembly in February 1947 asking for a total ban on foreign capital and management to prevent any alien hold on the Indian economy, C. Rajagopalachari, the Minister for Industries and Supplies in the interim government, intervened to oppose it on account of its excessively radical nature when the country was anxious about its production. 'This is not the time for making a rigid formula of any kind. While we must be guarded and wary to see that outdoors and windows are properly shut and opened, this is not the time when we can talk the language of narrow nationalism', he said.[27] Paragraph 10 of the industrial policy resolution of 1948 concerning foreign capital drew up a policy calling for its participation in development, but imposed conditions which were hardly attractive. It was felt that foreign capital was necessary for rapid industrial development as it offered the possibility of acquiring technical knowledge and capital goods. Nevertheless, in case of foreign equity, the effective control and the majority capital would remain Indian. Only in exceptional cases, in the national interest, could a loose interpretation of these rules be considered. Training of local personnel in all technical functions and in those related to management was the golden rule. The question of an eventual nationalization of foreign interests, or the possibility of a discriminatory treatment meted out to foreign enterprises in tax and regulatory matters, had not been broached in this resolution. The trend was finally to evolve towards adopting a more accommodating policy with regard to foreign investments, depending on the need for capital in priority sectors. However, the annual inflow of private capital had rarely exceeded the limit of Rs. 500 million, while foreign aid was to reach a level ten times as high.[28]

As the government's attitude towards foreign capital shows, particularly in the postponement of the programme for nationalization, the exercise of power compelled Nehru to display some pragmatism and flexibility. He was forced to play the role of a moderator between the opposing forces, but without losing sight of the ultimate objective which was to overcome the state of underdevelopment and sharply reduce the dependence of the country on the outside world through pursuing a policy of rapid industrialization. These objectives had willy-nilly to be achieved through the adoption of policies which would give to the state a dominant position in the economy, notably by raising the share of investments to be made in the public sector in the subsequent plans.

NOTES

1. Figures quoted by C. Bettelheim, *L'Inde Indépendante*, pp. 23 and 25, according to the *First Report of the National Income Committee*, published in April 1951.
2. A.V. Hill (ed.), *A Food Plan for India*, London: Oxford University Press, 1945, p. 1.
3. George Blyn, *Agricultural Trends in India, 1891-1947: Output, Availability, and Productivity*, Philadelphia: University of Pennsylvania Press, 1966, pp. 93-126.
4. B.M. Bhatia, *India's Food Problem and Policy since Independence*, p. 22.
5. P.A. Gopalakrishnan, 'India's Food Problem', *Eastern Economist Pamphlets*, no. 18, 1953, pp. 10 and 15.
6. D.K. Rangnekar, *Poverty and Capital Development in India*, p. 86.
7. C. Bettelheim, *L'Inde Indépendante*, pp. 23-5. An industrial establishment was one which employed ten or more workers using machine force or twenty or more without.
8. Planning Commission, *First Five Year Plan*, pp. 421-2.
9. See G.K. Shirokov, *Industrialisation of India*, pp. 47-9.
10. André Malraux, *Antimemoirs*, London: Hamish Hamilton, 1968, p. 140.
11. J.L. Nehru, *The Discovery of India*, pp. 407-8.
12. S. Chakravarty, *Development Planning*, p. 8.
13. INC (Indian National Congress), *Resolutions on Economic Policy, Programme and Allied Matters (1924-1969)*, p. 3.

14. For a study of the concept of planning in pre-Independence India, especially among the business community, see: Raghabendra Chattopadhyay, 'Indian Business and Economic Planning 1930-56', in Dwijendra Tripathi (ed.), *Business and Politics in India*, Delhi: Manohar, 1991, pp. 308-50.
15. INC, *Resolutions on Economic Policy, Programme and Allied Matters (1924-1969)*, p. 16.
16. Ibid., p. 29. In 1947, the public sector was restricted to the railways, posts and telegraphs, ordnance and aircraft factories, and some enterprises administered by the state, such as salt or quinine factories.
17. P. Thakurdas et al., *A Plan of Economic Development for India*, part II (Distribution—Role of the State), Bombay: The New Book Co., 1945, p. 24. See also P.S. Lokanathan, 'The Bombay Plan', *Foreign Affairs*, July 1945, vol. 23, no. 4, pp. 680-6.
18. As for Nehru himself, M. Brecher says that he had 'a deep-rooted emotional and ideological antipathy to private enterprise; he acknowledged its importance but kept it in a subordinate position as long as his power and vigour were unimpaired, i.e. until 1962-63'. M. Brecher, *Succession in India: A Study in Decision-Making*, London: Oxford University Press, 1966, p. 172.
19. *Monthly Abstract of Statistics*, vol. 4, nos. 1-2, January-February 1951, table no. 21, pp. 18-21.
20. Ibid., table nos. 22-3, pp. 22-3 and *Statistical Outline of Indian Economy*, table VI.33, p. 132.
21. *Jawaharlal Nehru's Speeches*, vol. 1, p. 109.
22. Ibid., pp. 142-3.
23. Planning Commission, *First Five Year Plan*, p. 422.
24. J.L. Nehru, *Glimpses of World History*, pp. 570-1.
25. National Planning Commission Series, *Industrial Finance*, Bombay: Vora & Co., 1948, p. 41.
26. *Eastern Economist*, 14 February 1947, p. 312.
27. *Legislative Assembly Debates*, 1947, vol. 1, p. 316.
28. NCAER (National Council of Applied Economic Research), *Development Without Aid*, p. 9.

CHAPTER 2

The Functions of Aid

IT WAS ONLY WITH the massive reconstruction aid granted by the United States to western Europe under the Marshall Plan, which marked the dramatic increase of government-to-government aid as a form of development financing on a vast scale, that India came to be really interested in the possibility of seeking external assistance to supplement its internal resources. In the 'Bombay Plan', reference had, in fact, been made to foreign borrowings, but these were to constitute just 7 per cent of the total outlay estimated at Rs. 100 billion. The remaining 93 per cent was to come from revenue drawn from a favourable balance of trade (Rs. 6 billion), from sterling securities (Rs. 10 billion), from the hoarded wealth of the country, mainly gold (Rs. 3 billion), and above all from created money (Rs. 34 billion) and from savings (Rs. 40 billion).[1] The two other plans presented in 1944, gave no role to external aid. In the 'People's Plan' of the Indian Federation of Labour under the leadership of M.N. Roy, the outlay of the order of Rs. 150 billion over a period of ten years was covered by the sterling balances, direct taxes, incomes from nationalized lands, and from the profits of public sector enterprises. The 'Gandhian Plan' drawn up by S.N. Agarwal depended solely on internal financing.

That the planners did not show much interest in obtaining funds from abroad was due largely to the existence of the sterling balances. The Indians counted on this a great deal to obviate probable deficits in the balance of trade at this stage of development when industrialization necessitated the import of capital goods, which could not be compensated for by a proportional increase in the value of exports of raw materials and primary goods.

These sterling balances had begun to accumulate under a financial agreement reached in April 1940, and represented mainly the purchases of goods and services made in India for war purposes.

IMPORTS OF IMPORTANT COMMODITIES

(*Rs. millions*)

	1950-1	1955-6	1960-1	1965-6
Machinery (other than electrical)	606	825	2,034	3,338
Grains	804	175	1,814	3,220
Base metals	454	921	1,698	1,662
Electrical equipment	238	376	572	878
Transport equipment	407	635	724	706
Crude, refined petroleum, and petroleum products	544	440	695	682
Raw cotton and waste	1,008	573	817	462
Raw jute	-	193	76	92
Chemical elements and compounds	85	213	393	359
Fertilizers	124	22	121	448
Medicines and pharmaceuticals	108	159	105	88
Others	1,434	2,256	2,348	2006
TOTAL	5,812	6,788	11,397	13,941

Source: Based on *Statistical Outline of the Indian Economy*, Table XIV.79, pp. 229-33.

These were to grow considerably after the United States joined the Allies in 1941 and when India became a base of operations for the eastern war zone. In exchange for bonds issued in pounds sterling by the British government in London, the Reserve Bank of India had advanced the rupees corresponding to the costs of these purchases. The sterling balances accumulated rapidly as the English pound had, since the start of the war, become virtually non-convertible. As a consequence of this development, India, a debtor country before the war, found itself, at the end of the worldwide conflict, Britain's largest creditor among the members of the sterling zone. The amount of the sterling balances on 15 July 1947 added up to £1,160 million.[2] The *Eastern Economist* estimated that if these sterling balances were to be made easily available, the need to rely on foreign funds 'may not be very large'.[3] If the sterling balances were indeed much needed for the programme of post-war industrial modernization, Indian business interests and financial authorities had long been questioning the room available for manoeuvre in the utilization of the large and growing sterling balances. Gaganvihari Lallubhai Mehta, then president of the FICCI and a future Indian ambassador to the United States, had already warned in 1943 that 'India's political status has tended to deprive her of any effective say in the disposal of her own foreign balances and it is apprehended that they might depreciate in value or not find convertibility or might be dissipated to India's detriment'.[4] The difficulties that the battered British economy confronted at the end of the war were bound to complicate the utilization of these foreign sterling balances when India was to gain Independence. Soon the shoe began to pinch, and the British wished to substantially scale back their debt and to impose restrictions on the use of the sterling balances, both in amount and in conversion into hard currency. Recourse to foreign aid, without yet becoming a pressing need, began to be considered by the government, all the more so as the financial situation as regards trade with hard currency areas was deteriorating. With the passage of time, aid began to occupy an increasingly important place in the development of the country and to fulfil several economic functions. It contributed towards increasing the rate of investment, offsetting deficits in the balance of trade, enabling transfer of technological know-how, and making good the shortage of food grains.

There could be no economic development and increase of national income without a high level of capital formation. The drafters of the First Five Year Plan recalled, in support of this assumption, that in the United States, between 1870 and 1900, this rate was of the order of 12 to 15 per cent of the national income. In Japan, the first three decades of the twentieth century witnessed a threefold increase in the national income as a result of an average rate of capital formation of about 14 per cent. In the Soviet Union, the rate of investment was evaluated as being of the order of 20 per cent of the national income for the period 1923-38, that is to say, during the first three five year plans. On the strength of these observations, the Indian planners considered that 'in underdeveloped countries with low standards of living and rapidly increasing population, a rate of growth commensurate with needs cannot be achieved until the rate of capital formation comes up to around 20 per cent of the national income'.[5] They could not but admit that this was then far from being the case. With a rate of savings of only 5 per cent in 1950-1 and on the basis of an annual rate of population growth of 1.25 per cent, the per capita income could barely be maintained at the existing level. It was, therefore, difficult to get out of the vicious circle in which a country finds itself when its national income is small, for it creates an equally low level of savings, and, therefore, of investments; these low rates are incapable of bringing about a perceptible increase in the national and the per capita incomes, without which the rate of growth stagnates. And then there was the additional strain of a rapid demographic expansion. Consequently, it became essential for the state to adopt an economic strategy likely to mobilize savings, so as to meet the imperative need for the growth of the national income and also to ensure the financing of public investments.

In December 1948, during a meeting of the Congress party in Jaipur, the economic programme adopted mentioned the necessity for the people to 'produce more, consume less and invest their savings in government securities and undertakings'.[6] Staking on tax receipts or restricting the supply of consumer goods could make it possible to increase the savings rate, the difficulty lying in the equilibrium to be established between bringing about a growing level of investments, and minimizing the hardships to be imposed on a largely impoverished population. While a totalitarian state could enjoin the sacrifices and tribulations necessitated by the rapid development of heavy industry, the Indian Constitution, recognizing the respect for fundamental rights and the existence of a multiparty system, ruled out forced savings. There was also the possibility of creating money for financing investments, but the risks of disruption in the monetary system and of inflationary pressures, inherent in a context in which the production would not satisfy the demand thus generated, restricted its use.

In the First Five Year Plan, Indian policy makers resorted to the notion of marginal propensity to save, a variant of the Harrod-Domar model on the average propensity to save which contends that *in tandem* with every increase in income there is an equivalent increase in savings in terms of percentage. According to the notion of marginal propensity, the fraction saved from the additional income is no longer simply equal to the rate at which the income has grown but is higher than it, thus testifying to the determination of an underdeveloped country, to sacrifice consumption within reasonable limits in the interest of achieving productive investment. The end objective of the policy implemented should be to ensure that a large proportion of the additional income resulting from development is saved and re-invested. An appeal was, therefore, made to undertake a prolonged period of austerity and to adopt a very slow increase in the level of consumption in order to increase the rate of capital formation. The planners estimated that the rate of savings had to cross over from 5 per cent to 6.75 per cent of the national income by the end of the first plan. This goal was a modest increase to begin with, but it was estimated that would keep on growing as and when the increase in investments was reflected in the national income and as it would simultaneously become easier to raise the rate of savings, which itself would lead to a more rapid increase in the national income. In 1951, the target was to achieve a rate of savings amounting to no less than 20 per cent of the aggregate national income by 1967-8.[7]

The growth model developed by Prasanta Chandra Mahalanobis and adopted for the Second Five Year Plan perpetuated the importance given to the mobilization of savings for financing the plan. The idea was that by giving priority to the production of capital goods over that of consumer goods, the propensity to save would tend to increase. A higher savings rate would inevitably follow from a higher share of capital goods in the gross national product for 'one cannot eat steel'.[8] However, there was a danger that with the demand for consumer goods remaining unsatisfied due to the low level of national production, this could lead to inflationary pressures and disturb the balance of trade.

Any significant result arising out of an attempt to raise the rate of capital formation by influencing the savings process could, therefore, only be a medium-term or a long-term measure. In the meantime, therefore, one had to rely on other sources for an increase in the rate of investment. Thus, the latter, at the end of the Third Five Year Plan rose to around 14 per cent of the national income while the rate of savings in 1965-6 was only 10.5 per cent. This difference had necessarily to be attributed to the fact that a part of the investments had been financed by getting loans and grants from abroad. These, in the course of the years, occupied an increasingly important part in the financing of public investments, particularly from the period of the Second Five Year Plan when an ambitious programme of investment, in excess of the level of savings, was drawn up. Aid was thus meant to hasten economic progress and to alleviate the cost which was paid in human hardship.

The objective of achieving a self-sufficient growth rate in which aid would become redundant was, nonetheless, not forgotten. Moreover, aid could not be considered as an ideal palliative. Apart from its eventual political implications, it could not be a perfect substitute for savings, all the more so as the amount of aid, its timing, and the conditions attached to it by the donors may not be in tune with the views and requirements of the receiving country. Foreign aid could also lead to a distortion of budgetary priorities since it is likely to go to sectors and areas which are accorded priority by the donor institutions rather than by the recipient nations. It was thus necessary to avoid an excessive dependence on external assistance in the developmental process. It was necessary also to keep in mind the danger of being encouraged to draw up development projects less in terms of their priority and more in terms of the probability of their being accepted for financing by foreign donors, or again of the risk of excessive indebtedness. Tiruvallar Thattai Krishnamachari, when he was Finance Minister, once noted that, even if aid was generously given, 'we have to ask ourselves whether we can afford to borrow beyond the point at which the returns we get of what we borrow, in terms of higher exports and lesser reliance on imports, are not commensurate with the additional burden of debt repayments'.[9]

Aid could serve as a supplement to savings so as to increase the volume of investments. It also often had the specific function of putting at one's disposal foreign exchange which would make it possible to finance investments in goods and services obtained from abroad not covered by exports revenues. The export-import ratio, which indicates the proportion of imports that can be financed from exports earnings, from the second plan onwards continued to deteriorate, crossing over from 85 per cent for the first plan to 57 per cent for the second, and it witnessed no notable improvement during the third plan when it was 61 per cent. Consequently, imports were partly financed from foreign assistance subsidies; this was all the more so when foreign exchange reserves were hitting rock-bottom levels. The reasons for this imbalance, over and above the inevitable economic fluctuations, rested on the structure of external trade in a country in which 90 per cent of the exports were in the nature of raw materials, primary goods, and agricultural products with low added-value and high price sensitivity. The three largest export products—jute manufactures, cotton (raw, yarn, and piece goods) and tea—alone accounted for almost 60 per cent of the total amount of goods exported in the late 1940s, and still for 45 per cent of the same in 1966.[10] The elasticity of demand for these types of items in the international market was relatively small. Even a decline in their value, resulting from an increased productivity or from devaluation, did not necessarily lead to an increased demand for them. An increase of income in the developed countries is not accompanied by a proportional increase in the demand for primary goods, contrary to what occurs in the case of manufactured products.

Account had also to be taken of the protectionist policies of the importing countries, of the development of substitutes, particularly in the field of textiles, or again of the loss of competitiveness which could arise out of inflation or out of low productivity, in the face of increasing competition from other developing countries.

It is also true that before the 1960s no government policy had really been framed for the promotion of exports. A contemporary analysis noted that:

> thus over the decade i.e., 1951-61, the country's efforts neglected the balance of trade question as being serious and the official policy hardly suggested using trade as an important lever to face the deteriorating foreign exchange situation at home or counter the swiftly shifting balances in the world-trade scene. Further, there was little appreciation of the correlation which foreign trade has with other vital sectors such as shipping facilities, financing and other servicing institutions. . . . *In fine*, not much was expected from trade as an instrument of economic growth during the first decade of planning nor efforts were [sic] made in that direction excepting on an *ad hoc* basis. There was hardly any trade plan and the trade policy of the country betrayed a lack of design and perspective.[11]

A policy for extending support to exports was formulated at the start of the third plan and it culminated in the second devaluation of the rupee in June 1966. Despite these steps, India's share in world exports kept on decreasing between 1950 and 1966, going down from 2.01 to 1.17 per cent.[12]

In order to minimize external interference, priority was given to a development policy oriented towards the domestic market and designed to promote an import-substitution strategy, notably in the case of capital goods. It was in this perspective that the concept of self-reliance was put forward, itself rooted in the Swadeshi movement which had been an integral part of the nationalist movement. The notion of self-reliance should not be merely equated with a closed economy or an economy aiming at restricting commercial intercourse, but rather with the determination 'not to be dependent upon external assistance for the import of its life-line supplies and to the extent possible, it should have the capacity to withstand the vicissitudes of international markets'.[13] But while waiting for the industrial structure of the country to achieve the level of diversification and production adequate enough to generate a notable and autonomous growth in national income and the surpluses required to alter the composition of exports in favour of 'non-traditional' goods, India could not easily do without foreign aid.

Foreign aid represented not only a mean to procure the capital to supplement internal resources and export earnings, but also to obtain from developed countries the technology and international expertise which India lacked; this could be achieved through the training of local personnel by foreign specialists, by deputing managerial and engineering staff to foreign countries to familiarize them with new technologies under cooperation agreements or by the setting up of various research and technology institutes within the country.[14] Technical assistance allocations, understood as being intended to raise output by changing the methods of production, nevertheless, constituted only a small part of the funds coming from foreign aid. During the decade 1951-61, they accounted for only 1 per cent of the entire authorized aid as against 85.2 per cent in the form of economic assistance intended to raise output by increasing the supply of capital; the remaining 13.8 per cent corresponded to a combined aid in the case of certain projects amalgamating technical and economic assistance.[15] However, the long-term incidence of technical assistance on development went far beyond these sole percentages.

There was finally the food aid that India had asked for in order to face the situation arising out of its inadequate agricultural production and which became, right from the time of the First Five Year Plan, an important element of foreign aid. This last type of aid also contributed to the development and modernization of the economy, when the rupees paid by India for the imports of agricultural products would be offered by the supplier country to the Indian government in the form of grants or loans, to cover the cost of development projects in the local currency.

Over and above the economic justifications of aid, political stakes were also involved. True, aid did not arouse in 1947 the same hostility as foreign private investments, fraught with grim reminders of India's colonial history. However, there was awareness in India that external assistance was no panacea for the country's deep-seated economic problems. It was clear that aid-giving countries were not impelled by purely philanthropic motivations and that by taking recourse to aid, the receiving country ran the risk of facing pressures to revise its political and economic orientations. In giving aid, the big powers were often impelled by reasons related to the geopolitical situation of the recipient country and the strategic support that they could hope to derive from it. The *raison d'être* of aid—that is to say, of contributing to the economic development of underdeveloped countries—often tended to give place to the idea of its being an instrument of coercion by the donor country. In 1956, Eugene Black, then President of the World Bank, underlined in a speech made in Washington, D.C. that:

> despite the existence of an unprecedented flow of development assistance out of the industrialized countries today, the real self-interest of these countries is all too often obscured by a welter of short-term political and economic aims. All too often development assistance is seen merely as a means of buying diplomatic friends or military allies. As a result, all too often development assistance lacks continuity and provides an inadequate basis for the advance planning of development projects . . . all too often development assistance is seen merely as a means of helping domestic manufacturers, producers and exporters find new business.[16]

In an article which appeared in 1945, the American economist Herbert Feis, who was a close collaborator of President Roosevelt, acknowledged that the disbursement of aid was governed by American economic and political interests. In response to the question, 'Shall we take political questions into account when making loans?', he replied: 'It seems plain that we must. Our economic prospects, our safety, the chance that decency will prevail in this world—all these will be affected by the use that foreign countries make of the economic strength for which we provide the nourishment.'[17] The predominance of bilateral aid over multilateral aid (the latter constituted only 12 per cent of the aid given during the first three five year plans) was certainly no stranger to the desire of the donor countries to keep a close check on the utilization of their assistance and to reserve to themselves the power to bind it to political or economic preconditions.

Nehru discussed at length the pressures related to receiving aid during the Cold War in a speech he made before the Constituent Assembly in March 1948 and which served as a frame of reference regarding government policy in the matter:

> I do not think that anything could be more injurious to us from any point of view—certainly from an idealistic and high moral point of view, but equally so from the point of view of opportunism and national interest in the narrowest sense of the word—than for us to give up the policies that we have pursued, namely, those of standing up for certain ideals in regard to the oppressed nations, and try to align ourselves with this great power or

that and become its camp followers in the hope that some crumbs might fall from their table. . . . We want the help of other countries; we are going to have it and we are going to get it too in a large measure. . . . Even in accepting economic help, or in getting political help, it is not a wise policy to put all our eggs in one basket. Nor should we get help at the cost of our self-respect. Then we are not respected by any party; we may get some petty benefits, but ultimately even these may be denied us.[18]

This statement of intent was put to the test over the coming years.

NOTES

1. *Economic Weekly*, 14 May 1949, p. 16.
2. In August 1939, India's sterling securities amounted to Rs. 670 million. By the end of the war, it had increased by some 2200 per cent to reach Rs. 1,507 billion. S.L.N. Sinha (prepared by), *History of the Reserve Bank of India (1935-51)*, p. 308.
3. *Eastern Economist*, 25 August 1944, p. 202.
4. *Speech of Mr. G.L. Mehta at the sixteenth annual meeting held on 27 March 1943 at Delhi,* Delhi: The Hindustan Times Press, 1943, p. 18.
5. Planning Commission, *First Five Year Plan*, p. 14.
6. INC, *Resolutions on Economic Policy, Programme, and Allied Matters*, p. 34.
7. Planning Commission, *First Five Year Plan*, p. 21.
8. J. N. Bhagwati and P. Desai, *India: Planning for Industrialization*, p. 118.
9. *Hindu*, 24 July 1965.
10. *Statistical Outline of the Indian Economy*, table XIV.78, pp. 224-8. The Partition had a two-sided effect on India's foreign trade. On the one hand, it diminished India's capacity to export many raw materials (raw cotton, raw jute, raw wool, raw hides, and skins) and, on the other hand, it increased its dependence on imports for those very items. In regard to jute—jute manufactures were the most important items of India's export trade-, a significant part of the export revenues went to pay for the import of raw jute from Pakistan. It was not before the 1960s that India's production of raw jute compensated the loss suffered at Partition (by the mid-1950s, in case of raw cotton).
11. S.L. Sharma, 'Shifts in India's Foreign Trade Policy', *Foreign Trade Review*, July-September, 1966, vol. 1, no. 2, pp. 165-6.
12. *Statistical Outline of the Indian Economy*, table XVI.88, pp. 260-6.
13. H.L. Bhatia, *Does Foreign Aid Help?*, p. 79.
14. Among the five pacesetter Indian Institutes of Technology, the one in Bombay received direct support from the Soviet Union and through the UN

Expanded Programme of Technical Assistance. The United States provided assistance to the IIT, Kanpur.

15. V.K.R.V. Rao and D. Narain, *Foreign Aid and India's Economic Development*, p. 7.
16. *Commerce*, 6 October 1956, p. 650.
17. Herbert Feis, 'Political Aspects of Foreign Loans', *Foreign Affairs*, July 1945, vol. 23, no. 4, p. 610.
18. 8 March 1948. J.L. Nehru, *India's Foreign Policy*, pp. 31-2 and 35.

CHAPTER 3

The Rationale of Non-alignment

BEFORE EXAMINING the orientations of India's foreign policy, it is fitting to call to mind Jawaharlal Nehru who was, in many ways, its chief architect and spokesman. The appointment of Nehru as Prime Minister of independent India, after he had held an equivalent position (vice-president of the Viceroy's Executive Council) in the interim government from September 1946 to August 1947, would not necessarily have taken place without the intervention in his favour by Mahatma Gandhi, who had decided to make him his 'political heir'. Sardar Patel, who controlled the apparatus of the Congress party, could as well have been chosen to accede to the position of the head of government. However, Nehru owed to no one the fact of assuming also the office of Minister of External Affairs. In 1935, he had lamented 'an astonishing ignorance or indifference to world happenings among our politicians'.[1] Now, for a year he had been in charge of External Affairs and Commonwealth Relations in the interim government and, what is more, he had been in charge, for twenty years, of shaping the foreign policy of the INC. While other nationalist leaders had shown interest in one or another specific international problem, Nehru had the distinction and experience of having integrated within a global perspective the specific attitudes adopted by post-colonial India. This made him the originator and the propagator of the Indian policy regarding international relations.

Jawaharlal Nehru had gained exposure to the external world during his childhood thanks to the efforts of his father Motilal. Motilal, a descendant of a Brahmin family of Kashmir, had settled in Allahabad, a city in north India, in 1886, three years before the birth of his son, to practice there as a lawyer. His skills as an orator had quickly won him renown and enabled him to acquire the means to lead a Westernized lifestyle which earned him the consideration of the British authorities. In 1905, he sent his son to pursue his studies in England where he remained for seven years, first at Harrow and later at Cambridge. During this period, Jawaharlal also visited Europe; he was to return later to the continent, once in 1926-7 and subsequently in 1935-6, for two sojourns of several months each. His studies over, he returned to India in 1912. Meanwhile, his father had become one of the most prominent leaders of the INC; he was elected president twice, in 1919 and 1928. For eight years, the future prime minister of India pursued his career at the bar in Allahabad but without any great enthusiasm. He was, in fact, increasingly drawn to the nationalist cause; eventually this deepening interest in political matters led him to rally to the side of Mohandas K. Gandhi and join the non-cooperation movement launched by the latter in 1920. From that date until his death, he hardly ever left the forefront of the Indian political scene, except during the numerous stays in prison that his activism earned him (between 1921 and 1945, he spent nine years in jail).

From the time when he represented the INC at the Congress of Oppressed Nationalities at Brussels in 1927 till his death in May 1964, there were few foreign policy resolutions of the INC, and later those of the Congress party, which had not been originated, moved, and drafted by Nehru. While the INC had begun to support the different nationalist movements in Asia right from the start of the 1920s, Nehru emphasized the fact that the success of the national movement for independence in India was due almost as much to the influence of the various struggles conducted against the imperialist powers throughout the world as to the fight conducted in India itself. Thus, in 1928, the Congress expressed its sympathy for the nationalist movements against Western imperialism in Egypt, Syria, Palestine, and Iraq. During the years that followed, the INC espoused the cause of peoples who were victims of fascism, this 'mirror of imperialism', whether it be Japanese fascism in China, Italian fascism in Abyssinia, or German fascism in Czechoslovakia.

During the seventeen years that he was prime minister and minister of External Affairs, it was Nehru's thinking that was reflected in India's foreign policy. His overwhelming influence should, however, not obscure the fact that some people whose advice was sought by the prime minister, as we shall see later, did at one time or another, also influence to some degree the conduct of this policy. While some politicians did contest the wisdom of some of the decisions of the prime minister, no one within the Congress or the government had ever really denied Nehru's ascendancy in this sphere. Indeed, important decisions on India's external policy were often taken without prior discussion by the Cabinet. There was, after independence, one man who perhaps had the power to oppose Nehru on international matters; this was Sardar Patel, whose strong anti-communism led him to harbour pro-Western sensibilities, but he remained largely preoccupied with internal affairs. Indeed, he did once convey to Nehru that, apart from privately expressed disagreements on some particular matters, 'I do not think in the pursuit of foreign affairs you have met any obstruction or opposition from me or any of your Cabinet colleagues'.[2] Potential opposition faded with Patel's death in December 1950. As for Parliament, its influence remained on the whole marginal (with the notable exception during the border conflict with China from 1959 onwards) on account of the large majority that the Congress party enjoyed within it; it was also due to the lack of familiarity of its members with international affairs. Moreover, there was an absence of any profound disagreement with the broad principles of Nehru's external policy.

These principles—call them non-alignment, peaceful coexistence, or opposition to colonialism—were regarded as axiomatic and enjoyed a wide consensus within political circles. Indeed, they have even survived their initiator in the conduct of India's foreign affairs. Admittedly, on the one hand, views were expressed within the rightist parties and by some socialist politicians in favour of a comprehensive rapprochement with the United States, and, on the other hand, the Communist Party of India was inevitably in favour of forging closer relations with the Soviet Union. This kind of debate might also have taken place within the Congress itself. But, on the whole, to question the principle of non-alignment involved a political risk—once it came to be clearly associated with national independence and seemed economically viable—that very few were ready to assume. There were fewer interrogations over the soundness of non-alignment than over the precise scope that this term should cover: should it be interpreted as strict neutrality or, at the other extreme, should it be seen as the possibility of a close collaboration with one of the Cold War camps without adhering to a system of military alliances, or was it possible to place oneself somewhere between these two ideological positions?

India's foreign policy, as it gradually evolved after 1947 was first of all the assertion of its free will. Two centuries of British colonial rule had only reinforced the determination of the new leaders of India to fiercely defend the independence of the country against interference from the big powers. There was, nevertheless, no question of isolation from the outside world; it was, in fact, the contrary that was true, for India intended to make its voice heard in the concert of the big nations. Nehru declared emphatically in December 1946:

> It is obvious that what we are going to do in India will have a powerful effect on the rest of the world, not only because a new, free, independent nation comes out into the arena of the world, but because of the very fact that India is such a country that by virtue not only of her large size and population but of her enormous resources and her ability to exploit those resources, she can immediately play an important and a vital part in world affairs.[3]

Over and above India, he desired to see the whole of Asia assert a distinct identity after several centuries of submission to the Western powers, and to present a united front against any form of neo-colonialism. In his inaugural speech at the Asian Relations Conference on 23 March 1947, Nehru described the new reality on the international scene resulting from the process of decolonization; he declared that the time was now past when the countries of Asia were governed from European capitals and proclaimed that henceforth they could no longer 'be used as pawns by others; they are bound to have their own policies in world affairs'.[4]

Some months earlier, in September 1946, in what appeared as the first statement outlining the principles of India's foreign policy, Nehru had warned: 'We shall take full part in international conferences as a free nation with our own policy and not merely as a satellite of another nation.' The corollary to the will to assert India's autonomy in international affairs and its refusal to take directions from any foreign power was the intention 'to keep away from the power politics of groups, aligned against one another, which have led in the past to world wars and which may again lead to disasters on an even vaster scale'.[5] Non-alignment was born out of India's determination to take its destiny back into its own hands by claiming the right to judge events according to their merits and in terms of national interest and not according to the requirements of one or another power.

When India attained independence a year later, on 15 August

1947, the international environment was dominated by the emerging East-West conflict. On the European continent, the blocs were getting crystallized. Truman had decided to apply the doctrine of containment towards communism. Abandoning eastern Europe to the Soviet camp, he undertook to deploy every means to prevent the spread of communism further towards western and southern Europe. The first concrete application of this strategy became evident when on 12 March 1947, Truman asked the US Congress to authorize financial and military assistance of $ 250 million to Greece and $ 150 million to Turkey while specifying that this step was only the beginning of the new policy shift; other states threatened by communist totalitarianism could receive similar attention. Thus, after the US Congress gave its legislative sanction, on 22 May, to the demand for funds submitted by Truman, George Marshall, Secretary of State since the start of the year, in a speech at Harvard University on 5 June announced the intention of the United States to help the economy of post-war Europe back on its feet. This was the European Recovery Programme which Marshall, in early January 1948, asked the Congress to ratify swiftly by allowing the initial sum of $ 6.8 billion for the first fifteen months of a plan meant to cover a period extending from 1 April 1948 to 30 June 1952. At the time of its merging into the Mutual Security Programme during the financial year 1951-2, the funds voted by Congress for the Marshall Plan had risen to $ 13.4 billion. The Soviet response to the Marshall Plan and to the strengthening of bonds between the countries of the Western bloc came with the creation of the Cominform, announced in early October 1947, and the adoption on this occasion of the Zhdanov report; this report presented the vision of a world divided into two camps: the imperialist, anti-democratic, aggressive camp was placed under the guidance of American monopolistic capitalism, and the anti-imperialist and democratic camp was led by the USSR. The Cold War was beginning to take a firm hold in Europe. It was not long before it extended to Asia with the victorious advance of the communist troops of the People's Liberation Army in China and the renewed activity of the communist movements in the colonies and in the newly independent states.

Despite inducements from the two blocs, India stuck to the principle of non-alignment. The division of the world into two blocs was the antithesis of the 'One World' concept, then defended by Nehru in numerous speeches, which the United Nations, of which

India was a founding member, was supposed to symbolize. Regional cooperation in Asia, which was the dominant theme of the Asian Relations Conference in the spring of 1947, was, moreover, to be in line with this perspective. During this conference Nehru stressed that 'in order to have One World, we must also, in Asia, think of the countries of Asia co-operating together for that larger ideal'.[6] Such cooperation appeared indispensable in order to more effectively resist pressures from the power blocs.

Indian leaders considered that the independence for which they had struggled long and hard would be hollow if the country was forced to enter into a system of alliances, within which the countries of Asia would be inevitably reduced to a state of subordination. Such a step would also betray the solidarity that should ideally exist between the decolonized countries in the face of any form of imperialism; it would also betray the confidence of the men and the women who had fought to liberate their country from the colonial yoke at great personal sacrifice. This quest for national independence was articulated by Nehru on the occasion when the Philippines was granted independence by the United States on 4 July 1946:

> We hope that this really signifies independence, for this word has become rather hackneyed and outworn and has been made to mean many things. . . . Some so-called independent countries carry on with what might be termed 'puppet' regimes and are in a way client countries of some great power.[7]

To Nehru's mind, a non-aligned external policy could not be confused with a neutrality in which, in the name of maintaining a strict equidistance, India would be obliged to refrain from taking sides in times of crisis between the two power blocs. It could well happen that in the event of a concordance of views, India would want to opt to vote by the side of one of the two military blocs. Intervening before the Constituent Assembly in 1948, Nehru explained this principle as follows:

> What does joining a bloc mean? After all it can only mean one thing: give up your view about a certain question, adopt the other party's view on that particular question in order to please it and gain its favour. It means that—it means nothing else so far as I can see because if our view is the view of that party then there is no giving up and we do go with that bloc or country or whatever it is. The question only arises when we are opposed to it on that point; therefore we give up our viewpoint and adopt the other one in order to gain a favour.[8]

Such an independence of views would not be to the liking of the superpowers, Nehru admitted elsewhere for at a time when the attitudes adopted by each of the blocs on international problems were more in keeping with the logic of confrontation than with an analysis of the real merits of each case, 'a country like India which talks in a different language is looked upon as a nuisance in every way; unfortunately, not only as a nuisance, but every group suspects it of joining hands with the opposite group'.[9]

Vengalil Krishnan Krishna Menon defined non-alignment as the logical extension of nationalism and, he specified, 'of the conflict between nationalism and military blocs, the fact that we had little in common with the *raison d'être* of the blocs'.[10] India refused to allow itself to be dragged into an ideological conflict which was not of its making. There was not in the Indian perception a Manichaean representation of the two superpowers. While the West was still often associated with an oppressive colonial system, racial discrimination, and economic exploitation of underdeveloped countries, the dictatorship of the proletariat advocated by the Communist bloc was also far removed from India's parliamentary democracy. Nehru took care not to indulge in any gratuitous comparison between the American capitalist economy and the Soviet communist system for neither one could serve as a model for India. During a meeting of the Commonwealth Prime Ministers in London in October 1948, he asserted that while many Indians were theoretically attracted to communism, they would not for all that ideological leaning be ready to live in practice under a communist regime. But, on the other hand, he added, that although Indians might envy the material prosperity of the United States, few would be inclined to accept the consequences following the application of the principles of American capitalism to India.[11] During the course of centuries, India had exercised a strong cultural influence on so many countries that it would not thereafter want to be reduced to a state where it would have to conform blindly to ideologies that had emerged in Europe within a very different environment. In fact, capitalism and communism appeared to Nehru to be ideologies inherited from the nineteenth century, which would have to reform themselves in order to survive, the former by allowing a growing intervention by the state in the economy in order to enable a more equitable distribution of wealth, and the latter by respecting individual liberty.

Not only did India not see itself fitting into either of the opposing blocs but the tensions between them also endangered the achievement of what the country then needed most urgently, namely, peace and international cooperation. The internal problems linked to a multi-ethnic, multi-religious and multi-lingual state and the expectations of the citizens for an improvement in their living conditions would be all the more difficult to meet as India would have to make its way in a world weighed down under the threat of a global conflict. None doubted that in this nuclear age, in the event of war no country would be spared, not only on account of its cataclysmic consequences but also because, as Nehru was ready to admit, it would be very difficult to remain neutral if a world war was to break out. By seeking to go beyond the bipolarity imposed by the Cold War and by calling for multi-directional cooperation, the non-aligned option was also perceived as the best means to work for peace. India sought to play an active role, particularly under the framework of the United Nations, in resolving conflicts, with the conviction that 'peace and freedom are indivisible and the denial of freedom anywhere must endanger freedom elsewhere and lead to conflict and war'.[12]

The East-West conflict was not the only source of tension around the world. The problems stemming from colonialism, racial discrimination, and poverty also demanded attention. As one of the first countries to throw off the colonial yoke, India felt that it held a particular responsibility to bring the concerned European powers to understand and appreciate the inevitability of decolonization and hence the obsolescence of colonial wars. One of the functions of the Asian Relations Conference of 1947 was to lend its support to the countries still subjected to foreign domination. The Asian Conference on Indonesia in January 1949, which also took place in Delhi to protest against the Dutch police action *vis-à-vis* the Republican government there, contributed to the diplomatic battle which was to lead the United Nations Security Council to find a rapid and peaceful solution to the Indonesian problem. On this occasion, Nehru spoke out strongly against Western colonialism:

> The freedom of a sister country of ours has been imperiled and a dying colonialism of the past has raised its head again and challenged all the forces that are struggling to build up a new structure of the world. . . . It is a challenge to a newly awakened Asia which has so long suffered under various forms of colonialism.[13]

The Indian government also raised its voice against racial segregation, whose capacity for giving rise to conflicts could not be underestimated for 'it is a continuous challenge to the self-respect of a vast number of people in the world and they will not put up with it. . . . And that conflict will not be confined to particular areas in South Africa or elsewhere; it will affect peoples in vast continents.'[14] In addition, the threats of destabilization created by the poverty prevalent in large parts of the world needed attention. Nehru appealed to the rich countries that when drawing up their monetary and financial policies, they should keep in mind the inequalities of development and the poverty-stricken multitudes who 'have suffered long enough' and who want the better things of life. If denied these opportunities, their anger might easily find expression in violence.[15] If the governments of the rich countries were to finally decide to concentrate a part of their efforts and their resources towards raising the standard of life in the underdeveloped countries, the risks of war in the world would thereby largely subside.

This ambitious international policy, which some might regard as idealistic for an economically and militarily weak state, rested on India's conviction that it had a leading role to play in Asia. Nehru based his policy on the fact that:

> whether you think in terms of China or the Middle East or South-East Asia, India immediately comes into the picture. It is so situated that because of past history, traditions, etc., in regard to any major problem of a country or a group of countries of Asia, India has to be considered. Whether it is a problem of defense or trade or industry or economic policy, India cannot be ignored.[16]

Nor did Nehru doubt that India would unavoidably be drawn as a mediator between the two antagonistic blocs and, on the strength of its refusal to align with either one of the military blocs, it could throw its weight in the balance in favour of peace.

Promoting peace was not only a moral imperative, it was also a *sine qua non* condition of development. To be durable, democracy in India had to be accompanied by economic growth and social progress without which the country's position and ability to resist the pressures of external powers would be weakened. A war or a tension-ridden world would enfeeble economic cooperation between the industrialized and the underdeveloped countries. The sums allocated to the procurements of armaments in the rich countries consumed valuable resources which should ideally be devoted to the economic aid packages for poor countries. The baneful effects of the arms race did not stop there. Trade would also be disrupted. At the end of 1950, when there was an extremely tense situation in Korea and a national emergency had been declared on 17 December in the United States, Nehru expressed his concern:

If the mighty production machine of America is turned towards war production, then it will not be able to supply the needs of other countries in terms of capital goods. If there is any surplus in the US, this will go to western Europe, which is considered the first priority from the point of view of a possible war. We are, therefore, not likely to get much or anything in the shape of machinery, etc. from the US. Inflationary tendencies will be more and more marked all over the world. The US will buy up raw material in all parts of the world and pay heavily for it. Thus prices will go up and will affect India too.[17]

Non-alignment made it possible to develop economic relations with other countries independently of their adherence to one or the other bloc, thus guaranteeing that the political independence of India would not be endangered by an exclusive economic dependence on any one country or on identification with any one of the Cold War camps. The diversification of the sources of external assistance guaranteed against any overwhelming dependence on one creditor and also satisfied the desire to maximize capital and technical know-how to meet the various forms of development-based needs. If Nehru noted one day that 'ultimately, foreign policy is the outcome of economic policy',[18] the establishment of a mixed economy—a middle path between the interests of the Indian bourgeoisie and the socialist ideals of the reformers within the Congress party, as well as between American liberalism and the Soviet state-owned economy—opened the path to non-alignment, as also did the concept of a pattern of a supposedly self-reliant economic development.

To opt for a policy of non-alignment meant explicitly not being able to count, in the event of external aggression, on the automatic support implied in the participation in a military alliance, and, therefore, indicated the need to rely more or less implicitly on a defense mechanism that would be dissuasive enough to discourage an eventual aggressor. Now, while the Indian government did not accept the idea held by Gandhi that non-violence was India's weapon, military expenditure had, nevertheless, to be kept to the strict minimum consistent with the absolute necessities of self-defense and had to be kept subordinated to the resources devoted to economic and social development. Financial considerations restricted the purchases of military equipment abroad, and military aid at the price of accepting military commitments would compromise the independence of the country. The alternative was to develop a national defense industry, which was not a priority consideration and which, in any case, would require several years to execute. The defense forces were indeed an extension of the industrialization effort. The role assigned to the Indian armed forces was essentially to be in a position to face a possible threat from Pakistan and eventually to give a hand to the police force in the maintenance of law and order.

The security of the country was to be built less on a military capability endowed with enough dissuasive force to compel a big power to keep itself at a distance than on political considerations designed to considerably reduce the threat of external aggression.[19] More than anything else, there was the conviction that no big power would risk a major military offensive against India, for, given its geo-strategic importance, this adventurism would inevitably invite the intervention of other great powers which would come to its help. The delicate world balance of power and the rivalry between the blocs were already guarantees against any foreign aggression. In a text dating back to 1931 and entitled 'The Defense of India', Nehru had dwelt at length on the fact that the force of dissuasion in India was built less on its military power than on what it represented on the international scene:

> If the domination of England over India ceases and India becomes free, what will be the reaction of other powers? It may be that some will covet her, but the master desire will be to prevent any other nation from possessing India. No country will tolerate the idea of another gaining dominion over India and thus acquiring the commanding position which England occupied for so long. If any power was covetous enough to make the attempt, all others would combine to prevent this and to trounce the intruder. This mutual rivalry would in itself be the surest guarantee against an attack on India.[20]

India's territorial integrity was, moreover, protected by the fact that the country had no enemies as implied in the very fact of non-alignment. Considering that an attack by the Western powers was highly improbable, the only countries which might possibly put military pressure upon India were, apart from the Pakistani threat, Communist China and the Soviet Union. India, if aligned with the West, would then more likely become a target for the communist powers. But with a policy of non-alignment and the strengthening of its internal position, it would be much more difficult for these powers to make any headway by propaganda and any aggression would be widely condemned. Incidentally, this approach generated some kind of acquiescence in the West. A January 1956 archival document relating to British and American interests in South Asia in the light of a new Soviet activism in the region assessed that 'a genuine neutrality, provided that it is not based on a complacent disregard of the true aims of Sino-Soviet communism, need not be inconsistent with the interests of the West. By its very neutrality, the neutral bloc enjoys a relatively high degree of security from overtly hostile Chinese or Russian action.[21]

If even these assumptions a *priori* were not to suffice in completely keeping all peril at bay, Nehru was convinced that a proper recourse to diplomacy would thwart any display of belligerence towards India. 'Security can be obtained in many ways'; he was to say,

> The normal idea is that security is protected by armies. That is only partly true; it is equally true that security is protected by policies. A deliberate policy of friendship with other countries goes farther in gaining security than almost anything else. Apart from this, from the larger point of view of the world also, we have laboured to the best of our ability for world peace.[22]

When confronted with the Chinese invasion of Tibet, Nehru was clear that India 'cannot have all the time two possible enemies on either side of India', and that Communist China would have to be dealt with diplomatically, notably because 'if we fall out completely with China, Pakistan will undoubtedly try to take advantage of this, politically or otherwise'.[23]

In 1947, Nehru had declared:

> Whatever policy we may lay down, the art of conducting the foreign affairs of a country lies in finding out what is most advantageous to the country. We may talk about international goodwill and mean what we say. We may talk about peace and freedom and earnestly mean what we say. But in the ultimate analysis, a government functions for the good of the country it governs and no government dare do anything which in the short or long run is manifestly to the disadvantage of that country. Therefore, whether a country is imperialistic or socialist or communist, its foreign minister thinks primarily of the interests of that country.[24]

Nehru had hence come to the conclusion that national interests, from the point of view of the geographic, historical, political, and economic conditions specific to India, would be best defended by an external policy based on non-alignment. This policy was not an end in itself but was also a means to fulfil objectives which themselves were interdependent: to establish political independence, foster economic development, promote peace, and ensure the security of the country. Nehru did not forget the fifth aim—which was to make India's presence felt on the international stage.

NOTES

1. J.L. Nehru, *An Autobiography*, p. 586.
2. To Nehru, 28 March 1950. Durga Das (ed.), *Sardar Patel's Correspondence*, vol. 10, p. 20.
3. 13 December 1946. J.L. Nehru, *India's Foreign Policy*, p. 8.
4. Ibid., p. 251.
5. Speech broadcast on 7 September 1946. Ibid., p. 2.
6. 23 March 1947. J.L. Nehru, *India's Foreign Policy*, p. 252.
7. *Selected Works of Jawaharlal Nehru*, vol. 15, p. 545.
8. 8 March 1948. *Constituent Assembly of India (Legislative) Debates*, vol. 3, no. 2, p. 1769.
9. 22 March 1949. J.L. Nehru, *India's Foreign Policy*, p. 46.
10. M. Brecher, *India and World Politics—Krishna Menon's View of the World*, p. 4.
11. Minutes of the fifth meeting of the Commonwealth Prime Ministers, on 13 October 1948. *Selected Works of Jawaharlal Nehru (second series)*, vol. 8, p. 280.
12. 7 September 1946. *Jawaharlal Nehru's Speeches*, vol. 1, p. 2.
13. 20 January 1949. J.L. Nehru, *India's Foreign Policy*, pp. 407-8.
14. 22 March 1949. Ibid., p. 48.
15. Remarks made at a joint annual meeting of the IMF and the IBRD on 6 October 1958. *Hindu*, 7 October 1958.
16. 22 March 1949. J.L. Nehru, *India's Foreign Policy*, p. 43.
17. 31 December 1950. J.L. Nehru, *Letters to Chief Ministers*, vol. 2, p. 302. India's attitude during the Suez crisis was largely dictated by the desire to achieve a solution that would not handicap India's development.
18. 4 December 1947. *Jawaharlal Nehru's Speeches*, vol. 1, p. 202.
19. When Nehru met Eisenhower in Washington D.C in December 1956, the former said, 'Neutrality has another advantage. India and China have 1800 miles of common border. Any attempt to maintain a defense of this long border would be such an expensive proposition as to render India completely unable to raise the standards of living of her people. Starvation and disease would make the nation even more susceptible to Communist

penetration.' Dwight D. Eisenhower, *The White House Years, vol. 2. Waging Peace 1956-61*, pp. 109-10.

20. 9 September 1931. Published in *Young India* in two instalments on 24 September 1931 and 1 October 1931. *Selected Works of Jawaharlal Nehru*, vol. 5, p. 557. C. Rajagopalachari, questioned by Robert Guillain, a French journalist specializing on Asian affairs, on the existence of a Soviet threat, replied that 'the Russians would neither like to, nor would they risk it, as they would have to confront England and America which would come immediately to our rescue'. *Le Monde*, 28-29 September 1947.
21. Brief for Washington talks, January/February, 1956: UK/US interests and objectives in South and South-East Asia in the light of new Soviet activity, Foreign Office minute, 27 January 1956. *PRO (Public Record Office)*, FO 371 123246.
22. 9 December 1958. J.L. Nehru, *India's Foreign Policy*, p. 79. Nehru illustrated this approach when he commented in the Lok Sabha, on 29 September 1954 : 'I suppose in the final analysis, no country can trust the other countries; or, if I may put it differently, no country should rely 100 per cent on trust alone. It has to think of possible developments, changes in views and policies, etc. . . . Therefore, it is not a question of my trusting any of these big or small countries; but it is a question of our following a policy which is not only right in itself but which makes it more and more difficult progressively for the other country to break trust. We need not live in a fairy world where nothing wrong happens. Wrong does happen. But we can create an environment wherein it becomes a little more dangerous to the other party to break away from the pledges given.' *Lok Sabha Debates*, vol. 7, part II, col. 3683.
23. 'Policy regarding China and Tibet', 18 November 1950. J.L. Nehru, *Selected Works of Jawaharlal Nehru (second series)*, vol. 15, part 2, p. 345.
24. 4 December 1947. J.L. Nehru, *India's Foreign Policy*, p. 28.

PART II

Questioning Aid From America (1947-1955)

CHAPTER 4

Unfulfilled Expectations

INDIA'S INTENTION in refusing the logic of blocs was to establish a policy of cooperation with the two superpowers which assumed the task of determining the direction of post-war international relations. With this perspective in mind, Nehru made renewed overtures to the Soviet Union. In his radio broadcast of 7 September 1946, after greeting the American people he immediately extended similar salutations to the Soviets, 'our neighbours in Asia and inevitably we shall have to undertake many common tasks and have much to do with each other'.[1] The USSR participated in the first diplomatic initiative taken by India in the form of the Asian Relations Conference held in Delhi from 23 March to 2 April 1947. Welcoming the Soviet delegates of the three republics of Trans-Caucasia and the five Central Asian republics which had been invited, Nehru saluted them as the representatives of republics 'which have advanced so rapidly in our generation and which have so many lessons to teach us'.[2]

The appointment of Henry F. Grady as the first American Ambassador to India was made in early April 1947. A few days later, a press communiqué dated 13 April announced an agreement between the Indian and Soviet governments over the exchange of diplomatic representatives at the highest level. India's determination to implement a policy of good relations with the USSR was seen also in the deputation to Moscow of the sister of the prime minister, Vijayalakshmi Pandit, to represent India. On 13 August, that is, two days before the proclamation of Independence, she presented her credentials. It was not till 1 January 1948 that the Soviet Ambassador to New Delhi, Kiril Vasilevich Novikov, reciprocated the gesture before the Governor General, Lord Louis Mountbatten.

The development of friendly and close Indo-Soviet relations was not simply a response to geopolitical considerations of proximity, or even those of domestic policy from the point of view of the activism of the Communist Party in India. While some Indian leaders did note the expansionist tendencies of the USSR, most did not regard the USSR as a direct threat to the sovereignty and the territorial integrity of India. Nehru refused to believe in the Red Peril decried by the West, remaining faithful in this belief to the views which he had expressed nearly twenty years earlier. At that time, brushing aside the possibility of conflictual relations between the Soviet Union and free India, he had written:

> The Tsar has gone but the rivalry between England and Russia continues and we are now told that India is threatened by the Soviet Government. . . . Ordinarily Russia and India should live as the best of neighbours with the fewest points of friction. . . . If we face the facts we can only come to one conclusion, and that is that India has nothing to fear from Russia.[3]

For Nehru, the Soviet Union was not the bogey denounced by the Americans. The issue of the age was, moreover, less the advance of communism than the end of imperialism and the elimination of mass poverty. Besides, the Soviet Union was regarded 'as a countervailing force in a world which was otherwise dominated by imperialists, ex-imperialists and neo-colonialists'.[4] It should be recalled that a number of Indians engaged in the struggle for independence had found themselves deeply attracted to the USSR. They were drawn by the swashbuckling anti-imperialist rhetoric of the Bolsheviks following the October Revolution, and similarly impressed by the proceedings of the first Congress of the Oppressed Peoples of the East held at Baku in September 1920 at which British imperialism was vehemently denounced. For Indian nationalists, this was an encouragement of their own fight for emancipation. In September 1928, Nehru, while addressing students in Calcutta, noted that Russia:

> stands today as the greatest opponent of imperialism and her record with the nations of the East has been just and generous. In China, Turkey and Persia of her own free will she gave up her valuable rights and concessions, while the British bombarded the crowded Chinese cities and killed Chinamen by the hundreds because they dared to protest against British imperialism. . . . Russia goes to the East as an equal, not as a conqueror or a race-proud superior.[5]

The Bolsheviks, for their part, had not yet reached the stage of irrevocably condemning the freedom movements led by the national bourgeoisie in the colonies. Lenin himself emphasized the necessity for the Communists to initially cooperate with the national bourgeoisie within the framework of a united anti-imperialist front. Incidentally, this stance conflicted with the radical theses of the maverick Bengali political thinker, Manabendra Nath Roy. At the time, Roy refused to grant any revolutionary credibility to the freedom movements led by the local bourgeoisie, which he regarded as showing solidarity with the feudal order. In February 1927, Nehru attended the Congress of Oppressed Nationalities organized in Brussels by the League against Imperialism, and supported by Moscow. A few months later, invited for the tenth anniversary of the October Revolution, he went to Russia where he remained for four days. This short but, as he himself admitted, exciting stay, became the subject of a series of essays in which he described the economic and social changes in the USSR and their relevance to India. The essays which appeared in the *Hindu* were later published under the title *Soviet Russia*.

While studying law in England, Nehru had shown an interest in the reformist socialism of the Fabians; by end of 1927, after another stay of twenty months in Europe, he grew interested in Marxist thought. While admitting that he was 'far from being a Communist' as he had been 'too much influenced by the humanist liberal tradition to get out of it completely',[6] he confided that reading Marx and Lenin had 'produced a powerful effect on (his) mind' and had helped him to see 'history and current affairs in a new light'.[7] During the 1930s, this man who has been described as 'India's greatest non-Marxist salesman of Marxism'[8] sought to promote within the INC, whose bourgeois character he criticized, the idea that political independence was not an end in itself and that it should be accompanied by radical social and economic changes.

Nehru noted with respect the efforts of the Bolsheviks to modernize the country, the successes and the failures of the remedies to resolve the problems raised by industrialization, land reform, and illiteracy, or the approach to the problem of nationalities and minorities. Nehru, then President of the Congress, addressing the delegates gathered at Lucknow during the 49th session of the INC in April 1936, expressed his admiration for the progress achieved in the USSR 'though often at terrible cost'; he said that he was convinced that 'the only key to the solution of the world's problems and of India's problems lies in socialism, and when I use this word I do so not in a vague humanitarian sense but in the scientific, economic sense'.[9] This was the time when the INC was beginning to adopt resolutions advocating a nationalized economy and the planned management of development.

Nehru always displayed a deep repugnance towards dogmatism, ruthless suppression of all contrary opinion, and the wholesale regimentation which took place in the Soviet Union, disapproving particularly of the bloodshed of the purges that formed part of the big Moscow trials. His long association with Gandhi had convinced him that the end did not justify the means. Nevertheless, in an autobiographical essay written in prison between June 1934 and February 1935, he described that the violence in the USSR as being 'aimed at a new world based on peace and cooperation and real freedom for the masses'. At a time while the capitalist West confronted a devastating economic depression—which contrasted sharply with the apparent success of the First Five Year Plan in the USSR—and had laid itself open to the rise of fascism, he admitted that 'in the balance, therefore, I was all in favour of Russia, and the presence and example of the Soviets was a bright and heartening phenomenon in a dark and dismal world'.[10] Nehru retained to some degree the optimism of these early years—whatever may have been his later disillusionment—which made him reluctant to openly criticize the Soviet Union; on the other hand, he never hesitated to censure and castigate the United States.

While the INC was making some timid advances towards socialism, the Soviet leaders, after the sixth Congress of the Third International in 1928, drawing a lesson from the failure of the Comintern policy towards China, had hardened their attitude towards the national bourgeoisie in the colonized countries. Reversing the Leninist policy in favour of a collaboration between the nascent Communist movement in India and the much better organized nationalist movement for leading a common struggle against imperialism, a call was given to the Communists to no longer enter into such an alliance, even temporarily. They saw themselves enjoined to fight not only the colonial authorities but also the bourgeois nationalist leaders of the INC, including at the same time its left wing under the guidance of Nehru, accused of leading the Indian masses up the garden path and of offering to enter into compromises with the colonizers. The seventh Congress of the Communist International in 1935 marked the return to a less sectarian attitude. The INC being the only mass organization fighting for independence with a national reach, Indian Communists were asked to work towards the policy of an anti-imperialist united front, within as well as outside the Congress. The INC, and above all its progressive wing, once again became respectable allies, in the same way as in Europe and elsewhere in Asia, Moscow spared the social democrats and nationalists and encouraged the formation of anti-fascist popular fronts. From the mid-1930s, Moscow paid less and less attention to the colonies except wherever it served the interests of its policy in Europe with regard to Hitler's Germany. Soviet propaganda carefully avoided any reference to the struggle conducted in India during the entire period when the Soviets were fighting by the side of the Allies.

The moral prestige of Soviet foreign policy was undermined by the Second World War. Indians were rapidly disillusioned by the opportunism and cynicism of the Russo-German Pact, the repudiation of the non-aggression treaties concluded with Poland and the Baltic states, and, above all, by the invasion of Finland by the Red Army, an act by which the USSR joined the ranks of the nations committing aggression. Whereas in early 1939, Nehru had written:

> Whatever doubts I had about internal happenings in Russia, I was quite clear in my mind about her foreign policy. This had been consistently one of peace and, unlike England and France, of fulfilling international obligations and supporting the cause of democracy abroad. The Soviet Union stood as the one real effective bulwark against fascism in Europe and Asia. Without the Soviet Union what could be the state of Europe today? Fascist reaction would triumph everywhere and democracy and freedom would become dreams of a past age.[11]

Disenchantment did not, however, lead to repudiation and the future prime minister of India continued to entertain hopes that the USSR would not be defeated in this fight. This expectation is seen in the Quit India resolution of 8 August 1942; while the AICC explained that the refusal of Great Britain to entertain the possibility of independence had led the INC to withhold its support to the war effort, it regretted, nevertheless, not being able to help 'China and Russia in their hour of need'.[12]

Noting the expansionist tendencies of the USSR towards the end of the war, Nehru began to worry over the future policy of this country, still 'shrouded in mystery' but whose well-known policy—'having as many friendly and dependent or semi-dependent countries near its borders as possible'—was hardly encouraging for world cooperation.[13] The pressures exerted by Moscow on Turkey and Iran following the war fuelled Nehru's apprehensions, even if he continued to believe that India was not directly endangered. Internally, the Congress leaders were deeply irked by the attitude of the Indian Communists who tended to consider the interests of the Soviet Union as paramount, overriding even those of the movement for independence after the entry of Nazi troops into Russian territory. On the other hand, the decision of the Indian Communists to not hamper the Allied war effort, after having earlier vehemently denouncing the 'second imperialist war' between 1939 and 1941, now earned them the appreciation of the colonial authorities; in July 1942 the British authorities lifted the ban imposed on the Communist Party of India in 1934. And this gesture of goodwill came a few days before the arrest and imprisonment of Congress leaders following their adoption of the Quit India resolution. The favourable attitude of the Communists towards the demand of the Muslim League for the creation of Pakistan was to further deepen the rift between the CPI and the INC, with the result that those Communists who were still members of Congress organizations were expelled from these bodies in 1945.

These last-mentioned events contributed towards tarnishing the image of the Soviet Union in India, as Nehru noted in a letter to V. K. Krishna Menon in May 1946:

> there has come about a certain change not only in Congress circles but elsewhere also in the attitude to Russia. This is chiefly the result of the feeling against the Communist Party of India. . . . Because the Communist Party is intimately connected with Russia that prejudice has been transferred to some extent to Russia. Also events in the Middle East, especially in Iran, have produced this result. It would be incorrect to say that there is any definite anti-Russian feeling, but it is true that the previous enthusiasm for Russia has considerably lessened.[14]

However, Nehru was careful not to condemn the Soviet Union irrevocably for the behaviour of the CPI or for its aggressive foreign policy. There were three main reasons behind his cautious approach. First, the left wing of the nationalist movement felt a definite admiration for the achievements of communism. Second, any hastily issued denunciation could ruin the policy of cooperation contemplated with Moscow. Third, in the immediate future, the Indians wanted to be able to count on Soviet support in their struggle for independence. At the United Nations Conference on International Organization in San Francisco in April 1945, Viacheslav M. Molotov, ending the silence observed by Moscow during the war, declared at a press conference that he hoped that the voice of independent India would soon make itself heard. By this observation, he denigrated the representativeness of the British-appointed delegation from India, itself abjured by the Indian nationalists who had sent an unofficial delegation headed by Vijayalakshmi Pandit.

In October 1946, on the occasion of the first session of the United Nations General Assembly, the Indian delegation representing the interim government had the opportunity of cooperating with the Soviet delegation, much to the annoyance of the Americans. Muhammad Ali Cureem Chagla, one of the Indian delegates, recalled:

> There was little or no personal or social intercourse between the delegates from the East and the West. But with us from India the Russian delegation was most friendly from the very start, and in many matters the two parties worked hand in hand. India received Russian support in most of the proposals that were put forward.[15]

They held convergent positions whenever there was a question of denouncing Western colonialism. The Indians did not fail to appreciate the Soviet support given to their resolutions relating to racial discrimination in South Africa, which was in contrast to the half-hearted response of the Americans in condemning the South African regime. These cordial working relations within the UN strengthened the hope of a possibility of achieving some significant economic and scientific cooperation. Consequently, Nehru suggested that Soviet scientists be invited to the Indian Science Congress which took place from 3 to 8 January 1947 in New Delhi. V. Volguine, Vice-President of the Academy of Sciences and leader of the Russian delegation, related at the end of his stay that Nehru had disclosed that those Indians longing for reforms saw in the USSR a commendable example from which India wanted to know more.[16]

However, for the time being, there was hardly any question of entertaining illusions over the possibility of receiving anything other than technical assistance from a war-devastated country where industrial production had fallen by half. When, following the indifference displayed by the United States, Nehru approached the Soviet government in September 1946, requesting food grains in order to meet the threat of famine weighing on several regions in India, the Soviets referred to a recent drought of their own as a reason for their inability to promise anything.[17] Along with this act, Nehru had raised the question of establishing diplomatic relations in the near future. To this end he entrusted Krishna Menon, then Secretary of the India League in London, with the task of meeting Molotov in Paris where the latter was attending the Peace Conference. Krishna Menon could not but be happy at the cordial nature of the conversation he had with the Soviet Foreign Minister and asserted that he was optimistic about the future of Indo-Soviet relations.[18] He met Molotov once again in the autumn of 1946 in London during the UNGA. On 1 December, the Indian government entrusted to K.P.S. Menon the responsibility of going to Moscow to discuss arrangements prior to the exchange of diplomatic representations.

In early 1947, the establishment of durable and friendly relations with Moscow, therefore, seemed to receive a favourable response from the Soviets. And yet some months later, when India became independent, this objective seemed already to be compromised. The Soviet leaders had actually felt a relatively secondary interest in the nature of their relations with India. Their attention was then concentrated in reinforcing their influence in eastern Europe and in extending it towards the western part of the continent. It was, moreover, the evolution of the situation in Europe and the rise of antagonism between the former Allies which came to determine the attitude of the USSR towards independent India, and not Nehru's professions of faith in neutrality. In mid-1947, against the background of the bipolarization of the world into military blocs, the acceptance by the INC of the Mountbatten Plan for the division of the subcontinent and the peaceful transfer of power aroused suspicions of a collusion between the Indian government and London. The hardening of the Soviet attitude was already perceptible in a paper presented by E. Zhukov, an eminent Orientalist, before the Academy of Social Sciences in May 1947. Zhukov described Gandhi as 'the apostle of backwardness', censured Patel for his anti-communism, and, more surprising, virulently criticised Nehru who had until then been hailed for his progressive ideas and for his posture of friendship towards the USSR. Now Zhukov accused Nehru who was previously 'well known for his anti-British activities', of working 'for the emergence of the Right . . . his later position corresponds to his support to the Indian bourgeoisie and to maintaining the ties with England'.[19]

Soon the Soviet leaders began to present Indian independence as being purely formal, regarding Partition as a manoeuvre of British imperialism to conserve its political, economic, and strategic links with India. They found proof of this in India's dominion status, the appointment of Mountbatten to the post of Governor-General (he occupied this position till 20 June 1948), the continuance of British generals and personnel in the Indian army, the presence of British officials in the state machinery, or again the role of British capital in the economy. The Soviets argued that London could not have achieved these aims without the complicity of the Indian bourgeoisie which had betrayed the interests of the nation by compromising itself with British imperialism on which it depended for its markets and its investments. They laid stress notably on the use by Britain of its debt to India to shackle this country to the sterling zone. The Constitution, when it was adopted in January 1950, was, in the view of Russian analysts, the outcome of this class alliance against the workers and the peasant masses since it equipped the Indian bourgeoisie with the means to keep itself in power. Further, 'by guaranteeing the inviolability of foreign property and foreign capital, the Indian Constitution perpetuates the dominant position of the foreign imperialists'.[20]

The dogmatism displayed in the Zhdanov report widened the gulf between New Delhi and Moscow. The attitude of 'whoever is not with us is against us' was increasingly in evidence and non-alignment did not fit into this black-and-white world-view. In contrast with the wide convergence of views of the preceding year, the USSR clashed several times with India during the second session of the UNGA in autumn 1947. For instance, India decided, albeit unsuccessfully in the end, to present itself as a candidate, with the support of the United States, for a seat as a non-permanent member of the Security Council, competing against Ukraine. They also had radically divergent positions over the 'Little Assembly' and over the setting up of a UN Temporary Commission on Korea entrusted with supervising the elections aimed at leading to the re-unification of the country and chaired by K.P.S. Menon. Finally, India abstained when the matter of the civil war in Greece was examined. If, as Vijayalaksmi Pandit claimed, the leaders in the Kremlin still had, at the time when she took charge in Moscow, 'the hope then that we would completely side with the Soviet Union',[21] they had to give up the idea of wooing India to their side and, therefore, they exhibited a hostile attitude towards New Delhi, which the Indian Communists were to emulate with revolutionary zeal.

In the wake of Independence, the Communists, under the leadership of Puran Chander Joshi, announced that they were ready to serve as a party offering fair opposition to the government, and even to support the progressive forces within the bourgeoisie against reactionary elements. This 'reformist' attitude lasted till the emergence of a new, more radical leadership during the second CPI congress held in Calcutta from 28 February to 6 March 1948; this event marked a return in actual practice to the sectarian line of the sixth Congress of the Third International. The government was henceforth accused of playing into the hands of business circles and the big bourgeoisie, in collusion with Anglo-American imperialism. The CPI from then on defended the path of armed insurrection led by the working class and ultimately resulting in the establishment of a people's democracy, a *sine qua non* condition for true independence. Although some strikes accompanied by violence, a few sporadic riots, and even political assassinations did take place, still no urban centre rose in revolt and the trend of strikes rapidly died out. The leadership of the CPI had obviously overestimated its ability to mobilize the working class against a party in power whose name was so closely associated with the freedom struggle. The government, under the guidance of Patel, acted with firmness against the agitation fomented by communist activists. Nehru also openly expressed his vexation at the CPI whose actions, he said, could only culminate in weakening the political and economic structure of the nation. In a letter to Mountbatten, Nehru explained that he had not 'the least feeling against Communism or against Communists as such. . . . But I must confess that the way the Communists are carrying on in India in the shape of the most violent activity and writing is enough to disgust anyone.'[22] The Communist Party was even banned in four provincial states and waves of arrests of militants took place in quick succession.

The failure of the urban-based radical line adopted by Balchandra Trimbak Ranadive was evidenced in the election in May 1950 of a new secretary general, Chandra Rajeshwar Rao. Until his elevation, Rao had been a local leader of the Communist Party in Andhra Pradesh, where an armed peasant uprising had taken place in the region of Telengana. But this insurrection lost the intensity it had initially had in 1946 when the peasants of this northern region of Hyderabad State had rebelled against the oppression of large landowners and had established village soviets. The 'police action' conducted by the Indian army in September 1948 to oust the Nizam of Hyderabad, who was hostile to the merger of his state in the Indian Union, provided the central government the opportunity to move into the nearby rural areas of Telengana and put down the peasant revolt. The uprising was not, however, completely suppressed and it took the form of an underground guerrilla movement. Taking a cue from this episode, the new Communist leadership adopted as its model the recent Chinese Revolution which seemed more adapted to a society that was still largely rural. The necessity of an armed struggle was reiterated but it was thereafter to be focused on the countryside. The Cominform journal, *For a Lasting Peace, For a People's Democracy*, rather half-heartedly, in its editorial of 27 January 1950, supported this change. The editorial noted that Indian Communists, basing themselves on 'the experience of the national liberation movement in China and other countries', had to fulfil the task of strengthening the alliance of the working class with all the peasantry and, more widely, to gain the support of all classes, parties, groups, and organizations willing to fight for India's independence. While the Indian Communists were not explicitly asked to adopt the path of armed struggle, it was recognized that this was at the time the main form of struggle in many colonial and dependent countries.[23] The leadership of the CPI did not manage, any more than the earlier one had, to set in motion the revolutionary dynamics which could pose a threat to the government. The line of insurrection commended from 1948 to 1950 proved very costly to the Communist Party. It recorded a sharp fall in the number of its members, which also affected the labour and peasant organizations affiliated to the party.

During this period, the very critical attitude of the Soviets towards India's internal and external policy did not change. Postponement of land reforms, stalling of nationalization, repression of Communist militants, compromises entered into with feudal princes, collusion between the national 'plutocracy' and foreign capital, all these were presented in the Soviet press as evidence of the sharply reactionary nature of the Indian government. E. Zhukov launched yet another diatribe against Nehru, accusing him of having become the 'shrewd valet of two masters—England and the United States—an ally of the Indian princes and the wealthy classes, a bloodthirsty destroyer of progressive forces in India'.[24]

The 'two camps' thesis defended by Stalin forbade any 'third option between imperialism and democracy'. According to the Soviet analysis, India had *de facto* affiliated itself with the Western camp. India's decision, in May 1949, to remain within the Commonwealth, was seen in accordance with this alignment. Moscow also saw proof of complicity between New Delhi and London in the attitude adopted by the Indian government during the months following the Conference of the World Federation of Democratic Youth held in Calcutta in February 1948 and the subsequent communist insurrections in the colonies and 'dependent countries' of South-East Asia. India sent arms to the Thakin Nu government which was facing disturbances triggered in April by the Burmese Communist Party, and, in this regard, later joined a plan set up within the Commonwealth for financial assistance to the nationalist regime in Rangoon. New Delhi also supported Sukarno in Indonesia after the outbreak of an armed uprising organized by the Communists in Java in September 1948 and which was mercilessly suppressed by the republican government. The Indian government was loath even to support the nationalist movements dominated by Communists in countries where they were pitched against the colonial authorities. Thus, it condemned the communist rebellion in Malaysia against British domination. As for its attitude towards Indochina, it abstained from clearly taking the side of the Vietminh, refusing to recognize the Democratic Republic of Vietnam while the latter had asked for its help, particularly during the Asian Relations Conference to which a Vietminh delegation had been invited. India balked at defending the Vietnamese cause in international fora while it firmly supported that of the Indonesian nationalists. In the case of Indochina, undoubtedly the pending settlement of the future of the French establishments in India had motivated the Indian government to exercise restraint, but it was also proof of the predicament in which New Delhi found itself over asserting a clear stand between a recognition of the legitimate aspirations of the different nationalist movements, when their spokespersons were local Communists, and its fear of a communist thrust in South-East Asia. About the Asian conference on Indonesia of January 1949, the Soviet press said that it aimed at setting up a reactionary Asian bloc led by India and inspired by London and Washington to constitute a front against the national liberation movements, after the successes met by the People's Liberation Army of China or again by the Vietminh in Indochina. After the fall of the Kuomintang, the US State Department was suspected of offering Nehru the vacancy left by Chiang Kai-Shek.[25]

On the particularly sensitive Kashmir issue, the USSR observed strict neutrality when the question was discussed in the UN by abstaining during voting on the resolutions. Yet, Moscow was more likely to champion India's cause, since it suspected the Anglo-American strategists to be in favour of this region, or at least the part of it almost bordering the Soviet Union, being united with Pakistan. In 1948, the Soviet Ambassador even informed a member of the Nehru cabinet that his country would be inclined to support India's position and would gladly help if their help was sought.[26] A Western diplomat pointed out that the Soviet position on Kashmir would not only serve Soviet propaganda in India, but more generally run the risk of turning to the Soviet Union a public opinion driven by particularly touchy nationalistic feelings.[27]

While readily admitting that the confrontation with the Communists on the home front, and the existence of truly closer political and economic ties with the Western camp could justify the displeasure of the Soviets, Nehru noted with some bitterness the repeated attacks against the Indian government, 'hostage to the Anglo-American bloc', published in the Soviet press; he saw the possibility of any constructive dialogue becoming increasingly remote. In the Moscow of the post-war years, when foreign diplomats were looked upon with suspicion by the Soviet authorities, Vijayalakshmi Pandit was treated with polite indifference by the Ministry of External Affairs. She complained of not being able to maintain regular contact with the Soviet leaders; during the time that she occupied her post from August 1947 to April 1949, she was never invited to meet Stalin. In New Delhi, it was observed that the Soviet Ambassador was more keen to conduct a dialogue with the Indian Communists than with members of the government. Writing to Krishna Menon on 26 June 1948, Nehru confided his disappointment:

> We want friendship and cooperation with Russia in many fields but we are a sensitive people and react strongly to being cursed at and run down. The whole basis of Russian policy appears to be that no essential change has

taken place in India and that we still continue to be camp-followers of the British. That of course is complete nonsense and if a policy is based on nonsensical premises it is apt to go wrong.[28]

Despite the constant denigration of his government and the support given to the CPI, Nehru seemed, nevertheless, not to attach more importance than was necessary to Soviet animosity and he did not doubt that, sooner or later, the USSR would end up by appreciating the independence of India's views in the matter of foreign policy. To an Indian diplomat who informed him about the virulent remarks being made against India on Soviet radio, Nehru replied:

the heat is not against us though it looks like it. The heat is against the British. The British have always tried to keep the Russians out of this subcontinent and the Russians cannot believe that that policy has changed. Let us wait and see. If we can show the world that we are, in fact, an independent country, the world will change its attitude to us.[29]

India's continuance within the Commonwealth was yet another reason why Nehru did not wish to burn his bridges with Moscow. He explained this in a letter sent in May 1949 to the Ambassador designate to Moscow, Sarvepalli Radhakrishnan:

one of the main reasons why I agreed to the recent London settlement was because I thought this would help in the preservation of peace and would give India a chance to make her influence felt in a little more than otherwise. . . . To put this across to the Soviet Government is of vital importance. . . . Thus, in a sense, our activities in Moscow bear directly on our work for world peace.[30]

Hence Nehru, biding his time until such a moment as the Soviets would be in a better frame of mind, and anxious not to aggravate the already strained relations between the two countries, wanted to revive the idea of contacts in non-political fields such as the signing of a trade treaty, the purchase of petrol, the sending of a cultural delegation, and the exchange of films.[31] The frigidity displayed by the Soviets was not without being reciprocated by Indians in government circles. Such a proposal had few buyers among the senior officials, who were more often prejudiced against communist Russia, or among members of the Nehru cabinet, not all of whom were convinced of the soundness of pursuing a closer relationship. Thus K.M. Munshi, who entered the government in May 1950 as minister of agriculture, categorically stated, 'USSR never has been a friend and never will be. Why should we lose the goodwill of friends without whom we cannot face Russian expansion?'[32]

Economic relations between the two countries were practically non-existent. Pre-war exports from India to Russia were negligible except for raw jute, jute goods, and small quantities of tea. India had allocated to Russia for 1947-8, 20,000 tons of raw jute and 16,000 tons of jute goods. Between 1947 and 1951, commerce with the USSR represented on an average less than 1 per cent of Indian imports and exports.[33] There had been a few barter agreements. The first one in July 1948 related to the supply of 50,000 tons of wheat by the USSR in exchange for 5,000 tons of Indian tea.[34] Two other barter agreements were signed in 1949 on the exchange of tea, jute, and other Indian raw products against 300,000 tons of wheat and 20,000 tons of maize. These agreements were to form part of more ambitious trade negotiations which, however, met with obstacles, notably because the Indians felt that the prices quoted by the Soviets were too high. As for the possibility of economic aid, it seemed incongruous considering the political relations between the two countries. During the conference of the Economic Commission for Asia and the Far East (ECAFE), held in June 1948 in Ootacamund, the Soviet delegate Novikov, then Ambassador to New Delhi, reiterated the Soviet policy towards granting assistance to underdeveloped countries.[35] He first strongly condemned Western aid and foreign capital as vehicles for the subjugation of the recipient country. He accused the West of giving aid in pursuit of the traditional policy of imperialism by perpetuating the asymmetrical international division of labour born out of colonialism, which requires that underdeveloped countries concentrate on the development of agriculture and mineral resources in order to enable the capitalist West to continue to import primary goods and raw materials at low prices, and export to them in return high value-added manufactured products. In an article in *New Times*, the Orientalist scholar Alexander Diakov accused the Indian government of being prone to accept the American 'subjugating' aid, with the result that India was placed not only under the direct economic and political dependence of London, but also of Washington.[36]

At Ootacamund, Novikov reasserted that all aid, whether economic or technical, to Asian countries should be accompanied by no political or economic strings and should be routed through the United Nations and its specialized agencies; this aid should, as a matter of priority, be centred on the development of heavy industry, which he accused the West of fighting shy of doing. Yet, apart from favouring the establishment of a committee for the promotion of national industries, the Soviet delegation did not make any substantial proposal. During a conversation with S.P. Mookerjee, Minister of Industry and Supply, Novikov did mention the need to increase bilateral trade relations and offered the services of expert engineers. But it was a short-lived proposal.[37] That there was some reticence from the Indian side is testified to by Yezdezard Dinshaw Gundevia, who relates that just before leaving for Moscow, where he had been appointed a counsellor at the Embassy, he had gone to the Commerce Ministry to meet C.C. Desai, Secretary, Trade and Commerce, to discuss the possibility of furthering business relations. Desai was succinct; he wanted to hear nothing of relations with 'these damned Communists'.[38] Nehru had even to issue a directive to one of his ministers not to discriminate against the Soviet Union for political reasons and to consider buying goods from it if these were cheaper than those available elsewhere.[39]

While the USSR expressed itself in favour of the principle of multilateral assistance within the framework of the United Nations, there was still the fact that the Soviets considered the international financial institutions connected with the development of poor countries to suffer from a grave flaw, that of being tools in the hand of Western countries desirous of pursuing their policy of subjugation and exploitation of Third World countries. Thus, the Soviet Union justified its refusal to contribute to the UN expanded programme of technical assistance and declined to participate in any of its projects.[40] The World Bank and the International Monetary Fund were presented as being financial instruments in the service of American interests. A Soviet analyst offered the following assessment:

> the chief channel of American penetration is the International Bank for Reconstruction and Development, which is a Wall Street affiliation in disguise. . . . The Indian authorities are deprived of the right of deciding how the funds should be placed, with the result that the dollars are employed to develop those branches of the economy in which the American monopolies are interested, that is, chiefly the production of strategic materials and their export to America. Another means used by the United States to enslave India is Truman's celebrated Point Four Program of 'technical aid' to underdeveloped countries. The credits granted under this form of 'aid' involve the control of whole branches of India's industry by American 'experts'.[41]

During the first years following Independence, Indo-Soviet relations were caught in a bind, which continuously pushed ever further the possibility of a rapprochement. The subversive activities of the Indian Communists and the initial hostility of the Soviet leadership, during the ideological dogmatism of the Stalin era, towards the Indian government left the latter no other choice but to turn exclusively to the Western countries to obtain the equipment, capital, and expertise required for development. Hence the inevitability of having to maintain close relations with the West, which resulted in reinforcing the animosity of the leaders of the Kremlin, subjecting to scorn the desire displayed by New Delhi to remain non-aligned with regard to the blocs. According to them, it ill concealed the duplicity of the Indian government and the fact that India basically belonged to the Western camp. Little importance was attached to Nehru's genuine desire to not become excessively dependent on the United Kingdom and the United States which would have endangered the application of the professed economic policy and the credibility of the principles of non-alignment which was then coming into being.

NOTES

1. *Jawaharlal Nehru's Speeches*, vol. 1, p. 3.
2. Inaugural speech made on 23 March 1947. Ibid., p. 299.
3. J.L. Nehru, *Soviet Russia*, p. 126 and p. 131. Already at the end of the nineteenth century, the leaders of the INC, then in its infancy, had expressed serious doubts about a Russian threat weighing on the subcontinent and they saw it more than anything else as a pretext of the British to satisfy their own expansionist ambitions.
4. D.K. Rangnekar, 'Economic Cooperation', *Seminar*, no. 73, September 1965, pp. 32-3.
5. Nehru was referring to the Russo-Iranian treaty of 1921, to the one signed the same year with Turkey, and to the Sino-Russian treaty of 1924. Presidential address at the All-Bengal Students Conference, 22 September 1928. *Selected Works of Jawaharlal Nehru*, vol. 3, New Delhi: Orient Longman, 1972, pp. 193-4.
6. J.L. Nehru, *An Autobiography*, p. 591.
7. J.L. Nehru, *The Discovery of India*, p. 29.
8. Bhabani Sengupta, *Communism in Indian Politics*, Delhi: Young Asia Publications, 1978, p. 21.
9. *Presidential Address—INC 49th Session*, Lucknow, Allahabad, 1936, pp. 5 and 15.

10. J.L. Nehru, *An Autobiography*, pp. 361-2.
11. J.L. Nehru, *Unity of India*, p. 116.
12. J.L. Nehru, *Selected Works*, vol. 12, p. 447.
13. J.L. Nehru, *The Discovery of India*, pp. 541 and 546.
14. J.L. Nehru, *Selected Works*, vol. 15, pp. 576-7.
15. M.C. Chagla, *Roses in December*, p. 244.
16. *New Times*, no. 12, 21 March 1947, p. 20. Remarks that are corroborated by the speech made by Nehru at the inauguration of the congress. *Selected Works of Jawaharlal Nehru (second series)*, vol. 1, pp. 380-1.
17. J.L. Nehru to Molotov, 21 September 1946. Ibid., pp. 486-7. Already in February of the same year, during a meeting of the UNGA in London, the Indian delegate, Ramaswamy Mudaliar, had unsuccessfully sought food grain assistance from the Soviets; at this time the Soviets had expressed their willingness to offer food assistance to France, where Communists were members of the government then in office. See M.S. Venkataramani, 'The Soviet Union and the Indian Food Crisis of 1946', *International Studies*, vol. 4, no. 4, April 1963, pp. 395-403.
18. *Hindu*, 1 October 1946. See also Nehru's letter to Krishna Menon and Molotov's message to Nehru, J.L. Nehru, *Selected Works of Jawaharlal Nehru (second series)*, vol. 1, pp. 508, 513 and 521. During his interview in Paris with Krishna Menon, Molotov had suggested that, if India desired, the Soviet government could provide experts for its military schools. This proposal did not go down well in the External Affairs Department.
19. E. Zhukov, 'On the Situation in India', *Mirovoe Khozyaistvo Mirovaya Politika*, August 1947. Quoted by R.K. Jain (ed.), *Soviet-South Asian Relations 1947-1978*, vol. 1, pp. 186-7.
20. T. Yershov, 'Indian Version of Bourgeois Pseudo-Democracy', *New Times*, no. 11, 15 March 1950, p. 4.
21. Vijayalakshmi Pandit, *The Scope of Happiness: A Personal Memoir*, New Delhi: Vikas, 1979, p. 237. For an insider account of the functioning of the Indian mission in Moscow during these years, see: Rajeshwar Dayal, *A Life of Our Times*, Delhi: Orient Longman, 1998, pp. 104-51.
22. 4 August 1948. *Selected Works of Jawaharlal Nehru (second series)*, vol. 7, p. 205.
23. *Pour une Paix Durable, Pour une Démocratie Populaire*, no. 64, 27 January 1950, p. 1.
24. E. Zhukov, 'Question de la lutte coloniale après la seconde guerre mondiale', *Voprosy Ekonomiki*, no. 9, 1949. Quoted by Hélène Carrère d'Encausse and Stuart R. Schram, *Le Marxisme et l'Asie 1853-1954*, Paris: A. Colin, 1965, p. 374.
25. *New Times*, 'Behind the closed doors of the Delhi Conference', no. 6, 2 February 1949, p. 17. When Nehru went to the United States in the autumn of 1949, the same journal ran the headline 'Chiang Kai-shek's successor', no. 42, 12 October 1949, p. 20.
26. Conversation between Syama Prasad Mookerjee and Novikov on 1 June 1948, reported by Nehru on 11 September 1948. *Selected Works of*

Jawaharlal Nehru (*second series*), vol. 7, p. 669. The USSR had great reservations at the time over Pakistan. It was only in April-May 1948 that the two countries exchanged notes with a view to establishing diplomatic relations. The Soviet leadership showed more interest in this country during the following year when it began to view with anxiety the forthcoming visit of Nehru to the United States. One reaction was to invite the Pakistani Prime Minister, Liaquat Ali Khan, to Moscow. This invitation lost its relevance after the failure of Nehru's visit to Washington in the autumn of 1949 and the forthcoming visit of Liaquat Ali Khan to the American capital.

27. Telegram of the French Ambassador in New Delhi, Daniel Levi, 1 March 1948. *Archives du Quai d'Orsay* (*AQO*), Nations-Unies et Organisations Internationales, 1945-1959, vol. 237.
28. *Selected Works of Jawaharlal Nehru* (*second series*), vol. 6, p. 465.
29. H.V.R. Iyenger, 'Evolution of Soviet Attitude to India', *Indian Express*, 29 January 1966.
30. Nehru to Radhakrishnan, 7 May 1949. *Selected Works of Jawaharlal Nehru* (*second series*), vol. 11, pp. 362-3.
31. Note to the Secretary General, 14 February 1949. *Selected Works of Jawaharlal Nehru* (*second series*), vol. 9, pp. 467-8. In this same note, Nehru admitted that his government had shown little enthusiasm over the matter of a trade treaty.
32. 29 June 1950. S. Gopal, *Jawaharlal Nehru. A Biography*, vol. 2, p. 100.
33. United Nations, *Yearbook of International Trade Statistics*, New York: Department of Economic and Social Affairs, Statistical Office, 1950 (p. 91), 1951 (p. 129), 1952 (p. 163), 1953 (p. 223).
34. The Indian Embassy in Moscow approached the Soviet government about the purchase of wheat in the autumn of 1947. The British Ambassador offered his assessment of the situation: 'If Mikoyan and Molotov follow their usual principles, sentiment would not be allowed to interfere with business, and the Indians would only get their wheat in return for goods required by the Soviet Union. On the other hand, the propaganda advantages of sending wheat to India may well prove decisive, although the Soviet government are probably by no means satisfied with the policies and behaviour of the present Indian government.' From Frank Roberts, British Embassy in Moscow, to Mr. Hankey, Foreign Office, 16 October 1947. *Public Record Office* (*PRO*), FO 371 63574.
35. *Hindu*, 8 and 11 June 1948.
36. A. Diakov, 'La Situation dans l'Inde', *Temps Nouveaux*, no. 23, 2 June 1948, p. 15.
37. Note drafted by Nehru on S.P. Mookerjee's interview with Novikov, 11 September 1948. *Selected Works of Jawaharlal Nehru* (*second series*), vol. 7, p. 669.
38. Y.D. Gundevia, *Outside the Archives*, p. 80. There were in the Foreign Service many former members of the Indian Civil Service who constituted an anglicized elite well disposed towards the West. A typical example is G.S. Bajpai, the Secretary General in the Ministry of External Affairs

between 1947 and 1952, who was considered by Western diplomats as a friendly interlocutor. This can also be said of his successor, N.G. Pillai. The fresh entrants brought into the Foreign Service after Independence were to be more in tune with the ideological and political orientations of Nehru.

39. Nehru to K.M. Munshi, 8 August 1950. S. Gopal, *Radhakrishan: A Biography*, p. 236.
40. After Truman's announcement in January 1949 of the Point Four Programme of technical assistance to underdeveloped countries, the US government proposed to the United Nations Economic and Social Council to provide assistance on a multilateral basis. In November 1949, the UNGA approved an expanded programme of technical assistance, which finally turned out to be a rather modest one.
41. A. Alexeyev, 'The Political Situation in India', *New Times*, no. 44, 31 October 1951, p. 7.

CHAPTER 5

From Ideals to Practice

UNTIL WORLD WAR II, Great Britain had jealously guarded the subcontinent against any attempt at intrusion by the United States into its affairs. In view of the possibility of the United States being drawn into a war with Japan, the State Department informed the British in May 1941 that the US government, whose diplomatic representation was restricted till then to consulates at Calcutta and Bombay, intended to initiate closer relations with India. This country was assuming new importance 'as a source of materials essential to the implementation of the coordinated programmes of the government of the United States for national defense and the extension of aid to the British Empire'.[1] Great Britain, heavily dependent on US assistance, was at the time in no position to refuse this request. In July 1941, an American diplomatic mission was opened in the Indian capital. Simultaneously, the United States allowed the British to establish the office of an Agent General for India, attached to the British Embassy in Washington, D.C. The Embassy intended to use this post to bolster American support of Britain's policies in India.

The wording of the Atlantic Charter, signed in August 1941 by Roosevelt and Churchill, and particularly the third point stipulating that the two parties undertake to respect 'the right of all peoples to choose the form of government under which they will live' and to see 'sovereign rights and self-government restored to those who have been forcibly deprived of them', raised the hopes of the Indian nationalists that the United States would support their cause.[2] However, Roosevelt showed no disapproval of the restrictive interpretation made by Churchill of point 3 of the Charter before the House of Commons in September 1941, where he said that it applied only to the European states occupied by the Nazis. Indian nationalists bitterly resented Roosevelt's stance. Still, Roosevelt, who had no particular sympathy for the British Empire and who had no doubt that it would break up once the war was over, raised the question of the political future of India during his meeting with Churchill in end of December 1941, but his intervention was in vain. The United States was moved by a greater sense of urgency at the time, primarily to avoid any quarrel with their British ally which might hamper the proper coordination of their joint policies in the conduct of the war.

After Pearl Harbor and the rapid military successes of the Japanese in the Asia-Pacific zone, the American attitude changed somewhat to move towards a direction more favourable to the aspirations of the Indian nationalists. After his visit to India in February 1942, Chiang Kai-shek in a message to Roosevelt noted the risk of giving this country into the hands of the enemy when Indian nationalists leaders asserted they were ready to fight by the side of the Allies, on condition that the British give them the means to take charge of their own destiny.[3] After the fall of Singapore on 15 February 1942, London accepted, *nolens volens*, the dispatch of a US technical mission (the 'Grady mission') entrusted with evaluating India's war potential and with submitting thereafter some recommendations making it possible for the American government to assess the aid, in the form of equipment and technical assistance, needed for developing the production machinery to meet the requirements of the war effort. The British Prime Minister reluctantly agreed to send Stafford Cripps, a Labour member of the War Cabinet, to negotiate with the leaders of the INC. The Indians interpreted this step as the result of American pressure.

On 23 March, a few days after Rangoon fell to the Japanese, Cripps arrived in Delhi. A little before that, Roosevelt had advised Churchill to hand over power to a temporary dominion government made up of representatives of all constituents of India's political life.[4] The proposals that Cripps had been assigned to make to the Congress leaders were not so far-reaching. They contained simply the promise of a dominion status at the end of the war, along with other provisions that were, however, unacceptable in the view of the Indians. Nevertheless, these leaders accepted the invitation to discuss their participation in the government. The negotiations failed despite the best efforts made by Colonel Louis Johnson, who had meanwhile arrived in Delhi as the personal representative of Roosevelt in order to work out an agreement that would be as favourable as possible to the nationalists. The Cripps mission stumbled over the intransigence of the British regarding the establishment of a truly national government in which would vest, notably, responsibilities in matters of defense. That Churchill was hardly inclined to make concessions to the nationalist leaders was *a posteriori* confirmed when he declared in November 1942 that he had not become 'the King's First Minister in order to preside over the liquidation of the British Empire'.[5] As Churchill made use of the failure of the Cripps mission to accuse the INC, before British and American public opinion, of playing into the hands of the Axis powers, Nehru wondered if 'all this [has] been done merely as a propaganda stunt for the people of the USA'.[6]

However, Roosevelt had not been duped by the British action.[7] But he was worried by the increasingly apparent Japanese threat weighing on India's north-eastern border and was definitely sensitive to Churchill's argument that to concede to the demands of the INC would dangerously disorganize the defense of the country, notably by reviving the antagonism between the Congress and the Muslim League. Consequently, he felt that this was not the time to intervene into the political situation in India. Therefore, when, following the vote by the AICC on 8 August 1942 of the Quit India resolution, the British proceeded to arrest Congress leaders and espoused a policy of repression of every popular demonstration, the American government chose not to interfere. American aid in men and in arms had by then already reached India, notably in order to conduct airborne operations of support to China. In these circumstances, the possibility of unrest arising out of the discontent of the nationalists disturbed both London and Washington. As long as the United Kingdom was in a position to control the situation in India so that the Allies could avail of some strategic benefits and the resources required for the war effort, the USA remained satisfied. Roosevelt only insisted that the American forces stationed in India should take part solely in the fight against the Japanese enemy and should not in any way be associated with internal law and order problems. Some 250,000 US soldiers were stationed in India during the war, mainly in the eastern part where the China-Burma-India (CBI) command was headquartered. They fulfilled engineering and supply functions in Bengal and Assam, notably airlifting supplies to the beleaguered Nationalist China.

This attitude aroused definite resentment against the United States, blunting the favourable impact that the Johnson mission had made on nationalist circles. Gandhi was hostile to the presence of

American soldiers who had been called to India at the invitation of the British government alone, and echoed the increasingly widespread sentiment among the Indians that the Americans were giving tacit support to the way the British were conducting themselves in India. Gandhi reproached the United States for making 'common cause with Great Britain', with the result that they could not therefore 'disown responsibility for anything that her representatives do in India'. Consequently, on the eve of the adoption of the Quit India resolution, he requested them 'to look upon the immediate recognition of India's independence as a war measure of first class magnitude'.[8] No less critical, Nehru declared during a press conference on 28 October 1945:

> In India, the United States has kept itself clear from all entanglements. We cannot blame it for this attitude, specially in wartime, but there has been something much more than this during the past few years—a passive and sometimes even an active support of British policy and British propaganda. . . . American policy in regard to India has been strangely subservient to British policy.[9]

George R. Merrell, the US permanent representative posted in Delhi, was to summarized the bitterness of the Indians in 1946:

> rightly or wrongly many of them gained the impression that the United States was going to 'liberate' them from British rule. When this hope was not realized, Indians were bitterly disappointed and in many cases not only decided to question the United States' 'sincerity' as a democratic nation, but began to class the United States with Britain as an imperialistic power.[10]

Four years earlier, in the wake of the Quit India resolution, Merrell had informed the Secretary of State, Cordell Hull, of the dangers that would accrue from this identification for 'our moral leadership in Asia and therefore American's ability to exert its influence for acceptable and just settlements in post war Asia'.[11]

The culpable indifference of the American government during the terrible famine of 1943 which decimated the population of Bengal, the very place where US troops were based, further tarnished the image of the United States in the eyes of the Indians. The famine began in October 1942 when a cyclone followed by tidal waves devastated the eastern districts of Bengal, causing considerable damage to crops. This situation had been aggravated by the stoppage of rice imports from Burma following its conquest by the Japanese, the presence of British and American contingents on Indian soil which led to the increased demand for foodstuffs, and the apathy of the colonial authorities in the face of the shortage when it would have been possible to have food grains brought from surplus provinces even after taking into account the wartime curtailment of transport facilities. Shortages in Bengal led to the hoarding of goods for the sake of safety as well as speculation. The information communicated to the State Department by the American mission in New Delhi and the US consulate in Calcutta underscored the gravity of the food situation but the warning went unheeded. When the India League of America referred the matter to the United Nations Relief and Rehabilitation Agency, dominated by the United States, with a request for assistance, it received the reply that as India had not been occupied by the enemy, it could not lay claim to any aid. It was only in the beginning of 1944, after the initiative taken by Karl Mundt, a Republican senator, that an amendment was voted by the US Congress, which aimed at lifting India's inadmissibility to food aid. This was a conclusive step since UNRRA paid attention to it, but it finally proved futile since Britain, not desiring to see this agency, and with it the Americans, operating in India, refrained from formulating an official request for assistance. As for the Roosevelt administration, it had obligingly remained content with the repeated assurances given by the British who were anxious to minimize the magnitude of the food shortage; they asserted that they were controlling the full situation which was far from being alarming, even though its own information gave no room for optimism. This response provoked Nehru into saying that the concept of the 'Four Freedoms' presented by Roosevelt in January 1941 during the annual State of the Union address to the US Congress—and including the freedom from want, lost all meaning when 'rich England, and richer America, paid little heed to the hunger of the body that was killing millions in India'.[12]

The generosity awaited from the US government was put to the test yet again when, following inadequate rainfall in 1946, the spectre of famine once again loomed large over India. Contrary to what had occurred three years earlier, the colonial administration, as also Wavell, the Viceroy of India, and even the Attlee Cabinet in London did not deny that there were difficulties in supplies, even going to the extent of drawing the attention of the US government and of the Combined Food Board to the disastrous food situation. The scant consideration that this board gave to the request for aid and the thoughtlessness with which Truman, who had been directly alerted, treated this problem, exasperated the Indians. The *Eastern Economist*, a periodical owned by the industrialist Birla, did not mince its words, noting that 'allocations which were made to us [by the Combined Food Board] were revised by President Truman's pressure applied in the true Nazi manner'.[13] Faced with the uncooperative attitude of the United States; Nehru, after he became head of the interim government, made inquiries in September 1946 from the Soviet government for the supply of wheat and rice.

While the US government, after the Cripps mission in the spring of 1942, had chosen not to intervene in the political arena in India, it had, nonetheless, tried hard to make some headway in the economic field which till then had been the prerogative of the British. The Indians did not fail to take note of this with some apprehension. It emerged from article VII of the lend-lease agreement signed between the United States and the United Kingdom in February 1942 that Washington desired the abolition of the system of imperial preferences which enabled Britain's trade with its colony to benefit from the most-favoured nation clause and which justified the existence of discriminatory trade practices with regard to foreign products other than British ones.

The free access to the Indian market demanded by the Americans was unanimously rejected, opposition to it coming as much from London as from the future leaders of independent India and from industrialists anxious to protect their enterprises with customs barriers. The matter became even more acute when the United States contemplated signing a separate lend-lease agreement with India, substituting for the sums transferred to India by the United Kingdom from its own lend-lease agreement with the United States. Girija Shankar Bajpai, the Agent General for India in the United States, informed Dean Acheson, the Assistant Secretary of State, that the application to India of article VII, which would logically result from a lend-lease agreement, might lead to the impression that the government of India, having won a certain independence in fiscal matters from the British, would now be ready to compromise it by signing an agreement of this kind with the United States. This seemed clearly inadmissible.[14] The Americans had no intention however, of making any concessions. Harry C. Hawkins, Chief of the Division of Commercial Policy and Agreements in the US State Department, pointed this out, asserting that:

a 'diluted' article VII would not only give the green light to an exaggerated Indian self-sufficiency program after Independence but also seriously weaken our existing position with other signatories of master agreements, particularly China, in which country there is already danger of an overdose of tariff protection on 'infant industry' grounds, and with other countries with which mutual-aid agreements are contemplated.[15]

Industrialists were not the last to declare themselves hostile to the imposition of article VII. The FICCI adopted a resolution to this effect, insisting that the country conserve its fiscal independence and make no commitment which, in exchange for a lend-lease agreement, could compromise the future development of India. William Phillips, who had succeeded Louis Johnson as the personal representative of Roosevelt in India, reported that the president of the FICCI, G.L. Mehta, had confided in him the disquiet of business circles with regard to US economic intentions then and after the war. These suspicions had emerged with 'the Grady mission and appears to have been accentuated by the presence of US troops'. To allay these suspicions, Phillips offered, with the approval of the State Department, to make it known that the Americans disclaimed any motives of 'economic imperialism' or 'exploitation' on their part.[16] Even so, this was indeed what Nehru feared, basing his misgivings on the fact that US manufacturers, whose production had increased considerably during the war, were going to be obliged, once peace had returned, to look for new markets for their products and hence oppose all protectionist measures in those countries that were their potential clients. 'The economy of the USA after the war will be powerfully expansionist and almost explosive in its consequences,' he noted pointedly, and went on to wonder: 'Will this lead to some new kind of imperialism? It would be yet another tragedy if it did so, for America has the power and opportunity to set the pace for the future.'[17]

The American attempts to negotiate a lend-lease agreement with India which would not leave out article VII finally came to naught in the face of the inflexibility of the Indians. There remained simply a mutual-aid agreement by virtue of which the United States would supply industrial and military equipment in exchange for Indian raw materials. The war had, nonetheless, led to a substantial increase in commercial intercourse between India and the United States, on account of the inability of the United Kingdom to maintain a normal trade with its colony. Imports from the USA into India had come to rank in value close to those from the UK, even occasionally exceeding them. As for exports, these continued to be steady *vis-à-vis* the United Kingdom but the United States emerged clearly as the second largest buyer of Indian goods.

The presence of large numbers of American troops during the war had also contributed to substantial net dollar incomes for India. Till 1946, India had a positive trade balance with the United States but it could not freely avail of the dollars thus earned for they returned to the sterling area dollar pool composed of the dollar earnings of the member countries and out of which requirements of dollars by each of these countries were to be authorized by the control authorities in London. During the period from September 1939 to March 1945, India's net contribution to the pool was of the magnitude of $ 300 million.[18] This development was all the more disquieting since India would require its dollar earnings for post-war reconstruction. Indeed, from 1947, India registered an almost continuous trade deficit with the United States. Some argued, at the end of the war, that the country should come out of the Empire Dollar Pool and hold its dollar earnings separately. On this point, the United States did not think differently. Given their desire to abolish all obstacles in the way of free trade, the Americans made the sterling area dollar pool one of their primary targets; they saw this large amount of sterling not convertible into dollars as an influence in diverting trade away from the United States. Thus, in the financial agreement signed on 6 December 1945 with the United Kingdom, Washington agreed to write off $ 650 million (the debt which Britain owed under the lend-lease agreement) and give another line of credit amounting to $ 3,750 million; London had to promised in exchange to gradually abolish the system of imperial preferences, work towards the free convertibility of the pound, and undertake the removal of any discrimination arising from the sterling area dollar pool so that each member country could have its sterling and dollar receipts at its free disposition for current transactions anywhere. London promised in addition not to use the funds that were being given to it to effect repayments to creditors of the sterling area. Nevertheless, so as to not endanger the financial stability of Britain, the Americans considered the proposal that the British debt, and, therefore, India's sterling balances blocked in London, should be, at least partially, cancelled as compensation for Britain's contribution to the defense of its colonies. The Indians were firmly opposed to any alleviation of the British debt, which led even Nehru to issue a clarification during his visit to the United States in the autumn of 1949:

> those sterling balances represent many things. They represent the goods which we produced and sold to America, to England, sold for dollars and sterling, sold for lesser prices than the market price. They represent the lack of the necessaries of life which India had to put up with, even food. They represent the final culmination of that great tragedy, the Bengal famine, in which three million people died. . . . So, when you think of those sterling balances about which there is often so much discussion, think of the price that India paid for them in blood and suffering.[19]

The American economic offensive aimed not only at the free access of their products into the Indian market but also at the opening up of India to private investments. At the time of India's independence, foreign capital invested in the country was still three-quarters British, only around 5 per cent of the investments being American. In view of this, the Americans suggested in 1945 that negotiations be resumed for a treaty of commerce and navigation aimed at drawing up a legal framework within which American interests participating in commercial and industrial activities in India could function. The first contacts in this matter had taken place in 1941, but came to a halt the following year when the British indicated their desire to suspend the discussions regarding the treaty until after the war.[20] The Indians, having already burnt their fingers over the experience of the privileges that colonial Britain had granted to its fellow citizens in spheres of economic activity, intended to keep a tight control in future over foreign investments. Representatives of the American government were told by Ardeshir Dalal, member of the Viceroy's Executive Council (Planning and Development), who was also a director of Tata Sons Limited, as well as one of the authors of the Bombay Plan, that India would be able, if necessary, to get along without foreign capital if the latter was unwilling to come in on a minority basis. 'With both Indian business interests and the Indian elements in the Government in such a hyper-nationalistic frame of mind', George Merrell felt it was preferable for the time being to give up the idea of a treaty of this type.[21]

The Americans attempted to entice Indians with prospects of economic assistance in exchange for a more tolerant policy likely to attract investors from their country. The daily *Hindu* dated

17 January 1945 reported that Palamadi Samu Lokanathan, who was then the editor of the *Eastern Economist*, had discussed with representatives of the US government and American businessmen the possibility of getting direct loans from the United States for the industrialization of India during the coming years, and has thereafter made it known that there would be 'many strings attached to them', among these being the assurance that the credits would not be used for building production that might interfere with US export goods. Such conditions were considered unacceptable, even without taking into account the possibility that these loans might be used for political ends, as shown in the Latin American countries. On his part, the Assistant Secretary of State, William L. Clayton, had promised Ardeshir Dalal that the Indian government could obtain credits from the Export-Import Bank but under certain assurances. Among these, it was demanded that the operation of import licensing be established on a non-discriminatory manner and done away with as soon as practicable, even if this meant the withdrawal of India from the sterling area dollar pool, or again that all new enterprises in which American capital was invested be not necessarily controlled by Indians.[22] Indians and Americans once again clashed during the formulation of the Havana Charter in 1946, which was to open the path to the GATT the following year in Geneva. The Indian representative defended the right of the developing countries to implement discriminatory measures with regard to foreign capital and to take protectionist measures to safeguard their national industries.

Despite several refusals, the Americans continued to insist that the Indians give them a certain number of guarantees as a precondition to private investment. A letter sent to Nehru in February 1947 by Westmore Willcox, the Chief of the US Foreign Economic Administration Mission to India, in 1945 and 1946, testifies to this. Nehru mentioned the matter to Asaf Ali, who had been appointed Ambassador to the United States after it had been decided in October 1946 to raise the diplomatic missions to the level of embassies, calling it 'an extraordinary letter asking us to give all manner of guarantees to American businessmen'.[23] There was also the question of tying the allocation of a loan to the grant of liberal terms to Americans wanting to start industries in India. Willcox had in particular suggested a twenty-year ban on the nationalization of American companies and that, if such an event were to take place, then the Indian government would buy out the American shareholders at a price determined by the foreign company.

In his reply to Willcox, Nehru reminded him that until such time as a general policy on foreign investments was laid down, the Indian position was the following:

> We would gladly welcome help from abroad in this process [of industrialization]. But we are equally anxious to prevent any foreign control of Indian industry. Naturally if foreign industrialists invest in India in money, brains or technique, they will require to be recompensed adequately. That we fully realize. But where there is any question of control by foreign interests, there is likely to be great opposition in India.

Nehru concluded by declaring that foreign cooperation in development must be 'within the terms of our own policy and with full freedom for us to do what we consider proper'.[24]

In the days that followed his arrival in India, Grady, the US Ambassador, reiterated to the National Foreign Trade Council the desirability of an early negotiation of a treaty of friendship, navigation, and commerce to establish a sound legal framework within which the growing interchange of commodities and the development of investments may be carried on. He asked also that the obstacles, such as the complicated tax structure, hampering the conduct of manufacturing activities in India by foreign companies be removed.[25] Mountbatten did not fail to note that the United States had chosen for Ambassador a man whose primary task was manifestly to push forward US trade interests. He commented that in the wake of Independence, foreign capital had definitely a role to play in the Indian economy and that this would be fulfilled either by the British or the Americans. If the Americans were to fill the void it would be regrettable not only for the British but also for the Indians, for undoubtedly the Indians would receive 'incomparably better treatment from British than from US firms'.[26]

If differences between Indians and Americans existed in economic matters, there were also disagreements on international policy issues. The Indians criticized the complacent attitude of the Americans in the face of the efforts of the European colonial powers to regain the parts of their empires which had been conquered by the Japanese. It was, therefore, with relief that the US government, spared from having to face yet another embarrassing confrontation with the Indian nationalists, welcomed the announcement made on

20 February 1947 by Clement Attlee that the British intended to leave India before June 1948. Washington, nonetheless, was anxious about its place in independent India. The US government suspected the interim government of entertaining pro-Soviet sympathies. The State Department was particularly vexed at the activities of the Indian delegation at the United Nations. The Indian press, echoed this feeling, noting that the Indian stance at the United Nations had resulted in a lack of cooperation from the United States authorities as regards the supply of machinery and other materials required for the development of the country.[27] John Foster Dulles, who had been part of the US delegation to the United Nations, even alleged on 19 January 1947 that the Soviet Union exercised a strong influence on the 'Hindu interim government'. The presence of a Soviet delegation at the Asian Relations Conference in Delhi could not but disturb the Americans to some degree. Now, as a diplomatic dispatch from the French Embassy in New Delhi noted, 'the British are to undertake a retreat from this region, whose magnitude is yet to be decided but whose effect will undoubtedly be to weaken imperial defenses and thereby the possibilities of resistance to Russian influence in this part of the world'. It could be felt that the British withdrawal would be compensated for by an increased American presence: 'It is assumed that Great Britain, along with the transfer of power to the Indian government, will have to accept, to the advantage of the American government, at least a partial transfer of its influence in this region of the world where it has been able till now to jealously guard an exclusive right of access.'[28]

To those who were worried at his government's goodwill vis-à-vis the Soviet Union, Nehru responded indirectly in a note addressed in January 1947 to Asaf Ali and to K.P.S. Menon in which he defined what India's attitude to the two giants of the post Second World War period should be:

> Our foreign policy will ultimately be governed by our internal policy. That policy is far from being communistic and is certainly opposed to the Communist Party in India. Nevertheless there is a great and growing feeling in India in favour of some kind of a vague socialist order of society. There is much goodwill for America and expectation of help from her in many fields, especially technical. There is also a great deal of sympathy for the work of the Soviet Union and the remarkable change that this has brought about among the people. The Soviet Union being our neighbour, we shall inevitably develop closer relations with it.

And by way of conclusion, 'We cannot afford to antagonize Russia. . . . Nor indeed can we antagonize the USA'.[29] As this note reveals, Nehru reasserted his refusal to choose between the two emerging superpowers, and stressed on the economic dimension of India's relations with the United States, despite the frictions this relationship caused. In fact, H.F. Grady, reporting on his talks with Nehru in June and July 1947, said that India desired, on the one hand, to receive expert assistance from the Americans for future government projects and, on the other hand, wished to import capital goods which the United States alone was quantitatively and qualitatively in a position to supply.[30]

In *The Discovery of India*, written in prison in 1944, Nehru, having in mind the recent past, noted that 'America is a curious mixture of what is considered hard-headed realism and a vague idealism and humanitarianism', and he wondered which of these traits would be the dominating tendency in the future or what would result from their mixing together.[31] Three years later, at the time of Independence, it was clear that in the matter of aid, no philanthropy could be expected from the United States. There would be no economic assistance unless it fitted in with American interests, whose incompatibility with the ideological orientations of the Indian government was already plain, as we have seen. Nevertheless, it was felt in New Delhi that the United States remained the only country able to offer a substantial development aid package, similar to the Marshall Plan for post-war Europe, and that it would be necessary to overlook disagreements and come to terms with the Americans since, at least in the near future, there seemed no possibility of securing assistance from the Soviets. G.S. Bajpai, who had become Secretary General in the Ministry of External Affairs, during a visit to the United States in the spring of 1948, identified two fundamental reasons preventing India from joining the Soviet bloc. The first factor was the democratic ideals of the government of India and its respect for individual liberty. 'Second, India can expect no effective assistance from the USSR in its primary objective of developing and strengthening itself economically and militarily. In fact, the United States is the only country in a position to aid India.'[32] This pragmatic assessment of India's needs embodied prospective dilemmas between economic contingencies and foreign policy stance.

NOTES

1. The Secretary of State (Cordell Hull) to the British Ambassador (Lord Halifax), 21 May 1941. *Foreign Relations of the United States (FRUS), 1941*, vol. 3, pp. 170-1.
2. Nehru was mistrustful of the possible discrepancy between the ideals of liberty and democracy professed by the American leaders and their practice as observed in their relations with foreign countries. During the Congress of Oppressed Nationalities in Brussels in February 1927, in a confidential report addressed to the Working Committee of the INC, he felt that 'the great problem of the near future will be American imperialism, even more than British imperialism. Or it may be, and all indications point to it, that the two will join together to create a powerful Anglo-Saxon bloc to dominate the world.' *Selected Works of Jawaharlal Nehru*, vol. 2, Delhi: Orient Longman, 1974, p. 281.
3. Chiang Kai-shek to Roosevelt, 25 February 1942. *FRUS, 1942*, vol. 1, pp. 604-6.
4. Franklin D. Roosevelt to Winston Churchill, 10 March 1942. Ibid., p. 616.
5. *New York Times*, 11 November 1942.
6. J.L. Nehru, *The Discovery of India*, p. 464.
7. See Roosevelt's letter to Churchill after the breakdown of the negotiations. *FRUS, 1942*, vol. 1, pp. 633-4.
8. 'To American Friends', *Harijan* (Ahmedabad), 9 August 1942. Earlier in the issue of 26 April, the Mahatma had written: 'We know what American aid [in soldiers] means. It amounts in the end to American influence, if not American rule added to British. It is a tremendous price to pay for the possible success of Allied armies.'
9. *Selected Works of Jawaharlal Nehru*, vol. 14, p. 458.
10. The Commissioner in India (Merrell), to the Secretary of State, 10 June 1946. *FRUS, 1946*, vol. 5, p. 91.
11. 11 August 1942. *FRUS, 1942*, vol. 1, pp. 712-13.
12. J.L. Nehru, *The Discovery of India*, p. 17. After the new Viceroy, Lord Wavell, informed him that a minimum of one million tons of food grains would have to be imported in 1944, Churchill had to make up his mind to ask Roosevelt for permission to use allied ships to transport Australian wheat to India. Roosevelt endorsed the inability expressed by the US Joint Chiefs of Staff in May 1944 to divert ships needed for military operations. M.S. Venkataramani, *Bengal Famine of 1943: The American Response*, pp. 64-8.
13. *Eastern Economist*, 10 May 1946, p. 769.
14. Memorandum of conversation by the Assistant Secretary of State (Acheson), 4 March 1943. *FRUS, 1943*, vol. 4, p. 259.
15. Memorandum by the Chief of the Division of Commercial Policy and Agreements (Hawkins), 25 January 1943. Ibid., pp. 250-1. See also conversation between Acheson and Bajpai of 30 March 1943, pp. 261-2.

16. Phillips to the Secretary of State, 9 February 1943, Ibid., pp. 251-2. The Acting Secretary of State to Phillips, on 6 March 1943. Ibid., p. 259. The Grady mission is the US technical mission which spent five weeks in India in April-May 1942 and to which reference has already been made. Henry F. Grady, the first US Ambassador to India, headed it. This mission met Indian government officials and industrialists. The industrialists were so suspicious of US intentions that Grady had to assure the FICCI on 8 May 1942 that the only objective of the mission was to examine how to accomplish an increase in the production of war materiel and that American capitalists had no intention of making use of this opportunity to establish themselves in India.
17. J.L. Nehru, *The Discovery of India*, p. 546.
18. S.L.N. Sinha (prepared by), *History of the Reserve Bank of India (1935-51)*, p. 369.
19. Nehru's speech before the National Foreign Trade Council and the Far East America Council of Commerce and Industry, on 20 October 1949. J.L. Nehru, *Visit to America*, New York: The John Day Co., 1950 p. 67.
20. Cordell Hull, *Memoirs*, vol. 2, London, 1948, p. 1483.
21. The Secretary in Charge at New Delhi (Merrell) to the Secretary of State, 27 February 1945. *FRUS, 1945*, vol. 6, p. 272.
22. The Commissioner in India (Merrell) to the Secretary of State, 18 July 1945. Ibid., pp. 276-7.
23. Nehru to Asaf Ali, 29 April 1947. *Selected Works of Jawaharlal Nehru* (*second series*), vol. 2, p. 591.
24. Nehru to Willcox, 29 April 1947. Ibid., pp. 589-90.
25. *Hindustan Times*, 20 April 1947.
26. Minutes of a meeting on industrial planning in the dominions of India and Pakistan, New Delhi, 11 September 1947. *Mountbatten Papers*, File no. 51. Nehru Memorial Museum & Library, New Delhi.
27. See Nehru's letter to Krishna Menon, of 29 January 1947. *Selected Works of Jawaharlal Nehru* (*second series*), vol. 1, pp. 587-8.
28. Dispatch of Henri Roux, French Chargé d'Affaires in New Delhi, 27 May 1947. *AQO*, Asie-Océanie, 1944-1955, Inde, vol. 66.
29. 22 January 1947. *Selected Works of Jawaharlal Nehru* (*second series*), vol. 1, p. 576.
30. The Ambassador in India to the Secretary of State, 27 June and 9 July 1947, *FRUS, 1947*, vol. 3, p. 157 and pp. 160-1.
31. J.L. Nehru, *The Discovery of India*, p. 539.
32. Memorandum of a conversation by the Acting Secretary of State (Lovett), on 2 April 1948. *FRUS, 1948*, vol. 5, p. 507.

CHAPTER 6

A Dialogue of the Deaf

WE HAVE ALREADY underlined how important it was for the Indian government to be able to draw from the sterling balances blocked in London. It was also essential to know the manner and method of their convertibility into dollars. The Anglo-American loan agreement had provided that the British government would enter into negotiations with the countries that were the holders of these sterling balances. Discussions between the British and the Indians took place in New Delhi in February 1947. The British delegation warned that the United Kingdom intended to put some restrictions on the withdrawal of sterling balances for the settlement of expenditures within, as also outside, the sterling area. The discussions were resumed in July 1947 in London, but in view of the far-reaching political changes in India, only an interim agreement was signed on 14 August 1947.

This agreement endorsed the impossibility of writing off any part of the debt incurred by Great Britain but fixed some limitation on the use of it. The agreement provided for two accounts to be opened by the RBI with the Bank of England. The no. 2 account was credited with the total amount of the sterling balances that India possessed, viz., some £ 1,160 million. As for the no. 1 account, established for current purposes, it was funded from withdrawals from the no. 2 account—after agreement between the two parties—, from income accruing by way of interest on the sterling balances credited in the no. 2 account and from the earnings of pounds sterling derived from current transactions. By virtue of the agreement, £ 35 million (the Indians had asked for £ 48.5 million in view of the high prices of food imports) were then transferred to the no. 1 account meant to meet the estimated deficit on the current account for the second half of the year. In addition, a working balance of £ 30 million was credited, to serve as a reserve to be utilized for meeting any temporary deficits.

After having accepted, under US pressure, a return to a free convertibility of the pound, the United Kingdom had to repudiate this measure from 21 August 1947, so as to put a stop to the severe depletion of its dollar reserves. If India's current earnings of sterling and the amounts released under the August agreement had not been rendered inconvertible, this new development did not fail to have an effect on the financial agreement on sterling balances when this was renewed on 15 February 1948 to cover the first six months of the year. In July 1947, the Indian delegation had estimated the dollar deficit for the second half of 1947 to be £ 15 million. But it turned out to be £ 38 million. As the British insisted that efforts be made by the Indian side to reduce to the maximum its expenditures incurred in dollars, a limit was thereafter fixed to the amount of convertible pounds. Out of the extra £ 18 million that the Indian government was authorized to draw from the sterling assets to cover any deficit till 30 June 1948, only £ 10 million could be converted into dollars. In the event that the convertible sterling balances were not sufficient to cover the trade deficit with the dollar area, it was suggested that India would turn to the International Monetary Fund.

The Finance Minister, Shanmukham Chetty, went to London to conclude, on 9 July 1948, a three-year agreement (up to the end of June 1951) governing the release of the sterling balances. No releases from the no. 2 account to the no. 1 account were provided for till 30 June 1949 in view of the large balance of nearly £ 80 million on the no. 1 account. On the other hand, during each of the two subsequent years, the RBI would be credited with £ 40 million on the no. 1 account. Hence, all in all, India could avail of £ 160 million over a period of three years, in addition to the receipts coming from an eventual positive trade balance with the sterling area. There was also an unpublished understanding that the second year releases (1949-50) could be anticipated if, in 1948-9, the balance at the no. 1 account fell below the working balance of £ 30 million. The agreement had also made it possible to assess the total amount of sterling resources figuring in the no. 2 account, once the share allocated to Pakistan had been subtracted, as also the sums due by India to the United Kingdom in respect of military stores and fixed assets left behind and provisions for pensionary liabilities. The sum arrived at was thus £ 800 million, the equivalent of Rs. 10.64 billion (the parity between the two currencies, unchanged till the devaluation of the rupee in June 1966, being Rs. 13.33 for £ 1).

If the agreement finally appeared relatively satisfactory because it extended over a fairly long period, thus making it possible to draw up the general lines of an import policy taking into account the sterling balances that England was putting at India's disposal for three years, a long-term solution to the problem of hard currencies deficit had not for all that been found. Till 30 June 1949, only £ 15 million ($ 60 million) would be convertible on the basis of an estimated hard currency deficit of $ 160 million which was to be covered, in addition to the convertible sterling, by borrowing from the IMF and by India's own earnings of hard currencies. While before the war about 10 per cent of India's external trade was conducted with the dollar area and the balance was positive, at the end of the 1940s it had exceeded 20 per cent and there was a deficit.

India's sterling assets were finally advantageous for Great Britain because they ensured continued close economic relations, notably a market for their manufactured goods, and eventually a means of pressure which it was in its interest to maintain as long as possible. Faced with a restriction on the drawings of hard currencies from the central reserves of the sterling area, India, which had been forced lately to buy from the hard currency countries certain commodities which the latter used to obtain traditionally from within the sterling area or from soft currency countries, required the United Kingdom government to help in securing those requirements from sterling area sources.[1] Some experts underlined the paradoxical situation in which India now found itself, obliged as it was to turn to the bodies which sprang from the Bretton Woods agreements—the IMF and the International Bank for Reconstruction and Development—while it owned fairly large sterling balances blocked in England and whose release and convertibility had to be carefully negotiated. The *Economic Weekly* criticized the government over its attitude on the hand-to-mouth system of annual negotiations for releases which some found too conciliatory:

> The Nehru Cabinet has succeeded in removing from public gaze the tempting mirage of the sterling balances. They seem to have disappeared from the picture altogether. We have come to accept, instead, the position of a debtor country in which we had been before, and we appear on the world scene as applicant for loans, instead of concentrating our efforts towards recovering what we had lent at such a heavy cost in terms of human lives and preventable misery.[2]

Confronted with a relative shortage of dollars along with poor local investments, some people within government and in business circles turned towards the United States, hoping to find there the funds and the capital goods which would help to face the challenge of development. Whether it be private investment, bilateral aid, or credits from the IBRD or the IMF within which Washington played a major role, American financial muscle seemed to be the unavoidable recourse to offset the investments and balance of payments problems.[3] This was a bitter pill to swallow for those who, like Nehru, were mistrustful of 'dollar imperialism', and who had already had, before Independence, a foretaste of American demands in exchange for financial support. The British also strengthened the fears of the Indians on this point, a fact which did not escape Grady's notice:

The British have been friendly, but have made no attempt to consult with us on common problems or to ask our advice . . . . On more than one occasion, Mountbatten has warned Nehru against dollar imperialism . . . the British are not happy about the strong position which we have in India, or about the weak position which they have. They are trying to salvage everything they can from the separation.'[4]

The hopes of those counting on American capital to bring some dynamism into a largely stagnant economy were thwarted, both in regard to aid as well as in the field of direct investments. An economy in which the state would own enterprises and regulate industrial activity was not very conducive to attracting foreign capital, or votaries of free enterprise. The industrial policy resolution of 1948 did not succeed in putting an end to American reticence, the powers of the state being still considered too dissuasive and the call for foreign capital too vitiated with prohibitive restrictions. The Indian government was, in fact, reduced to square the circle in its desire to formulate a policy with regard to foreign capital which was attractive enough in the eyes of potential foreign investors while making it possible also to control their activities in the name of national objectives and also in order to reassure local entrepreneurs.

Neither the US government nor private investors in America showed any eagerness to come to the assistance of India's economic development. No immediate communist threat justified the dispatch of urgent aid as had been done when hundreds of millions of dollars had been spent in the attempt to keep afloat the decaying regime of Chiang Kai-shek. East Asia, where American interests had been established over a longer length of time, had a higher geopolitical value in Asia than the Indian subcontinent. When Bajpai held talks in September 1947 with Grady about the possibility of American loans to India, he was advised by the latter to direct Indian industrialists to borrow from US commercial banks and the Indian government to approach the World Bank or the Export-Import Bank for its large public works.[5] Finally, the desire exhibited by New Delhi to keep itself away from the blocs was not appreciated by the Americans any more than by the Soviets. While the USSR disavowed any middle path between the socialist and the imperialist camps, the USA was no less incredulous and critical over the possibility of not taking sides in what was presented as a struggle between communist totalitarianism and the free world. The American government felt that India was attaching too much importance to the fight against colonialism, a form of imperialism that was in any case condemned to rapidly disappear, without seeing the far graver danger of Soviet hegemony and the movement which it was spearheading: the spread of international communism.

Indians had no doubt at all that it was non-alignment, or rather what was then called neutrality, that blocked the grant of aid from America, and this realization gave rise to attitudes in which the idea of economic realism came into conflict with the notion of political independence. An article in the *Hindustan Times* of 26 December 1947 thus felt that 'for a half-naked, half-starved country to take up a mighty pose and talk about its neutrality . . . is a pastime which is not only amateurish but may prove positively harmful to her real interests', and it called for a reorientation of external policy in the light of the hard realities in a clearly pro-Western direction. For the Indian Communists, American aid necessarily signified the surrender of one's sovereignty. There were also those for whom, in the context of a bipolarized world, the United States could not ignore the political future of India and would therefore be led to offer aid without New Delhi having to make any basic concessions. N.G. Ranga, a member of the Parliament's Standing Committee for External Affairs, argued along these lines; he felt that India could hope to obtain aid without having to give in to any pressure of a political nature from the Americans. The United States 'are sure to abandon any possible political ambitions of theirs and to offer the loans of their capital and skill along the Marshall Plan or through the World Bank if only to retain our goodwill and not to oblige us to seek the assistance of others'.[6]

New Delhi was no less critical of America's foreign policy than

Washington was of India's. Nehru was particularly disdainful: 'It is astonishing how naïve the Americans are in their foreign policy. It is only their money and their power that carries them through, not their intelligence or any other quality.'[7] India regarded the United States as being as responsible as the USSR for the tense atmosphere around the world, on account of its hegemonic aspirations. The Indians regretted that a frenzied anti-Communism governed all the decisions of the US State Department and led it to close its eyes to the acts of its European allies in the colonies, even helping them indirectly and giving them the means, with subsidies under the Marshall Plan, to pursue their policy of repression against nationalist movements overseas. It thereby compromised the basic principle of the people's right to self-determination, as it had done some years earlier in India in different circumstances. Even if the Indian government did not show any particular sympathy for the communist movements in South-East Asia, the Indians felt, nonetheless, that these were primarily the expressions of a nationalism being curbed by the colonial powers.

Another point of disagreement between the two countries was the question of Kashmir which was to endlessly embitter Indo-American relations. When New Delhi submitted to the UN Security Council a complaint against Pakistan for its support to the armed raiders who had invaded a part of Kashmir in October 1947, thus leading the Maharaja to sign the instrument of accession of this province to India, India never suspected that its action was going to turn against itself. Far from officially acknowledging the responsibility of Pakistan in the triggering of the first Indo-Pakistani conflict, the Security Council, guided by the views of the United Kingdom and the United States, set up a United Nations Commission for India and Pakistan. It was to work for the creation of conditions favourable to the holding of plebiscite in Kashmir supervised by the United Nations, to which New Delhi was opposed as long as Pakistani troops, both regular and irregular, would not first have withdrawn from the areas that they were occupying in Kashmir. The Indian government felt it had been tricked in the name of considerations which had nothing much to do with the question of the legality of the accession of Kashmir to India, and which arose more out of strategic calculations related to the emerging Cold War. The only positive development in the months that followed was the coming into force of a ceasefire on 1 January 1949.

It was clear in New Delhi that the Truman administration was seeking to show greater complaisance towards the theocratic regime in Pakistan. An explanation of the American attitude was perhaps the desire to be reconciled with the Muslim countries which were offended at Washington's pro-Israeli stand which found expression in the support for the partition of Palestine; and, above all, it ensued from the perspective of making Pakistan into a bulwark against a Soviet thrust towards the warm seas and from the belief that the US wished to establish bases in Pakistan in the event of a war with the USSR. The conclusions arrived at during a meeting of the US Joint Chiefs of Staff concurred with this view. While accepting that, in the event of war, the Soviets would probably not risk any substantial military effort in South Asia in view of its inaccessibility from the north and of the fact that more remunerative objectives existed in Europe, the Middle East and the Far East, they recognized that Pakistan was strategically positioned in the subcontinent within the context of a national policy of communist containment. A Soviet penetration in the region would deprive the United States of a source of supply of raw materials and would threaten the sea routes in the Indian Ocean. The strategic importance of the Karachi-Lahore area was not negligible, in spite of tremendous logistic difficulties, since it could serve as a base for air operations against the central USSR and as a staging area for forces engaged in the defense or the recapture of the oil-bearing regions of the Middle East.[8] The bonds that the United States developed with Pakistan began to increasingly influence Indo-American relations. The US Embassy in India cautioned against any financial aid to Pakistan which was not followed by a similar gesture towards India and, more generally, against all unequal treatment which might not only 'prejudice the prospects of negotiating a treaty of friendship, commerce and navigation with India, but also would have an adverse effect on all aspects of the United States of America relations with India'.[9]

Some in India hoped that the third conference of the Economic Commission for Asia and the Far East, held in Ootacamund from 1 to 12 June 1948, would provide the United States with a golden opportunity to announce a regional development plan on the lines of the European Recovery Programme which had come into force in April. The financial weekly *Commerce* wrote on this occasion that 'Asia and the Far East need a "Grady Plan" just as Europe has a Marshall Plan.'[10] A little before leaving his post as Indian envoy to the United States, Asaf Ali had mentioned in Washington the necessity 'to get all Asian nations' representatives together to catalogue their resources and needs as did the sixteen nations of Europe at Paris' in order to discover 'where and how their needs could best be secured. That is where the United States comes in, mainly as a supplier of goods.' He had just reiterated the views he had already expressed to officials in the State Department and other branches of the American government.[11]

At Ootacamund, in his inaugural speech of 1 June, Nehru spoke on the theme, one of his favourities, of an India cloaked in dignity accepting foreign aid only if there was no strings attached to it. 'We would rather delay our development, industrial or other, than submit to any kind of economic domination by any country. That is an axiom which is accepted by everyone in India', declared the Prime Minister. He pointed out that the donor countries would not for all that be indulging in an act of charity, considering the inter-dependence existing between countries on the global scale: 'Today, if one part of the world goes down economically, it has a tendency to drag others with it. . . . So it is not a question of the prosperous, merely out of the generosity of their hearts, helping those who are not prosperous, though generosity is a good thing. But it is a question of enlightened self-interest.'[12] The next day, the editorial of the *Hindu*, commending Nehru's speech under the title 'Asia demands Justice', expressed the view that the West was under a moral obligation to come to the help of India and that by giving assistance, the West would simply be atoning for all its years of colonial exploitation.

However, it was not long before disillusionment set in. As the discussions progressed, the Indian delegation saw its latest hopes for an offer of American assistance utterly shattered. The hard-hitting statement made on 7 June by the American Ambassador, during a meeting of the ECAFE's committee on industrial development, dampened their spirits. Not only was Grady silent on this point but he also set about criticizing the countries which shilly-shallied over foreign private investment. He conceded, probably with India in mind, that if a country fears the domination of foreign capital, it was perfectly logical for it to pass laws and make administrative provisions that would keep capital out. But, he pointed out, it was quite inconsistent for the leaders of a country to complain that such capital did not come in when they were taking measures and announcing policies which could have no effect other than to keep it out. He once again brought up the possibility of obtaining loans from private banks in capital-exporting countries, or even from the World Bank or the Export-Import Bank, and in special cases from the US Congress, but he added 'none of them is inclined to give away money or advance it under conditions which make it in effect a gift'. Ultimately, it was only from direct investments in enterprise that adequate supplies of capital could really be obtained.[13]

The Indians reacted rather strongly to the remarks of the American Ambassador. Thus, a member of their delegation, Sitarama Reddy, replying to the allegations made by Grady over the incoherence of the government policy, reasserted the determination of the state to oppose 'the growth of vested interests which may later prove harmful to our national economic or political interests'.[14] The same sentiments were echoed in most of the English language dailies. The *Amrita Bazar Patrika* commented that the recent past could not be ignored and that it should be clear to foreign investors or creditors that they would not be allowed, directly or indirectly, on the plea of security, to interfere in the management or manipulation of political events and affairs of the country.[15] However, the financial press did not share the deep indignation expressed by the other mainstream Indian journals at the remarks of the American Ambassador.

Commerce considered the assurance demanded by the American Ambassador concerning private investment as perfectly legitimate. This journal reflected the point of view of economic circles more dogmatically committed to liberalization and it adopted a more tolerant attitude towards foreign private capital, differing in this from the *Eastern Economist* whose views were closer to the official attitude of FICCI. Concerning the four possibilities mentioned by Grady for obtaining external financial assistance, the author of the article was not opposed to their order of preference, favouring loans from individual banks or from a consortia of banks, eventually from business firms prepared to invest overseas, since it involves little or no political or economic domination and would make it easier to get the capital goods as well as training and know-how for industries. Involving the World Bank was considered more hazardous for a country which is not keen to encourage private enterprise and which advocates a mixed economy. As for financial aid coming from the Export-Import Bank or sanctioned by the US Congress, it was unrealistic 'unless the Government of India is prepared to associate itself actively, or at least sympathize, with the foreign policy of the United States'. And those who criticized Grady's speech for not containing a concrete offer of aid, as George Marshall had done at Harvard University, were 'the very people who are not prepared either to face the political implications thereof or even to clarify their policy in regard to communism'.[16]

The *Eastern Economist* published in June, July, and August 1948 three articles on the relationship between foreign aid and India's foreign policy, with an interesting gradation showing the growing divorce between the official position and the attitude of business circles, and with them, certain sections of the right wing in the Congress, holding the view that non-alignment worked against the economic realities of an underdeveloped country. The first of these articles appeared the day after the ECAFE meeting. 'There can be little doubt, at least in the minds of those who have visited the United States, that a dollar loan would be immediately available if India could qualify on the political front', noted the author and proceeded to ask Americans not to let themselves be put off by Indian neutrality but to consider it in its historical context: 'The painful assertion of our political neutrality in the international sphere arises from no lack of friendship with the United States or of admiration for her tremendous achievements but from a fear that we may again only too easily become a pawn in another's game.' The author appealed to the Americans, once this attitude had been correctly understood, to take the first step, by offering assistance 'knowing that we cannot, because of our new-born pride, be beggars at her doors'.

In the second article which appeared on 2 July, the attitude which said: 'Please, understand our neutrality and do not take it amiss' disappeared and was replaced by a call for less idealism and greater pragmatism while demanding that the policy of neutrality be reassessed in view of economic imperatives, and since the Soviet Union was not inclined to help India it was necessary to show support for the Americans. 'It is suggested that we should redefine our foreign policy, giving it direction and positive purpose in the economic sphere . . . and accept constructive help where we can get it, without timid hesitation that we may endanger neutrality in others' eyes. In practical terms, this means a leaning toward the United States.' The third article openly called for India to come down upon the Western side of the political fence no longer only on account of the economic benefits that would follow, but as the clear manifestation of a determined opposition to communism and a logical outcome of the economic ties that already bound India to the Western world:

An 'independent' foreign policy—by which we can mean only that we shall not lean in any direction—can lead only to a Communist victory and in effect decree no neutrality but a leaning towards the USSR. . . . Economically we are already dependent on the United States and the United Kingdom for our capital equipment and, so long as we stay in the Commonwealth and the sterling area, we are already tied, however loosely, to British strings. To make that bond politically closer in an attempt to destroy the new enemy that confronts us is merely to recognize an economic fact already there.[17]

While the Prime Minister admitted that India's relations with the Western world were much closer than with the Communist bloc—India was then negotiating its continuance within the Commonwealth—and admitted a certain benevolent neutrality with regard to the West, he was not for all that inclined to cross over to take that one step separating India from alignment in its proper and precise form. A hard-headed Nehru explained this in a note to K.P.S. Menon:

If we line up on one side that potential importance and bargaining power (in world affairs) are lost. . . . The safest policy, therefore, appears to be is to be friendly to America, to give them fair terms, to invite their help on such terms, and at the same time not to tie ourselves up too much with their world or their economic policy. Keeping a free hand we will ultimately get more from them and at the same time get the friendship and cooperation of other countries also.[18]

The Americans, on the one hand, were promptly accused of being miserly when it came to giving aid to the underdeveloped countries of Asia while it was granting billions of dollars to western Europe under the Marshall Plan. And the argument according to which the reconstruction of the economies of western Europe would benefit Asian countries also by increasing the number of states likely to meet their needs of capital goods and aid, was considered in India as specious. But, on the other hand, they invited criticism sustained by the impression that, as a consequence of the Marshall Plan, the American domination in the foreign field was constantly growing. This issue was discussed when the US Secretary of State met Nehru in Paris in October 1948, on the occasion of a meeting of the UNGA. To resolve the dilemma, Marshall pointed out that government loans were much more likely to form the basis for charges of imperialism than private loans.[19] A report presented during the fourth meeting of the ECAFE, held in Australia from 29 November to 11 December 1948, had calculated at $ 13.6 billion over a period of about five years the amount of foreign exchange indispensable for the implementation of regional development plans. That was like building castles in the air, Nehru said, as long as the United States 'are not providing either machinery or dollar exchange for the industrial rehabilitation of Eastern countries', regretting once again that 'the habit of ignoring Asia still continues'.[20] The only interest that Washington seemed to take in this continent was primarily to give military assistance to reactionary and dictatorial regimes which had nothing in common with the democratic ideals proclaimed by the United States, whether it be the regimes of Chiang Kai-shek in China, of Elpidio Quirino in the Philippines, or of Syngman Rhee in Korea.

The year 1949 seemed to begin on a more auspicious note. On 20 January, President Truman, in his inaugural address, announced a programme for peace and freedom whose fourth point was 'a bold new program for making the benefits of our scientific advances and industrial progress available for the improvement and growth of underdeveloped areas'.[21] It was the first concrete sign of a global aid programme for the development of the Third World. Its scope was, however, limited. President Truman's Point Four Programme—it was passed by the US Congress only in May 1950—provided for the possibility of technical assistance to underdeveloped countries, on the whole not very costly, supplemented by the prospect of foreign direct investments.

In the days that followed the announcement of the Point Four Programme, a World Bank mission arrived in New Delhi. Indian officials were aware of the close bonds between the US government and the IBRD, and they hoped that the renewed interest that Washington seemed to evince in the advancement of underdeveloped countries would lead to a favourable consideration of their requests for loans from this agency—India had submitted a list of projects totalling $ 506 million. The *Economic Weekly* had just underlined the fact that 'India is desperately in need of dollars.'[22] In fact, by the end of March, the entire annual quota to which the country was then entitled from the IMF had been drawn, i.e. $ 100 million, a quarter of its total contribution. But the IMF could at best grant a lump sum financial assistance to help to tide over the liquidity crunch being experienced in meeting current expenditures. On 16 March, the Finance Minister, John Matthai, informed Parliament about the inadequacy of India's capital resources to finance all the nation-building schemes that were being contemplated, and he invited American capital and American enterprises to collaborate with Indian concerns.[23]

A few days later, the government clarified its policy concerning foreign capital, in a speech made by the Prime Minister on 6 April 1949. The objective was to reassure foreign investors. Nehru stressed that while the insistence on regulating the scope and manner of foreign capital arose from India's bitter historical experience of colonial subjugation, he assured the world that:

> circumstances today are quite different . . . Indian capital needs to be supplemented by foreign capital not only because our national savings will not be enough for the rapid development of the country on the scale we wish, but also because in many cases scientific, technical and industrial knowledge and capital equipment can best be secured along with foreign capital.[24]

As a consequence of this, there would be no discrimination towards foreign enterprises, which would be subjected to the same rules as the Indian undertakings. There would be no restriction on the withdrawal of foreign capital investments, and remittance of profits would only be subjected to foreign exchange considerations. Reasonable facilities for the remittances of proceeds and a fair and equitable compensation would be provided for foreign enterprises compulsorily acquired. Except in exceptional cases, the major interest in the ownership and effective control of an undertaking would be in Indian hands. While the stress laid on the Indianization of the personnel was reaffirmed, the government was agreeable to the employment of non-Indians, as a stopgap measure, in posts requiring technical skill and experience when Indians with the requisite qualifications were not available.

In September, the government even went as far as to announce that 'it will not be in the interest of the country to wait indefinitely till Indian capital is forthcoming'. In order to secure 'the maximum possible influx of foreign capital in the shortest possible time', the government did not consider that the granting of permission to allow non-Indian majority ownership, and in some cases even non-Indian effective control, particularly in the formative stages, could be considered *ipso facto* as detrimental to the national interests. These measures worried Indian industrialists who considered that the 'open door policy for foreign capital' was going too far. FICCI asked for a strict application of the industrial policy resolution of 1948, and even indicated a desire for a return to the still more restrictive recommendations made by the Advisory Planning Board in 1947. It did this so that foreign concerns would be prevented from establishing themselves in India for producing goods which were already being manufactured or which might be manufactured by indigenous enterprises.[25]

The Indian Ambassadors to the United States, Asaf Ali, Benegal Rama Rau, and Vijayalakshmi Pandit, on their part, and Nehru, on his part, did not hesitate to remind their interlocutors in the West that if India were to manage without aid, its economic development would be delayed and the risks of difficult political and social problems would thereby be multiplied, and this would be like playing into the hands of the Communists.[26] In May 1949, G.D. Birla, with the backing of the Indian government, went to the United States to acquaint himself with the mood of the American government and its businessmen and, at the same time, as a preliminary to Nehru's forthcoming visit, to pave the way for negotiations on American aid to India. He found the Americans overly concerned by possible nationalization, existing regulations, excessive taxes, and difficulties in bringing back profits. Birla pointed out to the Americans that a sum of $ 1 billion would be required in the years to come for the industrial equipment that India needed.[27] A British diplomat observed that:

> there was very little chance indeed of American big business putting money independently into India and that the International Bank and the American official world in general are pretty doubtful but realize the political importance of India and are prepared to risk a certain amount of money, provided it is not much. Above all the Americans are most anxious not to be caught again in India as they had been caught in China.[28]

Indeed, the US government restricted its support to the granting of some requests for loans from the IBRD; this materialized in two loans—the first ones—granted a little before Nehru's arrival in the United States.

In August 1949, while turning down some of the Indian projects as economically unsound, the World Bank offered a loan of an amount of $ 34 million for the development of Indian railways. It was meant for the purchase of locomotives, boilers, and spare parts from the United States and from Canada in order to alleviate the transport crisis. The second loan of $ 10 million for the purchase of American heavy tractors for use in land reclamation was granted in September. A third credit of $ 18.5 million was finalized in April 1950 to enable the construction, as part of the development of the Damodar Valley, of the Bokaro thermal station in Bihar; this was notably for the purpose of increasing the production of coal and minerals in the region. It was also meant to enable the Indian agency in charge of the work to honour a contract signed in 1948 with an American enterprise, by supplying to it the foreign exchange required for the import of the equipment. The United States had its own motives for supporting the Indian requests for credits from the IBRD; a policy statement of the State Department mentioned the need to reduce the utilization of foreign exchange for non-productive purposes, that is to say, for the import of food grains, and to increase and facilitate the export of important raw materials stockpiled in the United States.[29] The Indians continued, however, to feel that the World Bank had till then failed to fulfil its function. Thus, before the UN Economic and Social Council, Ramaswamy Mudaliar, the Indian delegate, denounced the conditions tied to the IBRD loans, notably the high rates of interest, the strict control over the use of the loans, and the requirement of serious assurances regarding the ability of the borrower state to reimburse the loans. He claimed that, 'even a private investor would be willing to take more risks than the International Bank at this time'. Mudaliar's criticism of the IBRD underlined the failure of this institution to play a more dynamic role in the development of underdeveloped countries.[30]

In response to President Truman's invitation, Nehru visited North America in the autumn of 1949. Noting the importance of this visit, the British High Commissioner in New Delhi stated that the Foreign Office had definitely a role to play since the US government might have thought of seizing this opportunity to substitute Britain as the leader in the formulation of the South Asian policy. 'I am doubtful whether the visit to America will necessarily produce the good results we desire if it is left entirely to the Americans and the Indians', Archibald Nye wrote. Nehru's trip was regarded as potentially the key factor in overcoming Indian suspicions of the United States and in persuading America to join with the United Kingdom in the economic development of India and in the rehabilitation of Southern Asia generally. After noticing that 'hitherto the Americans have been reluctant to discuss their Asian policies with us (perhaps because they have none!)', it was high time to have frank discussions with the State Department so that there is at least the beginnings of an agreed Anglo-American policy in the region for 'time presses and this opportunity is unlikely to arise again. Indeed if the Nehru visit is the failure or only a partial success, the long term prospects not so much for a psychological counter-attack against Communism but for resisting Soviet pressure in Asia might be bleak indeed'.[31]

The request for American support for India's economic development was one of the main subjects broached during Nehru's visit, which included numerous meetings with business circles. The tone was set by a remark, even if it was probably nothing more than a figure of speech, made by Nehru to Krishna Menon on the need to 'align with the United States somewhat and build up our economic and military strength'.[32] Nehru would have to deploy all his diplomacy and tact to underline India's need for aid without for all that appearing to overtly depend on American funds. This comes out from a note Nehru sent to John Matthai in which he expressed his intention of talking 'frankly, whenever occasion arises, about American help in various ways, but to talk rather in a confident tone conscious of India's position and with faith in India'.[33] Perhaps it was no coincidence that the new concessions offered in September to foreign capital (to which reference has been made above), as compared to the policy spelled out by Nehru in April, were announced a few weeks before this visit.

India had been blowing hot and cold on its need for dollars during the earlier months. As a direct consequence of larger imports than foreseen, notably following the relaxation of import restrictions—which had to be re-imposed in May 1949—and the ever larger purchase of food grains from abroad, there was a debit of $ 200 million in the trade balance with the dollar area for the financial year 1948-9 ($ 1 was worth Rs. 3.3 before devaluation in September 1949 and Rs. 4.76 after it).[34] To meet this large hard currency deficit that could not be fully financed by the $ 60 million of sterling assets that were convertible in accordance with the agreement of 9 July 1948 and by drawings from the IMF, London had agreed in February 1949 to advance India the necessary hard currency as an overdrawal to be reimbursed to the UK from the convertible sterling to be made available for the period 1949-50. In June 1949, John Matthai had asked B.K. Nehru to go to Washington to expedite the withdrawal of a new credit of $ 100 million from the IMF and to exert pressure on the State Department in order that the Export-Import Bank extend financial support to India. These requests were to remain a dead letter. Even though Matthai had informed the new American Ambassador, Loy Henderson, on 22 June about India's concern at the US representative opposing Indian application for dollar withdrawals from the IMF by which 'its dollar situation would become immediately desperate and its entire budget plans upset'. As for Nehru, he suggested that Vijayalakshmi Pandit should broach this problem directly with the Secretary to the Treasury.[35]

One of the remedies to the chronic shortage of dollars was to ask for a modification of the agreement of 9 July 1948 on the transfer of the sterling balances. A mission led by John Matthai went to London to hold discussions with the British government. Through an exchange of letters in early August 1949, Great Britain agreed to the £ 81 million drawn from the no. 2 account, to keep the no. 1 account at the minimum of £ 30 million, and for which no provision had been made in July 1948, thus regularizing the overdrafts made by India. As for the allocations of sterling balances provided for the second (1949-50) and third (1950-1) years, they were increased from £ 40 to £ 50 million. Another notable feature of the new agreement was that India was readmitted to the full privileges of the membership of the sterling area and thereby no quantitative restrictions were placed on the availability of the released balances for payment in hard currency areas. Nevertheless, the Indian government promised in exchange, along with the other member countries of the sterling bloc, to restrict its dollar imports between July 1949 and June 1950 to a level equal to 75 per cent of those of the twelve preceding months, outside of the imports which would be covered by eventual American loans. Consequently, India could expect to draw on the central reserve up to $ 140–$ 150 million, as compared with $ 60 million under the 1948 agreement.

John Matthai was then able to justify India's participation in the sterling area by giving as argument the fact that if, before the war, India was a net dollar contributor of the sterling area, this situation had been reversed and that it was now, next to the United Kingdom, the country making the biggest demands upon the sterling area dollar pool.[36] Apart from this, Great Britain had shown proof of a calculated generosity, manifesting a much greater understanding of India's past necessities than of its coming needs, in such a way as to maintain this country in the position of a seeker and thus force it to accept in a larger measure the settlement of its debts in British goods, or from other sterling area countries, and at a pace imposed by the debtor. The relatively positive scope of the agreement as compared to India's need for dollars was going to be partially endangered by the decision of the Indian government to devalue the rupee in September, this step being taken in the wake of the devaluation of the pound sterling by 30.5 per cent. This at least was the pessimistic conclusion arrived at by the *Eastern Economist*. It noted that the consecutive increase in the cost of all dollars imports, the repayment of loans contracted with the World Bank or with the IMF at higher dollar values, and the losses due to the depreciation of the sterling balances convertible in dollars, would not be compensated by a substantial rise in the volume of hard currency Indian exports on account of demand inelasticity.[37]

Just before his departure for the United States, Nehru, in a letter to the chief ministers of the different Indian states, emphasized that there was no reason for Indians to go to North America 'as beggars', and that aid, however desirable, should not be obtained at the cost of the surrender of one's sovereignty. It was in any case clearly in America's self-interest to help India, not only in economic terms, in the search for new markets for its exportable commodities, but also in political terms because 'India has much to give, not in gold or silver or even in exportable commodities, but by virtue of her present position. It is well recognized today all over the world that the future of Asia will be powerfully determined by the future of India.'[38] Now that India had acquired a relative political stability after two years during which the priority of the government was to consolidate the national integration and the institutionalization of the democratic structure with the adoption of a new Constitution, Nehru desired that the voice of an India which, in spite of its impecuniousness, would deal with the big powers on an equal footing, be heard on the international scene. This ambition arose out of the pivotal role that India was expected to assume in a widely decolonized Asian continent of whose interests it would be the spokesperson, this fact stemming out of the strength gained from its refusal of any patronage or tutelage resulting from a corrupting alignment.

Recent developments in Asia had certainly given India a new importance in the eyes of the Americans who had, moreover, just lost their monopoly over the possession of the atom bomb. It was with the victorious march of the Communists in China in mind and the fear of seeing this trend pursued in South-East Asia that the Americans welcomed Nehru on their soil on 11 October 1949. The idea that India could head an anti-communist front was gaining currency, as much in the press as in the remarks of American politicians, and there was hope of being able to convince Nehru of the correctness of containing communism by cooperating with the United States in a system of collective security directed against China and the USSR, within something like an Asiatic version of NATO. New Delhi had shown no indulgence not only towards the CPI, but also towards communist forces in South-East Asia. The American Federation of Labor was showing keenness to enter India and give help to the non-communist trade union movements.[39] The fact that the conference on Indonesia in Delhi, at the start of the year, had not been marked by any excessive outburst of anti-Western feeling and that contrary to the Asian Relations Conference of 1947, the Soviets had not been invited to it, and above all India's maintenance within the Commonwealth, seemed to constitute for the Americans the numerous pointers to the fact that the accusations sometimes aimed against India about its suspected sympathies towards the USSR, were no longer justified. An editorial in the *New York Times* greeted this last decision, which was ratified by the Indian Parliament on 17 May 1949, as a 'historic step, not only in the progress of the Commonwealth but in setting a limit to communist conquest and opening up the prospect of a wider defense system than the Atlantic Pact'.[40]

Nehru publicly expressed India's expectations:

> First, we would like one million tons of wheat to hold as a reserve to enable us to control the wheat crisis in India. Second, we want technical assistance. Third, we want financial terms, that is we can afford for our purchases in dollar countries, and we want to encourage private capital to be invested in India.[41]

These demands could not have caught the Americans by surprise for Chintamani Deshmukh, appointed financial representative of the government of India in Europe and America in August 1949, in addition to his capacity as governor for India on the IMF and the IBRD, had, prior to the arrival of the Prime Minister, prepared the ground by meeting government officials and businessmen.

The Indian government desired to obtain 1 million tons of wheat at a concessional price, over and above India's requirements for normal use, in order to be able to economize valuable foreign exchange, breakdown hoarding and avoid a new escalation in the price of food grains. This latter had not only a significant repercussion on the standard of living, for a large part of the household budget was spent on food items, but it also to a great extent determined the general price level. Following the soaring price of food grains in the first half of 1948, the government had decided in September to re-impose a ban on the movements of food grains, procure them at controlled prices and start rationing again. In view of the gravity of the food situation, the Indian government had taken steps in March 1949 (reviving the Grow More Food campaign, putting new land under crops, etc.) which, except in the event of extraordinary calamities, were to enable self-sufficiency to be achieved by the end of 1951. This would mean that the existing deficit of 6 per cent to 7 per cent between supply and demand would then be met. When Nehru requested the Americans for food aid, he was convinced at the time that what was being faced was just a passing crisis and that, within two or three years, India would be able to do without the import of food grains. In the end, despite wheat surplus reappearing in the American market with the decline of demand from western Europe, the visit did not bring about any concrete result in this field. At one point, the Americans made a counter-proposition that they could possibly give India 650,000 tons in exchange for strategic materials (manganese and mica). The proposition was not accepted since, in the absence of concessional price, India could not expect to export sufficient quantities of strategic materials to pay even for the 650,000 tons on the basis of market prices.[42] Ultimately, in end of December, negotiations for the supply of 1 million tons of wheat were called off, the price fixed by the Americans being considered too high to really have any effect on bringing down the price of food grains in India.

On the matter of private capital, differences persisted. During the formal discussions that had been held in Delhi in August and September 1949 between the US Embassy and the Ministry of External Affairs, the American negotiators had complained that the Indians not only wished to reserve the right to subject US investments to extensive screening but also seek to continue discriminatory measures against American business enterprises once they are established in India. Other problems, some linked to exchange control, expropriation, and territorial preferences, had also been evoked.[43] The Indo-American conference held in December 1949 in New Delhi left little doubt that American investors still considered the fiscal, political, and legislative climate and the hurdles of procedure as not being propitious to the promotion of foreign direct investment. George McGhee, Assistant Secretary of State for Near Eastern, South Asian and African affairs, on return from a journey which had taken him to South Asia in December 1949 and January 1950, expressed this as follows:

> Although there is evidence that there has recently been a shift in official opinion away from this line of thinking, present policies of the two governments (Indian and Pakistani) as we understand them, involve nationalization of certain key industries and rather extensive and restrictive controls over other major elements in their economies which we associate with the methods of socialism. . . . The real need of India and Pakistan for industrial development is equity capital, not loans.[44]

American investors, for whom statements of intent were not enough, still insisted on the conclusion of a treaty of friendship, commerce, and navigation, which alone, according to them, would lead to the creation of a framework favourable to business relations. The two parties were clearly not able to reach an agreement on its content. Despite that, the Americans consistently brought up this matter for discussion. In October 1949, they proposed yet another draft text, without, however, coming to an agreement. The Indian rapporteur to the economic session of the India-American conference of December tersely summarized the Indian fears noting that 'the minimum conditions sought by American private business through such instruments as commercial treaties had in effect the result of laying down the framework of economic policy for other countries'.[45]

Finally, government-to-government aid, which would have to be endorsed by the US Congress, was unlikely in view of the numerous disagreements that persisted over perceptions of international problems. Shortly before Nehru's arrival, Loy Henderson had proposed a five-year, $ 500 million economic aid programme for India aimed at increasing food production, besides endorsing India's request for one million tons of wheat. However, this proposal was unsuccessful. The US Ambassador had argued that:

> With the active friendship and effective aid of the Western world, India might possibly develop into a stalwart and worthy champion in Asia of collaboration with the West. Without such friendship and aid it might degenerate into a vast political and economic swamp, the unclean exhalations of which would pollute the international atmosphere for an indefinite period of time. It might without such friendship and aid, be transformed

into a totalitarian state which could cooperate with similar states against the free West.[46]

This scenario did not impress the officials of the State Department, who perhaps regarded it extreme in its cost evaluation and its prognostication. Speaking on the East-West conflict, in an address to the US Congress on 13 October, Nehru stated that 'where freedom is menaced or justice threatened or where aggression takes place, we cannot be and shall not be neutral'. This assertion delighted the American commentators who interpreted it as a lightly veiled attack against the Communist bloc. But a few days later he asserted that India had no intention of aligning itself with any camp.[47] On the subject of China, Nehru announced the intention of his government to shortly grant recognition to the communist regime installed in Beijing (which was done on 30 December), while the United States persisted obstinately in considering the regime of Chiang Kai-shek as the only legitimate in China.

The different interpretations of the recent developments in China were the cause of conflict between the Indians and the Americans. The US government considered the People's Republic of China as just a satellite of the USSR, against whose proselytism Asian nations had to be protected through programmes of military assistance. Nehru, on the other hand, was convinced that a hostile posture would only provoke China to throw itself into the arms of the Soviet Union which, despite the ideological affiliation, the PRC had no intention of doing. India was, thus, to oppose every attempt at regional grouping directed against Beijing. This was seen at the Baguio Conference in May 1950 which, at the invitation of President Quirino of the Philippines, brought together Australia, Indonesia, Thailand, Pakistan, Ceylon, the Philippines, and India. There the Indian representative, R. Mudaliar, had orders to stick to economic issues. Nehru believed that a kind of Chinese 'Titoism' would evolve as the new leaders of China were not willing to become subordinates of Moscow. But Indian leaders, beginning with Patel, did not, however, rule out the possibility of Chinese expansionism in the region, and fearing communist infiltration in the Himalayan border kingdoms, New Delhi signed treaties with Bhutan, Nepal, and Sikkim respectively in August 1949, July 1950, and December 1950. The main trait common to all these treaties was to reassert that the security of India was linked with the inviolability of the territories of all these countries.

Far from presenting himself as an adversary of China, Nehru fully intended to evolve a policy of cooperation with the PRC, thus putting the seal of friendship on Sino-Indian relations. While no doubt motivated by security considerations, Nehru was also convinced that there could be no Asian unity without close and friendly relations between India and China, the two largest countries of the continent. This regional unity would symbolize the possibility of transcending ideological differences within a renascent Asia. In Washington, Nehru also repeated that the best means to fight the spread of communism was not by the use of arms—an option which would definitely be repudiated by the Asian peoples in view of the support, past or present, brought by the Communists to the fulfilment of their legitimate national aspirations—but lay in the determination of the industrialized countries to help the underdeveloped countries in the eradication of poverty and to work for the end of colonialism.

Finally, there was still the thorny and persistent problem of Kashmir which complicated Indo-American relations. While Washington accused New Delhi of intransigence, the Indians were convinced that they had a strong case and that the United States were being totally partial towards Pakistan so as to turn it into a client state. India's suspicions were later strengthened by the elaborate courtesy shown to the Pakistani President Liaquat Ali Khan during his visit to Washington in May 1950. 'Neither pressure tactics nor lure of help will make us give up a position which we are convinced is right from every point of view', Nehru wrote to Krishna Menon shortly before he left for the United States.[48] There was nothing rhetorical about invoking a bargain, the terms of which would be the grant of aid in exchange for concessions on the question of Kashmir. Vijayalakshmi Pandit had already expressed the possibility of the United States exerting economic pressures 'in order to compel us to settle the Kashmir dispute'.[49] In fact, a note dated 6 May 1949 from Stephen J. Spingarn addressed to C.M. Clifford, a special adviser to President Truman whose assistant he was, noted that:

> India's current need of dollars suggests a possible means of expediting settlement of Kashmir crisis . . . India has serious balance of payment problems. If the United States should wish to exert pressure at this time to achieve a solution of the Kashmir question, it is in an excellent position to do so by instructing the US Executive Director of the Bank and the Fund that it is not favorably disposed toward the request to draw additional dollars from the Fund, or to obtain a loan from the Bank.[50]

While there may not be a direct link between this comment and the difficulty India encountered at the time in getting funds from the IMF, as already mentioned, the US government often reminded the Indian government that it would find it more difficult to justify to the US Congress the giving of economic aid as long as the problem of Kashmir, which was eating into India's financial position and undermining the political and economic stability of the subcontinent, had not been solved.[51]

As an exercise in public relations, the visit had been far from successful. George McGhee, Assistant Secretary of State for Near Eastern, South Asian and African Affairs, remarked that Nehru 'only succeeded in making himself so unpopular with Americans generally that it would later prove difficult to muster support for helping to meet India's urgent need for wheat'. Regarding the interaction between Nehru and Truman, they 'did not hit it off at all'.[52] The Secretary of State, Dean Acheson, said of the Indian Prime Minister that he was one of the most difficult men with whom he had ever had to deal. Without disregarding the importance of Nehru to India (so much so that if 'he did not exist—as Voltaire said of God—he would have to be invented'), Acheson was, nevertheless, convinced 'that Nehru and I were not destined to have [a] pleasant personal relationship'.[53] On the Indian side, Trilok Nath Kaul, then first secretary at the Embassy in Washington, offered his assessment of the atmosphere that prevailed at the talks between the two parties during Nehru's visit:

> In his talks with the US Government not much headway was made because the two sides were talking at different wave lengths—Nehru represented an ancient but resurgent young India, full of enthusiasm and idealism, talking in the larger perspective of history and looking forward to the future of mankind, propagating his passion for peace and cooperation rather than war and confrontation, his policy of non-alignment and anti-colonialism. The US side talked a different language in those days—danger from Russia and China, the need to save freedom and peace through NATO and more military alliances, dangling the carrot of the US aid in return for towing their line, wanting her big business tycoons to penetrate the trade, industry and economy of other countries. Nehru was the representative of a sensitive and proud people. He loathed this gauche and 'commercial' approach of the US and was more disgusted than impressed by it.[54]

Perhaps the Indian Prime Minister, educated in England, shared the opinion of the upper class Englishmen who held Americans in some scorn. First-hand impressions of Loy Henderson confirmed that the two sides were at loggerheads:

> The general impression left in America was that India was making no contribution to world problems, was unlikely to do so as long as the present policy persisted and that Nehru displayed little sense of practical realism. Nehru's discussions on political matters with responsible people in America had been very general, vague and inconclusive.

The Americans also felt that Nehru not only failed to persuade skeptical financiers and industrialists that the Indian market was worthwhile from the American point of view, but that he even 'made a very bad impression. He was both wooly and evasive'.[55]

The visit, which ended on 7 November, therefore, produced no tangible result in terms of foreign aid. However, it was now clear that Washington would extend no generosity in this field as long as the Indian government did not share the same viewpoints on the objectives of American foreign policy and did not give up non-alignment. The meagre subsidies allocated under the Point Four Programme could not satisfy the enormous need for capital felt by most Asian countries. When in June 1950 Truman signed the foreign aid bill for the coming year, the $ 35 million devoted to technical aid under the Point Four Programme appeared quite derisory compared to the $ 2.850 billion allocated to the Marshall Plan in Europe for the third year, or again compared to the $ 194 million in aid to Korea, to South-East Asia, and non-communist China.[56] The *Eastern Economist*, which could not be accused of anti-Americanism, also began to get exasperated at the absence of any American response:

> We have played our cards. . . . Our foreign policy has been revised; compulsory saving is being extended, only a gesture of the determination which we will show in helping ourselves. We have not drawn an equal reply from the United States, and there are many people in India who believe sincerely that the United States is pressing to hard a deal. . . . What assistance does the United States really intend to give in its scheme, often enough proclaimed, of giving help to underdeveloped areas? . . . There is growing a feeling that the Congress of the United States is being commercial with almost the same hard-headedness which characterized the British Government in the days of British rule.[57]

Questioned in Parliament over a remark made by Vijayalakshmi Pandit, who had declared in the United States that the Point Four Programme had become 'ridiculous', Nehru approved of this characterization by noting that it 'had been reduced to such small dimension as to make it without any great value'.[58] Some months earlier, the *Hindu* had expressed its indignation over the American policy in the region:

> If the success of the Communists in China has given a rude shock to the Administration, the reaction is still in terms of power politics rather than a proper appraisal of the needs of the Asian countries. . . . No wonder that US Chiefs of Staff are busy discussing what arms should be sent to South-East Asian countries menaced by Communism, while the US Administration could not agree on a proposal to make food grains available to the semi-starved countries of Asia at prices below the world levels. . . . It is not by military support to reactionary and effete regimes that the challenge of Communism can be met.[59]

The prospect of obtaining economic aid from the United States then appeared so remote that John Matthai declared in Parliament in March 1950: 'On the whole today I am more hopeful of obtaining capital assistance from the United Kingdom than from the United States.'[60] The Commonwealth External Affairs Ministers had taken a decision in January 1950 in Colombo to consider the possibility of economic cooperation for the development of South and South-East Asia in the hope of containing the spread of communism. Nehru had never hidden the economic gain that he expected would accrue from the participation of India in the Commonwealth. While it was still pending, he noted that 'the membership of the Commonwealth will not commit us to anything, but will place us in a favourable position in regard to securing economic, technical and other assistance from the Commonwealth countries and from the United States'.[61] Nehru also believed that a weakened economic connection with the Commonwealth would only drive India into an excessive dependence on American capital and products. This concern is evident in Nehru's letter to his sister in which he noted that 'an India which was isolated completely from the Commonwealth would inevitably have had to slope in some direction. Practically speaking, that is in terms of capital goods and money or credit required, that sloping could only have been in the direction of the US'. But, he specified, it would have been risky for India to lean too much towards the American side in the present context of uneasy Indo-US relations.[62]

The Colombo Plan, which came into force on 1 July 1951, was devised to assist, through financial and technical aid, the development programmes of India, Pakistan, Ceylon, Malaysia, and British

Borneo. The programme presented by India was a compilation of projects that were to be implemented in the First Five Year Plan. The total cost of the plan, spread over a period of six years (1951-7), was estimated at £ 1.868 billion of which £ 1.084 billion, that is almost 60 per cent, was to be met from external resources, including withdrawal from sterling balances, money put up by private investors, loans from the IBRD and gifts and loans from governments outside the area. Almost three-fourths of the expenses of the plan (£1,379 millions) and more than 50 per cent of its external financing were to be for Indian projects.[63] It was implicitly acknowledged by its planners that a substantial element of public external financing would be required and this meant a long-term aid from the US government since the non-Commonwealth countries could also participate in the implementation of the plan. But, in February 1951, Dean Acheson disclosed that the United States did not propose to contribute to any arrangement for financing the intended programmes of the Colombo Plan since it had its own plans.[64]

The agreement of 28 December 1950 signed between India and the United States under the Point Four Programme provided for putting some American experts at India's disposal and for deputing some Indian trainees to the United States. However, it did not arouse much enthusiasm considering the modest sum involved: a gift of $ 1.2 million. 'Technical assistance has all too often seemed to be a facile and easy substitute for a capital flow; and it has, therefore, been regarded with a certain amount of cynicism in all the underdeveloped countries', lamented the *Eastern Economist* on this occasion.[65]

Despite the evident coolness in Indo-American relations, New Delhi, confronted with a hostile Soviet Union, fully realized that it could not reasonably turn against the other superpower without risking international isolation on the one hand, and endangering its access to the benefits of American economic power, on the other hand. Radhakrishnan, the new Indian Ambassador to Moscow, learnt this to his cost when, after getting the signal favour of being received by Stalin on 14 January 1950, he suggested the negotiation of a treaty of friendship on the basis of good-neighbourly relations and mutual respect. Nehru informed him that it was hardly the proper time for this and furthermore, that such an initiative coming shortly after India's recognition of People's Republic of China, might be misinterpreted in the West and worsen India's already uneasy relations with the United States.[66]

Nehru also faced critics at home. Conservative politicians, whose influence had grown within the Congress after the departure in 1948 of the members of the Socialist Party, and then within the Cabinet after its reshuffle of May 1950, started for the first time to question the wisdom of Nehru's external policy, notably in relation to China. They also called for a more cooperative attitude towards the United States, thus hoping that India could profit from a part of the financial manna of American economic and military aid going to those Asian countries which were more receptive to the objectives of the US State Department. It was recorded by the British High Commission that:

> Some critics have begun to blame Nehru for the isolated international situation in which India finds herself, attributing this to his intransigent attitude on Kashmir, and to his cherished policy of non-attachment to blocs. Early in the quarter [of 1950] Sardar Patel was pressing upon him (and at the same time canvassing Congress and big business support) proposals to compromise by partition on Kashmir, and thereafter, enter into negotiations with Pakistan with a view to settling all outstanding questions including the economic deadlock resulting from Pakistan's non-devaluation of the rupee, and thus putting Indo-Pakistan relations on a firm basis.[67]

In June 1950, a sub-committee of the Cabinet for foreign affairs was set up. It consisted of Nehru, Rajagopalachari, Patel, and Gopalaswamy Ayyangar. Deepening opposition to the Communist bloc was fuelled by the outbreak of the Korean War, the Chinese invasion of Tibet, and the troubled situation in Nepal. For the first time India had to deal with an infringement of its interests, with direct implication for its security. The new mood had not gone unnoticed by foreign diplomats. The British High Commissioner in India observed that:

> Sardar Patel's impatience with Nehru's refusal to change his line was coming to a head. . . . He considered that measures should be taken to discourage further Communist aggression and infiltration and, to ensure India's defenses, consultations should be held with the United Kingdom and possibly the United States. . . . Mr. Rajagopalachari shared Patel's views on the necessity for a drastic modification of Indian policy, but hoped that this would be accomplished without any breach with Nehru.

It was, nevertheless, acknowledged that, if there was in Patel's mind a readiness to cooperate with the West in the defense of India, it never extended to an acceptance of commitments outside India's frontiers.[68]

The opposition within the Cabinet towards Nehru's foreign policy was seriously weakened with the death of its spokesman, Sardar

Patel, on 15 December 1950. The Deputy Prime Minister had just a few weeks earlier wished for a drastic revision of India's attitude towards Communist China, on the basis of Chinese duplicity and the fact that the combining of Chinese irredentism and communist imperialism was 'ten times more dangerous' than the expansionism or imperialism of the Western Powers.[69] More than ever, Nehru had a free hand in foreign affairs when he regained his authority over the Congress party by becoming its President in September 1951, after Purushottamdas Tandon, a protégé of Patel, was forced to resign.[70]

The pronounced communist presence in Asia during 1950 marked a distinct shift in America's policy of aid to India. The Truman administration, after worrying that aid to India would be wasted just as aid to China had been wasted, was slowly coming round to the idea that frowning upon foreign aid to India because of the governmental policies may run counter to their own global interests. The US Ambassador, taking for granted that India would not move from its neutral posture, even expressed the view that it was to the general advantage as its demands for equipment and all that would far outweigh the practical value of its assistance in case of a war.[71] The political and strategic advantage of denying India to Russia outweighed the military objective of having New Delhi on the side of the Western bloc. It may be recalled that three years after gaining Independence, India had still not received the least bit of bilateral aid from the United States. Without unquestionable signs of economic progress, India could well fall into the hands of the communists, carrying along with it other Asian countries. This analysis was fairly similar to the assessment made by Nehru at the same period who noted, when speaking of the communist countries, that India faced 'today a vast and powerful Soviet group of nations, which tends to become a monolithic bloc', pursuing a policy which is 'expansionist not only in the normal political sense but also in encouraging internal trouble in other countries'. He added: 'That internal trouble would not go far, if economic conditions were more or less satisfactory.'[72]

NOTES

1. From Stafford Cripps, Treasury, to R.K. Shanmukhan Chetty, 9 July 1948. *PRO*, FO 371 68906.
2. *Economic Weekly*, 26 March 1949, pp. 2-3.

3. J. Matthai was to acknowledge, about the IMF, that 'the real direction appeared to lie in the hands of the American Treasury and to be closely related to American's foreign policy'. *Economic Weekly*, 6 October 1951, p. 961.
4. Memorandum of conversation, by Joseph S. Sparks of the Division of South Asian Affairs, 26 December 1947. *FRUS, 1947*, vol. 3, pp. 177-8.
5. Grady to Marshall, 3 September 1947. Ibid. pp. 165-6.
6. *Eastern Economist*, 2 January 1948, p. 59.
7. To Vijayalakshmi Pandit, 25 March 1948. *Selected Works of Jawaharlal Nehru (second series)*, vol. 5, p. 576.
8. Memorandum from the Joint Chiefs of Staff, 24 March 1949, *FRUS, 1949*, vol. 6, pp. 30-1.
9. The Chargé in India (H. Donovan) to the Secretary of State, 26 January 1948. *FRUS, 1948*, vol. 5, pp. 495-6. See also similar remarks of H.F. Grady on 26 December 1947. *FRUS, 1947*, vol. 3, p. 177.
10. *Commerce*, 29 May 1948, p. 921.
11. *Hindu*, 28 March 1948.
12. *Jawaharlal Nehru's Speeches*, vol. 1, pp. 308 and 310-11.
13. *Hindu*, 8 June 1948.
14. *Hindustan Times*, 13 June 1948.
15. *Amrita Bazar Patrika*, 9 June 1948.
16. *Commerce*, 12 June 1948, pp. 1013-14.
17. *Eastern Economist*, 25 June 1948, p. 1123; 2 July 1948, p. 4; and 15 August 1948, p. 254.
18. Note to the Foreign Secretary, 12 August 1948. *Selected Works of Jawaharlal Nehru (second series)*, vol. 7, pp. 629-30.
19. The Secretary of State (Marshall) to the Acting Secretary of State, 16 October 1948. *FRUS, 1948*, vol. 5, p. 518.
20 23 December 1948. J.L. Nehru, *Letters to Chief Ministers*, vol. 1, p. 249.
21. Senate Committee on Foreign Relations and Department of State, *A Decade of American Foreign Policy, Basic Documents, 1941-49*, Washington, D.C.: US Government Printing Office, 1950, pp. 1366-7.
22. *Economic Weekly*, 15 January 1949, p. 2.
23. *Statesman*, 17 March 1949.
24. 6 April 1949. *Constituent Assembly of India (Legislative) Debates*, part II, vol. 4, 1949, pp. 2385-6.
25. *Commerce*, 24 September 1949, p. 546.
26. See *Statesman*, 8 October 1948, *Times of India*, 16 July 1949 and the minutes of the fifth meeting of the Commonwealth Prime Ministers, London, 13 October 1948, quoted in: *Selected Works of Jawaharlal Nehru (second series)*, vol. 8, pp. 279-80.
27. See the dispatch from Daniel Levi, French Ambassador in India, 28 May 1949. *AQO*, Asie-Océanie, 1944-1955, Inde, vol. 90.
28. Minute of a conversation between F.K. Roberts and Spottiswood of the IBRD, 1 August 1949. *PRO*, FO 371 75566.
29. Department of State Policy Statement, 1 December 1950. *FRUS, 1950*, vol. 5, p. 1477. Speaking on 25 April 1949 in the Senate, Democrat Hubert

Humphrey, an advocate of aid to India, was to remind that there were practical reasons for that: India is 'the second largest producer of vital manganese—and the first is the Soviet Union. She has twenty billions tons of unexploited iron ore and sixty billions tons of coal. Her steel production is seventh in the world and she produces nearly all of the world's mica, much of the tungsten, thorium (needed in atomic energy production) and lac (the basic ingredient of shellac).' *PRO*, FO 371 76096.

30. *Statesman*, 18 February 1950.
31. Sir Archibald Nye to Sir Percivale Liesching, Commonwealth Relations Office (CRO), 21 June 1949. *PRO*, FO 371 76090.
32. Krishna Menon reminded Nehru of these remarks in a letter dated 7 August 1952. S. Gopal, *Jawaharlal Nehru: A Biography*, vol. 2, p. 59.
33. 14 August 1949. *Selected Works of Jawaharlal Nehru* (*second series*), vol. 12, p. 404.
34. Reserve Bank of India, *India's Balance of Payments, 1948-49 to 1961-62*, table 16, p. 100. The Indian financial year covers the period from 1 April to 30 March. The American fiscal year covers the period from 1 July to 30 June.
35. Notes to Vijayalakhsmi Pandit, 22 June 1949 and to John Matthai, 23 June 1949. *Selected Works of Jawaharlal Nehru* (*second series*), vol. 12, pp. 396-8.
36. *Commerce*, 15 August 1949, p. 274. C.D. Deshmukh, *Economic Development in India*, p. 65.
37. *Eastern Economist*, 23 September 1949, p. 485. In fact, owing to the favourable balance of payments position during the year 1950-1, India did not use the sterling releases negotiated in July 1949, thanks to the outbreak of the Korean war. The decision to restrict dollar purchases to 75 per cent of the 1948 level was reviewed at the Commonwealth Finance Ministers' Conference in September 1950. The quantitative limitation was removed but the obligation still remained of ensuring the maximum economy in the members' dollar expenditures.
38. 2 October 1949. Jawaharlal Nehru, *Letters to Chief Ministers*, vol. 1, p. 471.
39. Suggestions for sending Indian trade unionists for study of trade union work in the United States seem to have elicited favourable responses if the silence was maintained on the US government funding. Reference was made to a conversation between Jayaprakash Narayan, leader of the Socialist Party and member of the Hind Mazdoor Sabha, and Ms. Faith Williams of the US Department of Labor. 'Attitude of the British Trades Union Congress towards the Indian National Trade Union Congress', K.D. Jones, United Kingdom High Commission in New Delhi, to R. Tuner, Ministry of Labour and National Service, 2 September 1949. *PRO*, FO 371 76098.
40. *New York Times*, 28 April 1949.
41. Remarks made during a press conference in Ottawa on 24 October 1949. J.L. Nehru, *Inside America*, New Delhi: National Book Stall, 1950, p. 89.

42. Letter to Premiers, 3 November 1949. Durga Das (ed.), *Sardar Patel's Correspondence*, vol. 8, Ahmedabad: Navajivan Publishing House, 1973, p. 399.
43. Remarks on Indo-American discussions relating to American investment in India. *FRUS, 1949*, vol. 1, Washington, D.C.: Department of State Publication, 1976, p. 650. In May 1950, the Government of India was to announce a relaxation of exchange control to permit freer repatriation of capital invested by other than residents of the sterling area, in respect of which repatriation had been liberally allowed.
44. Address to the Far East—America Council of Commerce and Industry, New York, 31 January 1950. *Times of India*, 8 February 1950.
45. *Indian-American Relations, Proceedings of the India-America Conference*, p. 20. The conference, co-organized by the Indian Council of World Affairs and the American Institute of Pacific relations, was held in New Delhi from 12 to 22 December 1949 and its objective was to explore political, diplomatic, economic and cultural relations by bringing together specialists from both countries.
46. Loy Henderson to James E. Webb (Under Secretary of State), 3 October 1949. 845.50/10-349, Record Group 59, Department of State Records, National Archives, Washington, D.C. Quoted in D. Merrill, *Bread and the Ballot*, p. 40.
47. *Selected Works of Jawaharlal Nehru (second series)*, vol. 13, p. 304. The new Indian Ambassador in the USSR, S. Radhakrishnan, who had arrived in Moscow in September, was summoned to explain who was the aggressor that Nehru had in mind. Telegram from S. Radhakrishnan to Nehru, 29 October 1949. S. Gopal, *Jawaharlal Nehru: A Biography*, vol. 2, p. 62.
48. 11 September 1949. *Selected Works of Jawaharlal Nehru (second series)*, vol. 13, p. 227.
49. Telegram from Vijayalakshmi Pandit to Nehru. *Selected Works of Jawaharlal Nehru (second series)*, vol. 12, p. 330.
50. Note to Clark M. Clifford, Stephen J. Springarn Papers, H.S. Truman Library, Independence, Missouri. Quoted by S.C. Mudumbai, *United States Foreign Policy towards India (1947-1954)*, p. 94.
51. See the report of the talk that Henderson had with Bajpai, communicated to the Secretary of State, 29 July 1949. *FRUS, 1949*, vol. 6, p. 1727. J.F. Dulles, crossing through Karachi in the spring of 1953 and who was asked by Muhammad Ali to put pressure on India on the problem of Kashmir, said nothing else, although refusing at the same time to tie American aid to India's concessions on Kashmir. Memorandum of conversation prepared in the Embassy in Pakistan, 23 May 1953. *FRUS, 1952-54*, vol. 9, part 1, p. 122.
52. G. McGhee, *Envoy to the Middle World*, p. 47.
53. Dean Acheson, *Present at the Creation: My Years in the State Department*, London: Hamish Hamilton, 1969, p. 336.
54. T. N. Kaul, *Diplomacy in Peace and War*, pp. 22-3.

55. Impressions of Pandit Nehru's visit to America given to the United Kingdom High Commissioner by the US Ambassador. To the Commonwealth Relations Office, 9 December 1949. *PRO*, FO 371 76097.
56. *Statesman*, 6 June 1950.
57. *Eastern Economist*, 18 November 1949, p. 765.
58. *Parliamentary Debates*, part 1, vol. 4, no. 3, 3 August 1950, col. 227.
59. *Hindu*, 20 February 1950.
60. *Statesman*, 21 March 1950.
61. 19 March 1949. *Selected Works of Jawaharlal Nehru* (*second series*), vol. 10, p. 147.
62. 8 June 1949. *Selected Works of Jawaharlal Nehru* (*second series*), vol. 11, p. 356.
63. *Economic Weekly*, 2 December 1950, p. 1135.
64. *New York Times*, 22 February 1951.
65. *Eastern Economist*, 5 January 1951, p. 7.
66. See Nehru's letters of 6 February and 5 March 1950 to Radhakrishnan. *Selected Works of Jawaharlal Nehru* (*second series*), vol. 14 part 1, pp. 204-5 and 543.
67. Sir Archibald Nye to the Secretary of State for Commonwealth Relations (P.C. Gordon Walker), 21 April 1950. *PRO*, FO 371 84200.
    Field Marshall Auchinleck, in a conversation with the French Ambassador to Pakistan, mentioned also that the late Patel, who favoured a solution in a spirit of conciliation on Kashmir, had come into conflict with Nehru. Telegram from Pierre Augé, 9 août 1951. *AQO*, Asie-Océanie, 1945-1959, Nations-Unies et Organisations Internationales, vol. 238.
68. Sir Archibald Nye to the Secretary of State for Commonwealth Relations, 15 January 1951. *PRO*, FO 371 92870.
69. Most notably, he wondered about the wisdom of India's support of the PRC's entry into the UNO. Letter to Nehru, 7 November 1950. Durga Das (ed.), *Sardar Patel's Correspondence*, vol. 10, p. 337.
70. During a meeting of the INC in October 1951, Govind Ballabh Pant was entrusted with the task of getting the party to endorse the government's foreign policy. On this occasion, he attacked those who felt that the country had much to gain by aligning itself with one of the great powers: 'Critics of our foreign policy should look to China's example where Chiang Kai-shek was given all kinds of foreign help and crores of rupees worth of material aid was given to him. But what happened ultimately. All this foreign help could not help Chiang Kai-shek to keep his Government going. All our critics, therefore, should take a lesson from Chiang Kai-shek's fate.' *National Herald*, 18 October 1951.
71. See dispatch from F.K. Roberts, Deputy High Commissioner in Delhi, to R.H. Scott, Foreign Office, 19 January 1951. *PRO*, FO 371 93074.
72 15 July 1950. J.L. Nehru, *Letters to Chief Ministers*, vol. 2, p. 141.

CHAPTER 7

Discord over Wheat

IN MID-JUNE 1951, the United States gave India food aid, in the form of a loan of $ 90 million (Rs. 903 million), for the purchase of 2 million tons of wheat. This loan could have greatly contributed towards burnishing the image of a magnanimous America coming readily to the assistance of a poor country confronted with its gravest food crisis since the Bengal famine of 1943, and thereby helped to improve the strained relations between the two countries over the issue of economic assistance. But the moral and diplomatic advantages that the US government may have expected to reap from its food aid were finally tempered. The major reason for this was the legislative procedure followed in the United States for the sanctioning of any large sums of money for public aid; the US Congress discussed the grounds for the aid and the terms under which it would be bestowed. For almost six months, the sittings of the concerned committees of both the House and the Senate and the Congressional debates reported by the press revealed the range of political opinion on this matter. These protracted discussions and procedural niceties delayed the decision and with the delay the hopes of an improvement in Indo-American relations came under a cloud.

On 16 December 1950, Vijayalakshmi Pandit communicated, on behalf of the Indian government, a request for food aid to the US government in the form of a soft loan for the purchase of 2 million tons of food grains. A succession of natural catastrophes had forced India to make this request. The poor monsoon of the summer of 1950 was followed by the inadequate rainfall of the north-east monsoon in autumn, which was particularly important for the rice crop in the state of Madras. To the drought were added floods in Punjab and an earthquake in Assam. The Union Minister of Food and Agriculture, Kanaiyalal Maneklal Munshi, assessed that the production of food grains in 1951 would be around 5.5 million tons less than in 1950, while there were in addition 5 million more mouths to feed every year.[1]

The precarious balance achieved between demand and supply through the import of three million tons of food grains on average per year during the previous year was now shattered. The stock of food grains fell between 1 January 1950 and 1 January 1951, declining from 1.6 million tons to around 700,000 tons. The authorities had been deluded by the objective of achieving self-sufficiency and had underestimated the need for the import of food grains. During the summer of 1950, the United States made use of $ 4.5 million out of the funds initially meant for China to subsidize the purchase by India of 627,000 tons of American sorghum.

To fight the threat of famine, it became urgent to import 6 million tons of food grains, the equivalent of around one-eighth of the expected domestic production, so as to not endanger the rationing system and to contain inflationary trends. On 19 January 1951, it was decided to reduce by 25 per cent the ration of food grains allocated to the people throughout the country. The Indian government assessed that at the current market rate the economy could pay for the import of a maximum of 4 million tons of food grains. Anything over and above this figure would involve a dangerous worsening of the balance of payments deficit and substantial drawings on India's sterling assets as well as on the sterling area dollar pool, which would seriously endanger the development programme contemplated in the Colombo Plan. Finally, it would bode ill for the work of the Planning Commission, set up in May 1950 and entrusted with fixing the targets for the First Five Year Plan. The difference of 2 million tons was, therefore, to become the subject of a request for aid from the United States in expectation of obtaining special and easy terms of payment. Without this assistance, it was near certain that famine would break out before the next harvest in October 1951. It was not easy for Nehru to make up his mind to ask for aid from the United States for he was acutely aware that he had allowed himself to be convinced by his advisers to ask for 1 million tons of food grains from the US government during his visit to America in the autumn of 1949, to end up by finally getting nothing. Indeed, just a few months before, he had reminded his sister, Vijayalakshmi Pandit, that US assistance should be dealt with the utmost care; he noted that 'recently we have seen that American help is often associated with political pressure, as in the case of Greece and

Korea. . . . There is a tendency in the US to treat the countries they help as some kind of clients to it, which are expected to toe their general policy.'[2] The situation was all the more difficult for Nehru as New Delhi and Washington had different perspectives regarding the situation in East Asia, where Indian diplomatic initiatives often exasperated the Americans.

Ever since it had recognized the People's Republic of China, the Indian government had endeavoured to prevent Communist China from being isolated in the international arena by championing its entry into the UNO. On 13 January 1950, India thus voted in favour of a Soviet resolution in the Security Council asking for the dismissal of the delegation from Nationalist China. Nehru made no secret of his belief that the island of Formosa, where Chiang Kai-shek's Nationalist government had installed itself, should return to the fold of mainland China. But it was above all the outbreak of the Korean War, triggered by the entry of North Korean forces into South Korea on 25 June 1950, which exacerbated the differences between New Delhi and Washington. It is true that India had supported the two initial American resolutions, those of 25 and 27 June, and this action had pleased the Truman administration. Nehru justified these decisions on the grounds that, faced with a premeditated aggression, the United Nations had reacted as it should have done on pain of losing all future credibility as regards its role in the maintenance of peace. The State Department had noted with some satisfaction that during Nehru's recent tour of South-East Asia:

> the theme of his speeches was a strong attack against Communism instead of against the continued existence of European colonialism in Asia which it might so well have been. . . . The tone of his speeches was set by an address delivered in India just prior to his departure in which he asserted that the Communist Party in India is purely terroristic . . . and warned that India would not permit interference from China or elsewhere.[3]

The satisfaction of the Americans, who might have believed that India's policy of rapprochement with the communist powers, was short-lived. When on 7 July the Security Council voted for the setting up of a United Nations force in Korea, at the head of which General Douglas MacArthur was appointed, India abstained and refused to contribute actively to the military assistance, sending just an army ambulance unit in Korea.

Fearing an escalation of the conflict, particularly after the dispatch of the Seventh Fleet to the Formosan Straits, Nehru communicated on 13 July an identical message to both Stalin and Dean Acheson; he asked for the admission of the PRC to the UN and an end to the Soviet Union's boycott of the Security Council so that it could, along with the United States, find a peaceful way out of the Korean conflict. The Americans immediately rejected the proposals for fear of appearing to give way to the Communist bloc's threatening posture in Korea. In the months that followed, India's policies were interpreted by many Americans as capitulation in the face of a conspiracy by the Communists to widen their ascendancy over the world. In September, India tabled a resolution, aimed at recognizing the PRC alone as representing China, but this was rejected by the UNGA. Subsequently, on 7 October, when the UNGA approved a resolution authorizing the troops of the United Nations to cross the 38th parallel, India abstained. The Indian government knew from a meeting of its Ambassador in Peking, K.M. Panikkar, with Zhou Enlai, on the morning of 3 October, that such a step would lead China to intervene militarily. This did indeed occur on 16 October, when some Chinese 'volunteers' crossed the river Yalu to go to the help of the North Korean troops. When the UNGA adopted on 31 January 1951 a resolution moved by the United States declaring Communist China guilty of aggression, after having rejected a compromise proposal presented by India, for the first time during this war New Delhi joined its voice to that of the Communist bloc to vote against the resolution.

In spite of the deep resentment that Nehru's attitude over the Korean conflict aroused in the United States—which therefore led to a certain initial wavering—the Truman administration agreed to consider the Indian request for food aid and admitted that the gravity of the situation necessitated that action be taken rapidly. India's request came at a time when the State Department was advocating the necessity of setting up a programme of economic and financial aid to India, although many Americans were disappointed and irritated by New Delhi's attitude of neutrality and the country's unwillingness to identify itself with the Western democracies with whom it had historical ties.

The idea of a programme of economic assistance to South Asia had been making some headway for a few months. In a memorandum to Secretary of State Dean Acheson sent shortly before the outbreak of the war in Korea, George McGhee considered as necessarily limited the scope of private investments, of the Point Four

Programme and of World Bank or Export-Import Bank loans; instead he underlined the need to develop a more ambitious policy of a long-term assistance programme in the economic advancement of South Asian countries.

> All are exposed to Communist pressures. India, Pakistan and Afghanistan constitute the only countries on the borders of the USSR and its satellites for which there is no program of United States economic assistance. Experience has shown that countries in such close proximity to the USSR orbit need the stiffening and confidence provided by the United States economic assistance.[4]

In August, it was the turn of the American Ambassador in India to stress that 'the most effective measure for improving the atmosphere would be the expression of readiness on our part to extend to India substantial economic aid'.[5] The Gray report released in November 1950 and favouring an increase in assistance to underdeveloped countries had elicited some interest in India. In early December 1950, a policy statement of the State Department noted that 'India has become the pivotal state in non-communist Asia by virtue of its relative power, stability and influence', but that on account of the prevalence of grinding poverty, 'it is likely that the present Government of India will lose power unless it can present the Indian people with definite progress in improving their social and economic conditions, and it is likely that a successor government would be less favorably disposed towards the United States than the present one'.[6]

While Congress was debating the question of food aid, the two governments exchanged notes on 7 and 16 March 1951 relating to mutual defense assistance, and an agreement came into force enabling India to become eligible for the acquisition of US military supplies and equipment in accordance with the terms of the Mutual Defense Assistance Act of 1949; this was done in order 'to maintain its internal security, its legitimate self-defense or permit it to participate in the defense of the area of which it is a part'.[7] A similar agreement had been signed some months earlier, on 15 December 1950, between the United States and Pakistan. New Delhi had earlier asked the United States several times, but without great success, to supply arms and ammunition to it. Washington had balked for a long time, arguing that in view of India's unstable relations with Pakistan, it did not wish to disturb the military balance between the antagonistic forces. India had approached the US government in January 1948 with a request for military planes and equipment, which was turned down. Two months later, the State Department imposed an informal embargo on the supply of military matériel to India and Pakistan until the situation in Kashmir had clarified. This decision showed that South Asia had not then acquired overwhelming military importance in terms of America's security requirements. Even after the ceasefire came into force on 1 January 1949, and the arms embargo was lifted one year after its imposition, the United States continued to hesitate to lest military equipment given to one country might be used against the other.[8] Requests for military supplies met with little success in spite of India's decision in July 1949 to extend the landing rights and transit facilities given to US military aircraft. The Korean War contributed considerably in allaying US hesitation although the continuing strained relations between India and Pakistan prevented their respective armed forces from being strengthened to the extent desirable if they were to play a significant role in a war against Communism. A regional policy statement prepared by the Office of South Asian Affairs considered that the time had come to meet 'as far as possible in the light of other demands of higher priority the requirements of the South Asian countries for military matériel not available from other sources'. However, the statement noted, that 'unless the Kremlin should adopt a more aggressive posture towards South Asia and the countries of the region should close ranks to meet this threat, matériel should be provided to the South Asian countries only on a reimbursable (non-grant) basis'.[9] When the Indians sought 54 Fairchild C-119 Packet transport aircraft, Donald D. Kennedy, of the same office, opined that India's military procurements must be perceived as sensible: 'India's expenditure of dollars on defense equipment should be kept to minimum because of difficulties such expenditure creates for future program of United States economic assistance to India'.[10]

Despite the congenial disposition displayed by the State Department and the White House, two months went by before President Truman took the matter before Congress while urging both houses to grant to the government the legislative means to act in such a way as to send the food aid required by India. This delay was largely due to the anticipation of a fairly frigid reaction from Congress considering the many differences that had cropped up between the two countries during the past year over foreign policy matters.[11] The Senate Foreign Relations Committee had already decided on 25 January to defer any action concerning the Indian request for assistance. Nevertheless, a few days later, on 30 January, a bipartisan group of twenty-four members of Congress took the initiative to write to the President, asking him to support the dispatch of food grains despite what they called 'the foreign policy pursued by the Indian government'. Intervening at a distance in the debate, the *Times of India* wondered: 'Are foodstuffs more explosive than munitions? And must a country be penalized merely for venturing to differ on some aspects of US foreign policy?' and concluded that 'any suggestion that foodstuffs will only be forthcoming for those who toe the Washington line wrongs America and does no service to this country'.[12]

Meanwhile, the State Department, seeking a precise assessment of the situation before proposing a bill to Congress, asked New Delhi for more information about the food deficit, the level of stocks, and even the eventual number of deaths if American aid was not forthcoming (the estimate given in reply was as many as 1 million and possibly even in excess of 2 million).[13] The American Ambassador in India warned in advance that any 'failure to respond generously and promptly will add grist to [the] mill to those elements unfriendly to the United States and will weaken those leaders and groups who continue [to] insist [on] close political and economic relations between the United States and India'.[14] The State Department, on the strength of the economic data now in its hands, concluded that India was not in a position to finance the purchase of a further 2 million tons without drawing excessively on its foreign exchange reserves. This would risk compromising the implementation of development programmes without which the stability of a non-communist government would be at stake. No one doubted that the Communist Party of India would be the first to take advantage of any popular discontent arising out of the drought. The first general elections were to take place during the winter of 1951-2.

A communist victory in India would not fail to help the spread of communism in the neighbouring countries of the subcontinent. The National Security Council reported in a policy statement approved by the President that:

> the loss of India to the Communist orbit would mean that for all practical purposes all of Asia will have been lost; this would constitute a serious threat to the security position of the United States. The loss of China, the immediate threat to Indochina and the balance of Southeast Asia, the invasion of Tibet, and the reverses in Korea have greatly increased the significance to

> the United States of the political strategic manpower and resource potential of the countries of South Asia and made it more important that this potential be marshalled on the side of the United States. India, especially, and Pakistan as well, possess leaders having great prestige throughout the whole of Asia; the future support of these countries diplomatically and in the United Nations is of great importance; India in particular has certain strategic materials of importance to our national defense.[15]

The statement stressed that if India turned to communism, the aircraft of Western countries would not receive permission to fly through the territory of a country at the crossroads of communication lines between Europe, Africa, and East Asia. Similarly, the use of the shortest sea routes between Suez and the Malacca Straits would be endangered.

Truman asked Congress for authorization to grant a gift of 2 million tons of grains, half of which would be loaded on American ships before 1 April, the cost of sea transport being borne by India. Funds would be appropriated immediately only for the first million tons, and the appropriation of funds for the balance would be deferred until the situation had been further clarified. The dispatch of food grains would be conducted under the Economic Cooperation Act of 1948 whose initial function had been the management of the US aid programme to western Europe. Truman suggested that a mission of the Economic Cooperation Administration be sent to India to supervise the distribution of the food grains and to participate, in cooperation with the Indian government, in the choice of the development projects that would be financed by the earnings derived from the sale of the food grains. The Indian people would also be kept informed through full and continuous publicity regarding the source of the grains.

On 15 February, the House of Representatives was informed of a bill which reiterated the provisions put forward by the President three days earlier. Wishing that all political bargaining be set aside right from the start, Loy Henderson intervened with the House Foreign Affairs Committee, to warn it that the 'Indian people would probably prefer to starve rather than sacrifice any of their political and economic independence.'[16] The latter approved a grain gift to 'help resist Soviet exploitation'.[17] Nevertheless, four Republican members (the Committee had 27 members) submitted a report in which they objected to the principle of a grant, which moreover India had not even asked for, preferring that the aid be in the form of a loan to be paid for with strategic materials. With the outbreak of war in Korea and American rearmament, the stocking of strategic minerals had become a matter of priority. The controversy over the terms of food aid was set in motion and it was to delay the delivery of food grains despite the deterioration in the supply position, particularly in Bihar and in the state of Madras. It was the debate on the propriety itself of giving aid to a country which was adopting policies opposed to those of the Americans in the United Nations and a country which was considered to be much too favourably inclined towards the Communist bloc, which was once again initiated in US Congress. The motivations of the Congressmen in favour of the dispatch of food grains were based on considerations no less realistic and as lacking in humanitarianism as those of the State Department. For instance, Senator Fulbright, giving his opinion before the Senate Foreign Relations Committee said plainly:

> If [our action] is humanitarian, I do not know why we are so much more humanitarian now than we were in 1943. We did not give it then. . . . If it is not justifiable on the ground of our policy with regard to the whole situation with Russia, I think it is hard to justify. . . . They had just as bad a drought (in 1943) as they have now. Millions died. . . . The real reason is because we don't want that government to collapse over there and the Communists make headway. . . . They shoot Communists when they find them. That is all to the good. Even though they do not like us, it is still better to have it that way than let the Communists run it.[18]

While awaiting the response of the United States to its request for aid, the Indian government had made contact with the countries likely to supply the remaining 4 million tons. American wheat was imported under the International Wheat Agreement. India signed an agreement with Pakistan on 25 February, ending the commercial warfare which followed the refusal by this country to devalue its currency, after the devaluation of the pound in September 1949; the agreement also provided for the supply of food grains to India. Contacts were made with Burma and Thailand for the import of rice and with Canada, Australia, and Argentina for the purchase of wheat. More unexpectedly came the offer in early February from the People's Republic of China to supply 50,000 tons of rice in exchange for jute and this offer was accepted. Shortly after this announcement, the author of an editorial in the *Economic Weekly*, expressed incredulity at the enormous progress that Chinese agriculture had made, and brought up the possibility of totalitarian regimes creating, for reasons of state, a surplus where none had existed; he finally claimed that it would ultimately be the Americans who would decide 'whether we will eat or starve'.[19]

Eager to expedite the legislative procedure and to avoid a bargaining process which could offend the sensibilities of the Indian government, the State Department let it be known that in 1950 India had exported to the United States over 580,000 tons of manganese (about one-third of America's imports), a mineral used mainly in the manufacture of special steels and imported in large quantities from the USSR till 1948, and 260,000 tons of mica. It made up around three quarters of India's total exports of these minerals. It was also added that these exports were constantly on the increase. As for monazite (which contains thorium) and beryl (the mineral source of the metal beryllium which can be potentially used as a moderator in nuclear piles), for which the US Atomic Energy Commission had showed a keen interest, there was officially an embargo on their export. But this embargo could be lifted, not under duress, but through negotiations conducted in a friendly environment engendered by a grant of food grains, more likely to kindle a receptive attitude in the Indian government than blackmail.[20]

In September 1948, just after the creation of the Atomic Energy Commission to develop its nuclear research programme, India had passed an act imposing an embargo on the export of fissile materials; this applied notably to monazite and beryl. In fact, the Indian government, at least unofficially, proved much more flexible in its approach than might have been suggested by its official declarations. At the time, the US government had already expressed its desire to secure the relaxation of the embargo on monazite and beryl, an increase in the export of strategic mineral resources for industrial and stockpiling requirements as well as for atomic energy purposes, and assurances from the Indian government that these would not be supplied to 'unfriendly nations'.[21] Loy Henderson was to report that Nehru had assured to him in March 1949 that his government would not oppose the import from India of beryl and monazite in 'reasonable amounts' by the United States, but that he would ask in exchange that Indian scientists be given the opportunity to work in the nuclear physics laboratories of the United States.[22] As concerns beryl, a secret five-year renewable agreement was concluded on 1 October 1950, providing for the purchase by the United States of 25 per cent of India's production of beryllium oxide.[23]

The Indians revealed their annoyance at the opposition in the US Congress to their request, as they believed 'with the casualness sometimes affected by the poor, that the grant was due to them. . . . They seem to ignore that the United States expect from all their actions, if not a benefit of a material nature, at least a moral return.'[24] In one of his regular communications to the chief ministers of the Indian states, Nehru showed his impatience and irritation over the controversy that the request for aid by India had raised in the Congress:

It is obvious that we cannot barter our freedom of choice in regard to our political policy for any gift from abroad. We have said nothing in criticism of what is happening in the American Congress in regard to this proposed food gift and we do not propose to say anything. But the manner in which this has been handled has hurt us.

He acknowledged, however, that in Washington, the State Department had done its best to get this grant through and that some American newspapers also had advocated this donation.[25] The *New York Times*, in an editorial entitled 'Clouding an Issue', had urged that niggling debate and dreary argument about American self-interest should no longer interfere with an urgent and grave call of distress:

We demean ourselves if we allow what should be a question of good morals to be placed on the bartering block of expediency. We believe that we should use the instruments of persuasion to convince Prime Minister Nehru that some of his judgments are ill-advised. But the delay in an act of mercy is no honorable instrument of persuasion.[26]

On news of the removal of MacArthur whom India distrusted, from his post on 11 April 1951, Henderson informed Bajpai that some moderation was desirable, both in the comments made in the press and in public declarations, if the adoption of the bill for food aid to India was not to be compromised. The American Ambassador feared, above all, a 'new display of the verbal exuberance of Pandit Nehru'.[27] The State Department began to give up all hope of placating New Delhi with a grant of wheat and even feared that the shilly-shallying of Congress would end up by making it lose all benefit of its generous offer in the eyes of the Indian government. It noted in a memorandum to Congress that in the event of a refusal to send food relief, tens of years would be required to remedy the harm thus caused to American prestige in India and in the whole of Asia;

for Asia was waiting to see if America would keep its food grains after having spent billions of dollars for the recovery of Europe.[28]

A new element intervened in the situation with the Soviet proposal, in March, to supply food grains. After China, this was the second communist country to propose its services to the Indian government. Till then, New Delhi had refrained from appealing for Soviet assistance for fear of jeopardizing all American assistance. The initiative came from the Soviets; in mid-March, their Embassy in New Delhi made an initial offer of 50,000 tons of wheat. In response, the government of India instructed its Ambassador in Moscow, Radhakrishnan, to contact the concerned ministries to find out the substance of the Soviet proposals. Few days later, Kumykin, the deputy minister of Foreign Trade informed him that the Soviet Union was ready to supply 500,000 tons of wheat on the basis of a barter agreement. In exchange, the Soviets wanted raw jute, rubber, raw cotton fibre, and shellac. Meanwhile, the Chinese had outbid all others by offering to negotiate the supply of 1 million tons of food grains in exchange for sterling. There was much talk of this in the media, the Indian press laying stress on the fact that these offers were being made on a strictly commercial basis and involved no condition of a political nature. These developments disturbed the Truman administration sufficiently enough to prompt the President to renew on 29 March, his call to Congress asking it to come to a favourable decision as quickly as possible as all delay would be to the advantage of Russian propaganda.

But even so, the Soviets proved to be tough negotiators, particularly compared to the Chinese, as Nehru noted:

> The Chinese offer is a more attractive one from the point of view of price. The difficulty there is that of shipping. . . . The Russian offer has one advantage—the Soviets will supply most of the shipping needed. But the price quoted for wheat is very high and there is an insistence on our supplying some commodities which we ourselves lack, like raw jute and raw cotton.[29]

In mid-April, the Indian government informed the Soviets that for the time being it only wished to negotiate the supply of 50,000 tons of wheat. A barter agreement for 100,000 tons of wheat was finally concluded on 22 June.[30] Out of its 1 million tons on offer, China had contracted, by the end of May, to supply 520,000 tons of food grains (450,000 tons of sorghum and 70,000 tons of rice) which thus made China the second largest supplier of food grains to India.[31]

After a six-week deadlock, the committees of both the House and the Senate approved bills, by the end of April, that were different from the original one; the most notable difference was the fact that the proposal for an outright grant was, at least partly, given up. The House bill provided for a loan of $ 190 million for the purchase of 2 million tons of food grains. It was felt desirable that a part of the repayment be made in unspecified strategic materials. The Senate bill adopted a middle position by proposing that these 2 million tons be given on a half loan, half grant basis. The provisions included in these bills—fairly usual terms embodied in US legislation providing for economic assistance to foreign countries—made many Indians sit up with a start. The Indian government asked its Ambassador to communicate to the State Department its hesitation and reservations concerning a certain number of these clauses. Thus, the reference to the suspension of aid, if it was no longer compatible with American foreign policy, was interpreted as an unacceptable means of exerting pressure on the Indian government over its political orientations. In the same spirit, New Delhi sought clarifications over the role of the ECA mission entrusted with determining the utilization of the counterpart funds, fearing that it would interfere in India's choice of development projects. As for the provisions envisaging a US supervision over the distribution of food grains to ensure notably that the latter would be done 'without discrimination as to race, creed or political belief', it appeared to question the efficiency and impartiality of the distribution system set up by the government.[32]

These provisions provoked a veritable hornet's nest in the press. The *Amrita Bazar Patrika* wrote on 3 May: 'These are conditions not only derogatory to India's self-respect and sovereignty but definitely detrimental to her policy of neutrality and the Indian nation will rather starve than swallow such insult'. Anti-American sentiment was prevalent among the public during this time. The indignation in official circles was tempestuous and the possibility began to be mentioned of doing without an aid granted under such humiliating conditions. Nehru proclaimed that the conditions laid down amounted 'practically to converting India into some kind of a semi-colonial country or at least a satellite in the economic sense. . . . I realize completely the consequence of our refusal of this gift. Nevertheless I cannot bring myself to agree to this final humiliation.'[33]

While the situation appeared to have reached a dead end, both in New Delhi and the US Congress where the fulminations of an incensed Nehru had heightened the tense atmosphere, the Indian Prime Minister made a speech on 10 May and, quite unexpectedly, opened the path for a final solution to the agreement on food aid. The assurances of the State Department as regards the real scope of the much maligned clauses, and even the persuasion of his advisers, notably Deshmukh and Bajpai, in the name of economic realities, broke the deadlock. Nehru declared before Parliament that there were 'no political or discriminatory conditions attached to these bills [before the US Senate and the House of Representatives], and, therefore, there can be no objection on this ground to our acceptance', while indicating his preference for the plan of the House of Representatives for a simple loan. Nehru, however, stated that monazite was 'a fundamental part of our foreign policy that such material as is particularly related to the production of atomic or like weapons should not be supplied by us to foreign countries'. At the same time, he announced that the first consignment of 50,000 tons of Soviet wheat had left the port of Odessa and was on its way to India.[34] This last remark was ill-received by some American senators, who recalled with indignation that their country had supplied to India since some months more than 100,000 tons of food grains per month on a commercial basis, and they protested against the unwelcome publicity that the Soviet supplies were receiving.

The final version of the bill was adopted by the Senate on 16 May; it gave up the earlier 'half loan, half grant' option and gave preference to a single loan of $ 190 million. It was also stipulated that the supply of strategic materials—monazite and manganese were specifically mentioned—would be included in the terms of repayment of the loan. As for the bill finally adopted by the House of Representatives on 24 May, it differed in the language and in the financial procedure used but it also made no specific reference to manganese or monazite, although mention was indeed made of a repayment of a part of the loan in the form of supplies of raw materials to the United States. In order to arrive at a consensus, the two bills were submitted for arbitration to a House-Senate conference. The compromise text was accepted in the House of Representatives on 6 June and in the Senate on 11 June. While the immediate and continuous transfer of substantial quantities of raw materials remained an objective, no specific request was expressly made. The bestowal of a loan instead of a grant, in accordance with New Delhi's wishes, had made it easier to arrive at a consensus.

On 15 June, President Truman signed the India Emergency Food Assistance Act of 1951. A loan of $ 190 million was given to India to enable it to buy 2 million tons of food grains in the United States before 30 June 1952. The loan was to be repaid in dollars over a period of thirty-five years with an interest rate of 2.5 per cent; the repayment of the principal was to begin in June 1957. Article 7 of the Act set up a special deposit account from the interest payments, not exceeding a sum of $ 5 million, due between December 1952 and January 1957 to initiate an educational programme. The terms of credit were to be governed by the Economic Cooperation Act of 1948, which Nehru accepted without enthusiasm. An administrator of the ECA arrived in mid-July to observe the distribution of the food grains and the implementation of the other clauses of the India Emergency Food Assistance Act. Not long after the bill was passed, a special US mission arrived in India to discuss with high-ranking Indian officials the question of increased shipments of strategic minerals, particularly beryl, manganese, mica, kyanite, and even monazite. In September, a representative of the Indian government went to Washington to conduct negotiations, which led notably to the shipment, heretofore prohibited, of 500 tons of monazite concentrate. India also informed the US that it does not intend to supply strategic and military items to China.[35]

It had, therefore, required four months before Congress could settle the matter of food assistance to India. Hence, the Truman administration, in an attempt to catch up with lost time, acted promptly so that the transportation of the food grains was not delayed any further. The bilateral agreement on aid was concluded the very day that the Act was ratified by Truman. The first ship was loaded at Philadelphia on 19 June. The amount of food grains delivered under the American loan rose to 1.05 million tons during the second half of 1951, i.e. 22 per cent of the total imports of 4.75 million tons that year. If we add around 1.5 million tons commercially imported from the United States, the total supply of American food grains in 1951 represented around 50 per cent of the total imports. As for the import of Soviet wheat, it did not finally exceed 100,000 tons. Radhakrishnan, however, had endeavoured to convince the Indian government that there was no harm in procuring the further 400,000 tons offered by the Soviets, if only, on the one hand, to build up stocks, and, on the other hand, to not offend the Soviets who had proved to be accommodating on this matter.[36] His plea went unheeded and despite Krishna Menon's support to this idea, the government preferred to put forward the excuse that the ports of the country were not in a position to handle any more grain. The Minister of Agriculture, K.M. Munshi, who was no friend of the Soviet Union, was extremely hostile to this proposal. Bajpai, for his part, highlighted the reduction in dollar-earning exports that a new barter agreement with the USSR would bring about.

While the United States had helped India to surmount the food crisis, the American Ambassador, questioned by the State Department over the fallout of the agreement, admitted that the hope of a more friendly attitude by Nehru towards the United States had vanished with the delay over the dispatch of the aid and after the criticism of India heard in Congress as also the debate over the terms of the aid. He expected that Nehru would continue 'on occasions [to] make remarks sharply critical of [the] American way of life and US governmental policies', and he recommended that in future the United States should be particularly careful to see that its aid should clearly denote a desire for cooperation and not for domination, so as to put an end to the current suspicions about American motives. Even then, to bring about a distinct improvement in Indo-US relations, it was necessary that the differences over the problems of Kashmir and the Far East should be toned down.[37] Indeed, Nehru, in a letter dated 6 August 1951 to Vijayalakshmi Pandit, reiterated his criticism of American support to undemocratic regimes, which were nevertheless 'faithful allies', and, more generally, of the American tendency to look 'at everything from a purely military point of view', the result of all this was that 'moderate tendencies and really democratic ways and policies find less scope and the fascists and the Communists hold the field against each other, ultimately probably leading to war'.[38]

It was not long before another controversy arose between Indians and Americans, this time on the subject of the Japanese peace treaty. This treaty was part of a first wave of military alliances in the Asia-Pacific zone, with the bilateral security pact signed on 30 August with the Philippines and the ANZUS pact of 1 September between the United States, Australia, and New Zealand. A second wave of alliances, extending to continental Asia, was conducted from the autumn of 1953 by the Eisenhower administration. The Indian government felt that the draft peace treaty could not profess to restore to Japan an honourable place within the international community. The islands of Bonin and Ryukyu, which had been put by the UNO under the 'strategic trusteeship' of the United States, were not restored immediately to Japan and the former reserved to themselves the right to retain military bases on Japanese soil. India also considered that conditions had not been created for a thorough settlement of the Far East question because the PRC was not invited to the negotiations. New Delhi objected to the fact that no mention was made of the cession of Formosa and the Pescadores to Communist China and of the confirmation of the acquisition by the USSR of the Kuriles Islands and South Sakhalin as had been decided at Yalta. Consequently, New Delhi refused to participate in the San Francisco Conference, which ended up with the signature on 8 September 1951 by 49 countries, of the Japanese peace treaty. In April 1952, the Indian government concluded a separate treaty with Japan.

As a result of these resolute policy positions, Nehru became the object of unkind comments in the United States. J.F. Dulles, who had been the main American negotiator at the San Francisco Conference, complained to Vijayalakshmi Pandit that India also seemed to have adopted the Chinese slogan of 'Asia for the Asians', and wished the end of American influence in Asia. She clarified that there was no anti-American bias in India and endeavoured to put Americans' mind at ease by reminding them that during the recent sessions of the UNGA, India had voted 38 times out of 51 with the United States, had abstained 11 times, and has differed only twice.[39] A few days earlier, Nehru had reassured the outgoing US Ambassador that in spite of marked differences of opinion between their two countries in regard to various matters, 'there was basic community of views, or, to put it differently, our differences were not deep but rather superficial and temporary'.[40] However, there was a recurrent perception that the United States was seeking to establish its hegemony in Asia.

Fortunately, this new frostiness in Indo-US relations did not have any adverse effect on the principle of aid to India. The Truman administration had resigned itself to supporting the Nehru government, more to prevent a deterioration in the economic situation and hence the possibility that the leadership of the country might pass into the hands of the Communists, with the baneful consequences that this development would bring for American strategic and economic interests in Asia, than in the hope of persuading the Indian government to join the American initiatives in the fight against communism. A CIA report, calling for a substantial aid extending over several years, was in keeping with this viewpoint.[41] Some Indian dailies reproached the American government of still not having given concrete shape to its declared intention of giving aid to India. The *Amrita Bazar Patrika*, widening the debate to cover promises of assistance in general, considered that for:

> the average citizen in this country, these words such as Colombo aid, US technical aid, US economic aid, have begun to be tyrannous and oppressive, seeing that there are less substance in them than words. So far as India is concerned, Colombo Plan is nothing more than an annual release by Britain of £ 35 millions of India's frozen sterling balance, besides a trivial food grant by Australia and Canada. The US technical aid is only a $ 17 million programme for India.[42]

In the *Times of India* of 27 July 1951, the editorial called on 'the somnolent pundits of Washington' to wake up to the elementary fact that the comparative progress of China and India would have 'far-reaching effects on the politics and economy of the East' and ultimately on 'the future of democracy in this part of the world'.

NOTES

1. Loy Henderson to the Secretary of State, Dean Acheson, 20 January 1951, *FRUS, 1951*, vol. 6, part 2, p. 2087.
2. To Vijayalakshmi Pandit, 9 May 1950. J.L. Nehru, *Selected Works of Jawaharlal Nehru* (*second series*), vol. 14, part 2, p. 379.
3. Memorandum by the Deputy Assistant of State for Near Eastern, South Asian and African Affairs (Hare) to the Secretary of State, 3 July 1950. *FRUS, 1950*, vol. 5, p. 1466.
4. Memorandum from the Assistant Secretary of State for Near Eastern, South Asian and African Affairs (McGhee) to the Secretary of State, 7 June 1950, *FRUS, 1950*, vol. 5, p. 169.
5. Henderson to the Secretary of State, 23 August 1950. Ibid., p. 1469.
6. 1 December 1950. Ibid., p. 1478.
7. Department of State, *Treaties and Other International Acts Series*, no. 2241, Washington, D.C.: US Government Printing Office, 1951, p. 1. In mid-1952, Indians sought to obtain some tanks and fighters. The first request was met and a large number of Sherman tanks were delivered. As for the second, some eyebrows were raised over it and the Indians had to

remain content with obtaining only some C-119 transport planes. It has also been argued that this agreement between India and the United States provided a legal foundation to their secret collaboration against Chinese expansionism and permitted large numbers of US military and intelligence personnel to expand covert operations in Tibet. S. Mahmud Ali, *Cold War in the High Himalayas—The USA, China and South Asia in the 1950s*, p. 25.

8. See for instance memorandum of conversation by Joseph S. Sparks of the Division of South Asian Affairs, 29 July 1948, *FRUS, 1948*, vol. 5, pp. 513-14. See also the note of the Ambassador in India, Loy Henderson, to the Secretary of State, 29 July 1949, *FRUS, 1949*, vol. 6, p. 1727.
9. Policy statement prepared in the Office of South Asian Affairs, 9 October 1950. *FRUS, 1950*, vol. 5, p. 252.
10. Telegram from Washington to the Foreign Office, 18 September 1952. *PRO*, FO 371 101139. India received 26 C-119G aircraft in 1954.
11. The opposition of the Indians to the new Anglo-American proposals on the question of Kashmir did not help in any way. Great Britain and the United States had drawn up a draft resolution in January 1951 opposing the convening by the Indian government of a Constituent Assembly in Kashmir. Moreover, New Delhi was enraged at the very fact that foreign troops could be sent there to supervise the plebiscite. Finally, in end March 1951, a resolution was adopted in the UN suggesting that a representative of the United Nations, entrusted with the demilitarization of the region, be sent and, in the event of a disagreement between the parties concerned, it was provided that recourse would be taken to arbitration by the International Court of Justice, in spite of India's opposition.
12. *Times of India*, 26 January 1951.
13. Loy Henderson to Dean Acheson, 2 February 1951. *FRUS, 1951*, vol. 6, part 2, p. 2107.
14. Loy Henderson to Dean Acheson, 20 January 1951. Ibid., p. 2089. In another communication dated 12 April, Henderson described C. Rajagopalachari, who succeeded Sardar Patel as Home Minister as being 'after Nehru the most influential member of the Cabinet and reputedly the leader of the pro-American group in the Cabinet'. Ibid., p. 2142. K.M. Munshi was among those who wanted a clear alliance with the United States. There was also a pro-American lobby within the Congress, which included M.R. Masani and N.G. Ranga. These four politicians were later founding members in 1959 of the Swatantra Party which was openly anti-communist and pro-West.
15. Draft statement of policy proposed by the National Security Council on South Asia, 22 January 1951. Ibid., p. 1651.
16. *Amrita Bazar Patrika*, 23 February 1951.
17. *New York Times*, 5 March 1951.
18. 19 April 1951. Executive sessions of the Senate Foreign Relations Committee, no. 164, 693-4 and 696. Quoted by R.K. Jain (ed.), *U.S.-South Asian Relations 1947-1982*, vol. 1, p. 180.

19. *Economic Weekly*, 17 February 1951, p. 169.
20. Declaration of William Thorp, Assistant Secretary of State for Economic Affairs, 21 January 1951, US House, 82nd Congress, 1st session, Committee on Foreign Affairs, Hearings, India Emergency Aid Act of 1951, pp. 47, 66, 96-101. Quoted by R.K. Jain (ed.), *US-South Asian Relations 1947-1982*, vol. 1, pp. 169-70. Letter of the Chairman of the US Atomic Energy Commission, Gordon Dean, to Acheson, 19 February 1951. *FRUS, 1951*, vol. 1, pp. 694-5.
21. 'Current US Objectives with Respect to Indian Atomic Energy Raw Materials', memorandum prepared by the Office of the Under Secretary of State (Lovett), 17 September 1948. *FRUS, 1948*, vol. 1, part 2, pp. 758-65. *Amrita Bazar Patrika*, 5 April 1951.
22. Record of a conversation of the US Ambassador with Nehru on 6 March 1949. Department of State, Division of Communications and Records, Under Secretary's Office, USA. Quoted in J.L. Nehru, *Selected Works of Jawaharlal Nehru (second series)*, vol. 10, pp. 427-8.
23. Memorandum by the Deputy Assistant Secretary of State for Near Eastern, South Asian and African Affairs (Jernegan) to the Acting Secretary of State, 29 September 1954. *FRUS, 1952-1954*, vol. 11, part 2, pp. 1767-70. In a conversation with the Counsellor of the US Embassy on 25 May 1951, Nehru indeed asked him if the US had taken away the 400 tons of beryl that India had agreed to supply them, before adding that there were also some rare earths that India was prepared to let them have. Note to Secretary General, MEA. J.L. Nehru, *Selected Works of Jawaharlal Nehru (second series)*, vol. 16, part 1, p. 92.
24. Dispatch from Daniel Levi, French Ambassador in India, 29 January 1951. AQO, Asie-Océanie, 1944-1955, Inde, vol. 66.
25. 10 April 1951. J.L. Nehru, *Letters to Chief Ministers*, vol. 2, pp. 370-1.
26. *New York Times*, 6 April 1951.
27. Telegram from the French Ambassador in India, Daniel Levi, 13 April 1951. AQO, Asie-Océanie, 1944-1955, Inde, vol. 66.
28. *Le Monde*, 6 April 1951.
29. 21 April 1951. J.L. Nehru, *Letters to Chief Ministers*, vol. 2, p. 378.
30. Y. D. Gundevia, *Outside the Archives*, pp. 91-2.
31. *Hindustan Times*, 24 May 1951.
32. Memorandum of conversations between Vijayalakshmi Pandit, B.K. Nehru, McGhee and Matthews on 14 and 18 April 1951, by J. Robert Flucker of the Office of South Asian Affairs. *FRUS, 1951*, vol. 6 part 2, pp. 2144-50.
33. To Vijayalakshmi Pandit, 11 April 1951. J.L. Nehru, *Selected Works of Jawaharlal Nehru (second series)*, vol. 16, part 1, p. 72.
34. *Times of India*, 11 May 1951.
35. 'The Position of USA with Respect to South Asia', memorandum by the Deputy Under Secretary of State (Matthews) to the Executive Secretary of the National Security Council (James S. Lay), 13 November 1951. *FRUS, 1951*, vol. 6, part 2, p. 1696.

36. Radhakrishnan to Nehru, 6 June 1951. S. Gopal, *Radhakrishnan: A Biography*, pp. 238-9.
37. Loy Henderson to the Secretary of State, 7 June 1951. *FRUS, 1951*, vol. 6, part 2, pp. 2167-8.
38. To Vijayalakshmi Pandit, 6 August 1951. J.L. Nehru, *Selected Works of Jawaharlal Nehru (second series)*, vol. 16, part 2, p. 612.
39. Vijayalakshmi Pandit's report of interview with Dulles, 4 October 1951. S. Gopal, *Jawaharlal Nehru: A Biography*, vol. 2, p. 138. *Times of India*, 20 September 1951.
40. Nehru's note on his talk with Loy Henderson, 15 September 1951.. J.L. Nehru, *Selected Works of Jawaharlal Nehru (second series)*, vol. 16, part 2, p. 627.
41. Memorandum by the Central Intelligence Agency, 4 September 1951. *FRUS, 1951*, vol. 6, part 2, p. 2179.
42. *Amrita Bazar Patrika*, 4 August 1951.

CHAPTER 8

A Troubled Equation

THE DEBATES IN THE US Congress over India's foreign policy and the controversy raised by the terms of the food assistance that had preceded the wheat loan of 15 June 1951 revealed valuable lessons to Indian policy-makers. Consequently, the experts who drew up the First Five Year Plan emphasized that there were 'obvious risks in excessive reliance on foreign aid which depends on the domestic political situation in lending countries and which might be interrupted by any untoward international developments'.[1] To avert this danger, they displayed their preference for credits coming from international organizations, while at the same time acknowledging they would have to come to terms with an aid programme that would still be largely bilateral. This assumption was not without reason, since multilateral aid was to constitute only 15 per cent of the total aid during this First Plan.

If foreign aid was not to be recommended on political grounds, it appeared unavoidable on economic grounds, and it was acknowledged that the First Five Year Plan could not be implemented in its totality without it. The final version of the plan, covering the period from 1 April 1951 to 31 March 1956, was adopted by Parliament in early December 1952. Its primary characteristic was the relatively modest objectives, particularly when compared to the 'Bombay Plan'. The national income at the end of the plan was expected to increase by 11 per cent, not a stupendous proposition considering that the population growth rate was anticipated at 6.5 per cent. The level of public expenditures, estimated finally at Rs. 20.69 billion, was restricted by a small savings rate (5 per cent of the national income), by the inflationary trends which limited opportunities for the creation of money, and, to a certain extent, even though the foreign exchange reserves were still adequate, by the unhappy situation regarding the balance of payments which had been constantly experiencing a deficit since Independence. Admittedly, the trade boom resulting from the stockpiling induced by the Korean War had led to an increase in both the volume and the value of India's exports. This, combined with the devaluation of the rupee and a stricter control of import licenses for goods from the dollar area, did improve the foreign trade balance, leading to a surplus in the balance of payments on the current account of Rs. 389 million in 1950-1. For the first time since Independence, there was a net credit in the current transactions with the dollar area to the extent of Rs. 295 million. However, these gains proved temporary, and right from the following year, 1951-2, India recorded a deficit of Rs. 1.63 billion on total current transactions following a slowing down in the demand for India's main export items and an upward movement of world prices. This deficit would have been even higher without the US wheat loan.[2] These were the reasons that led the planners to expect an annual deficit of Rs. 1.8 to Rs. 2 billion for the remaining years of the plan, of which Rs. 500 million were expected to be financed out of withdrawals from sterling balances and the rest through foreign aid and private foreign investment as well as commercial borrowings.

Three-quarters of the public expenditures to be spent on development were to come from internal resources originating from savings from the current revenues of the central and state governments (Rs. 7.38 billion), from private savings absorbed through loans from the public, small savings, deposits, funds, etc. (Rs. 5.2 billion), and finally from deficit financing up to Rs. 2.9 billion corresponding to the anticipated releases of sterling balances assimilated with past savings of the community.[3] Seven and a half per cent of the outlay in the public sector (Rs. 1.56 billion) was to be financed from loans and grants already received, essentially Rs. 900 million from the US wheat loan, Rs. 250 million from assistance under the Indo-American Technical Cooperation Agreement signed in January 1952, and Rs. 120 million from the Commonwealth assistance under the Colombo Plan. To balance expenditures with revenues, there still remained to find Rs. 3.65 billion.

No specific target had been fixed in the matter of foreign aid. The projects included in the plan laid emphasis on agriculture and were biased in favour of labour intensive schemes requiring mainly domestically available resources. Hence, they necessitated only a comparatively modest amount of foreign exchange, about

Rs. 4 billion, which was covered by the sterling balances and external assistance. It was also necessary to take into account the requirement of foreign exchange for all the non-plan expenditures, such as those resulting from expanding domestic incomes which would, in turn, generate additional demand for commodities which may have to be met by imports from abroad insofar as additional supplies were not available domestically. Nevertheless, the planners remained confident that, even if further external assistance was not forthcoming, these problems were manageable, and could be solved without compromising the targets of the overall development programme. This would mean either taking recourse to a larger mobilization of internal resources, by taxation, borrowing, and larger deficit financing, or adopting measures aimed at holding down or reducing consumption.[4]

The plan laid stress on the development of the rural areas and on rural infrastructure. About one-third of the outlay in the public sector was devoted to agriculture, community development, and irrigation. The government hoped to increase productivity and hence reduce its imports of food grains which, since Independence, constituted the foremost item imported, with the notable exception of the year 1950-1 when the import of raw cotton was higher. As compared to 1949-50, the reference year considering the abnormally low results of 1950-1, the production of food grains was to increase by 14 per cent, i.e. it had to reach 61.6 million tons by the end of the plan, a level of production which, it was thought, would allow India to be nearly self-sufficient. Commercial crops were also accorded importance, because in order to reduce the dependence of the textile industry on imported raw materials, the goal was to achieve an increase of 42 per cent and 63 per cent in the production of cotton and jute respectively between 1951 and 1956.[5]

Transport, communications, and social services took up almost half the expenditures of the public sector, of which one-tenth went to building additional power capacity. The programme for industrialization was a modest one. Only 8.4 per cent of the public outlay was reserved for the development of the industrial sector. The major part of the investments was to be borne by the private sector supplemented in some cases by foreign private investment and by the state which took upon itself a special responsibility for the development of key industries such as iron and steel and chemicals.

This plan, on the whole, met the approval of the Americans who had insisted several times on the necessity of paying greater attention to agricultural development. However, George V. Allen, when he was the American Ambassador to India (1953-5), warned that this insistence of the Americans lacked the proper psychological approach for it led the people in underdeveloped countries to think that the United States was opposed to their industrialization, and he criticized this as 'a policy on a par with colonialism—a policy which the United States should turn its back on resolutely'.[6] When the draft plan became known, the *Pravda* pointed to the meagre amount of investment devoted to industry and to the absence of any radical land reforms, all of which, it predicted, would keep the Indian economy in its rural-based and backward state. The *Pravda* concluded that this was 'nothing more than the imperialistic plan of Mountbatten'.[7]

The American wheat loan was followed by negotiations between the two countries to further bilateral economic cooperation. These talks came to a successful conclusion on 5 January 1952 when a five-year agreement was signed in New Delhi. It was renewed in 1957. The Americans hoped that this agreement would contribute in helping India to strengthen its foundations and to set itself firmly on the path of development while adhering to the principle of a liberal economy. An Indo-American Technical Cooperation Fund (Fund A), financed by an initial grant from the American government of $50 million drawn on the Mutual Security Programme, was established for the realization of cooperation projects. It was agreed that this fund would be used for the procurement of goods, materials, and contractors' services from sources outside India and would be jointly administered by the Director of Technical Cooperation, attached to the US diplomatic mission in New Delhi, and by an officer appointed by the Indian government. The United States also accepted to bear the cost of the salaries and expenses of all technical experts employed for the programme by the US government, as well as the expenses related to the training facilities of Indian nationals abroad and the costs of technical assistance provided by the US government through contracts with private agencies. To cover these costs, $ 4 million were allocated in addition to the $ 50 million already allocated in Fund A.

The Indian government instituted a Special Development Fund (Fund B), into which were apportioned sums of an amount equal at least to the American contribution to Fund A and covering the rupee expenses of the duly agreed projects.[8] The Indian government also took upon itself the responsibility of constituting a central committee entrusted with laying down the broad policies and providing the general supervision under which the agreed upon projects of technical supervision were to be executed. It was understood that the American director of the Technical Cooperation would be consulted with respect to all programme recommendations of the committee and that his concurrence was required each time allocations from Fund A were involved.

The reactions to this agreement were generally favourable in India. Commentators inevitably noted that the sum of Rs. 250 million offered by the United States—was rather modest compared to the military and economic assistance given to countries in western Europe and East Asia. But more noteworthy was the fact that the agreement constituted a significant upturn in terms of the scope and the duration of the assistance provided until then under the Point Four Programme.

Still, some Indian commentators expressed their reservations. The *Amrita Bazar Patrika* wondered if help from the leader of one of the two blocs would not have some undesirable hidden strings attached to it and asked 'how far it is likely to jeopardize or even influence the independence of the country's foreign policy and how far that assistance is likely to entrench itself as a powerful foreign capitalistic interest in the domestic sphere'. The editorialist was particularly worried by the preamble laying stress on the agreement between the Indian and the American governments in regard to a joint endeavour to promote international understanding and maintain world peace and, as a corollary to it, to undertake such action as they may mutually agree upon to eliminate causes of international tension. As there was considerable difference of opinion over the various means for the promotion of peace, particularly when political issues relating to the Far East and South-East Asia were involved, he expressed the fear that this political background might create obstructions almost at every step.[9] But, on the whole, the satisfaction of being able to count on American aid at a time when the outlay of the First Five Year Plan was being debated and the assurances of the American Ambassador, Chester Bowles, that this aid was absolutely free from political strings, largely swept aside the apprehensions regarding the content of one or another clause of the agreement. The *Economic Weekly* felt that the fears based on the old 'Trojan horse' theory of foreign capital, which might be put forward, were unfounded.[10]

The most virulent attacks came obviously from the Communists for whom no American aid could ever be respectable for its final aim was to coerce the recipient country to join in the American-led struggle against the spread of communism, and to influence the economic orientations of the government for the benefit of the interests of American monopolists. The communist member of Parliament, Hirendra Nath Mukherjee, endorsed the remarks made by the Gandhian Kishorlal Ghanshyamdas Mashruwala who denounced the Indo-American Technical Cooperation Agreement as 'virtually a charter to the US to establish herself in India, first as a trading concern and then as India's political boss. The government of India has agreed to place at the disposal of the US all its administrative machinery and to become her advertising agency.'[11] Addressing Parliament, Jawaharlal Nehru denied that India had entered into the American orbit and asserted categorically that the Indian government would not buckle under any pressure over its political options in exchange for aid: 'There have been times when one word from us would have brought us many of the good things of life. We preferred not to give that word. . . . If at any time help from abroad depends upon a variation, howsoever slight, in our policy, we shall relinquish that help completely and prefer starvation and privation to taking such help.'[12] And yet during this period, an instance arose when the political conditions implicit in American aid did manifest themselves, an event which led the Indian government to strike a compromise with its American counterpart to circumvent the suspension of the aid. This instance did not arise out of a specific interpretation of the Indo-American Technical Cooperation Agreement, but emerged from the enactment of American legislation on foreign aid.

On 21 July 1953, George Allen, who had by then succeeded Chester Bowles as US Ambassador to India, informed the State Department of a communication from the Consul General in Bombay that 2,248 pounds of thorium nitrate, a highly strategic material according to American classification, was being loaded on a Polish vessel going to Communist China and that it was consigned by the Indian Rare Earths Limited, a joint stock company of the government of India and the Travancore-Cochin state, based at Alwaye.[13] The Americans were astonished. Two years earlier, in July 1951, Nehru had authorized a denial when there were rumours in the United States that India was shipping strategic materials to the

People's Republic of China,[14] even though the Indian government had abstained from the vote in the UNGA, on 18 May 1951, for an embargo on the export of strategic materials to the PRC. But above all, the American Embassy reminded the Indian government that under the Mutual Defense Assistance Control Act, better known as the 'Battle Act', signed into law in October 1951, any nation trading embargoed materials with the USSR and its satellites, including the PRC, would have all US economic or military assistance terminated. The US government had indeed inquired, a few weeks after the signing of the Indo-American Technical Cooperation Agreement, as to what action New Delhi proposed to take in this matter. Indignant at this request, Nehru responded that India could not give any guarantee or assurance to Washington, either written or oral, regarding the export of articles prohibited under US law.[15]

In end July, George V. Allen proposed that the thorium nitrate consignment be off-loaded from the ship at Colombo. In response, Nehru again swore that India would never submit to the derogation to its national sovereignty in permitting American law to determine with whom and in what commodities India could trade, and, therefore, it contested any obligation resulting from the 'Battle Act', but it could consider cooperating with the US in the future about the disposal of thorium nitrate.[16] Not much noise was made over the matter at the time. The Americans in charge, who did not want to throw their country's aid to India in the balance, preferred that the contentious issue should not be brought to the notice of the US Congress. They argued that a stoppage of aid would not fail to weigh on the already tense state of Indo-American relations, and that this would be especially unfortunate at a time when India was going to be the chairman of the Neutral Nations Repatriation Commission (NNRC) for Korea; they noted that 'political considerations strongly support our taking the position that the present shipment is not in violation of the provisions of the Battle Act'.[17] Finally, the State Department had no desire to put the Indian government in the ticklish position of having to publicly acknowledge the existence of political strings tied to the aid. A compromise was ultimately worked out. The Indian government, not wanting to commit itself in writing to a ban on the export of strategic materials to the communist countries, promised stricter administrative controls to prevent such an imbroglio from occurring again. As for the United States, it made an effort to make a pre-emptive purchase of India's production of thorium nitrate; this was spelt out in a memorandum of commitment concluded at the end of 1954. At the beginning of 1955, a paper prepared by the Office of South Asian Affairs reviewed this matter:

> As part of our policy to eliminate trade between India and the Communist bloc in strategic materials, and to assure the US adequate supplies of such materials, we have arrangements with the government of India on beryl and thorium nitrate. Constant vigilance, however, is necessary to assure, insofar as it lies within the power of the US, that India's actions do not conflict with the provisions of the Battle Act. India's cooperation with regard to exports has been carried on in an informal . . . manner. This cooperation has been at least adequate, though problems involving specific shipments or groups of shipments continue to arise. So far, we have been able to adjust to them on an *ad hoc* basis.[18]

A contract was to be signed on 14 December 1955, stipulating the purchase from India of 230 tons of thorium nitrate.

One of the main promoters of the Technical Cooperation Agreement of 5 January had been the former Connecticut governor, Chester Bowles, who became US envoy to India in September 1951. After $ 54 million had been secured to Fund A at the time of signing the agreement, he was back in Washington as early as mid-January to plead in favour of a four-year aid plan for a total amount of $ 1 billion. Meeting Truman, the Secretary of State, Senators, and officials of the State Department, the Pentagon, the CIA, and the Mutual Assistance Administration, he did his utmost to convince them of the need to agree to an increased assistance for India. He proposed for the fiscal year 1952 an amount of $ 250 million. The sum of $ 125 million was for agricultural commodity transfers (grains and cotton) which India bought in large quantities from the United States and whose sale in India could provide the rupee finance for Fund B of the Indo-US Technical Cooperation Agreement, notably for meeting the local costs of an expanded community development programme. The other half would be for capital goods and materials and the deputing of engineers and technicians to India. Bowles felt that a financial effort of this magnitude would be reasonable and, at any rate, it was smaller than what Congress would be willing to give if the situation were to deteriorate and the prospect of India sliding towards the Communist bloc were to become more likely.

In a communication to the State Department after his return to New Delhi, Bowles warned that the

> survival of a democratic Indian government over the next five years is

definitively unlikely unless bold steps are taken now to sharply increase food production and strengthen the economy. Recent Communist successes in South India indicate how rapidly [the] political and economic situation here could disintegrate. Failure of Indian democracy would in all probability result in disaster substantially greater than Communist victory in China since Southeast Asia and the Middle East would become impossible to hold once India is lost.

Ultimately, 'a Communist sweep in Asia would gravely undermine our position in Europe'. Since one could not expect from democratic India the same level of sacrifices that China could force upon its population, it was up to the United States to try to fill the gap between the two countries' capacity to mobilize resources. 'The total four-year cost for 360 million Indian people is no more than the amount spent on economic aid to Greece and the annual total economic and military aid committed to Formosa, an island of 8 million which symbolizes Communist victory in China', Bowles noted.[19] In another dispatch to the Secretary of State, Dean Acheson, he emphasized that the dollar cost of helping France in Vietnam to stop the military advance of the Communists in Indo-China approached $ 500 million annually, or double the amount that he was requesting for India for the next fiscal year.[20] During his visit to Washington, Bowles responded to the sworn opponents of non-alignment by stressing the advantages that India's neutrality offered to the West by keeping this country outside the Soviet sphere of influence without imposing too heavy a burden on America. He stated that 'a more marked closeness towards the Western bloc could one day lead the leaders in New Delhi to ask for actual protection, which the government of the United States is not in a position to provide'.[21]

In Washington, without questioning the necessity of actively assisting Indian development, there was arguably less pessimism as regards the stability of the Nehru government. A National Intelligence Estimate drawn up in June 1953, and for which the State Department, the CIA, and the services of the armed forces had been consulted, minimized the communist threat in India. This evaluation was based on the results of the first general elections. On the Left, the CPI which had turned to the parliamentary path, after the failure of the armed struggle movement, and the Praja Socialist Party were not in a position to seriously challenge the Congress government in the foreseeable future. As far as rightist groups were concerned, such as the Hindu Mahasabha and the Bharatiya Jan Sangh, they were unlikely to score more than successes at the local level. The Congress party was indeed expected, even if Nehru died and provided that it held together, 'to secure a plurality if not an absolute majority in the 1957 elections'.[22]

The general elections of the winter of 1951-2 was the first occasion since Independence when the party leaders could assess their support among the electorate. The Congress emerged as the major victor, with 45 per cent of the votes in its favour. It had 364 elected representatives, i.e. 74 per cent of the 489 seats of the Lok Sabha, the lower house. By concentrating their efforts on their pockets of influence in the three states of south India (Hyderabad, Madras, and Travancore-Cochin) and on West Bengal, the Communists succeeded in getting 26 candidates elected while they had obtained a little more than 5 per cent of the votes on the national scene; as a result, the Communists emerged as the second largest parliamentary group in the Lok Sabha. The two socialist parties—the Socialist Party and the Kisan Mazdoor Praja Party—which later merged in September 1952 under the name Praja Socialist Party, received a total of 16.4 per cent of the votes; however, on account of their lack of unity, they had only 12 and 9 members of parliament respectively. The Hindu nationalist parties, the Hindu Mahasabha and the Bharatiya Jan Sangh, between them gathered 4 per cent of the votes and 7 of their candidates were elected.

Nevertheless, at a time when Communist China was fighting the US-led United Nations forces in Korea, any aid plan for foreign countries submitted for approval to the US Congress was more likely to be voted on the grounds that a communist threat, whether real or supposed, endangered the recipient country. Addressing a joint meeting of the Foreign Relations Committees of the Senate and the House which were examining the mutual aid programme for 1952-3, Dean Acheson defended the necessity to grant aid to India by citing the 'unexpected strength' displayed by the Communists in the recent elections and emphasized the need to not be deluded by the notable victory of the Congress party, for 'unless the Prime Minister Nehru can show substantial progress in economic development over the next five years, the likelihood is that [in] the next elections the democratic forces will be endangered either by the extremists of the Right or by the Communists'.[23]

The new legislative framework, following the adoption by the US

Congress of the Mutual Security Act in October 1951, witnessed an increased proportion of funds allocated to military aid as compared to economic assistance. The Mutual Security Programme brought together administratively the economic and military aid given till then separately under various foreign aid programmes (the military aid of the Mutual Defense Programme, the economic assistance to Europe, and the Point Four Programme). Western Europe remained the primary beneficiary of American aid, receiving 80 per cent of the total aid budget of $ 7.33 billion voted by Congress for the fiscal year 1952. For the Asia and Pacific zone alone (about 10 per cent of the total aid), priority was given also to the strengthening of the military capacity of the US allies since two-thirds of the aid was of a military nature, a distribution based on the conviction that the Korean War was only a prologue to a series of communist offensives in Asia.[24]

The plan for aid to India proposed by Chester Bowles, therefore, was largely against the prevailing trend of the order of priorities of the foreign aid budget. In June 1952, he returned to the United States to defend anew the cause of his aid programme, but without any greater success. Meanwhile, the Truman administration considered it politically injudicious to further increase the budgetary expenditures right in the middle of an election year, and asked Congress to sanction an aid of $ 115 million meant strictly for developmental assistance and thereby ruled out any supply of food grains which would have been required to be enacted as a specific piece of legislation. Finally, the aid granted to India for the fiscal year 1953, declined after having been scaled down to $ 77 million following a reduction of 32.5 per cent voted by Congress in the foreign aid budget. It declined even further, after new cuts were made by Congress, to $ 45 million, which was less than one-fifth of what had been initially demanded by Bowles, and was less than the amount of the preceding year.

The news of the victory of the Republican candidate, Dwight D. Eisenhower, in the presidential elections got a cold reception in India. In light of previous debates in the US Congress, the Republicans had earned the reputation of being even more hostile to the principle of non-alignment than the Democrats. The appointment of John Foster Dulles, as Secretary of State, at the head of American diplomacy did not bode well for a renewed cordiality in Indo-American relations. During the electoral campaign, he had shown a desire to replace the policy of containment towards communism with the policy of a rollback, a line in total opposition to the efforts of India on the international scene to promote the cause of peaceful coexistence. As Count Stanislas Ostrorog, the French Ambassador to New Delhi, noted in the eyes of the Indians Dulles was the 'representative of an authoritarian doctrine which, in a new form, takes over the imperial ambitions of the West and tends to establish American hegemony in Asia'.[25]

Dulles's militaristic rhetoric, along with the election of a high-ranking general who had been the supreme commander of the NATO forces in Europe in 1951, led to the fear that the military component of the aid budget might be increased even further. This possibility seemed even more imminent since the Republicans, who were in a majority in both the houses of the 83rd Congress, were also considered to be more tight-fisted in matters of foreign economic aid and were ardent advocates of its replacement as far as possible by foreign direct investment. On this latter point, the Indian weekly *Commerce* shared similar doubts and reservations regarding the capacity of underdeveloped countries to manage government-to-government aid without falling into indolence and complacency, or encouraging the party in power to try costly fads, to launch uneconomic ventures, or to try to win public opinion through stunts.[26]

However, it must be acknowledged that in the case of India, private American capital was not in a position to replace, even partially, public funds. The Industries (Development & Regulation) Act of 1951 had made American investors fear the growing interference of the state in the management of private enterprises. From early 1948 to mid-1952, out of the 108 new projects involving foreign private capital approved by the Indian government, only 13 were American; the lion's share went to British private capital with 69 registered projects. The major part of American private investment was made in the oil industry.[27]

As it happened, the agreement signed on 30 November 1951 with Stanvac (Standard Vacuum Oil) for the setting up of a refinery in the Bombay region revealed the extent of the concessions that the Indian government was ready to make to foreign companies in those sectors considered as enjoying high priority. In the wake of the Second World War, the Indian government had felt, as much for strategic reasons as for the need to save foreign exchange, that it would be desirable to install refineries in India in order to be able to locally refine the crude oil that was imported. The production of refined oil in the country was then equal to less than 10 per cent of the consumption. Only one refinery existed, dating back to 1920; it was situated in Digboi in Assam, and was operated by the Assam Oil Co., a subsidiary of Burmah-Shell. Moreover, the turmoil in Iran had introduced an element of uncertainty into the import of Persian oil. Hence, this American company obtained the assurance from the Indian government that there would be no nationalization for twenty-five years, and if that situation were to change subsequently, a reasonable compensation would be granted. The Indian participation in the capital would not exceed 25 per cent. Facilities were offered for the repatriation of the annual profits in hard currency. The company could use its own fleet of tankers for its imports of crude oil—with a ten-year exemption of customs duty—coming generally from deposits situated in the Middle East which the company controlled. The latter could fix the price of the refined products at a level equal to that of equivalent imported products. Finally, it was exempted from a certain number of controls stipulated in the Industries Act of 1951. Similar conditions, which also contravened the industrial policy resolution of 1948 to the same extent, were granted to the Burmah Shell and Caltex companies, in December 1951 and in April 1953 respectively, for the construction of two other refineries, one in Trombay, near Bombay, and the other at Vishakhapatnam (Andhra Pradesh).

FICCI regularly warned the Indian government against adopting a 'liberal' policy towards foreign capital in fields where Indian capital was already engaged as it would adversely affect the indigenous industries. It argued that foreign investment should be allowed only in specialized industries, requiring higher technical skills, which had not already been developed in the country, and also in those industries where domestic capital was 'definitely shy over a period of years'.[28] Negotiations on an Indo-US treaty of friendship, navigation, and commerce were still at a dead end. So much so that in March 1953, the Americans suggested another draft treaty of friendship and establishment, setting aside the clauses concerning trade and navigation and focusing basically on the problem of American investment in India; the objective was to create conditions to facilitate the flow of private capital into India.

When Bowles left India in the spring of 1953, he had raised the Indians' hopes of receiving a substantial economic aid but his administration was not able to actually dispense this package. There was even greater disappointment in store for India as Indians had come to increasingly identify Washington's aid policy with the growth of the military potential of American allies on the periphery of the communist world. G.L. Mehta, the new Indian Ambassador in Washington, in a speech which sounded like an indictment of this policy, expressed his anger against a defensive approach which considered the granting of development aid to poor and underdeveloped countries as a matter of secondary importance.

> These problems would have confronted us even if the teachings of Karl Marx had not influenced Lenin or Mao Tse-tung. They will have to be solved, Communism or no Communism. . . . To seek to explain the tremendous upsurge in Asia in rigid categories of Communism and anti-Communism is to oversimplify the problems. . . . Anyone acquainted with Asia and Africa knows that a military solution cannot endure, that safeguard against external aggression are less important than measures of economic amelioration to prevent disruption and subversive forces working within. . . . Neither air bases nor atomic weapons can ensure stability or progress.[29]

In the early part of 1953, Indian newspapers announced the probable participation of Pakistan in an organization for the defense of the Middle East, an idea that Great Britain and the United States had been, in fact, seriously considering since the autumn of 1951. The Indian government, which had heard about talks between Americans and Pakistanis concerning a military aid programme, had already informed the State Department of its disapproval. The State Department could not praise Pakistan enough since the officially professed neutrality of this country did not have the doctrinaire nature of India's non-alignment and also because its leaders had repeatedly demonstrated their friendship for the United States in many ways, including effective cooperation at the United Nations and in connection with the signing of the Japanese peace treaty.[30] Evidence of the excellent relations between America and Pakistan was seen when Pakistan experienced a grave shortage of food grains after two years of inadequate rainfall. It took just fifteen days, from the time Eisenhower sought emergency assistance from the US Congress on 10 June 1953 to the moment President signed into law a grant of 610,000 tons of wheat to Pakistan. This brief lapse of time compared favourably with the shilly-shallying of Congress two years earlier regarding the wheat loan to India.

The decision to grant military aid to Pakistan also had its detractors. Among the critics was Bowles who felt that Washington had everything to lose as a result of a deterioration of its relations with New Delhi and out of the souring of Indo-Pakistani relations which would not fail to follow. In addition, there was the risk arising from the dispute between Pakistan and Afghanistan over the Pakhtoon question and the recognition of the Durand line which might result in the forging of a closer relationship between Kabul and Moscow. More generally, Bowles stressed the artificial nature of the friendly relations between countries based on aid:

> Contrary to the assumptions of some diplomatic and military strategists, foreign aid will not enable us to purchase Allies and friends. We can no more buy the loyalty of a free people than we can buy the loyalty of a free individual. Nor will foreign aid even assure us the gratitude of destitute people in Asia, Africa or South America.[31]

As the Truman administration neared the end of its term, no final decision was taken on the proposed military aid programme to Pakistan. Summing up the American dilemma, Nehru noted that India counted for them and that they would not easily take the step in favour of a military alliance with Pakistan, but 'if military opinion is dominant, they might very well override political considerations'.[32]

The distinct possibility of a substantial military aid to Pakistan rapidly re-emerged with the arrival of the Eisenhower administration. Dulles, accompanied by Harold E. Stassen, Administrator of the Mutual Security Agency, visited several states of South Asia, the Near East and the Middle East in May 1953. He visited India from 20 to 22 May 1953. This was the first visit ever paid to India by a US Secretary of State. Dulles concluded from his visit that a regional defense organization in the Near East was for the time being impractical on account of the attitude of the Arab League countries, which were more preoccupied with their quarrels with the United Kingdom and with Israel than with an eventual communist threat. But the 'northern tier' countries were more receptive to the American line concerning the need to counter the Soviet danger. Turkey, a member of NATO since 1952, did not need to be convinced. Iran, after the fall of Mossadegh and the return of the Shah in the summer of 1953, was likely, once the internal situation had stabilized, to fall in line with America's strategic designs. Finally, there was Pakistan whose leaders showed more and more eagerness to obtain a more liberal supply of defense equipment from the United States. Since

1951, there had been suggestions on various occasions of Pakistan's willingness to give valuable military support to the Western allies. The Governor General, Ghulam Muhammad, and the Commander in Chief of Pakistan's armed forces, Ayub Khan, were scheduled to visit Washington in November 1953, with the intention of convincing the State Department that it should pay no heed to India's recriminations.[33]

In the autumn of 1953, the American government had reached certain decisions even while it still continued to weigh the pros and cons of the matter. On 18 November, Eisenhower announced during a press conference that the United States was examining the consequences of a military pact with Pakistan. The assessment of the intelligence agencies had indicated the probable nature of Indian reactions to a US-Pakistan military pact:

> The inclusion of Pakistan in Western regional defense and military assistance arrangements would almost certainly evoke strong Indian resentment, not only because of its implications for the Kashmir dispute but also because it would tend to increase Soviet military interest in the subcontinent. Western efforts to counter the Indian reaction are unlikely to be very effective. Although India would probably feel compelled to build up its own military forces to maintain a balance with Pakistan, it would probably reject any Western offer of military aid on the same terms as that given Pakistan as involving unwanted military or political commitments. Offers to guarantee borders or other Western efforts to assure India against possible Pakistan aggression would be unlikely to overcome India's resentment.[34]

A second report dated 15 January 1954, drawn up six months after the first, enumerated the repercussions that a US-Pakistan pact would have on Indo-American relations. These included the possibility that India would be disposed to undercut and embarrass the United States, that India would refuse to negotiate the proposed treaty of friendship and establishment, and that official and private American activities in India would encounter growing difficulties with government officials and the general public. The Americans also anticipated that it would probably increase Indian interests in trade with the Communist bloc and strengthen India's conciliatory attitude towards China. But non-alignment would, nevertheless, not be called into question as a result of the US-Pakistan military rapprochement. Finally, 'except possibly as a result of a cumulative series of frictions and disagreements, India would be unlikely to refuse US economic aid'. The analysis concluded in favour of granting military assistance to Pakistan for fear of weakening the pro-Western moderate elements in control in Karachi to the advantage of the reactionary religious elements which were opposed to close ties with the West and which favoured a more militant policy regarding Kashmir. It was, moreover, too late for the United States to move back without appearing to give in to India's protests, to which were joined those of the Soviet Union and China. Furthermore, a retreat might lead to a crisis of confidence among the allied countries. In any case, the Americans did not expect that giving up any military agreement with Pakistan would arouse a significantly more cooperative attitude from the Indian government towards America's security policy.[35]

In January 1954, the Americans decided to seize the opportunity of signing an agreement with Pakistan interwoven into a future regional defense pact and fitting in with the broader framework of a *cordon sanitaire* of military bases bordering the communist world. Dulles, who disliked India's non-alignment, had undoubtedly influenced this policy shift. The Vice President, Richard Nixon, on his return from a long tour of Asia in the autumn of 1953, also felt that a defense agreement with Pakistan, an outspokenly opponent of communism, was an opportunity to be seized to counterbalance India's neutralist influence in the continent.[36] On a personal level, he had no kind words for Nehru, with whom he had two private meetings, and whom he described as 'the least friendly leader' he had met on this trip. This was in sharp contrast with the positive impression made by Ayub Khan whom Nixon described as strongly pro-American and fiercely anti-communist.[37] In November 1953, Dulles informed Nehru that the disparity in population and area between India and Pakistan ruled out any reasonable possibility of Pakistan exploiting American assistance to threaten India and that consequently the United States could not indefinitely postpone the military strengthening of a vital area because of the unfriendly relations between these two countries.[38]

This was enough to provoke one of Nehru's characteristic outbursts against American foreign policy: 'The Americans cannot think of anything else but of getting bases all over the world and using their money power to get manpower elsewhere to fight for them. . . . The military approach is dominant in US politics and there is an almost total unawareness that human beings count and might even make a difference.' Nehru did not exclude the possibility that one of America's objectives in granting military aid to Pakistan was to bring pressure upon India to compel her to change its policy of non-alignment.[39] The signs of a deterioration in Indo-American relations had become all too evident. In August 1953, the United States exerted pressure on its allies in the United Nations to ensure, largely at the urging of Syngman Rhee of Korea, that India was to be kept out of the international conference on Korea that had been called during the signing of the armistice at Pan-Mun-Jon on 27 July. India bitterly resented this action since it had through its efforts at mediation, contributed towards ending the deadlock over the problem of the prisoners of war, and moreover, India headed the NNRC itself. India suspected that by restricting the participation at the conference on Korea to the warring powers alone, the United States wanted to avoid any discussion on the overall problems of East Asia as well as to exclude the possibility of seeing an Indian representative add his voice to those who might sought to establish a link between the settlement of the Korean question and the entry of Communist China into the UNO or those who wished to bring in the problem of the status of Formosa.

Nehru showed an increasingly defiant attitude towards American activities in the region. He had several times reminded the United States that its unfriendly attitude on the Kashmir issue was an obstacle to more cordial Indo-American relations. He suspected the Americans of having encouraged Sheikh Abdullah to adopt a pro-independence stance—which led to his arrest in August 1953—and of plotting in Nepal, which was then seeking to establish some political stability: 'I have no doubt that American agents have been the cause of some mischief both in Kashmir and Nepal. I have little doubt that it is American help that has brought about the last change in Iran', charged Nehru, in a reference to the overthrow of the government of Mohammed Mossadegh. 'With all this background, I am not prepared for an instant to accept an American nominee whoever he might be', concluded Nehru, referring to Admiral Chester W. Nimitz, who had been appointed as plebiscite administrator in Kashmir by the UN Secretary General in March 1949 and whom Nehru wished to be replaced by a person hailing from a less directly involved country.[40] He considered inappropriate the sending of Indian defense officers to the United States or the coming to India of US officers.[41] Even American activities of non-political and non-military nature in India exasperated the prime minister. Referring to the interest paid by India which, under the India Food Emergency Act of 1951, was made available by the US Congress to the State Department for educational purposes (exchange of students, supply of technical books, etc), Nehru advocated caution since the Americans tended to produce the impression of having partly taken charge of many activities which normally the government should do.[42]

On 24 February 1954, Eisenhower officially informed Nehru of the American decision to extend military aid to Pakistan and assured him that the agreement was for defensive purposes and was not directed in any way against India. He promised that if American aid to any country, including Pakistan, were to be misused and directed against another in aggression, all appropriate action would be taken immediately to thwart such aggression. He promised to recommend to Congress a continuation of substantial economic and technical aid to India, proposing finally to consider favourably any Indian request for military assistance of a type contemplated by the Mutual Security legislation.[43] Nehru rejected this offer of assistance, about which he was to say later that it was almost like adding insult to injury, that is, 'the injury was supply of military aid to Pakistan against us and the insult would be that, when we were protesting against it on principle, to ask us to break our principle'.[44] He denounced this development as one that went against the movement for independence which had aroused the people of Asia and one of whose symbols was the withdrawal of foreign troops, emphasizing that, whatever the motive, 'the return of any armed forces or any thing like it from any European or any American country is a reversal of the history of the countries of Asia'.[45] On 19 May 1954, a mutual assistance pact was signed between the United States and Pakistan, the Americans supplying military equipment and training.

Politicians and the press in India were outraged by the announcement of the agreement on military aid to Pakistan, and a wave of anti-Americanism swept over Indian public opinion. The security of the country was at stake, there being no doubt in India that the Pakistani leaders were less interested in fighting communism than in securing an underwritten collective defense of their territory against any Indian attack and in strengthening their military potential *vis-à-vis* India. Indians were also convinced that the Americans would not be able to prevent the Pakistanis from using the arms supplied against India in an offensive manner, for 'no one has yet invented a gun that could fire only in one direction' as Krishna Menon said ironically.[46] As regards the American promise of imposing sanctions against Pakistan should the need arise, Nehru pointed out that the United States had not condemned the Pakistani aggression in Kashmir in 1947. Anticipating that the military aid would be relatively large, for the United States would not otherwise have taken the risk of provoking India's hostility, New Delhi felt itself bound to respond by developing its own military strength. The possibility of a settlement of the Kashmir question became thereby even more remote, and the US personnel working there under the UN observer team were declared *persona non grata*.

Over and above the strictly bilateral implications, the US military assistance to Pakistan also meant the irruption of the Cold War at the very doorstep of India, and a barrier in the creation of a zone of peace in Asia arising out of India's refusal to participate in the Cold War strategies of the two superpowers. Nehru once again raised his voice against the militarist approach which had led the United States:

> to support reactionary as well as colonial regimes in various parts of the world. Some of the symbols of the 'free world', for which America stands, are Syngman Rhee, Chiang Kai-shek and Bao Dai. . . . In North Africa, French colonialism is directly or indirectly supported by the United States. In Spain, the fascist regime has entered into an alliance with the US. This process is now continuing in Western Asia, often at the expense of the United Kingdom.[47]

It was the application of the old Monroe Doctrine to all non-communist countries, Nehru wrote elsewhere.[48]

The question now arose of how opportune it would be for India to accept American aid at this juncture. Although this aid was of a different purpose and consequence, could India morally shout itself hoarse in denouncing the military aid granted to Pakistan by the United States and still accept from this country a not negligible economic aid, without being accused of duplicity? In January, with the prospect of US arms support to Pakistan looming large, Nehru had called for restraint, holding that 'we should not go out of our way to say that we will not accept American aid, but we might be a little cautious about it'.[49] He later wished that the number of Americans coming to India as well as the number of Indians going to the United States for training under various schemes should be limited.[50] There were at least two good reasons for not discontinuing US aid. The diplomatic argument was that such a rejection would be interpreted as a hostile gesture against the United States and would further exacerbate the friction between the two countries.[51] Then there was the economic imperative, and 'amid all the furore over India's condemnation of United States aid to Pakistan the Nehru government blandly ignored extremist agitation for the repudiation of United States economic aid to India'.[52]

The swearing in of the Eisenhower administration did not have any notable repercussions on the aid given by the United States to India. In July 1953, Dulles, while addressing the budgetary commission of the Senate, recommended an aid of $ 110 million to India for the fiscal year 1954, while underlining that there was a *de facto* competition between India and Communist China as to whether a pluralist regime or the police state, collectivist, and totalitarian methods could achieve better results in bringing about development. The outcome of this competition would not only affect the 800 million inhabitants of these two countries, but it would also influence American interests, and it justified the appropriation, at least on a modest scale, of some technical and external resources to permit India to go on with its five year plan.[53] The US would give an aid of $ 87.2 million to India. This was surely less than what the Indian government had proposed, but it was still almost twice the amount allocated during the preceding financial year.

For the first time, a distinction was made under the MSP between economic aid, which went by the name of development assistance, and technical assistance which covered the expenses borne on foreign experts, the deputing of Indians overseas to receive training, and the supply of educational equipment. The first rose to $ 60.2 million, and the second to $ 27 million. Similarly, from 1954 onwards, the scope of American bilateral aid, focused till then basically on agricultural development (community development projects, irrigation works, supply of chemical fertilizers, etc.) widened to cover transportation and power development, the supply of railway material and steel, and a contribution to dam and hydroelectric development such as the Rihand river valley project in Uttar Pradesh.

New Delhi could do no more than proclaim that in the new atmosphere, it would be better for India to progress a little more slowly than to allow itself to depend on others. Dwelling on this point during his address to the FICCI in March 1954, Nehru insisted that India could not really progress if it went about on 'crutches' all the time, and he stressed the necessity to rely above all on its own strength for 'no country which depends mainly on other countries for her defense, security and general well-being can hope to go far in achieving anything substantial'.[54] This declaration of intention did not prevent the Finance Minister, Chintaman Deshmukh, from asserting in June that the availability or the absence of foreign assistance 'might particularly make a difference' in the Second Five Year Plan.[55] In autumn, Deshmukh went on a six-week visit to Europe and the United States to meet with bankers, businessmen, and industrialists to propagate India's development plans.

The gulf widened a little more between the Indian and the American governments with the creation, on 8 September 1954 in Manila, of the South-East Asian Treaty Organization (SEATO), which Krishna Menon then called 'the modern version of a protectorate'.[56] India had refused to go to the Philippines capital. After France's withdrawal from Indochina, which had been settled during the Geneva conference, the American reaction was not long in coming and it took the form of an alliance providing the basis for an eventual Western military intervention. Nehru criticized SEATO as a serious blow struck against the 'Geneva spirit', and South-East Asia, which ought to have been one of the major areas of peace, was thus practically converted into an area of potential war.[57]

In addition, with the signing of mutual defense pacts with Nationalist China on 2 December 1954 and with South Korea fourteen months earlier, the United States had succeeded within three years in drawing almost all the non-communist countries of East Asia and South-East Asia, with the notable exception of Indonesia, into the Western collective security arrangements. Pakistan would be the link between SEATO and a Middle East defense system. This system came into being on 24 February 1955 with the signing of the Baghdad Pact between Turkey and Iraq; Great Britain joined in April, followed by Pakistan on 23 September 1955, and by Iran in early November. The United States, without explicitly being a member, participated in the deliberations of the pact. The American policy of containing communism, therefore, took the form of a vast arc on the periphery of the communist world, covered by a network of military pacts and alliances extending from western Europe to the Far East.

Nehru did not fail to underline the fragility of these military alliances. First, they represented the antithesis of the assertion of nationalism in Asia by transforming states sometimes newly liberated from the colonial yoke into countries that had become satellites of the United States. Second, the Western leaders continued to maintain their dealings with dictators who enjoyed no popular support at home. In a way the *coup d'état* in Iraq in 1958 and the subsequent withdrawal of this country from the Baghdad Pact were to prove him right. Some Indian analysts felt that the very idea of granting military aid to small, recently independent, underdeveloped countries was unwise and the tying up of such countries in military pacts was futile. Militarily, they could never offer enough aid to make a difference in the event of a general conflict. But locally, since they always had some feud of their own with a neighbour, the local enemy would then be tempted to go and knock at the doors of the other superpower for assistance. A case in point was that of Pakistan and Afghanistan.[58]

The foreign policy positions of New Delhi and Washington had never been as far removed since Independence as they were now. During discussions on the foreign aid budget for 1954-5, some Senators accused the Indian government of playing into the hands of the Communist bloc by its virulent criticism of American foreign policy. The Americans were irritated by the six-point proposal made by Nehru in April 1954 for a peaceful settlement of the Indochina question, as well as by India's decision to forbid US planes carrying French troops to Indochina from flying over its territory. It was also said that 'the ordinary man-in-the-street is getting fed up, both with India's captious criticisms of the United States and with her failure to pull her weight in the present struggle. Mr Nehru's self-righteous attitude causes particular annoyance'.[59] George Allen, who succeeded Chester Bowles as US Ambassador to India, intervened before US Congress to warn against the catastrophic effect that a break in the economic assistance to India, so close on the heels of the decision to grant military aid to Pakistan, could have, as this would create the impression that the United States had come to rely entirely on a military policy in tackling world problems.[60] Dulles, defending the $ 105 million aid to India asked for by President Eisenhower, noted that it was essential to continue to help India 'if for no other reason than to serve our enlightened self-interest. It would be a tragic day for us if the confidence which India's people have in their democratic institutions should fail.'[61] US Congress voted $ 85.6 million of aid to India ($ 72.5 million for economic aid and $ 13.1 million for technical assistance), i.e. an amount almost identical to that of the preceding year. For the first time, it was stipulated that around half the economic aid would be in the form of agricultural surpluses, basically wheat and cotton under Public Law 665. A second innovation was a change in the nature of the economic aid given under the Indo-American Technical Cooperation Agreement since it was decided that three-quarters of it would be in the form of loans. According to the Soviet economist, V.I. Pavlov, this shift away from economic assistance, whose majority portion had been in the form of grants, to an aid made up largely of loans was proof of the obvious connection between the aid given by the United States and the imperialist designs of its foreign policy. Faced with 'the obvious failure of US attempts to draw India into aggressive blocs', it was no longer necessary for Washington to show proof of its generosity.[62]

At the time when a rather ambitious Second Five Year Plan was being drawn up, requiring a larger amount of foreign aid, the higher authorities in India did indeed expect to count on the cooperation of the United States and they let this be known to H. Stassen, who now headed the Foreign Operations Administration (the successor agency to the Mutual Security Administration). Stassen, who passed through India in February 1955, perhaps talked to the Indians about his plan for a regional development programme for Asia, including the SEATO member countries and the neutral States whose economic future was important to the United States. As a result of Stassen's initiative, the US Congress voted an Asian Development Fund whose very modest budget was fixed at $ 200 million over a three-year period. This, nevertheless, provided New Delhi with the opportunity to organize, during the first week of May 1955, a conference at Shimla to which were invited nine Asian nations (Cambodia, Indonesia, Japan, Laos, Nepal, Pakistan, the Philippines, South Vietnam, and Thailand) to discuss foreign aid and to reflect, in particular, on the utilization of this new aid fund. It was meant for the development of intra-regional trade and the setting up of a machinery to provide credit to enable Asian countries to tide over short-term balance of payment difficulties resulting, for instance, from price fluctuations affecting raw materials.[63] That these countries, which had been exulting a few days earlier at the first Afro-Asian conference in Bandung over the idea of the renaissance of Asia and Africa rid of Western domination, had now gathered together to discuss American financial aid showed that they tacitly acknowledged the inevitability of economic dependence. A report of the State Department reviewing Indo-American relations between

May and November 1955 noted that Indians were showing a greater acceptance of the value of economic cooperation with the United States. As evidence of this shift in attitude, the report cited the Shimla conference, India's request for a larger number of additional American technicians to work in the country, and the suggestion of a joint Indo-American economic assistance to Nepal to minimize Communist China's potential political and economic influence in that country.[64] It was in vain that in May 1955, C. Rajagopalachari, protesting against the manufacture of and experiments in nuclear weapons, urged the Indian government not to nullify the earnestness of its condemnation of atomic weapons nor to render its displeasure into hypocrisy by accepting financial assistance from the United States. C. D. Deshmukh had made it clearly known that this proposal to refuse US aid was entirely inappropriate: 'Whether we are capable of rejecting foreign assistance is the test of our solvency . . . it is not merely a question of stinting yourself.'[65] American aid had an intrinsic advantage; it covered dollar exchanges that Indian resources could provide only with difficulty. As for Nehru, in his reply to Rajagopalachari, he reiterated that India was ready to do without any US aid but objected that it would ultimately serve India ill to appear to be systematically hostile towards the United States; he emphatically asserted that 'an act must bear some relation to the existing circumstances'.[66]

While Washington's attempts to convince New Delhi to share the attitudes of the Western bloc on the international scene had not met with success, the Americans, nevertheless, were able to derive satisfaction from the lack of cordiality in the relations between New Delhi and Moscow. However, from the mid-1950s, this situation was no longer true. There were increasing signs of an emerging Indo-Soviet relationship, which began with an offer of aid from the Soviets. The Americans feared that this Soviet offer was a more insidious manoeuvre by the USSR to spread its influence in the Indian subcontinent.

NOTES

1. Planning Commission, *First Five-Year Plan*, p. 26.
2. Reserve Bank of India, *India's Balance of Payments, 1948-49 to 1961-62*, table 1, p. 85, and table 16, p. 100.

3. In February 1952, India and Great Britain had been concluded a final agreement. The agreement covered a period of six years—from 1 July 1951 to 30 June 1957, on the expiry of which the no. 1 and the no. 2 accounts were to be amalgamated. In addition to the sterling balances available under the earlier agreement and which had not been utilized, the Indian government could thereafter count on six annual withdrawals of £ 35 million (Rs. 465 million), with the possibility for advance transfers or the carry forward of undrawn releases. Furthermore, £ 310 million was transferred from the no. 2 to the no. 1 account to be held by the RBI as a currency reserve which could be utilized only in the case of extreme necessity after consultation between the two governments.
4. Planning Commission, *First Five-Year Plan*, pp. 62-3.
5. Ibid., p. 208.
6. *Commerce*, 23 October 1954, p. 778.
7. *Pravda*, 21 June 1951. Quoted by J.A. Naik, *Soviet Policy towards India*, p. 40.
8. *India, Bilateral Treaties and Agreements*, vol. 1: 1947-1952. Policy Planning and Research Division, Ministry of External Affairs, Government of India, Delhi: Siba Exim, 1994, pp. 442-8. After a visit to India in 1951 by its president, Paul G. Hoffman, the Ford Foundation opened there its first office abroad.
9. *Amrita Bazar Patrika*, 8 January 1952.
10. *Economic Weekly*, 12 January 1952, p. 31.
11. *Parliamentary Debates*, House of the People, part II, vol. 6, no. 11, 16 December 1952, col. 2472.
12. Reply to a debate on foreign affairs in the Lok Sabha, 12 June 1952. J.L. Nehru, *India's Foreign Policy*, p. 63.
13. The Ambassador in India (Allen) to the Department of State, 21 July 1953. *FRUS, 1952-1954*, vol. 11, part 2, p. 1696. Earlier that year, Nehru had been told of a Chinese demand for thorium nitrate. He had then, taking into account the US position on this matter, preferred to postpone any decision regarding a shipment. J.L. Nehru, *Selected Works of Jawaharlal Nehru (second series)*, vol. 21, pp. 121-2.
14. Telegram from Nehru to B.N. Rau, 24 July 1951. S. Gopal, *Jawaharlal Nehru: A Biography*, vol. 2, p. 137.
15. Note, 26 March 1952. J.L. Nehru, *Selected Works of Jawaharlal Nehru (second series)*, vol. 17, pp. 492-3.
16. George Allen to the Secretary of State, 28 July 1953, *FRUS, 1952-1954*, vol. 11, part 2, p. 1701. Note to the Foreign Secretary, 28 July 1953. J.L. Nehru, *Selected Works of Jawaharlal Nehru (second series)*, vol. 23, p. 492.
17. Memorandum by the Assistant Secretary for Near East, South Asian and African Affairs (Byroade) and the Assistant Secretary of State for Economic Affairs (Waugh) to the Under Secretary of State (Smith), 31 July 1953. *FRUS, 1952-1954*, vol. 11, part 2, p. 1705.
18. Briefing paper prepared in the Office of South Asian Affairs, 19 January

1955, *FRUS, 1955-1957*, vol. 8, p. 276. The issue was again raised when India got notice of the US intention to terminate by 30 September 1956 the gentleman's agreement regarding he export of beryl ore to the United States. Homi Bhabha proposed that, in view of the export restrictions imposed by the Battle Act, India should propose to the US that either beryl ore should be diluted from it or they should not terminate the agreement. Nehru's first reaction was to consider the first option as improper but also to stress that the 'American Battle does not govern us'. Note to Homi J. Bhabha, 7 December 1955. J.L. Nehru, *Selected Works of Jawaharlal Nehru* (*second series*), vol. 31, p. 402.

19. Chester Bowles to the Department of State, 21 February 1952. *FRUS, 1952-1954*, vol. 11, part 2, pp. 1635-7.
20. Chester Bowles to the Secretary of State, 28 October 1952. Ibid., p. 1676.
21. Telegram from Stanislas Ostrorog, French Ambassador to New Delhi, 28 January 1952, following an interview with Chester Bowles. *AQO*, Asie-Océanie, 1944-1955, Inde, vol. 66.
22. 'Probable Development in South Asia', 30 June 1953. *FRUS, 1952-1954*, vol. 11, part 2, pp. 1075-6. A State Department paper issued by the US Information Agency on 7 October 1953 considered that 'the Congress party, with Nehru at its head, represents the only force in India capable of giving that nation effective leadership. It is not too much to expect that if such leadership were suddenly taken away, events might lead to successful efforts to establish a number of independent states, and/or a radical shift toward Communist control of the government(s).' *PRO*, FO 371 106857.
23. *Statesman*, 15 March 1952. Chester Bowles warned the Americans against supporting some Hindu right-wing nationalist parties, such as the Jan Sangh, on account of their anti-communism and their hostility to Nehru's 'neutralism': 'Their ideology is almost as racist as Hitler's. They advocate turning India into a communal Hindu State with a much 'firmer' policy towards Pakistan.' If they were to take on an important role on the national scene, renewal of communal clashes would inevitably follow between Hindus and Muslims along with an intensification of the Kashmir dispute and finally the emergence of political, economic and social conditions which would turn many Indians towards Communism.' Memorandum from Bowles to Acheson, 6 December 1951. *FRUS, 1951*, vol. 6, part 2, p. 2197.
24. Department of State, *Statistical Review of the Foreign Aid Programs, 1945-1955*, American Foreign Policy 1950-1955 (Basic Documents), vol. 2, parts X-XX, Washington, D.C.: Department of State, Publication 6446, 1957, p. 3158.
25. Dispatch of Stanislas Ostrorog, 21 April 1953. *AQO*, Asie-Océanie, 1944-1955, Inde, vol. 66. In a conversation with Mao Zedong, Nehru once referred to Dulles as 'narrow-minded and bigoted. He thinks everyone must agree with him and a man like him might make any move.' Minutes of talks with Mao Zedong, 23 October 1954. J.L. Nehru, *Selected Works of Jawaharlal Nehru* (*second series*), vol. 27, p. 34.
26. *Commerce*, 17 April 1954, p. 717.

27. Study prepared by the staff of the National Security Council, undated. *FRUS, 1952-1954*, vol. 11, part 2, p. 1105. It was estimated that the total capital owned abroad in Indian industry was no more than 16 per cent. 'India—Progress and Plan', *The Economist*, 22 January 1955, p. 18.
28. *Statesman*, 28 May 1953.
29. *Statesman*, 7 January 1954. G.L. Mehta, an economist and businessman, former chairman of FICCI (1942-3), and member of the Planning Commission, was appointed Ambassador to Washington in mid-1952. The choice of such a candidate indicates the importance India attached to economics in relations with the United States.
30 Memorandum by the Acting Secretary of State to the Executive Secretary of the National Security Council (Lay), 19 August 1952. *FRUS, 1952-1954*, vol. 11, part 2, p. 1062.
31. Chester Bowles, *The New Dimensions of Peace*, New York: Harper & Brothers, 1955, p. 339.
32. Note to the Foreign Secretary, 25 November 1952. J.L. Nehru, *Selected Works of Jawaharlal Nehru (second series)*, vol. 20, p. 536
33. Chester Bowles recounted how the entourage of Ayub Khan informed the press that the State Department was reluctant to conclude a military alliance with a nation of 100 million 'hard-fighting Muslims' eager to take on whatever Communists the Americans might designate. This manoeuvre was not lacking in skill at a time when, at the height of McCarthyism, rumours were rife about the infiltration of communist elements into the State Department. C. Bowles, *Promises to Keep*, p. 478.
34. National Intelligence Estimate, 'Probable Developments in South Asia', 30 June 1953. *FRUS, 1952-1954*, vol. 11, part 2, p. 1087.
35. Special National Intelligence Estimate, 'Probable Repercussions of a US Decision to Grant or Deny Military Aid to Pakistan', 15 January 1954. Ibid., pp. 1843-5.
36. *New York Times*, 10 December 1953.
37. Richard Nixon, *The Memoirs of Richard Nixon*, London: Sidgwick & Jackson, 1978, pp. 131-3.
38. G.L. Mehta's telegram, 16 November 1953. S. Gopal, *Jawaharlal Nehru: A Biography*, vol. 2, p. 186.
39. 15 November 1953. J.L. Nehru, *Letters to Chief Ministers*, vol. 3, pp. 441-2. The Canadian High Commissioner in India, Escott Reid, shared a common impression, saying that the United States had in mind to put India in a position where it would have no recourse but to make a military agreement with the US, which would ultimately lead to India becoming an ally of the United States and the source of a mass army for the West in a third world war. E. Reid, *Envoy to Nehru*, p. 104. It is doubtful that the State Department, in light of the aforementioned documents, did really entertain such hopes.
40. To Mohan Sinha Mehta, 28 August 1953. J.L. Nehru, *Selected Works of Jawaharlal Nehru (second series)*, vol. 23, p. 354. Existing distrust over US activities in the region was to grow after the US-Pakistan agreement of

February 1954 on military aid. J.L. Nehru, *Selected Works of Jawaharlal Nehru (second series)*, vol. 25, pp. 489-90.

41. Note to the Minister of Defense Organization, 8 July 1953. J.L. Nehru, *Selected Works of Jawaharlal Nehru (second series)*, vol. 23, p. 489.
42. To C.D. Deshmukh, 7 May 1953. J.L. Nehru, *Selected Works of Jawaharlal Nehru (second series)*, vol. 22, p. 132.
43. Eisenhower to Nehru, 24 February 1954. Statement in the House of the People, 1 March 1954. *Parliamentary Debates*, House of the People, 1954, part II, vol. 1, no. 12, cols. 963-5.
44. Remarks made during a press conference in New Delhi. *Hindu*, 21 July 1961.
45. 22 February 1954. *Parliamentary Debates*, House of the People, vol. 1, no. 6, part II, col. 433.
46. Quoted by T.N. Kaul, *Reminiscences, Discreet and Indiscreet*, p. 164.
47. 15 March 1954. J.L. Nehru, *Letters to Chief Ministers*, vol. 3, p. 503.
48. 14 April 1954. Ibid. pp. 518-19.
49. To T.T. Krishnamachari, 25 January 1954. J.L. Nehru, *Selected Works of Jawaharlal Nehru (second series)*, vol. 24, p. 454.
50. 26 April 1954. J.L. Nehru, *Letters to Chief Ministers*, vol. 3, pp. 530-1.
51. Nehru's meeting with G. Allen, 24 April 1954. J.L. Nehru, *Selected Works of Jawaharlal Nehru (second series)*, vol. 25, p. 495.
52. *New York Times*, 7 March 1954.
53. *Report of the Investigations Division of the Senate Appropriations Committee*, April 1954, Washington, D.C.: US Government Printing Office, 1954, p. 7. Radio Address by John F. Dulles on his recent trip to the Near East and South Asia, 1 June 1953. *PRO*, FO 371 106857.
54. *Times of India*, 7 March 1954.
55. *Hindu*, 9 June 1954.
56. *Amrita Bazar Patrika*, 28 August 1954.
57. Speech during debate on foreign affairs in the Lok Sabha, 29 September 1954. J.L. Nehru, *India's Foreign Policy*, p. 89.
58. See Taya Zinkins, 'Indo-American Relations', *Economic Weekly*, January 1956 (annual number), p. 69.
59. Telegram from the British Ambassador in Washington (R. Makins) to the Foreign Office, 26 April 1954. *PRO*, FO 371 112212.
60. *Hindu*, 30 May 1954.
61. *Hindu*, 5 June 1954.
62. V.I. Pavlov, *India: Economic Freedom versus Imperialism*, p. 119.
63. *Economic Weekly*, 28 May 1955, p. 636.
64. Instruction from the Department of State to the Diplomatic and Consular Offices in India, 20 January 1956. *FRUS, 1955-1957*, vol. 8, p. 304.
65. *Hindu*, 8 and 10 May 1955.
66. To Rajagopalachari, 9 May 1955. J.L. Nehru, *Selected Works of Jawaharlal Nehru (second series)*, vol. 28, p. 213.

PART III

Aid as Component of East-West Competition (1955-1961)

CHAPTER 9

Rouble Diplomacy

THE INITIAL SOVIET policy was to give the nationalist governments in the recently decolonized countries the cold shoulder and instead to support local insurrectionary communist movements. This stance led the USSR to be isolated on the diplomatic plane from a large part of the Third World. The Soviet leaders adhered to the pure and simple application of the bipolarity to Asia, while denying the possibility that post-colonial states led by their national bourgeoisie could hold views differing from those of the big powers of the Western bloc to whom they supposedly owed allegiance. But the extension of the Cold War to Asia revealed that the geopolitical reality in the post-war period was far more complex than a simple East-West division.

The Soviets were eventually led to reconsider non-alignment as being other than the India's willingness to toe the line of the Western bloc albeit in a disguised manner. The Soviet decision to reassess the situation stemmed from the failure of Nehru's visit to the United States, as also the differences between the two countries over the question of the entry of Communist China into the United Nations and over the Korean War. India's initial support to the first two resolutions deeming North Korea as the aggressor and asking all members to render assistance to the UN and South Korea was coolly received in Moscow. But Nehru's attempts at mediation to achieve a negotiated settlement of the Korean conflict, illustrated first by the proposals sent to Dean Acheson and to Marshall Stalin, to which the latter responded favourably, and then by his disapproval of the crossing of the 38th parallel by the United Nations troops, were noted with interest in the Kremlin and gave the lie to the belief that India was a hostage to the Anglo-American way of thinking. This impression was reinforced by the refusal of India, in January 1951, to condemn Communist China in the UNO and by its decision not to sign the Japanese peace treaty on the grounds that it was flawed and inadequate, a reason that was largely similar to the criticism offered by the USSR.

The Soviet Union food offer in March 1951 at a time when the US Congress was dilly-dallying over the dispatch of food grains to India, attested to a new solicitude evinced by the USSR in India's affairs and provided the Soviet Union with the opportunity to score a public relations coup over the United States in the view of Indian public opinion. In August 1951, the French Ambassador to Moscow noted that:

> the constant interest that the Soviet press has shown in India has notably increased during these last few months. Without going to the extent of making polite advances to the government in New Delhi, propaganda has however taken a generally more benevolent turn and seems to have cut down on the tales of shooting, persecution and famine to the benefit of demonstrations meant to highlight the common interests and sympathies between the people of the two countries.[1]

In 1952, the USSR displayed increasing signs of its growing interest in forging closer relations with India. In January, the USSR finally ended the silence it had observed in the UN over the problem of Kashmir. During a meeting of the Security Council, the Soviet delegate, Jacob Malik, without openly taking the side of India denounced the Graham Plan (named after the UN representative for India and Pakistan appointed to suggest a plan for demilitarizing Kashmir) as being nothing more than a new attempt by the United States and Great Britain to convert this strategic region into an Anglo-American protectorate where the two countries could set up their military bases and station their troops.[2]

One event in the developing Indo-Soviet relations in particular attracted attention not only in India but also abroad. On the eve of his return to India, Radhakrishnan, the rather successful outgoing Indian Ambassador, was invited on 5 April 1952 to meet Stalin. The chairman of the Soviet of Ministers of the USSR hardly ever deigned to meet Ambassadors, not even once. Also, the granting of a second audience to the eminent philosopher-diplomat became a talking matter for the Western press, and the Stalin-Radhakrishnan meeting was interpreted as Moscow's desire to make New Delhi a mediator between the blocs within the context of a peace offensive by the Kremlin.[3] Gundevia, who was then a counsellor at the Indian

Embassy and attended the meeting, reports in his memoirs that Stalin concluded the conversation by declaring that India and its Prime Minister were not among the enemies of the Soviet Union.[4] Apparently, the time when the Soviet press denounced Nehru as the lackey of Anglo-American imperialism was now forgotten. Less than a year later, it was the turn of Radhakrishnan's successor, K.P.S. Menon, to be received by Stalin, and this honour came just fifteen days before the Soviet leader's death, on 5 March 1953. Soon after, the Soviet Union proposed, although unsuccessfully, the name of Vijayalakshmi Pandit to succeed Trygvie Lie as the head of the United Nations.[5]

After Stalin's death, the Soviet Union rapidly recognized the potential geopolitical importance of India and at the same time set aside the post-war sectarian view of 'whoever is not with us is against us' to be replaced by 'whoever is not against us is with us'. From the moment that Moscow sought to strengthen its relations with non-communist Asian countries, New Delhi became the natural choice as the first capital for the launch of this new diplomatic offensive. It most effectively answered reasons of security at a time when American diplomacy found itself engaged in a policy of military alliances in Asia directed against the Communist bloc. The Indian government had proved its determination not to give in to Western dictates by refusing to adopt a narrow anti-Sovietism and had put itself at the head of those countries in Asia which refused to adhere to the American system of alliances. India, therefore, constituted for the USSR a prospective ally in the face of Moscow's experience of what seemed like an intimidating encircling by the imperialist camp.

The new Soviet leadership also appeared determined to show greater flexibility in tackling the causes of East-West tension. This attitude was seen notably in the matter of Korea. In May 1953, to New Delhi's satisfaction, Russia did not oppose China's official suggestion that the prisoners of war, who refused to go back to their country, should be entrusted to the care of troops supplied by members of a Neutral Nations Repatriation Commission whose creation India had advocated to the United Nations in November 1952. This proposal had, at that time, been severely criticized by Andrei Y. Vyshinsky, the head of the Soviet delegation, and peremptorily rejected. The way was thus cleared for breaking the deadlock over negotiations, leading to the signing of the armistice on 27 July. When in end August, the UNGA decided on the names of those countries which would be invited to the political conference on Korea, the USSR voted in favour of India's participation but it did not gather the required majority. Some days earlier, on 8 August 1953, the Soviet Prime Minister, Georgi Malenkov, speaking before the Supreme Soviet, paid a notable tribute to India's contribution to the search for a peaceful solution to the war in Korea, and more generally to the maintenance of peace in Asia. He also expressed the hope that in future 'the relations between India and the Soviet Union will continue to develop and strengthen with friendly cooperation as their keynote'. Commenting on the general content of Malenkov's speech, K.P.S. Menon underlined the moderate nature of his remarks; the Soviet leader did not say a single word which might be construed as an encouragement to the anti-government activities of communist parties abroad, or which could be interpreted, as Stalin's speech at the 19th Congress of the Soviet Union in October 1952 had been, as an interference in the internal affairs of other countries.[6]

The year 1954 saw a notable improvement in the relations between the two countries whose viewpoints converged on several international policy issues. The USSR joined India in protesting to Pakistani leaders against Pakistan's military pact with the United States. Soviet leaders and the Soviet press showed an increasingly high esteem for both Nehru and his foreign policy. For instance, over the years the level and extent of the Soviet official hierarchy which attended the celebration of India's Republic Day at the Indian Embassy rose markedly. At the Geneva conference on Far East, where he had the opportunity to converse several times with Krishna Menon, the emissary of the Indian government, Molotov declared himself in favour of the idea that India be chosen to preside over the proposed international commissions for supervision and control of the implementation of the Geneva agreements.

Nehru's China policy, which irritated the Americans a great deal, evoked favourable comments in the Soviet Union. Sino-Indian rapprochement was confirmed with the agreement on Tibet signed on 29 April 1954, by which New Delhi recognized the sovereignty of China over this region and gave up the rights in Tibet that it had inherited from the British. But most important was the fact that the preamble to the agreement enumerated the *Panchsheela* [the five principles], which appeared again in the joint communiqué published at the end of Zhou Enlai's visit to Delhi in June. The five principles in question were: mutual respect for each other's territorial integrity and sovereignty, mutual non-aggression, mutual non-interference in each other's internal affairs, equality and mutual benefit, and peaceful coexistence. The *Panchsheela* seemed to prove the correctness of the Indian approach—that security in Asia could only be obtained by first enlarging the area of peace—while the American policy strove to do the opposite, that is, extending the area of military security (SEATO was on the cards) with the hope of obtaining peace thereafter. 'From this emerges on the Indian side a tendency towards self-congratulation on the grounds of superior moral purpose,' resulting from 'the positive and constructive approach of Asian statesmen in contrast to the negative and essentially sterile methods of the West,' remarked a British diplomat.[7] Anyway, the *Panchsheela* was greeted in the Soviet Union as an important step towards the peaceful coexistence of states following different political, social, and economic systems, thus bringing back on the agenda a proposition dear to Lenin. When the UN Disarmament Commission resumed discussions after the US exploded the hydrogen bomb in March 1954, the Soviet Union criticized as one-sided the proposal made by the United Kingdom to include the United States, the USSR, Canada, France, and themselves in a new subcommittee in charge of giving concrete shape to the prohibition and elimination of weapons of mass destruction; instead the USSR suggested, although unsuccessfully, that the membership be enlarged, notably to include India.

Although satisfied with the USSR's change of attitude, the Indian government burnt its fingers in the past with the wavering attitude of the Soviet leadership, and it, therefore, waited for the new orientations of Moscow's foreign policy to become stabilized. The Indians preferred to proceed with caution on the path of a reconciliation with the Soviet Union, knowing that this could undoubtedly provoke hostile reactions in the West. Moreover, New Delhi considered it desirable that this Indo-Soviet reconciliation be part of an overall process of relaxation of tension between the two blocs. When the Soviet Ambassador produced before Nehru a draft bilateral treaty referring to the cultural, scientific, and technical relations between the two countries and, most important, incorporating in its preamble the five aforementioned principles, the Prime Minister declined to accept this proposal as:

> there was the chance of any such agreement between us at the present moment giving rise to misunderstandings and apprehensions in the minds of many people. We had just accepted chairmanship of the International

Supervisory Commissions in Indo-China. We do not wish to do anything which might take people doubt our neutral position.[8]

Still, Nehru was wholly receptive to the idea of receiving technical and scientific help from the Soviets even if that meant the presence of Russian experts in India; he dismissed the fears of the Intelligence Department as exaggerated. He explained his position in the following words: 'In these international matters, there is always an element of risk in whatever one might do. The friends of today might be the enemies of tomorrow. Our main objective is to build up India and we should take advantage of any proposal to that end.' He was all the more dispassionate about Soviet overtures as internally the government had 'rather undermined the Communist position in India'. Even the visit of Indian communist leaders to Russia seemed to have become beneficial since 'they are toned down by the praise they heard of India everywhere there'.[9]

In his public utterances Nehru was almost uniformly disparaging about the Indian Communists, denouncing the CPI as a 'foreign party' subject to the orders of Moscow and describing its militants as 'reactionaries' for their Marxist orthodoxy. With the new team in place in Moscow the trend in Indo-Soviet relations was changing. During the eighteen months that followed the death of Stalin, fourteen Indian delegations representing the field of culture, industry, and sports went to the Soviet Union at the invitation of the local authorities.

In the light of the facts mentioned above, it was logical that India should be one of the first countries to benefit from the USSR's offers of economic cooperation to underdeveloped countries. This economic offensive of the Soviets was dictated by two considerations. The first was linked to the anticipated surplus in the production of capital goods and the necessity of seeking new markets in exchange for the raw materials that lacked in the USSR. The second more political concern was aimed at reducing the dependence of underdeveloped countries on the capitalist world for their trade outlets and for the capital and machinery required for their development, and therefore at taking away from the West the weapon of economic aid as a means of political pressure.

Ever since the founding of ECAFE, the Soviet delegates at its meetings had restricted themselves to voicing violent criticism against the exploitation of the underdeveloped countries by the Western powers. The Indian delegates were exasperated by the relentless negative criticism of Western aid and despaired of a more constructive attitude from the USSR. The Indians were increasingly unwilling to hear Soviets say that by accepting this aid India was placing itself in the hands of the imperialists.[10] A first step in the direction of a more practical position was finally taken at the ECAFE conference in Singapore in October 1951, when the Soviet representative stated that, on a mutually advantageous basis, his country could supply South Asian and East Asian countries with capital goods, fertilizers, food grains, etc., in return for staple commodities.[11] The relations proposed to be developed then remained strictly commercial ones.

The offer was renewed in January 1952 when, at the International Industrial Fair held in Bombay, and less than a week after the signing of the Technical Cooperation Agreement between India and the United States, the Chairman of the USSR Chamber of Commerce, M.V. Nesterov, declared that his country was in a position to provide India with industrial equipment and agricultural machinery, fertilizers, consumer goods, etc. In exchange the Soviet Union was interested in receiving jute, tobacco, shellac, textiles, spices, copra, etc. And what was most important, he announced that his country would be ready to accept payment in any currency.[12] On 2 December 1953, the first trade agreement, of a duration of five years, was signed between India and the Soviet Union. True to their earlier declarations, the Soviets agreed to supply India with industrial goods in exchange for India's traditional export items. Article VI stipulated that the trade between the two countries would be conducted in rupees—an important clause considering India's chronic shortage of hard currency—and hence the State Bank of the USSR would maintain one or more accounts in Indian banks. Any balance in the rupee accounts could be converted on demand into pounds sterling. The exchange of letters accompanying the agreement also contemplated the possibility of the Soviets giving the technical assistance covering not only the equipment delivered under the said agreement but also the planning and execution of various additional projects.

Some months earlier, on 15 July 1953, at the 16th session of the United Nations Economic and Social Council, the Soviets announced, for the first time, their intention of making a financial contribution to the Expanded Programme of Technical Assistance to underdeveloped countries. Although it was a very modest contribution—4 million non-convertible roubles (about $ 1 million) which could only be used to obtain Soviet goods and services—it was nonetheless proof that the USSR was now ready to support the development of non-communist countries. This decision was inevitable if the Soviet leaders truly wanted to awaken the interest of these countries to their offers of cooperation. In the same month, the newly arrived Soviet Ambassador, Ivan A. Benediktov, met Nehru to push the idea of more significant trade relations between the USSR and India, particularly the possibility of selling Russian wheat; this proposal received positive consideration from the Indian side.[13] In January 1954, Moscow granted for the first time a loan to a non-communist Asian country. The beneficiary was Afghanistan which received a loan of $ 3.5 million.

But the first country to receive Soviet technical and economic aid on a truly significant scale was India. Nehru had always desired diversification of the sources of aid for that would enable India not to be exclusively dependent on a single country or on one bloc alone. In 1954, the political and economic situation was such as to make India receptive to Soviet offers of assistance. The growing disagreements between India and the United States on the approach to East-West conflicts in Asia had engendered some uncertainty over the magnitude of the aid. This was likely to vary from one year to the next according to the goodwill of the US Congress when it deliberated on the foreign aid bill. There was also the possibility that the Americans would hesitate to grant economic aid for industrial development projects in the public sector. This factor had to be kept in mind, particularly as India proposed to pay special attention to these projects in the Second Five Year Plan. This was the period just before the Lok Sabha adopted, on 21 December 1954, a resolution stipulating that the objective of the economic policy of the government was to work towards a 'socialistic pattern of society'.

In the First Five Year Plan, the state had undertaken to play an active part in the development of the steel sector to which the Soviets proposed to make a contribution. The steel industry was then dominated by two private enterprises, the Tata Iron and Steel Company (TISCO) and the Indian Iron and Steel Company (IISCO) which belonged to the Birla group. According to the industrial policy resolution of 1948, steel formed part of those sectors for which the state was to take charge of future development, if need be with the cooperation of the private sector. There was no question of nationalizing the existing private steel companies, which were even allowed to develop their production capacity (to this end IISCO obtained a loan of $ 31.5 million from the World Bank in December 1952), but the government contemplated the setting up of at least two steel plants in the public sector. In 1948, the Indian government had already engaged three foreign consultancy firms, including the American company McKee, to conduct a preliminary study concerning the construction of a steel mill, but the plan had then been temporarily shelved.

It was not till 1952 that the Indian government seriously reconsidered this matter and decided to start negotiations with foreign enterprises. Contacts were made with Japan, the United States, the United Kingdom, West Germany, and France. The following year, the Indian government decided to choose the German firms Krupp and Demag, and an agreement for providing expertise was concluded in December 1953 for the construction of a steel plant at Rourkela in the Sundergarh district of Orissa. A delegation led by Sucha Singh Khera, Secretary, Ministry of Production, was sent to the Soviet Union to examine the possibility of cooperation in steel manufacture. The Germans were still working on a preliminary report when Soviet experts arrived in India in November 1954. Jawaharlal Nehru had just returned from a visit to China where he had clearly been very impressed by the extent and scope of the Soviet help to the Chinese in the industrial field.[14]

On 2 February 1955, an Indo-Soviet agreement was signed in principle for the setting up of a plant with a capacity of one million tons of steel ingots per year to be erected at Bhilai in the Durg district of Madhya Pradesh. The investments required were assessed at Rs. 1.1 billion. The Soviets declined to participate in the capital, the management, or the profits. The designing of the plant and the heavy equipment would be of Soviet make, but the Soviet organizations promised maximum fabrication of components in India consistent with work efficiency and the maintenance of the time schedule (in fact, 90 per cent of the equipment required for the production of the steel mill was imported). The Soviet engineers and technical advisers would associate Indians at all stages of construction and train personnel and staff for the steel work in both Russia and India.

During the signing of the agreement, the Minister of Production, K.C. Reddy, praised the speed with which the Soviet experts had succeeded in submitting a preliminary report acceptable to the government and hailed this contract which would make it possible in future to minimize dependence on foreign assistance, and perhaps even render it superfluous for similar projects. The Indians were grateful to the Soviets for showing less hesitation than the West in sharing their technical know-how.[15] The responsibility entrusted to the Indians in the process of erecting the plant right from the initial phase impressed the Indian politicians and bureaucrats who were hostile to the patronizing attitude of the much reviled Western colonialists. The Soviets submitted their detailed project report on 9 December 1955. The final contract was signed on 8 March 1956. It anticipated that the first deliveries of equipment would be made towards the end of June 1956 and that the steel mill would be operational by 1959.

A loan of Rs. 631 million covering the cost of the industrial equipment supplied by the Soviet Union was given. The Soviet credit carried interest at 2.5 per cent per annum and the repayment period was 12 years, starting from one year after the delivery of each individual consignment of equipment. In September 1959, the repayment period was extended since it would be 12 years thereafter, starting from one year after the completion of the delivery of all the equipment for any particular project. Both the payment of interest and the repayment of principal were made in rupees, which were to be utilized by the Soviet authorities for the purchase of Indian goods in accordance with the trade agreement concluded between the two countries. These terms were renewed in all the Soviet loan agreements to India with just one exception: a loan meant for some drugs projects in 1959 which was repayable in seven years. While the Indian authorities welcomed Soviet aid, they did not for all that ignore American aid and they even displayed some concern over American reactions to the offers of assistance from the Soviet Union. C.D. Deshmukh, during his visit to Europe and the United States in the autumn of 1954, went to a great deal of trouble to dispel any impression that India might show special consideration to the USSR in order to secure Soviet capital.[16]

This Soviet entry in the industrialization process also served as a wake up call to Indian financial circles. Some observers were critical of this support towards the strengthening of the public sector and they expressed doubts over the technical competence of the Soviets. B.M. Birla, one of India's foremost industrialists, went to the United Kingdom, Germany, and the United States in the autumn of 1954 to try to obtain assistance and finance for setting up a plant in the private sector to produce one million tons of rolled steel products annually. It turned out to be a waste of time for the Birla project was rejected by the Indian government on the grounds that there was not sufficient provision in it for adequate state control. Furthermore, the Indian government was not willing to allow a private enterprise steelworks to be built if a government guarantee was required on any foreign investment. New Delhi approached the United Kingdom to know if it would be interested in supplying a steel plant in the public sector on the lines offered to Birla. Responding positively, London sent a steel mission to India in April 1955 under the technical cooperation scheme of the Colombo Plan. As for the Americans, they were still reluctant about supporting industrial development projects in the public sector. On the other hand, they responded to requests for loans from Indian industrialists. Preliminary discussions were thus initiated between B.M. Birla and the Export-Import Bank for expansion plans. In May 1955, it was the turn of fellow industrialist J.R.D. Tata to go to the United States in the hope of convincing the Americans to grant financial assistance in expanding the capacity of TISCO. According to Tata, this would enable the United States to counter the recent Soviet initiative and contribute towards showing what private enterprise could accomplish in India, with results comparing favourably with those of the Bhilai steel mill. This argument found some positive response within the State Department which recommended to the Export-Import Bank that it considers Tata's request sympathetically. Ultimately, negotiations fell through because of divergence on the rate of interest (the Indian side wanted a lower than usual rate to compensate for the more expensive American equipment) and it was the World Bank which, in June 1956, approved a loan of $ 75 million to pay for some of the foreign exchange costs of goods and services needed to boost TISCO's output. This loan was the biggest given till then for an industrial project in Asia by the IBRD.[17]

An agreement in principle with the Krupp and Demag consortium was concluded in July 1955 and the detailed report was accepted by the Indian government in February 1956. The agreement with the Soviets had sounded alarm bells in Britain and contributed towards activating negotiations for the construction of a third steel mill in the public sector. The final evaluation relating to the construction of a steel plant at Durgapur in the Burdwan district of West Bengal was submitted in May 1956 and an agreement with a consortium of

British firms was concluded on turn-key basis on 31 October 1956.[18] The Indian government had been able to make use of the conditions offered by the Soviets to obtain from the Germans and the British a greater flexibility in the negotiation of the agreements and they finally made up their mind to enter into a collaboration which conformed almost entirely with the conditions fixed by the Indian government, limiting their role to the supply of equipment and technical assistance but without any participation in the capital (contrary to what had been originally anticipated, Krupp and Demag decided to opt out of equity participation in the new public undertaking, Hindustan Steel Limited). With the progressive start of operations of the three integrated steel plants in the public sector of an initial one million ton capacity each and the increase in the production capacity of IISCO and TISCO, the government hoped to boost the production from 1.7 million tons of steel ingots in 1955 to 6 million tons by the end of the Second Plan.

The USSR intended to make a success story of Bhilai, its first major work undertaken in a Third World country outside the limits of the communist world.[19] The agreement of 2 February 1955 put the official seal in a concrete form, on the end of Soviet antagonism towards India; it was the first of a series of important events on the bilateral plane during this year which marked a turning point in Indo-Soviet relations. Fifteen days later, Molotov, speaking before the Supreme Soviet hailed the development of Indo-Soviet relations and recognized India as a country with its own on the international scene: 'It is a fact of great historic importance that colonial India is no more, and there is an Indian Republic instead . . . India's international prestige as a new and important factor of peace and friendship among nations is steadily rising.'[20]

The Soviets had thereby come to acknowledge that the position of imperialism in independent India was no longer what it had been in the colonial period. They thus implicitly admitted that former colonies could claim an independence not simply in name, even though the proletariat and its vanguard, the Communist Party, were not at the helm of affairs. The opportunity arose of splitting the bourgeois world and undermining the influence of the imperialist powers in Asia. The Orientalist, A. Diakov, who had in the past written much to denounce the willing dependence of the bourgeoisie in power on Anglo-American imperialists, now took to speaking well of this same national bourgeoisie: 'The peace-loving policy of the

Indian government is supported even by certain circles of the Indian bourgeoisie, including the big bourgeoisie, for this policy not only guarantees India's not being dragged into war, but also secures the possibility of smashing out of the grip of economic dependence on the Imperialist powers.'[21] To judge the evolution of the Soviet perception of the leadership in India, it is worth recalling that three years earlier, another Soviet commentator had written: 'The encouragement given by India's rulers to the penetration of foreign monopoly capital is on all fours with their general line of foreign policy and their support of the Anglo-American imperialist bloc.'[22]

On 7 June 1955, 'the reddest of red carpets' was unrolled in Moscow to welcome Jawaharlal Nehru with a consideration unprecedented for a foreign dignitary. He was starting a 15-day visit which was to take him to the main republics of the Soviet Union, including those of Central Asia. It was the first official visit by a head of government of a non-communist Asian country since the visit of the King of Afghanistan, Amanullah, in 1928. The Indian Prime Minister, who had since Independence occasionally expressed his hope to be invited by the Soviet government, was also on this occasion the first non-communist leader to address the Soviet people at a public gathering in a large stadium in Moscow.

Moscow could be grateful to the Indian government for having opposed the creation of SEATO and the conclusion of the Baghdad Pact. The recent Bandung Conference which had taken place from 18 to 24 April had further intensified the interest of the Soviet Union in India. While the unity flaunted at the end of this conference which brought together 29 Asian and African countries in this Javanese city, was quite fragile, Afro-Asian cooperation appeared, nevertheless, to have received a boost after having gradually fallen into abeyance during the years which followed the Asian Relations Conference of 1947, with the extension of the Cold War to Asia. Diplomatically, the Soviet Union consoled itself for not having been invited, by considering the importance that a collaboration between the Asian and African states could represent, particularly within the United Nations. For their opposition to colonialism and to racial discrimination would lead them to raise their voice against the Western powers. Then, the ten principles approved at the end of the conference were based on the *Panchsheela*. Moreover, the conference was a diplomatic success for China, which had been invited largely thanks to the intervention of Nehru. The conciliatory attitude shown by Zhou Enlai, particularly with regard to those among the representatives who were most mistrustful of Chinese Communists, had enabled China to gain respectability and to come out of its diplomatic isolation. What the PRC had succeeded in doing in Bandung—developing relationships with a number of non-communist countries of the Asian continent—the Soviets, in turn, also hoped to achieve, this again with non-aligned India playing the role of facilitator. Nikita S. Khrushchev unambiguously expressed his feelings on this point:

> Our friendship, as we understand it, should not be confined to friendly contacts with one, two or several States. We want friendship with all States. That is why we are glad of the friendly relations which our friends are developing with other States, including some with which we, for one reason or another, perhaps have somewhat strained or cool relations. Through the friend that we consider India to be we hope to improve our relations with those States.[23]

While Moscow rejoiced at the acceptance of peaceful coexistence in Asia, the diplomatic activity displayed by Beijing had the makings of a struggle between the two giants of communism to gain influence in this part of the world, at which the Soviet leaders began to get alarmed. Hence they conceived of the idea of playing the India card, using it not only as a 'springboard' for making a multiplicity of contacts with the states of Asia, but also in helping to contain China's hegemonic proclivity. This action was reminiscent of that of the Americans who, in 1949, had desired to make India a sentinel of the West in the face of the new People's Republic of China. The new role that Moscow intended that India should play in Asia did not really surprise Nehru, who had never believed in a durable alliance between the USSR and China. He had even mentioned this to Dulles during the latter's visit to New Delhi in May 1953, when he assured him that 'Communist China will divorce itself from Soviet Russia within fifteen or twenty-five-years. Already the ties are weakened by the death of Stalin. Soviet Union wants to keep China dependent upon the Soviet Union as its spokesman, and does not want China's admission to the United Nations in reality.'[24]

The Indian Prime Minister who had wanted his visit to the USSR to take place in a climate of thawing of the Cold War so as not to be suspected of partiality, could draw some moral comfort from the recent foreign policy decisions taken by the Soviet authorities, such as a proposal for disarmament, which pointed towards a détente.

The Austrian state peace treaty was signed on 15 May. Also, in that month, a high-level Soviet delegation, headed by Khrushchev, visited Belgrade to put an end to the quarrel with Yugoslavia, and at the beginning of June Moscow expressed a desire to establish diplomatic relations with the Federal Republic of Germany. One of the major topics for discussion with the Soviet leaders in Moscow was the Geneva Summit Conference, with the participation of the Big Four Powers (United States, USSR, Britain, and France) to be held in July 1955. At the same time, the tension between the United States and China, arising out of the shelling that Beijing had decided to conduct in the autumn of 1954 on the coastal islands controlled by Formosa, had somewhat decreased, and the PRC government announced on 31 May, following the mediation of Krishna Menon, the release of the four US airmen taken prisoner during the Korean War.

Politically, Nehru's visit to the Soviet Union was considered a success. The Indians present underlined the fact that the Soviets had never shown the least intention of persuading India to modify its foreign policy, leave alone putting any pressure on it to do so. The final communiqué, whose drafting was left to the Indians, repeated the *Panchsheela* which was thereafter to constitute the cornerstone of Indo-Soviet relations. And there was even an important addition as regards the third principle concerning non-interference in each other's internal affairs for any economic, political or . . . ideological reason, a direct reference to the Cominform. This was, however, an almost redundant clarification since Nehru considered that the acceptance by Moscow of the 'five principles' was not compatible with the functioning of the Cominform and that, in the light of past experience, as long as Soviet external policy required that good relations be maintained with a foreign government, Moscow would sacrifice the interests of the CPI:

> They (the authorities of the Soviet Union) wanted to utilize Communist parties elsewhere for their political purposes where this was considered necessary. Where this came in conflict with their national policy, they cared little for the Communist group in another country, even though they might have some vague sympathy for it.[25]

The importance given to India can be gauged by the fact that not only did Bulganin suggest a six-power conference, including apart the Big Four, China, and India, to discuss the Far East but also, and even more significantly, that he proposed suggesting at a later stage India's inclusion as the sixth member of the Security Council. Nehru found both proposals too premature, and, regarding the second one which was not time-bound, considered that the necessity to get China admitted to the UN came first and foremost.[26]

The decision of the Soviet leaders to consider India as figuring hereafter among the 'peace-loving nations' had indeed had a fall-out on India's political life. Moscow put pressure on the Communist Party of India to give support to Nehru's foreign policy. The leadership of the CPI was initially reluctant about dissociating the government's foreign policy from its domestic policy, still considered to be reactionary and favourable to big capital and to the landed oligarchy. It was during the third CPI Congress in Madurai in January 1954 that, for the first time since Independence, the Communist party acknowledged that the foreign policy contained some positive elements, such as its constant opposition to the tactics of American imperialism in the region. The rapprochement China, then the following year with the Soviet Union led to a more open support given by Indian Communists to Nehru's diplomacy. The CPI had not yet arrived at the end of its agonizing soul-searching since, at its fourth Congress in Palghat in April 1956, it approved, after Moscow had done so, some aspects of the government's economic policy.

The development of cultural, economic, and technical cooperation figured among the objectives that the two countries set themselves to achieve in their bilateral relations. The two parties asserted that the fact that each adhered to 'a system which is moulded by its own genius, traditions and environment' would not be an obstacle to such a cooperation. During his visit, some industrial sites were shown to Nehru, and even a nuclear power station near Moscow, with the will to convince him of the capacity of the USSR to help in India's programme of industrialization. To Bulganin's assurance that his country would be ready to give all possible help in India's industrial development, Nehru mentioned that tools and drilling apparatus for exploiting mineral resources were needed as well as assistance in prospecting.[27] Louis Joxe, France's Ambassador to Moscow, stressed the fact that since the USSR was keen to maintain its role as a great Asiatic power and wanted to counterbalance the Chinese influence in Asia, it was on the economic plane that it had the greatest chance of succeeding. 'China is still incapable of playing a role in this field, besides the non-communist countries of Asia feel less apprehensive over a Russian penetration than over a Chinese penetration.'[28] The plan frame of P.C. Mahalanobis, approved by the National Development Council in early May 1955, and fixing the broad lines of the Second Five Year Plan, opened vast possibilities for cooperation between the two countries. The director of the Indian Statistical Institute in Calcutta, a close economic adviser of Nehru since the autumn of 1954, who was said to be influenced by Soviet thought in the matter of planning (he was a member of the Indian cultural mission which visited the USSR in June-July 1951 at the invitation of the Union of Soviet Writers), had submitted on 17 March to Nehru his recommendations for the formulation of the Second Plan. Its main thrust was, first on the rapid development of heavy industry, indispensable to an accelerated growth of the economy and to the consolidation of the economic independence of the country, and, second on the strengthening of the public sector, not only in industry but also in certain commercial activities, in the banking, and in the insurance sectors.[29] In July 1955, the largest private bank in India, the Imperial Bank of India, was nationalized, giving birth to the State Bank of India and it was soon the turn of the life insurance industry to become state-owned.

While Nehru travelled across the USSR, an Indian mission consisting of specialists in mines, energy, aeronautics, and chemicals, also visited research institutes, factories, and dams and examined the possibilities offered for the training of Indians in various technical fields. The expenses on this visit were borne by the USSR in the framework of the Soviet contribution to the expanded technical assistance programme of the United Nations. Other Indian missions followed and they generally returned from the Soviet Union with the conviction that Soviet products were technically acceptable. In October, the Union Minister of State for Natural Resources, Keshava Deva Malaviya, persuaded of the urgency of putting an end to the expensive monopoly of the Western oil companies, announced on his return from Moscow that Soviet specialists would arrive shortly to assess India's requirements and the assistance they could provide for the full development of its mineral oil industry.[30] Acknowledging that India was becoming increasingly associated with the Soviet Union in regard to the development of industries, Nehru warned that 'we cannot afford to make ourselves appear cheap. I think the Russians can give us a great deal of help and we should take it. But the Russians, like may others, tend to go further than they are intended to.' What Nehru had in mind was not so much proselytism, but their general attitude to countries: 'Even in China the Russian experts and technicians there tend to take up a superior attitude to the Chinese and expect special favors, even special status. That is so in the East European countries also.' He consequently advised to proceed with a certain restraint in order to maintain self-respect and independence.[31]

On Nehru's invitation, Nikolai A. Bulganin, the Soviet Prime Minister, and Nikita S. Khrushchev, First Secretary of the Communist Party, came to India on 18 November 1955. The American military authorities had just announced that they were going to spend $ 20 million to improve airfields and other military installations in Pakistan. In between the three-week visit in India the two Soviet leaders went to Burma during the first week of December. Remembering the fervour with which the Soviet crowds had welcomed Nehru's visit, the Indian government, reciprocated by giving the Soviet leaders a very warm welcome. This visit further strengthened links between the two countries.

Over and above a largely convergent analysis of the international situation, Nehru nevertheless did not lose sight of the necessity of not appearing in the eyes of the world to compromise on non-alignment which had built the prestige of India on the international scene. 'So far as India's policy of non-involvement is concerned, there has been and will be no change, and the fears of Western countries in this respect have no foundations. But it may be true that the strong and angry reaction in certain Western countries may itself tend to make India more friendly to the Soviet Union.'[32] Besides, Nehru expressed his disagreement at the use of Indian platforms for virulent outbursts against the West to which the Soviet guests replied it was the Russian nature to react impulsively and violently to the deep hostility of the Western leaders.[33] The American Embassy in New Delhi noted besides that Indian officials at highest levels 'have gone out of their way to ask Embassy officers not to read undue significance into hospitality extended to Russian'.[34] A Western diplomat even considered that the Soviet courtship may have misfired to a certain extent:

> Indians still measure Europeans by the yardstick of the British, and the vulgarity of the Soviet leaders, the boorishness of their large and speechless retinue, their crumpled shapeless clothes and strange antics were, on the whole, regarded askance. I have no doubt that the visitors put on a deliberate act, designed to appeal to the 'people' over the heads of their westernized leaders. It may have served some purpose, but I am inclined to

> think that the class of person to whom that appeal was directed is still too ignorant of the world at large to have been seriously influenced by the demagogy of Marshal Bulganin and Mr. Khrushchev or even to be fully aware of identity of its new friends. Nor do the more educated seem to have been converted.[35]

The Indian government could not but be pleased by two of the stands taken in the course of the thirty-two speeches made by the two Soviet leaders during a visit which took them to much of the big cities of India. The first related to the recognition by the Soviet government of the accession of Kashmir to India. On 10 December, at Srinagar, Khrushchev said that he was convinced that the people of Kashmir considered themselves as an integral part of the Indian Republic. The Soviets were above all anxious to see this region under the control of a friendly government, all the more so after the signing of the mutual defense pact between the United States and Pakistan. The second stand concerned the Portuguese enclaves of Goa, Daman, and Diu which the Soviet leaders wanted to see rapidly transferred to India. By conforming to what the Indians wanted to hear being said on points they considered particularly sensitive and on which the West was seen as unsympathetic—such as the respectability of non-alignment or the fact of Goa and Kashmir being a part of India—the Soviet leaders earned the gratitude of the Indian government. Even the question of the links of the CPI with the Soviet Communist party received again a favourable response when Khrushchev assured Nehru that his country would do nothing to encourage the CPI to conduct anti-government activities which might endanger good relations between India and the Soviet Union.[36]

The two countries also discussed the future of economic colla-briefly. Bulganin announced at a rally in the Ramlila Maidan in Delhi on 19 November that his country was ready to share its experience in industrial activities and in the field of power production, including the use of atomic energy for peaceful purposes.[37] Khrushchev paid a tribute to the clear-sightedness of the Indian government for its desire to not make its economy dependent on foreign capital. Agricultural machinery worth Rs. 5 million to equip a state-owned mechanized farm in Suratgarh was offered as a gift. The joint communiqué on economic relations between the two countries, published on 13 December, provided, on the one hand, for the purchase of capital goods by India, particularly for oil extraction and for the mining industry, and, on the other hand, the import, over a period of three years, of one million tons of rolled ferrous metals. Moscow promised to considerably increase its purchases of Indian raw materials and manufactured goods. It was hoped that the total value of such purchases, including the sums which may be required for the maintenance of Soviet official organizations in India, would be equal to the total value of the goods purchased by India in the USSR. In order to meet the increase foreseen in the volume of trade, it was considered necessary to establish regular shipping lines between the ports of the USSR and India.[38]

Nehru was keen to project the assistance offered by the Soviets as a commonplace event and gave it the same importance as American or British aid, regarding it as merely a welcome contribution to India's industrial and technological development. He even viewed as an advantage the fact that the Soviet equipment was less sophisticated and finally better adapted to Indian needs.[39] These promises of Soviet aid came just at the right moment. Escott Reid, the Canadian High Commissioner in New Delhi, reported that the informal overtures that India had made over the past year or two to the United States, the United Kingdom, and Canada seeking a very substantial line of credit to cover requirements during the Second Five Year Plan had failed to elicit any positive response.[40] The amount of aid to India voted by the US Congress for the financial year 1956 was less than that of the previous year.

There were many who feared that Soviet political influence would go hand in hand with Soviet aid—an anxiety reflected mostly in business circles. Talking to the annual general meeting of the Associated Chambers of Commerce on 12 December at Calcutta, the Minister of Commerce and Industry, T.T. Krishnamachari, justified the recourse to Soviet aid. He noted the shyness of foreign capital in coming into India and recalled that the government was still as determined as ever to not surrender its liberty in exchange for aid: 'I know that if we could change our international policy we should get aid—in almost fantastic proportions—but we refuse that type of aid from one quarter and we are not likely to accept similar aid for similar consideration, from any other quarters.'[41] The aid offered by the Soviets gave rise to several favourable comments. Thus, the *Eastern Economist*, a journal which could not be accused of pro-Soviet sympathies, recognized that, even keeping in mind the long procedure because of the need of parliamentary sanction, the negotiations with Western countries were often dilatory by reason of the fact that they try to mould Indian requirements into their surplus areas, while the Soviets seemed prepared to cut their own cloth in order to meet India's needs: 'Partly because of this readiness to adapt their programme to our needs, Russian negotiators have created a far more favourable impression in New Delhi than their Free World counterparts.'[42]

The Soviets never lost the opportunity to show themselves up as sympathetic defenders of the interests of underdeveloped countries against the greedy rapaciousness and the cynicism of the West. Khrushchev expressed what many Indians felt when he declared to the Supreme Soviet on 29 December 1955:

> They (the colonialists) release funds for what they call 'economic aid', give 'free' arms to certain countries. But in payment for these arms the States which receive them must supply the colonialists with cannon fodder and raise great armies, thus exhausting their own people. The colonialists give one dollar in the form of 'aid' in order later to receive ten dollars in exchange by the exploitation of the peoples who have accepted that 'aid'. . . . The monopolists have therefore enough funds to give what they call 'aid' to those countries which the United States draws into its sphere of influence. In reality this is not aid but throwing crumbs from the master's table on terms equal to slavery.[43]

The 20th Congress of the CPSU in February 1956, by condemning Stalin, by defining a new framework for East-West relationships in which the war between the socialist camp and the imperialist camp was no longer inevitable, by erecting the principle of peaceful coexistence as a basic rule of Soviet external policy or again by recognizing to each country the possibility of finding its own path—and notably the parliamentary path—towards socialism (the Cominform was dissolved on 17 April), removed a certain number of ideological obstacles towards a consolidation of the bonds between New Delhi and Moscow. Nehru hailed 'a significant process of adaptation and adjustment' based upon 'a more realistic appreciation of the present world situation'.[44] The importance of the non-aligned countries had been underlined during the twentieth Congress and it was for their intention that the concept of a 'zone of peace' had been advanced, encompassing, by the side of the countries of the socialist camp, the nations which refused to lend their support to the aggressive tactics of imperialism. Contrary to Zhdanov in 1947, Khrushchev did not make it a condition for these nations that they would have to break with the capitalist camp if they were to belong to the zone of peace. In his report, Khrushchev had renewed Soviet support to the development of the former colonies and semi-colonies of Asia which, although not a part of the world socialist system, could profit from its progress. He stressed that those countries needed no longer to beg for modern equipment from their former oppressors since they could obtain the same in the socialist countries without any commitment of a political or military nature.[45]

At the end of March 1956, Anastase Mikoyan, travelling from Karachi, made a halt at New Delhi, if only to reassure its interlocutors, uneasy at the idea of a thaw in Soviet-Pakistan relations.[46] He discussed with Nehru, T.T. Krishnamachari, and K.D. Malaviya the recent changes in the USSR as well as the projects for cooperation then under examination. Mikoyan repeated on this occasion that his country was inclined to collaborate in the setting up of a national oil industry and reassured that Russia would increase its purchases in India to balance the bilateral trade. The *Economic Weekly* hailed the fact that the monopoly of the West as the supplier of capital goods and know-how was coming to an end while underlining that 'technical advice, facilities for training as also capital goods were all this time a monopoly of the West which was extracting far too exacting a price. Now with Russia as a competitor in the field, the West will have to be reasonable in its dealings with underdeveloped countries.'[47]

India, in the eyes of the Soviet leaders, had come full circle: from the status of an agent of American imperialism to the status of a dependable friend of the Soviet Union. Summarizing this rapid turn of events, the *Eastern Economist* recalled that on 2 December 1952, while commenting in the United Nations on an Indian resolution on the repatriation of prisoners of war in Korea, Andrei Vyshinsky said about the Indians: 'At best you are dreamers and idealists. At worst you do not understand your own position and camouflage horrible American policy'. Three years later, on 21 December 1955, on his return to Moscow, Marshal Bulganin announced: 'They (the Western countries) do not like our friendship with India, Burma and Afghanistan. But we like it and it suits us.'[48]

NOTES

1. Dispatch from Yves Chataigneau, 21 August 1951. *AQO*, Asie-Océanie, 1944-1955, Inde, vol. 68.

2. It is interesting to note that for Nehru the prospect of having to depend on the Soviet veto in the Security Council on a matter as important as the question of Kashmir was reluctantly contemplated at the time. On the one hand, it complicated this problem by integrating it within the disputes between the two blocs, and on the other hand, the Soviets might be tempted to ask in exchange for the support of India on other matters. The military alliance between the United States and Pakistan was to sweep aside a large part of this reservation.
3. *Le Monde*, 8 April 1952. Radhakrishnan refuted any Soviet proposal in this direction.
4. Y.D. Gundevia, *Outside the Archives*, p. 109.
5. *Le Monde*, 22-3 March 1953.
6. K.P.S. Menon, *The Flying Troika*, pp. 57-9.
7. G.H. Middleton, Acting British High Commissioner in Delhi, to the Secretary of State for Commonwealth Relations, 1 July 1954. *PRO*, FO 371 112210.
8. To K.P.S. Menon, 8 August and 30 August 1954. J.L. Nehru, *Selected Works of Jawaharlal Nehru (second series)*, vol. 26, pp. 516-7 and 520-1.
9. This stands in sharp contrast with what Nehru had then to say about some of the American personnel in India: 'In the present context, the danger to security comes much more from American agents who are spread out in vast numbers all over this country and not merely confined to technical jobs. There is no doubt that they bribe heavily and influence even our Press. They go all over our border areas, wherever they are allowed. They create disaffection with our Government and our policy and they are known to have been in close contact with the communal organizations.' To K.N. Katju, the Home Minister, 28 August 1954. Ibid., p. 519.
10. See Alvin Z. Rubinstein, *The Soviets in International Organisations*, pp. 155-6.
11. See the article by M. Nesterov, President of the USSR Chamber of Commerce, 'Economic Co-operation Desirable and Possible', *New Times*, no. 51, 19 December 1951, pp. 5-9.
12. *Amrita Bazar Patrika*, 11 January 1952.
13. Note, 20 July 1953. J.L. Nehru, *Selected Works of Jawaharlal Nehru (second series)*, vol. 23, p. 495.
14. During a press conference on 13 November 1954, after his return from China, Nehru disclosed that he had visited a new plant built by the Soviets at a fairly rapid speed and yet of good workmanship. J.L. Nehru, *Press Conferences 1954*, Delhi, pp. 34-5.
15. *Statesman*, 3 February 1955; *Amrita Bazar Patrika*, 4 February 1955.
16. *Commerce*, 23 October 1954, p. 778.
17. Memorandum of conversation by J. Robert Flucker, 25 May 1955 and letter from the Chairman of the Operations Coordinating Board (Hoover) to the President of the Export-Import Bank (Edgerton), 6 June 1955. *FRUS, 1955-1957*, vol. 8, pp. 288-9. In December 1956, IISCO received, for the second time, a loan from the World Bank, of an amount of $ 20 million.

18. Gundevia, then Deputy High Commissioner in London, reported that when it was decided that the British would construct one of the steelworks, Lord Alec Douglas Home, Secretary of State for Commonwealth Relations, rejoiced at the fact that the Germans were also involved in the construction of a plant as 'Nehru might otherwise have given away the whole show to the USSR!'. *Outside the Archives*, p. 359.
19. Inevitably studies were carried out on the comparative advantages of the three steel plants of Bhilai, Rourkela and Durgapur. All three were commissioned in 1959. The credit offered by the Soviets was the most attractive compared to the German loan carrying interest at 6.3 per cent per annum and repayable over a period of three years with a grace period of three years and to the British credit carrying interest at 5.5 to 6 per cent per annum repayable over a period of 11 years with a grace period of eight years. The aid component *stricto sensu* was highest in the Soviet loan, even though subsequently the Germans and the British did accept to reschedule the repayment in convertible currency of their loans.

    The Soviets, more than their 'rivals', sought to utilize local talent during the course of the work. However, Indian engineers were associated mostly in the construction of the steelworks and only marginally in its designing. It appears that in terms of deadlines, costs of production, profitability of the steelworks or again collaboration between foreign technicians and Indian personnel, as well as in terms of training, Bhilai produced better results than the other two steelworks. But, it is also true that at Bhilai, the technical procedures were less sophisticated—notably as compared to the German project—and hence made adaptation quicker for the personnel in charge of its utilization. By opting for a less complex project, the Soviets incurred smaller construction costs (the cost of the Soviet project was the one that underwent the lesser upward revision) and they had less operational problems. See M.S. Stanislaus, *Soviet Economic Aid*, chapter 8; P.J. Eldridge, *The Politics of Foreign Aid in India*, pp. 140-3; M.I. Goldman, *Soviet Foreign Aid*, pp. 85-91, or again the article by Bernard D'Mello, 'Soviet Collaboration in Indian Steel Industry, 1954-1984', *Economic and Political Weekly*, 5 March 1988, pp. 473-86.
20. *New Times*, supplement to no. 7, Second Session of Fourth Supreme Soviet of the USSR, 12 February 1955, p. 13.
21. A. Diakov, 'Indiia v Bor'be Za Mir', *Sovetskoe Vostokovedenie*, no. 1, 1955, pp. 36-43. Quoted by R.B. Remnek, *Soviet Policy towards India*, p. 130. Even Gandhi did not escape a re-evaluation of his political role. Thus Zhukov (who had described him in 1947 as the apostle of India's backwardness) acknowledged that he had been mistaken by the religious appearance of Gandhism. It provided with an excuse for criticizing Gandhi's actions when, in fact, despite certain defects, Gandhism was a genuinely popular anti-imperialist movement. E. Joukov, 'Le Rôle Historique du Mahatma Gandhi', *Temps Nouveaux*, no. 6, 2 February 1956, p. 16.
22. A. Alexeyev, 'The Political Situation in India', *New Times*, no. 44, 31 October 1951, p. 9.

23. Speech by N.S. Khrushchev delivered at the fourth session of the Supreme Soviet of the USSR, 29 December 1955. N.A. Bulganin, N.S. Khrushchov, *Visit of Friendship to India, Burma and Afghanistan, Speeches and Official Documents,* Moscow: Foreign Languages Publishing House, 1956, p. 274.
24. Memorandum of a conversation by the Secretary of State, 21 May 1953. *FRUS, 1952-1954*, vol. 9, part 1, p. 115.
25. 2 August 1955. J.L. Nehru, *Letters to Chief Ministers*, vol. 4, p. 230.
26. Minutes of meeting with Soviet leaders, 22 June 1955. J.L. Nehru, *Selected Works of Jawaharlal Nehru* (*second series*), vol. 29, pp. 228-31. It was said that, informally, suggestions had been made by the United States that China should be taken into the United Nations but not in the Security Council where it would be replaced by India. This was unacceptable to India for it would mean falling out with China, a great country which has every right to be in the Security Council, and even if India ought to be there, but only at a later stage. Note, 1 August 1955. Ibid., p. 303.
27. Minutes of the meeting with Soviet leaders, 10 June 1955. Ibid., pp. 218-19.
28. Telegram from Louis Joxe, 22 June 1955. *AQO*, Asie-Océanie, 1944-1955, Inde, vol. 68.
29. See P. C. Mahalanobis, *The Approach of Operational Research to Planning in India*, pp. 91-2 and 96-7.
30. *Hindu*, 22 October 1955.
31 Letter to K.D. Malaviya, 25 October 1955. J.L. Nehru, *Selected Works* of Jawaharlal Nehru (*second series*), vol. 30, pp. 429-30.
32. 20 December 1955. J.L. Nehru, *Letters to Chief Ministers*, vol. 4, p. 310.
33. Record by the British High Commissioner (MacDonald) of a conversation between Nehru, Mountbatten, R. Pillai and himself, 17 March 1956. *PRO*, FO 371 123587.
34. Telegram from the Embassy in India to the State Department, 25 November 1955. *FRUS, 1955-1957*, vol. 8, p. 299.
35. Dispatch from the Acting United Kingdom High Commissioner (G.H. Middleton) to the Secretary of State for Commonwealth Relations, 17 January 1956. *PRO*, FO 371 123587. If the demeanor of the Soviet leaders was unsophisticated, on their side, the hosts had chosen to give a proletarian flavor to the visit with the decision to rename 'Queen's Way', one of New Delhi main artery, Jan Path (People's Road).
36. Talks with the Soviet leaders, 12 December 1955. J.L. Nehru, *Selected Works of Jawaharlal Nehru* (*second series*), vol. 31, p. 345.
37. *Hindu*, 20 November 1955.
38. Joint Indo-Soviet communiqué on economic relations between India and the USSR. Visit of Bulganin and Khrushchev in India, Burma and Afghanistan. N.A. Bulganin, N.S. Khrushchov, *Visit of Friendship to India, Burma and Afghanistan, Speeches and Official Documents*, pp. 306-7.
39. 30 December 1955. J.L. Nehru, *Letters to Chief Ministers*, vol. 4, pp. 330.
40. E. Reid, *Envoy to Nehru*, p. 137.
41. *Hindu*, 13 December 1955.

42. *Eastern Economist*, 30 March 1956, p. 514.
43. Speech by N.S. Khrushchev delivered at the fourth session of the Supreme Soviet of the USSR, 29 December 1955. N.A. Bulganin, N.S. Khrushchov, *Visit of Friendship to India, Burma and Afghanistan, Speeches and Official Documents*, pp. 270-2.
44. Statement in Lok Sabha, 20 March 1956. J.L. Nehru, *India's Foreign Policy*, p. 578.
45. Action report of the Central Committee of the CPSU to the XXth Congress of the Party presented by N. Khrushchev. *Notes et Etudes Documentaires*, 14 March 1956, no. 2156, La Documentation Française, pp. 9-10.
46. Even after the signing of the military alliance pact between Pakistan and the United States, the Soviets tried to maintain contacts that were as cordial as possible with the Pakistani leaders, even proposing economic assistance. This offer was refused till the early 1960s.
47. *Economic Weekly*, 7 April 1956, p. 408.
48. *Eastern Economist*, 30 December 1955, p. 983.

CHAPTER 10

Overcoming the Differences

THE AMERICAN PRESS had used fairly harsh words against Nehru at the time of his visit to the Soviet Union in June 1955, accusing him of having sided with the Soviet positions to a greater extent than was expected from a self-proclaimed non-aligned country in a conflict which remained basically between democracy and totalitarianism. Thus, the *New York Times* noted that 'it is a pity that Mr. Nehru's contribution to this ideal [to contribute to world peace and to act as a mediator or pacifier between the two giant powers] should have been a general acceptance of the Soviet policies'. Then came the terse conclusion: 'He said as he took off from Moscow: 'I am leaving part of my heart behind.' We might be forgiven for thinking that he also left a part of his common sense behind.'[1] The Americans pointed, in particular, to Nehru's barely veiled criticism of Washington's policy in South Vietnam, and of US support of Prime Minister Ngo Dinh Diem; this appraisal was conveyed in the Indo-Soviet joint declaration, which displayed anxiety over the progress of the implementation of the Geneva agreements which were apparently 'in some danger of being obstructed by new and unexpected developments'.

Washington followed the visit of Bulganin and Khrushchev to India with much interest. A report of the State Department published in March 1956 noted with concern the establishment of closer Indo-Soviet relations: 'The Soviet Union has presented a challenge of unprecedented proportions for India's political sympathies and diplomatic support. While India will continue to maintain that its policy is one of "non-alignment", it may identify itself even more with the Communist Bloc positions on current problems.' It was also noted that for the first time India was seriously considering the purchase of Soviet arms.[2] The Americans broached this latter point at the time when Dulles passed through New Delhi on 9 and 10 March 1956, in the wake of the SEATO conference in Karachi.

The US Secretary of State had taken the initiative to visit the Indian capital evidently motivated by the desire to prevent India's foreign policy from leaning towards the Soviets and to smoothen out a number of misunderstandings, notably to defend himself from charges of having supported the Portuguese on the question of Goa. During their meeting, Nehru and Dulles only succeeded in agreeing to disagree. Neither held the other in high esteem and Nehru once described Dulles as 'a Methodist pastor and combined rigidity with self-righteousness'.[3] Nehru deplored that the question of Kashmir had been mentioned in the communiqué published at the end of the SEATO meeting. According to Nehru, this reference betrayed the bias of SEATO in favour of Pakistan over a bilateral issue which had nothing to do with the declared objectives of the organization. Nehru also deplored that India was obliged to increase its defense expenditure on account of the military aid that America was giving to Pakistan, while Dulles reasserted, without however being convincing, that the United States would firmly oppose any belligerent action by Pakistan towards India.[4] At the end of March, Nehru conveyed to the United States that the question of holding a plebiscite or engaging arbitration in Kashmir had lost much of its relevance. Above all, Nehru still reproached Dulles for conducting a diplomacy incapable of adapting to the recent changes that had occurred in the Soviet Union. Dulles remained obviously convinced that to thwart the spread of communism, only a firm stand with the communist leaders backed by a system of military alliances was likely to work. In June 1956, Dulles described neutrality as an obsolete concept, and went on to say that, except under very exceptional circumstances, it was an 'immoral and short-sighted conceptions'.[5]

Working, however, on the principle that it was better to deal with a democratic government, however vehement its criticism of US policies might be, than with a communist regime, Washington chose to accept the challenge thrown by the Soviets. The State Department discussed the ways in which the US should respond to the initial offers of Soviet aid to India. A few days before Khrushchev and Bulganin arrived in India, Nelson A. Rockefeller, Special Assistant to the President, wrote to Eisenhower recommending that he send a message to the Indian Prime Minister saying that the United States had been proud to contribute to India's advancement in agricultural development and was interested in helping to promote its industrial growth over the next five years. Informed of this, the Under Secretary, Herbert Hoover Jr., protested against such an action which might either give India the impression that it could count upon a sizeable amount of aid—which would be very presumptuous—or, in the absence of any specific pledge, seem like a crude manoeuvre to counter the importance of the Soviets' visit. In either case, Hoover argued, it would lead to unwanted effects on Indo-American relations.[6]

In November 1955, the State Department discussed the amount of aid to be granted to India for the fiscal year 1957 and decided to ask for $ 70 million in development assistance. The aim was to check the erosion of economic aid to India which, for the current year (1956) had declined to $ 47.2 million. There was near unanimity on this figure of $ 70 million for diverse reasons. The first reason was political: 'Loss of US economic support could well throw Indian leaders into dependence on Soviet aid for their Plan.' Then there were economic grounds:

> At the moment, the financial problems inherent in the plan are resulting in conflict between moderate leaders in India who wish to pursue a conservative financial and political policy and radical elements who demand increased state control of the economy to assure success. A reduction in US aid at this time would play into the hands of these radical elements and could set Indian economic policy on a more dangerously socialistic path for the future.

The lone hostile voice was that of a participant who expressed during this debate an opinion often heard at the time in the US Congress; this dissenting person felt that US assistance would only serve to strengthen an unfriendly government and suggested that consequently aid be withheld so that the Indian government realized where its real interest lay.[7]

At the time of the visit of Bulganin and Khrushchev, the American Embassy in New Delhi cautioned the State Department not to say or do anything that might signal that the United States had less interest in the welfare of India than in the past. John S. Cooper, the new American Ambassador posted there since April 1955 and a former Republican senator from Kentucky, warned that any new American retraction in the matter of aid would immediately be made good by the Soviets: 'It would be dangerous to seek comfort in the hope that the Russians may promise aid which they will not deliver . . . their understanding of India's importance in their global strategy is such that they will make prodigious effort to make good on promises.'[8] It was particularly in response to the extension of Soviet aid to newly independent countries that President Eisenhower, in his State of the Union address delivered on 5 January 1956, asked Congress to grant limited authority to make longer-term commitments for assistance to projects, requiring a period of years for planning and completion, to be fulfilled from appropriations to be made in future fiscal years.[9] The issue of giving an assurance of continuity in economic assistance for development programmes was regularly raised but each time it met with hostility from Congress which jealously wanted to preserve its hold over aid funding through annual budgetary appropriations. The threat of a new form of Soviet penetration into underdeveloped countries gave additional ammunition to those in charge of defending the aid budget before Congress. George Allen, who had become Assistant Secretary for Near Eastern and South Asian Affairs, intervened before the Senate Foreign Relations Committee to fuel its mistrust, if it was still needed, of an aid which would have not been inherently bad if it did not appear obvious, in the light of the history of Soviet aspirations, that the objective was 'first of eliminating all Western influence from the area [Asia and Africa] and, second, of dominating it themselves'; only the tactics had changed markedly.[10]

The repeated warnings of the United States against taking recourse to Soviet assistance which, they claimed, concealed sinister motives seemed to the Indians too prejudiced to be honest. *Commerce* rejected all attempts as ill-advised and in any event infructuous which aimed at persuading underdeveloped countries 'not to accept Russian business offers or economic aid by painting a dark picture of the consequences to them, as is being done by some US spokesmen'. The journal argued that the United States had only to blame themselves since they had made 'the mistake of rendering financial assistance more and more on political considerations, and less and less on economic. Pakistan, though only a third of India's size, is today getting US aid on a scale which is three times that given to India. Three years ago, the reverse was true.'[11]

One of the major events in India in the year 1956 was the publication of the Second Five Year Plan, covering the period from 1 April 1956 to 31 March 1961. The Planning Commission would certainly not have risked doubling the public outlay if it had not been encouraged to do so by the good economic results of the First Five Year Plan. Most of the objectives of the First Plan had been often nearly or fully achieved, and sometimes even surpassed. Of the first three plans, the first was *de facto* the one whose results converged most with the targeted objectives. National income had increased by 17.5 per cent and not 11 per cent as had been initially estimated; the investment rate had exceeded the anticipated 6.75 per cent to reach 7.3 per cent. The success of the plan was due largely to good harvests which greatly contributed to the favourable economic climate, which in turn encouraged industrialists to utilize their production capacity to the full. Consequently, industrial production had increased by 39 per cent during the First Plan.

Three good monsoons in succession enabled the production of food grains to soar. In 1955-6, 64.9 million tons of food grains were harvested, which was 3.3 million more than anticipated in the estimates made in 1952. This notable achievement was, nevertheless, below that of the two preceding harvests, while a record production of 68.8 million tons of food grains had occurred in 1953-4. As a result, there was a clear reduction in the imports of food grains—they declined from 4.8 million tons in 1951 to 600,000 tons in 1955; this in turn resulted in an unforeseen improvement in the balance of payments situation. There had been a deficit of Rs. 423 million in the balance of payments over the entire period of the First Five Year Plan. This was a very small deficit in the light of the alarming predictions of the planners who had anticipated an annual deficit of Rs. 1.8 to Rs. 2 billion. In fact, the year 1951-2, which served as a reference year, was the only year in the whole plan when there was a deficit. The foreign trade balance with the dollar area was itself on the positive side during the last three years. There was also a second important factor which explained the good performance of the balance of payments situation; this was the delay in the implementation of the plan projects, with the result that the import of capital goods really took off only during the last year of the plan. Consequently, the drawings from the sterling balances did not exceed Rs. 140 million, while a decrease to the extent of Rs. 290 million of these assets had been anticipated in 1952.

This delay in the commencement of a certain number of development projects, particularly those in the steel and heavy electrical sectors, was also translated into a reduced need for foreign aid. The aid utilized amounted to Rs. 2 billion (as against more than

Rs. 14 billion during the Second Plan), of which 45 per cent was on account of the single American wheat loan. The amount of aid utilized was the equivalent of 10 per cent of the public expenditures undertaken within the plan. American aid had constituted 70 per cent of the aid utilized during the First Five Year Plan. Moreover, the loans from the World Bank, which worked in close collaboration with the American government, had constituted 17 per cent of the aid utilized. The rest came essentially from the aid given under the auspices of the Colombo Plan. Two-thirds of American utilized aid had taken the form of deliveries of food grains.[12]

Considering these statistics, the publicity given in India to the first offers of Soviet aid outraged many Americans. The Americans reproached the Indians and their Prime Minister for their lack of gratitude for American aid which in terms of quantity was far greater than the Soviet offer. Subimal Dutt, who was the Foreign Secretary between 1955 and 1961, confided that he had often heard the Americans complaining that Nehru was not sufficiently appreciative of the massive aid given by their country. Dutt recalled for instance that Lester Pearson, the Canadian Secretary of State for External Affairs, echoed this criticism when he remarked in December 1955 that the Soviet Union got more credit by sending seven petroleum geologists at government of India's cost than the Western countries had ever received despite scores of specialists sent to India at their own expense.[13] Indignant at such 'a financial approach', Nehru pointed out that the United States and the United Kingdom are largely wrong 'in judging of the feelings of other countries'; he explained:

> The Russians are cleverer and more understanding. It is not money that goes far in creating impressions, but the policies pursued. The USA and the UK created adverse impressions in India by their policy of military alliances in South East Asia and the Middle East, by the military aid given to Pakistan, by their passive support of Pakistan in Kashmir, and their general policy relating to Goa. Nothing could have been more calculated to irritate Indian opinion than Mr. Dulles's amazing statement on Goa.[14]

This last reference was to the joint communiqué issued at the end of the meeting between Dulles and the Portuguese Foreign Minister, Paulo Cunha, in December 1955. The communiqué noted that the two countries had discussed the allegations made by Khrushchev and Bulganin in India on the 'Portuguese provinces in the Far East'. This designation of Portuguese possessions which followed from a

Portuguese constitutional amendment in 1951 which substituted the word 'colony' by 'province', was immediately interpreted in India as tacit support extended by the Americans to Portuguese colonial possessions in Asia.

In the draft Second Plan brought before the public in February 1956—the content of the final version adopted in December by the National Development Council differed little from the draft—stress was laid on the need to speed up the growth of the economy and to increase the potential for production in order to achieve a faster pace of development in the subsequent plans. The national income was to be raised by 25 per cent. The outlay in the public sector was fixed at Rs. 48 billion (about $ 10 billion). Public funds devoted to industry and mining constituted 18.5 per cent of the total public expenditure. This percentage was lower than had been foreseen in the plan frame of Professor Mahalanobis—26 per cent of public development expenditure[15]—resulting most likely from the pressures exerted by business circles and relayed by the right wing of the Congress against giving excessive priority to the public sector in the process of industrialization. This figure of 18.5 per cent being devoted to industry represented in absolute value an amount that was seven times higher than the expenditure actually incurred on this sector of the economy during the First Plan. On the other hand, while the state expenditure on agriculture, community development, and irrigation still took up some 20 per cent of the plan outlay, its increase was more tardy than that of the overall public expenditure. The main thrust of the plan was on transport and communications, which took up almost 30 per cent of the public expenditure. As regards the scheme of financing, more than 80 per cent of the central and state governments' developmental programmes, aggregating Rs. 48 billion, was to come from internal resources. About 17 per cent of the finance for the public sector (Rs. 8 billion) was to be raised abroad and a gap of Rs. 4 billion was to be covered by additional measures to raise domestic resources.[16]

With the increased public outlay and, even more than that, the importance attached to industrialization, the Second Plan would inevitably make heavy demands on the foreign exchange reserves. It was understood that in the foreign trade sector, purchases of machinery, vehicles, and metals would represent some 50 per cent of the total imports, clearly reflecting the emphasis on the development of basic industries. The balance of payments deficit for the entirety of the Second Plan was assessed at Rs. 11.2 billion. It was anticipated that a part of the deficit would be financed by drawing down the foreign exchange reserves, lowering them to a reasonable level equivalent to six or seven months' imports. Also, Rs. 2 billion or so of the sterling balances could safely be drawn from these reserves to meet part of the foreign exchange requirements of the plan. The amount of foreign capital for the investment programmes in the private sector—coming notably from the World Bank—was estimated at Rs. 1 billion. The planners calculated that the aid already assured was at Rs. 1.7 billion; this figure was arrived at by adding the external assistance not utilized during the First Plan to the net accretion of resources coming from the Soviet and British credits for the steel plants. There still remained Rs. 6.3 billion (around $ 1.3 billion) to be found.[17] This amount was far higher than the foreign aid available during the First Plan period and it gave rise to skeptical comments. Thus, the *Hindu* wrote the possibility of obtaining:

> a four-fold increase in external aid, after the government's strident declaration about its intention to nationalize insurance and sectors of private trading, is either a juvenile piece of make-believe or a pious expectation that the contenders in the 'Cold War' will outbid each other in coming to the rescue of India's democratic socialism.[18]

C.D. Deshmukh, the Finance Minister, himself conceded that while it was reasonable to hope for Rs. 4 billion in the way of foreign aid, or maybe even a little more in very favourable circumstances, it was 'somewhat exaggerated optimism' to expect Rs. 8 million.[19]

On the heels of the draft plan, on 30 April 1956, a new industrial policy resolution was announced, in line with the perspective of a socialistic pattern of society, modifying the earlier policy resolution of 6 April 1948. All industries of basic and strategic importance, or in the nature of public utility services, would be in the public sector, as well as other industries which were essential and which required investment on a scale which only the state could assume. Three categories were defined. The first category included the industries whose future development was to be the exclusive responsibility of the state. They were larger in number as compared to the industrial policy resolution of 1948, with the addition notably of the exploitation of mineral resources and the production of electrical equipment as well as heavy machinery for basic industries. Nevertheless, the state did not contemplate nationalizing the already existing privately-owned concerns in these fields, nor did it preclude their expansion. It even considered securing the cooperation of private enterprise in the establishment of new units when the national interests so required. In the second category—which truly indicated the widening of the sphere of intervention of the state in industrial production—were industries in whose development the public sector would generally take the initiative in establishing new undertakings. Private enterprises would also be allowed to develop, either on their own or with state participation. It concerned notably the sectors of machine tools, chemicals, non-ferrous metals, pharmaceuticals, fertilizers, and road and sea transport. Finally, in the third category were the remaining industries whose development was left to the initiative of the private sector, though it would also be open to the state to start any industry in this category. Even though the new industrial policy resolution intended to expand the public sector, its reception was relatively favourable among industrial and financial circles. The path leading to a veritable socialization of the economy promised to be long, the setting up of an extensive programme of nationalization was no longer on the current agenda, and the feeling prevailed that there was a wide flexibility as regards private enterprises, even those included in the industrial sectors subjected to public initiative.

These developments were analysed in a report presented by a World Bank mission which came to India at the start of the summer. Its conclusions were repeated in a letter that its president, Eugene Black, sent in early September to T.T. Krishnamachari. The main criticism concerned the under-utilization of the potential of private enterprise, which was subjected to too many controls, in the economic development of the country. The industrial policy resolution also came in for censure since, if it was implemented to the letter, it would impose additional burdens on the already overstrained financial and administrative resources of the public sector. For this same reason the public expenditure programme provided for in the plan was considered too ambitious to be completed within five years. Consequently, it was strongly recommended that the technical cooperation and financial support of foreign private enterprise be sought by offering it more attractive conditions. Commenting on these remarks, Nehru only saw in them the traditional opposition of the Americans to all measures aimed at strengthening the public sector.[20] In his reply, the new Indian Finance Minister asserted that while the Indian government had no intention of changing its economic policy, the private sector was not being segregated, and he cited as proof of this its buoyancy and confidence. He also gave the assurance that the Indian government intended to review the policies and procedures that inhibited foreign direct investment, while specifying at the same time that the opposition to its participation in Indian enterprises did not come from the government but from Indian industrialists themselves. This accommodating posture could be due to the emerging foreign exchange problem which obliged the government to re-examine development projects in terms of their capacity to generate hard currency or to help in saving on the same. Moreover, he informed Eugene Black that he had requested Braj Kumar Nehru, Secretary for Economic Affairs in the Finance Ministry, to remain in Washington after the annual meeting of the World Bank in order to initiate discussions about the Second Plan projects which might eventually be financed by the IBRD.[21]

The direction in which the economic policy of the Indian government was evolving and the trend towards establishing closer relations with the USSR were factors which further complicated the task of the Eisenhower administration. The US government had to convince a Congress that was touchy about the undermining of economic liberalism in India and of which some members considered Nehru a crypto-communist, to vote in favour of the $ 70 million of aid recommended for the fiscal year 1957. The American Embassy in India inevitably considered this amount insufficient and asked for a reassessment of the US aid programme for India in the light of the 'forceful new communist programme of economic penetration', and suggested a total programme, over a period of up to five years, for some $ 500 million in development assistance and a minimum sale of $ 300 million in surplus agricultural commodities, which were at the time the subject of negotiations. The half billion dollars were to come, on the one hand, from five annual installments of $ 75 million each and, on the other hand, from a long-term moratorium on India's repayment in kind of the US lend-lease silver due in 1957 (226 million ounces of silver, valued at some $ 120 million, had been lent to India during Second World War). This moratorium was meant to enable India to draw down an equivalent amount of its own foreign exchange being heretofore used for currency backing. Finally, the technical assistance would continue on a grant basis at $ 10 million per year.[22]

These various proposals met with different fates. The US Treasury was opposed to a moratorium on the lend-lease silver debt and in April 1957 India announced its repayment, while the attempt at a legislative endorsement of a financial commitment towards India over a period of several years was considered not advisable at this time by the State Department.[23] For the fiscal year 1957, the US Congress voted a $ 65.3 million aid allocation to India, barely a little higher than the $ 60 million given the preceding year. Only the proposal concerning the sale of agricultural surpluses to India received a positive response. On 29 August 1956, the first Indo-American agreement was signed under the Agricultural Trade Development and Assistance Act of 1954, known as Public Law 480.

When it was voted on 10 July 1954, PL-480 was primarily meant to solve the problem of American agricultural surpluses. The problem had been temporarily solved in the wake of the Second World War by the dispatch of massive exports towards the West European countries under the Marshall Plan, but it reappeared in 1949 although once again it was provisionally solved with the war in Korea and the constitution of stocks of food grains in these countries. From 1953, the surpluses again became a cause of anxiety at a time when the underdeveloped countries, which were potential importers, faced a shortage of hard currency. Consequently, the US Congress amended the Mutual Security Act in July 1953 by voting article 550, authorizing the sale of surplus agricultural commodities, of a maximum value of $ 250 million, to be paid for in local currencies. PL-480, voted the following year, was initially meant to encompass a volume of surpluses of a value of $ 700 million over a period of three years but it was subsequently amended twice, and in August 1956 it covered a volume of surpluses equivalent to $ 3 billion. With this law, initially motivated by domestic considerations arising out of the accumulation of surpluses stored at the government's expense, the US government saw also a way of serving its political interests abroad.[24] And in the case of India, PL-480 could contribute towards alleviating the disastrous effects of the military alliance with Pakistan on Indian leaders. The PL-480 programme offered a sizeable advantage to the American government in the sense that, of all the main types of US foreign assistance, it was the only one which was not subjected to a more or less minute scrutiny by Congress during its annual budget allocations. It was easier for members of Congress to approve food aid, which meant in effect to giving to Third World countries domestically unmarketable surplus commodities, rather than to allocate additional credits in the development aid budget. Furthermore, to deflect accusations of unfair competition and price distortion, the supplies, under Title I, were made on the condition that links between the importing country and its traditional suppliers should not be disrupted. The need to come to the help of the 'starving children' of the Third World—and also of American farmers—was an easier message for the American taxpayer to accept than the transfer of public money to governments whose loyalty was questionable.

Despite the good results obtained in the production of food grains during the second half of the First Plan, the Indian Minister of Food and Agriculture had never given up the idea of taking recourse to regular imports to build up stocks. While population growth, urbanization linked to industrialization, and rising incomes implied an increased demand, the fact remained that the climatic conditions still continued to largely determine the level of production and could lead to large fluctuations in supply from one year to the next. There were two ways to meet the need for cheap food grains in the urban areas: either by higher productivity resulting from land reforms and from investments and incentives boosting the production level, or by the import of food grains from abroad at a price reasonable enough to not impose a heavy burden on the foreign exchange reserves. The first proposal would have meant reviewing the property ownership system in the countryside on the one hand, and, on the other hand, giving preference to agriculture as compared to industry in the order of priority of the Second Plan. When confronted by the vested interests in the Congress party which felt threatened by land reforms, it was politically far more expedient to favour the second proposition. Consequently, in the spring of 1954, even before the vote on PL-480, the Indian government requested the United States to consider a three-year programme involving 4.5 to 5 million tons of wheat on preferential terms, which would make it possible to hold the price line while limiting the foreign exchange costs of such imports.[25] In May 1955, negotiations were started for an agreement under PL-480.

The draft plan, which anticipated an increase of 15 per cent in the production of food grains, had hardly been made public when, an upward revision of this objective became unavoidable to prevent any uncontrolled increase in the price index. In December 1956, the

Planning Commission was to fix the target for the increased production of food grains at 25 per cent, but without really giving itself the means to do so since there had not been at the same time any addition in the funds allocated to agriculture in the plan. While the projections concerning domestic production seemed at best rash, those announced for the import of food grains during the Second Plan—6 million tons—appeared all the more optimistic as they represented in volume half the amount imported during the First Plan.[26]

It was in this context that a PL-480 agreement was signed on 29 October 1956. Covering a period of three years ending on 30 June 1959, it provided for the sale of agricultural commodities of a value of $ 302.9 million and the payment by the Americans of 50 per cent of the freight charges.[27] The total value of the agreement rose to $ 362.4 million (Rs. 1.72 billion) which made it at the time the largest agreement ever entered into by the United States with a foreign country under PL-480. The imports related to 3.5 million tons of wheat, 190,000 tons of rice, some milk products, cotton, and tobacco. The procedure to be followed was that whenever an American ship unloaded its cargo of surplus agricultural commodities in an Indian port, the Indian government would deposit the rupee equivalent of the dollar cost of these commodities—before their sale in the Indian market—and half the freight cost in the US government account in the Reserve Bank of India. A major portion of these rupee deposits was given as loans or grants to the Indian government for financing mutually agreed upon development projects. The loans were repayable (generally over a period of 40 years) either in rupees, or in dollars, the choice being left to India. The rates of interest till 1960 ranged from 3.5 per cent to 5 per cent, and were subsequently lowered to 0.75 per cent or 1 per cent. The balance was retained by the US government for its own use in India or, after the Congress voted the Cooley amendment in 1957 (named after Harold D. Cooley, the Chairman of the House Committee on Agriculture), to assist industrial collaboration agreements concluded between private American and Indian partners. On 31 March 1966, the deposits credited to the account of the American government in the Reserve Bank of India by way of PL-480 had been distributed in the following manner: 54 per cent on loans and 26 per cent on grants to the Indian government for development projects, 13 per cent on US uses in India and 7 per cent on 'Cooley loans'.[28]

The agreement did not enable a reduction in the foreign exchange deficit during the Second Plan. The Ministry of Food and Agriculture noted that even after this agreement, the import of 6 million tons of food grains was still contemplated. The Indo-American agreement made it possible at least not to make the burden weighing on the foreign exchange reserves any heavier. It also had a dual anti-inflationary effect, on the one hand, it increased the supply of food grains for consumption and on the other hand, it put at the disposal of government, by the sale, the rupees that it would otherwise have had to procure by taking recourse to increased taxation, to borrowings and to the creation of money. It could contribute notably towards making good a part of the Rs. 4 billion not covered by receipts in the plan.

At the time when signs indicating a serious foreign exchange crisis were increasing, many believed that the question of American aid for the Second Five Year Plan would be among the main subjects broached during Nehru's visit to the United States in December 1956. The visit was initially scheduled for July, just after the Commonwealth Prime Ministers' Conference in London, but it was postponed on account of Eisenhower's illness.[29] It was a fortuitous delay as it enabled Nehru and Eisenhower to meet at a time when the recent international events—the Anglo-French expedition in Egypt and the Soviet intervention in Hungary—had brought the two countries somewhat closer to each other.

As regards the Suez crisis, Nehru expressed some reservations over the nationalization of the canal company when it had been announced by Gamal Abdel-Nasser on 26 July 1956, a week after the decision of the United States to abandon the idea of participating in the construction of the Aswan Dam, ruling out at the same time any possibility of a World Bank credit to the Egyptian government for its construction. Wanting to prevent Nasser from becoming 'the instrument' of Soviet ambitions in the region, Dulles had initially supported the idea of American aid in order to counter the agreement on the delivery of arms by Czechoslovakia to Egypt and the offer of a loan of $ 200 million from the Soviets. But he had subsequently revised this stand after having estimated that the withdrawal of all aid would be a good means to show to Nasser America's disapproval of his policies, and the Americans thought, moreover, that the USSR may not be in a position to finance the dam.

Without contesting the right of the Egyptian government to nationalize the canal, the absence of any dialogue over this decision concerning an international shipping lane was considered by New Delhi as being regrettable, to say the least. The Egyptian decision surprised Nehru. Some days earlier, while the Indian Prime Minister and the Egyptian President had travelled together by air from Brioni where they had attended, with Marshall Tito, a meeting heralding the non-aligned movement, Nasser had apparently mentioned his intention of abandoning the Aswan Dam project. Nehru had approved of this decision at the time, feeling it was wiser to opt for a large number of small projects rapidly implemented and yielding quick results rather than undertaking a gigantic enterprise which would require many years to complete and which would vest any country providing assistance with a commanding control over Egypt's economy.[30]

When Great Britain and France's stormy reactions to the nationalization of the Suez Canal Company threatened to end up in an armed confrontation, the Indian government sought to mediate between the positions adopted by the Western powers and Egypt during the London Conference (16-23 August), which the latter declined to attend. India was directly concerned with the solving of the crisis. Nearly 69 per cent of its export trade and over 61 per cent of its imports passed through the Suez Canal and any disruption in the traffic passing through the canal would hamper the implementation of the Second Five Year Plan. The alternative sea route, around the Cape of Good Hope, would entail higher freight rates and insurance charges; there would also be a probable shortage of merchant ships as well as delays in deliveries.[31] To defuse the crisis, India advocated a negotiated settlement which provided for the operation of the canal by Egypt, assisted by an international advisory body representing the canal users. While the American attitude differed from the Indian plan in the sense that they favoured some kind of international control over the waterway, the Americans did not adopt such a hard line in their stand as their European allies who were determined to force the Egyptian leader to bend to their wishes. The Americans were also as decided as the Indians in their desire to prevent any escalation of the conflict which could assume the nature of a colonialist escapade. This latter possibility was bound to provoke the ire of the Arab nations and would hence compromise the objectives of American policy in the Near East which aimed at the defense of US oil interests in the region and opposed any Soviet penetration which might replace the loss of British influence. This preoccupation was to lead to the Eisenhower doctrine, enunciated on 5 January 1957, which proposed economic and military assistance to any country or group of countries of this region willing to avail of it.

When the Anglo-French military intervention began on 31 October, the Indians, protested against this action as evidence of an outdated imperialism, and found themselves siding with the Americans to condemn this action and to demand the withdrawal, as quickly as possible, of foreign forces from Egyptian soil. This concordance of views on an international problem was at the time a sufficiently rare event to be described as noteworthy, even if the motives of the two countries did differ. The economic consequences that the Indians feared from the closure of the canal did follow; it was reopened in March 1957 after it had been cleared of the demolished ships blocking the passage. Nevertheless, T.T. Krishnamachari attempted to adopt a reassuring stance by insisting that the lengthening of shipping schedules and higher costs would not cause serious dislocation to the Second Plan as it was still in its initial stages.[32]

As regards the events in Hungary, the American government expressed its satisfaction at seeing the Indians putting the Soviet Union in the dock for a change. Nehru even went to the extent of declaring on 5 November 1956, during the inauguration of a UNESCO conference in New Delhi, that 'these five principles [*Panchsheela*] are also words without meaning to some countries who claim the right of deciding problems by superior might', after having expressed his anxiety at seeing 'in Egypt, as well as in Hungary, both human dignity and freedom outraged'.[33] He repeated thereafter that the Hungarian people should be allowed to freely decide their future and foreign troops should withdraw from their territory as soon as possible. No doubt Washington would have preferred that India not confine itself to verbal disapproval alone and that it adopt as decisive a position in the United Nations as the one it had displayed during the Suez crisis, by voting along with the West to unmistakably condemn the Soviet Union. On 4 November, India abstained during an American resolution condemning Soviet intervention, asking for the immediate withdrawal of its troops and the dispatch of a UN mission to investigate the situation in Hungary. India attracted particular disapproval for being the only non-communist country to have voted, on 10 November, against a resolution insisting that elections be held in Hungary under the auspices of the United Nations. Krishna Menon, the leader of the Indian delegation at the UNO, considered it inadmissible that the consent of the new Hungarian government was not sought. This decision was often explained as stemming out of India's opposition to what would have been a regrettable precedent which could be applied to decide the future of Kashmir. During the votes that followed on various resolutions, the Indian delegation abstained more often than not, joining generally only in those resolutions of a humanitarian nature and concerning the fate of Hungarian refugees. New Delhi's stance could be explained firstly by the desire not to be dragged by the United States into Cold War dialectics which would have frozen the attitudes on both sides and from which the Hungarians would have been the first to suffer. It was also probable, from a more prosaic point of view, that the political and economic advantages accruing from the closer relations of New Delhi with Moscow may have influenced India's attitude towards the Hungarian crisis in faraway eastern Europe, a region Nehru's where New Delhi was weakly represented.

On the eve of visit undertaken by Nehru to the United States, from 16 to 21 December 1956, the American Embassy in New Delhi sent a note to the State Department which analysed both the national and international context of this visit as well as the areas that it would open up for bilateral relations. The note observed that the United States enjoyed greater prestige in India than it had for several years, at a time when the USSR and Britain were found to be discredited and when India's relations with China were also no longer as cordial as before—this reference being to several disagreements on the international situation noted during the recent meeting between Nehru and Zhou Enlai in New Delhi. Moreover, India was experiencing a growing shortfall of foreign exchange requirements and these were jeopardizing the success of the plan. It was up to the United States to extract political mileage from this situation arising out of this combination of facts:

> We feel overall objective of talks should be to lay foundation for anchoring India more firmly to the West and of orienting India's external policy in directions which will, in turn, permit the American public opinion and Congress to support India by lines of credit substantial enough to assure Indian capacity and confidence in keeping abreast of China by democratic norms.[34]

To sooth Nehru's sensitivities, Eisenhower was advised to take the initiative to discuss the objectives of the plan and to make suggestions concerning the aid that the United States could offer, even if no immediate commitment was made:

> We feel strongly that a 'moment of history' has arrived which if seized and exploited, can give the United States a much firmer anti-Communist and anti-Red China counterpoise in India. . . . If India were convinced of our enduring interest in seeing her through the critical years ahead, India might be expected to ameliorate some of her present objections to American policy, especially as regards Pakistan, SEATO, the Baghdad Pact. Risks are involved but it appears to us that the risks are greater of losing India through failure to exploit the opportunities now presented.[35]

Armed with past experience, the State Department clearly had nevertheless little illusion that it would be able to persuade the Indian government to significantly modify its policy in exchange for larger American aid. This is seen clearly in a document which, while it recognized that in the absence of strong political and military ties, economic relations did assume a special importance, also acknowledged that non-alignment had taken firm roots and that the United States had relatively little 'leverage' over India, except perhaps in the matter of its growing need for foreign economic assistance. Having said this, 'the present level of US assistance, though substantial, is small in comparison with India's total economic development expenditure and can exert little if any influence on its policy outlook'. This also applied to the present level of Communist bloc assistance to India, the State Department noted. It finally drew from this the following conclusion: 'It is not clear whether any increase in magnitude would have any effect on India's policy outlook.'[36] The opportunity to put this speculation to the test was not long in coming.

NOTES

1. *New York Times*, 24 June 1955.
2. Progress Report by the Operations Coordinating Board, Department of State, 30 March 1956, *FRUS, 1955-1957*, vol. 8, p. 7
3. Minutes of the meeting with N.A. Bulganin, Moscow, 8 June 1955. J.L. Nehru, *Selected Works of Jawaharlal Nehru (second series)*, vol. 29, p. 208.

4. Memorandum of conversations between Secretary of State Dulles and Prime Minister Nehru, 9-10 March 1956. *FRUS, 1955-1957*, vol. 8, pp. 307-11, and Nehru's two notes on his talks with Dulles. S. Gopal, *Jawaharlal Nehru: A Biography*, vol. 2, pp. 274-5. The American Ambassador, Ellsworth Bunker, expressed his astonishment, during a talk with G.D. Birla on 1 April 1957, that so much noise was being made in India over military aid to Pakistan for, in spite of this, India remained, in terms of military power, '2.5 to 3 times stronger than Pakistan in every field and in the Air Force too'. He added that it would be suicidal for Pakistan to launch an offensive as Indians 'would crush them in a week's time and knowing this how could Pakistan venture to start aggression'. Nehru, to whom these remarks were reported, protested against the comparison of the military forces presented by Bunker, arguing that, 'Pakistan's Air Force is rapidly becoming as big as ours and better from the point of view of quality of aircraft..In regard to the Army too, their mechanized wing is in many ways much better and stronger than ours as they have got the latest type of tanks'. Nehru Family and Ghanshyam Das Birla, *A Unique Collection of Living Letters*, Delhi: Vision Books, 1986, pp. 100 and 102.
5. *Hindu*, 13 June 1956.
6. Letter from Nelson A. Rockefeller to the President, 7 November 1955 and reply from Hoover, 14 November 1955, Department of State, Central Files. *FRUS, 1955-1957*, vol. 8, pp. 296-7.
7. Memorandum of a conversation on economic assistance to India, 18 November 1955. Ibid., pp. 297-8.
8. Telegram from the US Embassy in India to the Department of State, 25 November 1955. Ibid., pp. 298-300.
9. Paul E. Zinner (ed.), *Documents on American Foreign Relations 1956*, New York: Harpers & Brothers, 1957, p. 3.
10. *Hindu*, 10 May 1956.
11. *Commerce*, 14 July 1956, p. 57.
12. Ministry of Finance, Government of India, *External Assistance, 1965-66*, Appendix II, pp. 168-71.
13. S. Dutt, *With Nehru in the Foreign Office*, p. 239.
14. 21 December 1955. J.L. Nehru, *Letters to Chief Ministers*, vol. 4, p. 324.
15. P.C. Mahalanobis, *The Approach of Operational Research to Planning in India*, p. 110.
16. Planning Commission, *Second Five-Year Plan*, pp. 26-7 and 40.
17. Ibid., pp. 51-4.
18. *Hindu*, 14 February 1956.
19. *Hindustan Times*, 16 April 1956.
20. 14 October 1956. J.L. Nehru, *Letters to Chief Ministers*, vol. 4, p. 457.
21. *Hindu*, 12 October 1956. It was obviously with the objective of reassuring foreign investors that the government, during the nationalization of the Kolar gold fields in the state of Mysore at the end of 1956, had granted a generous compensation to the British company which operated them.
22. 'A Feasible Program of US Economic Assistance for India', paper prepared

by the American Embassy in India, 13 March 1956. *FRUS, 1955-1957*, vol. 8, pp. 314-15.
23. Summary minutes of a meeting of the ad hoc committee on Ambassador Cooper's India aid proposals, Department of State, 3 May 1956. Ibid., pp. 317-18.
24. The law, as voted by Congress, had, among its objectives, to promote the economic stability of American agriculture and the national welfare, to make maximum efficient use of surplus agricultural commodities in furtherance of the foreign policy of the United States, to use foreign currencies which accrue to the United States under this Act to expand international trade, to encourage economic development, to purchase strategic materials, to pay United States obligations abroad, to promote collective strength, and to foster in other ways the foreign policy of the United States. 'Agricultural Trade Development and Assistance Act of 1954, as amended in 1955: Public Law 480 (83rd Congress 2nd session)' in: Department of State, *American Foreign Policy, Basic Documents, 1950-1955*, vol. II, parts X-XX, op. cit., pp. 2941-7.
25. Briefing paper prepared in the Office of South Asian Affairs, 19 January 1955. *FRUS, 1955-1957*, vol. 8, p. 276.
26. Planning Commission, *Second Five-Year Plan*, p. 52.
27. Of the total tonnage of the PL-480 commodities 50 per cent were to be transported in US vessels. The freight cost in respect of the tonnage transported in US vessels was initially paid for in rupees at international freight rates. From June 1965, India was to settle this payment in dollars.
28. Ministry of Finance, Government of India, *External Assistance, 1965-66*, p. 93. The Cooley amendment, when voted, mandated that up to 25 per cent of counterpart funds could be made available to American companies operating overseas. Soon after, the Industrial Credit and Investment Corporation of India was set up to channel loans—using some of the counterpart funds—to private industries.
29. The postponement of the visit was godsent for Dulles who was apprehensive that the inclusion of Krishna Menon—the *bête noire* of the Americans who accused him of being pro-communist—in Nehru's party would 'louse it up terribly'. Memorandum of a telephonic conversation, 14 June 1956 (Eisenhower Library, Dulles Papers, White House Telephone Conversations). *FRUS, 1955-1957*, vol. 8, p. 319. Gromyko, who considered Krishna Menon as 'personally friendly toward the Soviet Union', also commented that 'he vehemently rejected the idea that the USA should not be thought of as a colonial power' with their unashamed exploitation of backward countries. Andrei A. Gromyko, *Memories*, London: Hutchinson, 1989, p. 243.
30. Telegram to Ali Yavar Jung, Ambassador to Cairo, 27 July 1956. S. Gopal, *Jawaharlal Nehru: A Biography*, vol. 2, p. 277.
31. *Eastern Economist*, 9 November 1956, pp. 698-9.
32. *Hindu*, 1 December 1956.
33. J.L. Nehru, *India's Foreign Policy*, pp. 171-2.

34. Telegram from the Embassy in India (Bartlett, US Commercial Counsellor) to the Department of State, 7 December 1957. *FRUS, 1955-1957*, vol. 8, pp. 320-21.
35. Ibid., p. 325.
36. Operations Coordinating Board Report, Department of State, 3 July 1957. Ibid., p. 355.

CHAPTER 11

The Road to Washington

NEHRU AND EISENHOWER met in an atmosphere which allowed them to better appreciate each other's outlook despite the persistence of political disagreements between their countries. This augured well for Indo-American relations which showed promise of being less strained during Eisenhower's second term. From this point of view, Nehru's current visit to the United States was more beneficial than his earlier visit in the autumn of 1949 whose results had not matched expectations. It is true also that, meanwhile, the illusions that each might have entertained about the political options of the other had faded away. On the matter of aid, Eisenhower questioned Nehru about the Second Five Year Plan and promised that the United States would lend its support. However, no commitment was made, leaving the Indians in a state of uncertainty at a time when the financial situation was worsening.[1]

At the end of 1956, India's foreign exchange reserves had fallen to an alarmingly low level. Six months after the beginning of the Second Five Year Plan, three-fourths of the Rs. 2 billion of sterling balance which the government intended to use for financing a part of the foreign exchange deficit anticipated during the Second Plan, had already been drawn.[2] In end November 1956, T.T. Krishnamachari while alluding to the rapidly decreasing foreign exchange reserves, warned that 'it is obvious that this rate of drawal cannot be sustained for any length of time . . . it would be necessary not only to economize on imports and to increase our exports, but also, in addition, to take active steps to secure the necessary quantum of supplementary resources from abroad.'[3]

It became a matter of urgent necessity to mobilize foreign aid. B.K. Nehru visited several European capitals at the end of 1956 to ascertain the possibility of obtaining some credits. His efforts were not very conclusive at the time and this led the Indian government to count basically on the United States and the World Bank. T.T. Krishnamachari had already rejoiced at the fact that the IBRD had decided to take some interest in financing several development projects (second expansion programme of the IISCO, projects in the field of hydroelectricity and transportation) and had expressed the hope that the flow of funds from the World Bank would commence at the earliest practicable date in view of the very considerable drain on foreign exchange resources.[4]

The results of foreign trade over the first year of the plan (1956-7) strengthened doubts about the capacity of the country to implement all the development projects that the plan encompassed. Imports had increased by 43 per cent as compared to the preceding year, their value going up to Rs. 11.02 billion as against Rs. 7.83 billion anticipated. Even though exports had been higher than expected, they were far from enough to compensate for this increase. The main reasons put forward to explain this growing imbalance between imports and exports were the increase in the price of imports arising out of the existence of inflationary trends in most of the main exporting countries since 1955 and aggravated by the closure of the Suez Canal, the underestimation of the expenditure on armaments following American military aid to Pakistan, the imports of food grains by the state and of industrial capital goods by the private sector, and then the cumulative effects of the successive measures of imports liberalization since 1954. As a consequence, the deficit of Rs. 2.1 billion anticipated in the balance of trade for 1956-7 had actually more than doubled.

Such a result called for corrective measures. Hence, restrictions were imposed on imports. It was decided that public as well as private enterprises could henceforth obtain foreign exchange for the import of capital goods only in cases where this was covered by foreign aid or investments or took place on the basis of deferred payments. Special dispensations were, however, provided in three cases: when the projects were considered as high priority (steel, coal, transport, and energy); when the projects had reached a stage of implementation in which the major part of the foreign exchange expenses had already been incurred; and finally in the case of projects which, once completed, would pay off as external exchange earners or savers.[5] It was also decided to mobilize internal resources by raising new taxes and by effecting budget economies in public expenditure not related to the plan.

The United States was not altogether indifferent to the difficulties encountered by India. A report of the National Security Council, written in January 1957, reiterated the need to support the 'moderate, non-communist' government of Nehru despite the existence of an undeniable dilemma:

The Indian policy of non-alignment will on occasion bring India into opposition with US programs and activities, and a strong and increasingly successful India will add weight to this opposition. Nevertheless, over the longer run, the risks to US security from a weak and vulnerable India would be greater than the risks of a stable and influential India. . . . It would appear that Western sources of aid other than the United States will fall short of the mark. It is in our interest that India should substantially achieve the broad aims of the five year plan, in terms of increases in output and employment, and should continue to make an effective assault upon its development problems.[6]

A study on the foreign assistance programmes to South Asia, conducted at the request of the US Senate, had stressed the necessity of organizing economic and technical aid for the long haul. To cut down on costly and wasteful yearly negotiation on every project, it recommended that longer commitments to particular programmes and projects were desirable 'in order to fit our aid more effectively into the five-year development plans of the receiving countries, as well as to insure the most effective allocation of available funds'.[7] These statements of intent had yet to take concrete shape in proposals for aid that would eventually meet with the assent of Congress.

An interdepartmental working group entrusted with considering the timing, the form and the amount of economic aid to India, and representing the State Department, the Treasury, and the International Cooperation Association was set up in March 1957. By early May, the group had prepared a preliminary report on India's economic problems. After having taken into account the foreign assistance forecasted during the Second Plan (including the aid given by the United States under the MSP and that of the IBRD), the deficit that remained uncovered by foreign aid was estimated at $ 700 to $ 900 million (between Rs. 3.3 and Rs. 4.3 billion). This estimate was lowered to fall within a bracket of $ 300 to $ 500 million by the IBRD by taking into account only what were considered the most essential projects. There were differing views over the means to be deployed to help India. The State Department defended the necessity for additional assistance to India which the Treasury, hostile to any increase in the overall aid budget, accepted on condition that it be done by reallocation of funds originally intended for other areas. John Hollister, Director of the ICA, who had some reservations with regard to India, pleaded that a more detailed study be made of the suitability of the objectives of the Second Plan and that greater attention be paid to foreign private investments.[8]

In May 1957, B.K. Nehru, who had just been nominated Secretary to the government of India in the Department of Economic Affairs, went to the United States to assess the chances of obtaining additional aid. He drew before the Americans an alarming picture of the financial position of the country and stressed the urgency of supporting its development, even if only to enable the completion of those projects that were in the process of being implemented, failing which the government would have to face an uncontrollable political and social situation. For some time now, G.L. Mehta, India's Ambassador to Washington, D.C., and high-ranking officials of the State Department had established a dialogue on this matter. Mehta insisted that before any formal request was made by the Indian government, the ground should be carefully prepared and talks should be confidential in order to avoid the repetition of an embarrassing situation, similar to that arising from the grant of the wheat loan of 1951, which had been preceded by interminable and often distressing debates.[9]

At the end of April 1957, $ 650 million had already been drawn from the foreign exchange reserves, as compared to the $ 420 million that had been anticipated for the entire duration of the Second Plan. They would soon be reduced to their minimum legal level as provided for in the Reserve Bank of India (Amendment) Act, 1956 (the RBI was bound to hold at least Rs. 4 billion in foreign exchange and a minimum of Rs. 1.15 billion in gold). B.K. Nehru explained that crossing this level would amount to jeopardizing the stability of the rupee. In addition, India had already borrowed $ 127.5 million from the IMF. Admitting that it would be difficult to get any specific legislation in favour of India from the US Congress, he suggested the possibility of further PL-480 assistance and a larger share of the proposed Development Fund.[10] Finally, Nehru expressed the hope that the Eisenhower administration would intervene with the World Bank so that it would agree to give larger loans to India.[11]

B.K. Nehru was still in Washington when the new American

Ambassador to New Delhi, Ellsworth Bunker, went there to defend, as Chester Bowles, George Allen, and John S. Cooper had done earlier, the cause of aid to India at a time when this country was going through a bad phase. He held talks to this end with President Eisenhower, John F. Dulles, Eugene Black, officials of the State Department, and members of Congress. Bunker felt that he detected in his interlocutors a relative sensitivity to the difficulties that the Indian government was facing and a certain inclination to come to its aid, even among those members of Congress who were not known to have pro-India sympathies and in spite of the existence of a 'great resentment at Krishna Menon'. Nevertheless, Bunker did not entertain too many illusions that a special legislation in favour of India would be adopted during the current budget session. On his return to India, Bunker drafted a report about these consultations. In this, Eisenhower was quoted as arguing that the United States were 'better off with India following its policy of non-alignment than were she to join up actively on our side, with the consequent added burden on the American taxpayer and 2000 miles more of active frontier'.[12] Over and above the strictly material considerations, Eisenhower seemed more generally to have come to the conclusion that a non-aligned India could play a useful diplomatic role in promoting America's interests through its moderating influence in view of East-West frictions. During his meeting with Nehru in New Delhi in December 1959, the American President dissociated himself from those critics in the United States who deplored India's policy of 'neutrality', and he found no fault with India's desire to keep itself out of military alliances. He gave the assurance that in no event would such a policy come in the way of close ties between their two countries.[13]

During the summer of 1957, State Department officials continued to examine India's case. As had happened after the first general elections of 1952, the second general elections held in March 1957 supplied a further argument in favour of support for helping in remedying the financial situation by brandishing once again the bogey of a communist thrust. This was despite the fact that the Congress party had won by a comfortable majority, having procured 371 seats in the Lok Sabha out of a total of 494. The Socialists were, once again, divided. The Hindu nationalist right-wing parties, registered a slight increase in terms of the number of votes, but they did not succeed in gaining more seats than they had won during the earlier general elections, and they continued to remain relatively marginalized on the political scene. Similarly, the Communist Party of India, although remaining the foremost opposition party with 27 elected members, was not in a position to pose a serious threat to the party in power. Nevertheless, to the alarm of the State Department, the Communist Party had, with 9 per cent of the votes cast, almost doubled its score of 1952 and it was in a position to form the government in Kerala.[14] The State Department drew from this electoral victory in an economically depressed state, the lesson that this could well be repeated, if the Second Plan was to fail, in the 'strategically situated province of Bengal' where also the Communists had made advances. The State Department fretted that: 'This could trigger off a chain reaction which would lead to growing extremism and separatism in other parts of the country. The chances of chaos and a Communist advent to power in the sub-continent would be vastly increased.'[15]

Aware that the extent of reduction of development expenditures by the Indian government would depend for a large part on the American aid that it could hope to receive, several recommendations, largely akin to those expressed by B.K. Nehru, were put forward within the State Department. The first consisted in an increase of around 1 million tons in the deliveries of wheat under PL-480 sales, meeting thereby the expectations of the Indians. Despite a reasonably good harvest in 1956-7 which enabled the production of food grains to reach the 1953-4 record level, demand still exceeded supply with inflationary consequences. While the agreement of 29 August 1956 provided for the delivery of agricultural surpluses for the coming three years, barely ten months after it had been signed, on 1 July 1957, almost half these surpluses had already been utilized by India and there was reason to believe that they would be totally exhausted in less than two years. Two other recommendations of the State Department concerned the grant of credits from the new Development Loan Fund as well as by the Export-Import Bank, an agency more accustomed to lending money to the private sector. There was talk also of supporting India's request for funds from the World Bank. Finally, preparatory studies would also be undertaken regarding a possible request to Congress for a special legislation to provide additional resources to India during its next session in January.[16]

As on each occasion when foreign aid became a pressing need, the debate was revived in India over the belief that the Second Plan was going to be the major casualty of New Delhi's non-alignment. For the *Economic Weekly*, the critical assessment of the government's foreign policy had no solid basis. As proof, it was mentioned that, with the exception of Britain, no other country had received as many credits as India from the IMF, or again that, among Asian countries, India had been the major beneficiary of World Bank loans. 'New Delhi's foreign policy of non-alignment and the Soviet aid in men, money and equipment have, in no way, affected Washington's aid policy to India', which could compare favourably with that conducted with any other Asian country.[17]

'Because of this foreign exchange difficulty we have been cutting our plans and projects down to the bone, and sometimes a bit of the bone is taken off too', Nehru noted in September 1957.[18] In mid-August, the Finance Minister had announced that the statutory minimum level of foreign exchange of Rs. 4 billion had to be relaxed. As the drain on foreign exchange reserves continued, the government in the end decided to prescribe a minimum reserve of gold and foreign securities of Rs. 2 billion (of which the minimum gold reserve remained at Rs. 1.15 billion) under the RBI (Amendment) Ordinance, 1957 issued on 31 October. The government also announced a new import policy for the coming six months aimed at economizing the foreign exchange reserves without compromising, as far as possible, industrial activity. India could dip into the reservoir of capital of the sterling area, but its needs exceeded not only its own resources (the sterling balances) but also the capacity of British credit. Moreover, London, still apparently rankling over the Indian affront in the Suez affair, showed little eagerness to give loans to India. The British authorities had paid little heed to Nehru when two months earlier, in July, he had passed through London for the Commonwealth Prime Ministers Conference and expressed on this occasion India's desire to obtain credits from Great Britain to the tune of £ 200 million to help it tide over the foreign exchange difficulties in the next year or two.[19] The British Treasury, on its part, did not view favourably this chasm carved into the flanks of the gold and dollars reserves of the sterling area when it already had great difficulty in balancing the accounts in these reserves.

On 13 September, the Minister of Planning, Gulzarilal Nanda, declared in the Lok Sabha that the balance of payments deficit during the plan could be expected to be of the order not of Rs. 11 billion but of Rs. 16 billion. He announced that after taking into account the external assistance already committed, the borrowings from the IMF, and the drawings from the sterling balances which were already much higher than anticipated and which would have to be drawn further, the country might yet have to find resources of the order of Rs. 7 billion (nearly $ 1.5 billion). This was the minimum amount required for implementing the high-priority iron and steel, mining, transport, and ancillary power projects, which involved more than two-thirds of the foreign exchange expenditure contemplated in the plan.[20] The planners, the government, and the country were getting ready to resolve the dilemma between 'need' and 'reluctance' in their approach to foreign aid.[21]

Ironically, T.T. Krishnamachari was the representative of this commanding evolution in policy which dictated that need prevail over reluctance. It was he who had declared in December 1955:

> Personally I am very much against going and asking for foreign aid. In one sense I suppose it is a projection of one's individual. I hate to beg, though I am a born Brahmin and mendicant. I refuse to permit any of my colleagues to go and beg and say 'We wish to go through this plan, and therefore, will you help us?'. We know that we won't ask for aid. For, naturally, a man who gives us aid lays down his terms. . . . The fight that we had to put up for this attainment of liberty is still fresh in our mind and we shall not barter an inch of that liberty—not for a mess-of-pottage. Those of my colleagues who feel that foreign capital is necessary—indeed it is inescapable if we have to go through this plan—I beseech them not to go with the begging bowl.[22]

On 17 September, the Finance Minister left Delhi for a visit of more than two weeks to the United States to participate in the annual meetings of the IMF and the World Bank and, above all, to meet high-ranking government officials, politicians, bankers and industrialists. T.T. Krishnamachari also intended to visit Canada for the Commonwealth Finance Ministers Conference and on his return to stop over in Great Britain and in the Federal Republic of Germany. Almost at the same time, the ICA reiterated that the only aid acceptable in the state sector would be for railways, road and port infrastructure, irrigation, and power. American aid would not be given to finance any state-owned industrial or mining enterprises but only for fostering the private sector. This policy was to govern all government aid agencies so that US money would not be used to strengthen socialism. For New Delhi, this statement merely signified the pursuit of the present policy for, if supplies of steel for industrial purposes were excluded, American aid had been going essentially to the aforementioned sectors, apart from the community development projects, public health schemes, or technical assistance. It was, nevertheless, necessary to conclude that numerous industrial development projects in the public sector would come under the category declared taboo.[23]

While it was clear that the reluctance to ask for foreign aid had to be set aside in the face of economic contingencies, Nehru did not intend to let it have the slightest effect on his foreign policy, thus disappointing those who would have liked him to be a little more moderate in his speech on such matters so as to increase the chances of getting a large amount of aid from the United States. On 2 September, after Syria, supported by the Soviet Union, triggered a new crisis in the Middle East where the two superpowers were competing for influence, Nehru renewed his criticism of the Western powers' policy of military alliances to prevent Soviet interference for having *a contrario* exacerbated the tensions between the blocs in the region. A week later, he declared in the Rajya Sabha—and this was something that Washington was not easily willing to accept—that no durable settlement would see the light of day in West Asia if the Soviet Union was kept out of the picture, just as a solution to the problems in East Asia could only be found after the official recognition of China.[24]

T.T. Krishnamachari reminded his American interlocutors that the level of aid that India had been used to receiving till then would not be sufficient to run the economy at full capacity. It was imperative to find another $ 1.4 billion, without which the government might have to cut by 40 to 50 per cent imports of raw materials which, he stressed, knowing that this argument was weighty, would cause the private sector to suffer after being already affected by a reduction in public expenditure for power projects. T.T. Krishnamachari indicated on 25 September 1957 during a meeting in the State Department that, if it had been said that hitherto India has never asked for aid from anyone [*sic*], 'now, I can make a formal request'. At which Dulles, probably savouring a moment contrasting with the usual Indian sense of self-importance, replied that this would be premature as long as the chances of getting the request favourably acted upon had not been clearly assessed.[25]

The Indian Finance Minister did not remain content with asking for public aid alone but also, to quote a British diplomat, went daringly far in his attempts to allay American suspicion about Indian economic policies. His observations or insinuations that India had no serious intention of nationalizing anything important, that the United States was more socialistic (in terms of publicly owned industrial capacity) than India and that Indian socialism relied on private enterprise, apart from startling many Americans, excited violent criticism of him from leftist factions in India.[26]

He gave reassurances over the opportunities offered to American private investors, in spite of the reluctance of the Indian private businessmen themselves to face foreign competition within India. An agreement had just been reached between the two countries, on 19 September, designed to encourage new investments by private American capital in business enterprises in India. It made provision for the US government to guarantee that Indian currency receipts from new or expanded private American investments in India could be converted into dollars. A delegation of Indian industrialists headed by G.D. Birla spent nearly six weeks in America at the same time to back up the request for aid by the Finance Minister in creating a favourable climate which could not only pave the way to a governmental loan from the US Congress but also promote ways and means to increase the foreign exchange resources in the private sector by opening up new markets for export products, by securing suppliers' credit from and by attracting foreign investments through joint participation in Indian projects.[27]

After the decision of the US Congress to restrict the credits allocated to the DLF for the first year of its existence to $ 300 million instead of the $ 500 million asked for by the Eisenhower administration, and to commit itself during the following fiscal year (1959) to authorizing $ 625 million instead of the $ 750 million desired, the impossibility of meeting India's needs without resorting to a special Congressional authorization made itself more and more clearly felt for, even by combining the mutual security assistance, the Export-Import Bank loans, the PL-480 programme and all other American resources, the total sum would not suffice to put the mind of the Indian government at ease over the chances of success of the Second Plan. The Director of the Office of South Asian Affairs issued a reminder that it was up to the free world to act to ensure that India's economic development should be at least comparable to that of China where, it was estimated, the Soviets had committed to investing something like the equivalent of $ 2 billion.[28]

In early November 1957, Dulles addressed a memorandum to Eisenhower citing the recommendations of the State Department on the aid to be given to India. It referred to a National Intelligence Estimate of 8 October which, examining the repercussions of a failure of the Second Plan on the Indian political scene, had concluded that such a failure:

> would hasten the disintegration of the Congress party and threaten the continuance of democratic government. There is now no other coherent opposition force except the Communists, and they would stand to make important political gains from the collapse of the Congress party. Success with the Plan would probably permit the Congress party to retain power in the 1962 elections and would provide the kind of environment in which a moderate conservative party could emerge when and if the present Congress party breaks up.[29]

The American Embassy in New Delhi, for its part, again demanded a large increase in aid, submitting at the same time some economic objectives to be achieved alongside, such as the conclusion of a treaty of friendship, commerce, and navigation which had been postponed many times since Independence, the signing of a double taxation agreement (which was done in November 1959) or again encouragement to be given to the Indian government to further favourable actions towards the private sector and foreign direct investment. There were some other recommendations which were more openly political in nature: thus, loans, financing projects which would benefit the Congress party wherever there was a communist presence, or a major programme in cooperation with the US foundations, the AFL-CIO, and private US firms, to help strengthen the non-communist labour movement in India by training Indian labour leaders in the United States and India and by familiarizing them with labour-management relations in the United States.[30]

The meeting to decide the measures to be taken following the aid proposals made by the different services of the State Department took place on 12 November 1957. In addition to President Eisenhower, those who participated were John F. Dulles, Vice President Richard Nixon, and officials of the State Department. The possibility of asking Congress to vote for a specific loan to India was ruled out, if only because of America's own financial difficulties and the fact that the US government had reached its debt ceiling. Further more, the Secretary of State explained that the chances of success were practically nil on account of India's behaviour being 'very offensive on the Communist issue, and because they have gone out of their way to insult us on many occasions'. He also thought that any special programme for an individual country, and particularly for India, might have a bad effect on the whole Congressional effort at a time when the government of Félix Gaillard in France was in deep trouble and would need substantial assistance. The alternative considered was to have the DLF finance projects to the order of $ 50 to $ 75 million per year—almost similar to the the amount received by India till then under the MSP—and to convince the Export-Import Bank to give loans of between $ 150 and $ 200 million. Finally, the Germans would be asked to examine the means of covering through loans India's trade deficit with the Federal Republic.[31] The Americans were increasingly insistent that other Western countries assume a larger share of the burden of aid to India. Some argued that German businessmen drew profits from purchases by India of capital goods financed through subsidies from American aid programmes, while at the same time the government in Bonn showed little eagerness to assist India. Probably no other country had a bigger stake in the soundness of the Indian economy than the United Kingdom; at the end of 1955, 82 per cent of the capital invested in India by overseas concerns was British and 22 per cent of India's total annual trade was conducted with the UK. India's ability to pay for these imports was a matter of great concern. Another concern was the need to ensure that shortage of foreign exchange did not lead to a diversion of its trade to the Eastern bloc countries under bilateral arrangements.[32]

The American government decided in favour of a moderate increase in aid to India, giving up, at least for the time being, the idea of advocating to Congress a substantial augmentation. The US Secretary of State expressed the view that the impact of a major aid to India on Turkey, Iran, and Pakistan should not be lost from sight. These countries might feel discriminated because of their unstinting support to America's foreign policy when India was criticizing it. Dulles, moreover, considered it necessary to assure Feroz Khan Noon, Foreign Minister of Pakistan, that the aid given to India would remain relatively modest. The Americans also argued that it was in the interests of both the US and Pakistan to ensure that India should turn as little as possible towards the Soviet Union for assistance.[33] In the event of any aid being given to India, Pakistan could not be left with the feeling that India got more out of its non-alignment and it would then be a good thing to explain to the leaders of the two countries that Congress would be more likely to react favourably to the intended aid proposals that there were improved prospects of an agreement to halt the arms race or to make progress on the Indus waters issue and the Kashmir problem.[34] On the latter point, the Indian response was invariably that the US had made the Kashmir issue harder to solve because of their military aid nurturing Pakistan's bellicosity.

In mid-January 1958, the American government announced an aid of $ 225 million to India. The sum of $ 150 million would come from the Export-Import Bank of which, for once, two-thirds would go to the public sector, and $ 75 million would come from the DLF. This was the first time that the two agencies were granting credits to India. This sum, as *Commerce* commented, was not very large when viewed against India's need of foreign exchange and the US capacity to help, but it was some $ 160 million more than the amount the US government had been sparing for India every year during the past five years under the Indo-American Technical Cooperation Programme.[35] B.K. Nehru, at the head of a delegation of Indian officials, went to Washington during the days that followed, to begin negotiations on the projects which could be financed from these loans. An agreement relating to the line of credits offered by the Export-Import Bank was signed on 12 June. Its object was the acquisition of American capital goods for irrigation programmes, development of transport and power projects in the public sector, on the one hand, and for mining and other industries in the private sector, on the other hand. A few days later, on 23 June, agreements were concluded for the utilization of the DLF loan repayable in rupees. They covered basically the development of rail and road transport.

The increasingly active pro-Indian lobby which was emerging within Congress found this financial effort still insufficient. Thus, John F. Kennedy, the Democrat senator from Massachusetts, a member of the Senate Foreign Relations Committee, supported by Republican senator and former Ambassador to India, John S. Cooper, put forward on 25 March 1958 a resolution in which the US Congress would solemnly assert that it was in the interest of the United States to join with other nations in providing support of the type, magnitude, and duration which was adequate to assist India to complete successfully its current development programme. Kennedy emphasized the fact that India, with its 400 million inhabitants, containing nearly 40 per cent of all the free people of the uncommitted world, i.e. more than the population of Africa and South America put together, presented the example of a decisive experience for strategic reasons and because, from Casablanca to the Celebes, all uncommitted nations were watching the progress made by India and comparing it with that of China. The Russians were attempting to repeat their hold over China in other parts of Asia and Africa and, for the success of their enterprise, were counting on India's disappointment, on the inadequacy of Western assistance, on the failings of the democratic method of planning, and on the weakness of a free economy.[36] Most observers then acknowledged that the economic performances of the communist regime in China were higher than those achieved by India (this was before China suffered the reversals caused by the 'Great Leap Forward' of 1959-60). The communist model could appear all the more attractive in Third World countries that the USSR could claim, with the launching of the first Sputnik into space on 4 October 1957, that it had an edge over the United States in the scientific field.

Kennedy, moreover, warned against an aid which would be subject to political conditions that the recipient countries found difficult to accept: 'Our friendships should not be equated with military alliances or "voting the Western ticket." To do so only drives these countries closer to totalitarianism or polarizes the world in such a way as to increase rather than diminish the chances for local war.'[37] The action undertaken jointly with John S. Cooper was not entirely fruitless as the Kennedy-Cooper resolution was adopted by the Senate, which was something relatively unexpected and which would have been inconceivable a year earlier. However, it was finally rejected at a joint session of the Congress on 17 June 1958 on the plea, also advanced by the State Department, that it was not desirable to single out any one country in matters concerning the legislation on foreign aid.

In April 1958, an article appeared in *Foreign Affairs*, written by the American economists, Max F. Millikan of the Massachusetts Institute of Technology and Walt W. Rostow; the latter was known for his theory on the stages of economic growth and was later special advisor to the White House from 1961 to 1968. These authors developed the thesis that the amounts of foreign capital being productively absorbed in underdeveloped countries were initially limited by shortage of skills, administrative capability, infrastructure, or the absence of a growth-oriented political leadership. Technical assistance and a modest aid should suffice for a few years while waiting for the country to be technically and politically ready for the take-off leading to a self-sustaining growth process. The authors considered that India had already entered this critical turning point. For a decade or so, during the take-off phase, requirements for foreign capital would be at a maximum before the country's own rising income would provide the resources which could be ploughed back into investment to stabilize growth. Once the take-off has occurred, the country can rely on external capital from private or other orthodox sources. In the meanwhile and in addition to the immediate aid for the Second Plan, US loans on something like the order of $ 500 million per year would be necessary for the duration of the next five year plan and perhaps for some time thereafter. If foreign capital in adequate amounts was not forthcoming, 'not only will Indian development be threatened, but also a chance will have been missed for a practical demonstration of the complementarity of public and private activities which would be enormously persuasive in other underdeveloped countries with socialist preconceptions'.[38]

A debate then took place among economists in the United States regarding the relevance and the nature of aid to India. Some economists saw in India's mixed economy an alternative to the Chinese model of development for Asia, whereas the liberal thinkers, hostile to any form of interventionism, postulated that the growth of the relative share of the state in the economy was a near inevitable consequence of foreign aid. Milton Friedman described the American aid programme as being baneful as it would contribute towards eventually strengthening the public sector through unviable 'monument building', and would reduce the pressure on the government to maintain an environment favourable to private enterprise. Foreign aid would only speed the communization of the underdeveloped world since, he added, 'democracy and freedom have never been attained or maintained except in communities in which the bulk of economic activity is organized through private enterprise'. In response to Friedman's thesis, Charles Wolf argued that the private sector would be the first to fall victim to a halt in aid, for two reasons. The first was that 'the *étatisme* which understandably worries Friedman would very likely be greatly increased in a country like India, if foreign economic aid were eliminated or sharply reduced, by drastic efforts to capture private savings for public investment projects'. A second reason arose out the observation that public projects provided benefits also to the private sector by widening the market for its output and by improving the supply of inputs which are complementary to private enterprise (irrigation, river-valley developments, etc.). P.T. Bauer, the British economist of Hungarian origin, was closer in his approach to Friedman, but he did not adopt as extreme a position; Bauer suggested a modest programme differing 'from the recent and current proposals for the underpinning of Indian economic planning directed specifically towards the establishment of a socialist economy in India'.[39]

The foreign exchange crisis led the Planning Commission to re-examine some of the objectives of the plan in a study published in May 1958. The amount of public expenditures remained fixed at Rs. 48 billion despite the upward revision of the cost estimates (Rs. 54 billion), calling therefore for a reallocation of outlays which benefited mainly industry and mining, even though these were sectors in which American aid or aid from the World Bank could hardly be counted upon. A total outlay of Rs. 45 billion would be committed towards programmes directly related to increase agricultural production, 'core' projects, and those projects which had reached an advanced stage of execution. For the remaining Rs. 3 billion, projects could be undertaken only to the extent to which additional resources became available.[40]

It was acknowledged that not only had the amount of foreign exchange required for the implementation of the new development projects been underestimated, but this was also true for the value of the imports of raw materials and of semi-manufactured products required for the working of the recently created industrial units, resulting in a heavier deficit than anticipated in the trade balance. It rose for 1957-8 to Rs. 5.64 billion, almost double the figure advanced in the Second Plan (Rs. 3.03 billion). As compared to the previous year, imports had grown twice as faster as exports. During the first two years of the plan, the foreign exchange reserves held by the RBI had fallen from Rs. 7.46 billion on 31 March 1956 to Rs. 2.67 billion on 1 April 1958.[41] It now became imperative to conserve and even to reconstitute these reserves, if only to prevent capital outflow or to meet the commitment of payment of interest and the repayment of the principal of the foreign loans which would become fairly heavy from 1960-1. The authorizations of external assistance during the first twenty-four months of the plan had risen to Rs. 5.65 billion, which was larger than during the entire duration of the First Five Year Plan.[42] In addition, a credit of Rs. 950 million ($ 200 million) had been utilized from the IMF. Future prospects seemed gloomy. The Planning Commission admitted that the short-fall in foreign exchange could not be considered as a short-term phenomenon arising from some temporary imbalance in the system but that it was directly related to the large and continuing needs of the developmental process itself. As there was not much to be hoped for out of receipts from exports, at least in the near future, it was indispensable to re-impose strict regulations on imports together with a suitable phasing of the development programmes themselves, not only during the Second Plan but even beyond that period.[43]

Indian policy makers again set out to Western Capitals. With the objective of facilitating exchange of information on the economic situation in India and to speed up negotiations with international institutions and foreign countries willing to give loans, the Indian government decided also to strengthen its economic representation in the United States and in Great Britain. It appointed a Commissioner for Economic Affairs in Washington, entrusting the responsibility to B.K. Nehru, a man whose familiarity with international financial affairs dated back to the sterling balances negotiations and his appointment as India Director of the World Bank and financial adviser at the Indian Embassy in Washington in end 1949. He did not fail to issue a reminder that 'India constituted in population 40 per cent of the underdeveloped world and, from the point of view of influence, 60 per cent'.[44] B.K. Nehru was in Washington when discussions took place for the first time, from 25 to 27 August, between representatives of the Federal Republic of Germany, the United Kingdom, Japan, Canada, and the United States, and officials of the IBRD and the IMF to examine ways for joining together to come to India's help. The World Bank consortium renamed itself the 'Aid to India Club' and was an American device to get other Western countries to bear more of the aid burden. The new aid consortium assessed the aid required to implement the Second Five Year Plan at $ 940 million; it promised, during this first meeting, to offer an initial contribution of $ 350 million, which would enable India to pay its outstanding bills for the coming six months. The delegates of these countries also promised moreover to meet every year to examine the additional aid they could furnish till the end of the plan.[45] This decision worked towards increasing India's creditworthiness and taking the drama out of the forthcoming visit to the United States of the new Finance Minister, Morarji Desai, to discuss India's financial problems.

The American contribution to this joint initiative for aid took on the form of a fresh loan coming under the DLF. Regarding the wheat loan of 1951, the US government administration deferred the repayment of the 18 semi-annual installments of interest and principal due from December 1958 to mid-1967 (around $ 62 million). It resulted from this deferment that the terminal date of repayments was postponed from June 1986 to June 1995 without any additional interest. Finally, a third agreement under the PL-480, that of an amount of $ 239 million, was signed on 26 September 1958. This covered the delivery of maize, sorghum, and, above all, 2.8 million tons of wheat. A second agreement for the supply of the same food grains had been concluded three months earlier, on 23 June, for an amount of $ 57 million. The Indian government sought this type of agreement involving a foreign exchange expense confined to half the cost of the freight charges for transporting these food grains from the United States. This was all the more desirable as the production of food grains had fallen by 10 per cent in 1957-8. The food situation was grave enough to become a cause of anxiety for Nehru who noted:

> It is perfectly clear that unless we produce enough food to enable us to put an end to all food imports, we shall not be able to produce a worthwhile third five year plan. Our whole future thus resolves round this question of food production and our filling the gap before the second five year plan comes to an end.[46]

It was at the end of 1958, when the Planning Commission was attempting to save what could still be salvaged of the original plan (a document of the Finance Ministry entitled 'Plan Resources and Outlay: A Review' then considered the possibility of having to restrict the public expenditure to Rs. 42 or 43 billion) that the first signs of an improvement in the financial situation began to be discerned. There was a promising harvest, industry began to pick up, the measures taken to mobilize internal resources were beginning to bear fruit, inflation was declining as was the balance of payments deficit, thanks partly to the drastic cut in import allocations decided in the spring of 1958. At the same time, the disbursement of new credits started gathering momentum. There was a clear slowdown in the fall of the foreign exchange reserves. The worst of the crisis was over. The economic results at the end of the third year of the plan in end March 1959 confirmed this improvement. The national income, after having declined in 1957-8 for the first time since the advent of planning, took an upward turn and exceeded the 1956-7 level. Although exports, affected by the economic recession in the United States, had been on the decline, the deficit in the trade balance was reduced by 20 per cent on account of the notable reduction in imports. A record level of 77 million tons had been achieved in the production of food grains during 1958-9. For the first three years of the plan, the aid acquired rose to Rs. 9.62 billion rupees, and to Rs. 11.6 billion if the aid that had remained unutilized during the First Plan was also added, which already came to much more than the Rs. 8 billion provided for in the text of the Second Plan.[47]

Some months earlier, on 6 October 1958, while inaugurating in New Delhi a joint session of the World Bank and the IMF, being held for the first time in a Third World country, Nehru expressed his disagreement with the idea that a bipolar world resulted from the East-West confrontation, preferring instead a North-South divide. 'I think the major division of the world today and the real division is the division of the industrialized and developed communities and the undeveloped communities,' he said. He further elaborated:

> When you take some Communist state like the Soviet Union, which has become an industrialized state, or the many non-Communist states which are highly industrialized, though they may differ in their politics or economic theories, in the final analysis they worship the same gods. They worship the god of industrialization, the god of the machine, the god of higher production through utilization of nature's power resources to the greatest advantage. How to do it, they may differ. But they form more or less the same part while the undeveloped countries struggle for a bare subsistence.[48]

As proof of the growing interest in the United States in India's problem of underdevelopment, a conference on Indo-American relations was organized on 4 and 5 May 1959 in Washington by the Committee for International Economic Growth, a private body entrusted with exploring the means of adapting US external economic policy to the global evolution. It was presided over by Eric Johnston who had played a significant role in the creation of the DLF in 1957. The conference brought together 88 Americans and Indians belonging to political, business, and academic circles. Among the American participants were Richard Nixon and J.F. Kennedy, the two presidential aspirants, Chester Bowles, Hubert Humphrey, Averell Harriman, and M.F. Millikan. On the Indian side, were B.K. Nehru, M.C. Chagla, the recently appointed Indian Ambassador, Asoka Mehta, the parliamentary leader of the Praja Socialist Party, H.V.R. Iyengar, the governor of the RBI, and I.G. Patel, the alternate executive director of the IMF. The American speakers made conventional references to the importance of private capital, both national and foreign, in the development process, and the Indians made the no less hackneyed efforts to deny any cold-shouldering of the private sector. Nevertheless, the imperative necessity of helping India was more clearly evident than in the past among the speakers, both among the members of Congress invited and among the government representatives, and notably on the part of Nixon known more till then in India for his defense of military aid to Pakistan in 1954 and his opposition to 'neutralism'.[49]

In February 1959, Kennedy and Cooper had sponsored in the Senate a new resolution saying that the DLF should be enabled to grant long-term loans unhampered by the hazards of annual appropriations and the American government should invite other democratic nations to join in a mission to consult with India on the detailed possibilities for joint action to assure not only the fulfilment of the Second Plan but also the effective design of the Third Plan. The resolution was adopted by the Senate on 10 September after having been amended at the request of the State Department to include all of South Asia. It was understood that the mission would be sponsored by the World Bank. Morarji Desai, who was passing through the United States in early October 1959, announced that the Indian government found it strange that a legislature of one country should decide on the sending of an international mission to another country, but was nevertheless ready to receive it.

The growing place taken by foreign aid in the economy generated more and more questions on the forms that it took. On the American side, Douglas Dillon, the US Under Secretary of State for Economic Affairs, expressed the desire that in future the United States 'identify [themselves] more directly with certain specific projects which will be known as the projects that the USA has financed . . . certainly the Soviets have operated that way and have gained a lot of propaganda advantage from doing it'.[50] Among the criticisms often heard in Congress, there were those obviously which advocated that a larger share of the DLF credits go to help private industry rather than back state socialism. This theme was reiterated by successive managing directors of the DLF during their visits to India and, as in the case of Vance Brand in January 1960, it gave rise to an exchange of bitter sweet comments with in the Indian government.[51]

A typical instance of the shape that this dispute took is seen in the negotiations relating to the construction of fertilizer factories. At the invitation of the Indian government, a Ford Foundation mission came to India in 1959 to study the agricultural sector. Among the recommendations made in the report on food production, emphasis was placed on the need to generate a much faster agricultural growth rate to achieve a target of 110 million tons of food grains to feed an estimated population of 480 million by 1966. Stress had notably been laid on the necessity of substantially increasing the availability of fertilizers. The planners did not remain indifferent to these recommendations. In accordance with the industrial policy resolution of 1956, the public sector would be primarily responsible for the production of fertilizers. The overall investment devoted to this effort was to be increased from Rs. 300 million in the Second Plan to Rs. 2.25 billion in the Third Plan, of which almost half was in foreign exchange. The overall fertilizer output was thus to be increased from 165,000 tons of nitrogenous and phosphatic fertilizers in 1960-1 to about one million tons in terms of nitrogen (730,000 in the public sector) and 400,000 tons in terms of phosphate by 1965-6.[52] But the Americans insisted that a large share in this programme to be given to the private sector. Following this, when the DLF authorities granted a loan of $ 30 million, on 29 December 1960, for the construction of a public sector plant at Trombay, it was conditional on New Delhi's readiness to clear the way for Indo-American collaboration in the private sector in setting up a number of fertilizer plants. It was even announced at the time that 'five sites have already been identified as suitable for private fertilizer plants and other sites are under consideration'. The Americans also insisted that the price policy be revised so as to ensure a fair profit return to the foreign private capital to be invested in fertilizer production.[53]

In India, the tardy utilization of a part of the highly coveted American aid, even taking into account the inevitable bureaucratic red tape, gave rise to much questioning. This was the case for the line of credit supplied by the Export-Import Bank. Only 23 of the $150 million provided for in the agreement concluded in June 1958 had been utilized by end of March 1960.[54] This response seemed less due to the fact that these loans were not repayable in rupees, as against the DLF credits, than to the overall higher prices of American capital equipment (the loans of this agency were tied to purchases in the aid-giving country). The utilization of the different loans of the DLF which could serve to cover purchases anywhere in the world was more rapid. Now, in October 1959, the American government took the decision to channel the aid given under the DLF towards acquisition of goods and services in the United States. This was a consequence of the growing deficit in the American balance of payments position, and a way also of making an increase in the aid budget more acceptable. Morarji Desai admitted that the order, so far had been placed often in countries other than the United States and he concluded from this that 'the new policy would mean that the effective aid received in the form of commodities will be less'.[55]

In view of the foreign exchange problem, the Indians were more and more inclined to look for aid from the West which would be tied less to projects than to the overall programme of development. As long as India availed of sufficient foreign exchange, it mattered relatively little that the loans were tied to the implementation of projects. But these reserves being now reduced to the minimum, it became more and more difficult to cover the expenditure directly linked to development but outside of projects, such as debt servicing and, above all, maintenance imports, i.e. imports of raw material, spare parts, fertilizers, oil, manufactured goods, etc.

When President Eisenhower came on an official visit to New Delhi from 9 to 14 December 1959, the Indian leaders had two things in mind: the necessity of finding resources for the Third Five Year Plan and the emergence of a Chinese threat on the northern border. The deterioration in the relations between India and China since the start of the year ensured a warm welcome to Eisenhower from the Indians, surpassing even the reception given to Khrushchev and Bulganin in November 1955. The correspondence between the Indian and Chinese authorities concerning the border incidents which had started less than three months after the signature of the Sino-Indian agreement on Tibet and which had become, over the years, more and more frequent, had recently been made public. The Chinese had till then evaded the border issue—Nehru had not been very inquisitive as well—and declared that not much importance should be given to the existence of Chinese maps (while giving as an argument that these were reproductions of maps drawn under the former regime) in which large border territories which India claimed were shown as forming an integral part of China. The Chinese Communist Party officially recognized for the first time that a dispute existed over the demarcation of the border when Zhou Enlai, in January 1959, wrote to Nehru to inform him that in Beijing's view the Sino-Indian border had never been officially demarcated and he denied the validity of the treaties referred to by India. The Tibetan uprising and the flight of the Dalai Lama to India shortly afterwards, in March 1959, had also contributed to the worsening of the relations between New Delhi and Beijing. These developments did not displease the American government, one of whose representatives admitted that 'from the standpoint of the United States, it is a hopeful sign that the Indian government is becoming somewhat alarmed over Red China operations'.[56]

When the border incidents, coming soon after the crushing of the Tibetan uprising, were revealed in Parliament in September 1959, this had a very dampening effect on politicians, on the press, and on Indian public opinion. The '*Hindi Chini Bhai Bhai*' (Indians and Chinese are brothers) slogan, which had flourished after *Panchsheela* had been adopted by the two countries, had now seen its day. Nehru, who fostered the policy of friendship with China, became the target of severe criticism for having taken an attitude considered too conciliatory with regard to the PRC and with not having prepared the Indian army to face a Chinese threat. More and more, influential politicians within the government and the non-communist parties turned towards the United States to seek support, and they urged that any attitude be avoided which might cause the Americans irritation. An article in the *Economic Weekly*, reflecting the general mood of anxiety in the country, accused Nehru of having taken

> the fraternal goodwill of the Chinese too readily, and too literally, for granted; and that his anxiety to steer clear of both camps in the Cold War has now left us without the requisite military strength, or alliances, with which to face the Chinese with confidence. Indeed, it is even felt that if India were a member of some strong military alliance, its frontiers might never have been flouted by China in the first place.[57]

Some no longer hesitated to denounce the futility of non-alignment and saw in the Chinese attitude a display of the hegemonic trend inherent in communism, thus throwing discredit at the same time on the USSR.

New Delhi was grateful to Eisenhower whose moderating influence over the 'hawks' in the State Department was now appreciated. After the death of Dulles in May 1959, he had introduced a more constructive approach towards peaceful coexistence—he had met with Khrushchev in the United States in September—and he did not entertain any hostility towards India's foreign policy. The continuance of military aid to Pakistan, confirmed by another agreement signed on 5 March 1959, a few months after the military coup which had brought General Ayub Khan to power in Karachi, was relegated to the background among India's preoccupations, although Nehru expressed to Eisenhower the fear of 'a stab in the back' by Pakistan while India was facing a Chinese threat.[58] There were many who expected that Eisenhower would bring up the Sino-Indian dispute, which he did in a very cautious manner—while avoiding any commitment on the validity of India's claims—when he declared in Parliament that his country had always repudiated the settlement by force of international issues and quarrels.[59]

Nehru and Eisenhower also discussed the Second and Third Five Year Plans, and while they did not expressly tackle the question of economic aid, they did urge the necessity of making progress in development projects. Nehru even suggested that cooperation be developed in the field of atomic energy. The American Ambassador had already notified that any agreement in this regard would give a boost to the United States 'in the propaganda battle concerning US scientific capabilities in comparison to the Soviets' and would 'put US first in the field of Indian nuclear power as opposed to the Soviet influence in the rival field of public sector oil development'.[60] India's first major power reactor at Tarapur, north of Bombay, was acquired from the General Electric Company and financed with a $ 72 million loan following a cooperation agreement signed in August 1963; the United States promised, moreover, to supply the enriched uranium required for its functioning for thirty years.

Five months after his visit to India, on 4 May 1960, Eisenhower put his signature by the side of that of Sadashiv Kanoji Patil, India's Minister of Food and Agriculture, below the text of the fifth agreement concluded between the two countries for the sale of agricultural surpluses under Title I of PL-480.[61] This new agreement concerned the delivery of 16 million tons of wheat and 1 million tons of rice. Its value rose to $ 1.28 billion dollars (Rs. 6 billion). It was an unprecedented agreement from several points of view. It was the largest ever agreement signed under PL-480 since its creation in 1954, almost four times higher than any earlier agreement. It was also the first to extend over a period of four years and was aimed not only at offsetting the shortage of food grains, but above all at reconstituting substantial food reserves. By the side of the 3 million tons of wheat which had to be utilized annually to cover the shortage of food grains, 4 million tons of wheat and the entirety of the rice were meant to augment the stocks. This agreement was primarily a statement of failure indicating the inability of the country to achieve self-sufficiency. This had led the Indian government to turn once again to the United States in 1959 in the hope of obtaining the assurance of being able to import food grains on preferential conditions over a period of several years so as to build up reserves. India's request had greater chances of being heard as agricultural commodities continued to accumulate in American grain silos.

Although the decline in the foreign exchange reserves had distinctly slowed down (they had diminished by Rs. 160 million in 1959-60 as against a decline of Rs. 2.6 billion in 1957-8), it nevertheless continued to persist. India became more and more dependent on foreign aid and this fact was fully kept in mind in the draft of the Third Five Year Plan published in June 1960. The Planning Commission admitted that in the face of the uncertainties existing over the prospects of aid, it would be necessary for the country to resign itself to undertake foreign exchange expenditure only

> on the basis of external resources that are clearly in sight. The fact that the commencement and execution of projects both in the public and private sectors will depend upon the external assistance that is forthcoming highlights the need for keeping ready, well in advance, a sufficient number of projects that can be executed as soon as the necessary foreign exchange has been secured.[62]

It was precisely to secure aid for the Third Five Year Plan that Morarji Desai went once again to Washington and to London in the autumn of 1960. At a meeting of the National Press Club in the American capital on 27 September, he said that India would require $ 1 billion annually of external assistance during the coming decade before being able to develop satisfactorily on its own.[63] There was a feeling of relative optimism after the six-week visit to India in February-March 1960 of the three-men committee appointed by the World Bank—an outcome of the Kennedy-Cooper resolution—and headed by Oliver Franks, an Englishman. They gave general approval to the first outline of the Third Plan and recommended that the IBRD continue to assist India on a generous scale. Soon after, another World Bank mission reported that India demonstrated a capacity to make good use of foreign aid, while insisting that henceforth this aid should be extended in a form that did not add to the already heavy burden of debt repayment.

The Indians did not hesitate when required to use the threat of Soviet aid in order to obtain more assistance from the West. In September 1960, during a press conference in Paris, at the end of a meeting of the Aid to India Club during which the request for aid had only been partially met, B.K. Nehru declared that if the Western countries did not respond to India's need, it would have to turn to Moscow: 'We accept all aid that is offered to us, wherever it might come from. If the USSR were to offer to finance the whole of our development plan, it would be welcome.'[64] This was improbable for India's need greatly exceeded the amount of the loans that the Soviets were in a position to offer. However, such remarks were symptomatic of the development of Indo-Soviet economic cooperation and of the advantage that the Indians could draw from this in their negotiations with the West. The strengthening of bonds between Moscow and New Delhi also had a definite influence on Sino-Indian relations.

NOTES

1. Nehru's report to Cabinet on talks with Eisenhower, 29 December 1956. S. Gopal, *Jawaharlal Nehru: A Biography*, vol. 3, p. 41. Memorandum of a conversation, Department of State, 13 May 1957. *FRUS, 1955-1957*, vol. 8, p. 342.
2. *Commerce*, 10 November 1956, p. 882. Since 1 April 1956, the withdrawals of sterling balances had considerably increased, to rise to some £ 120 million at the end of October (as against £ 105 for the entire First Five Year Plan).
3. *Hindu*, 1 December 1956.
4. *Hindu*, 7 December 1956.
5. *Hindu*, 7 June 1957.
6. National Security Council report, 10 January 1957. *FRUS, 1955-1957*, vol. 8, pp. 35-6.
7. Regarding the allocation of US aid to India, it was recalled that between 1952 and 1956, the United States contributed $ 326 million in assistance to

India. Of this total, 42.9 per cent was for agriculture and mineral resources; 20.6 per cent to industry and mining; and 20 per cent for the development of transportation. The balance was applied to health and sanitation, community development, and education. *South Asia (Afghanistan, Pakistan, India and Ceylon): Report on United States Foreign Assistance Programs*, prepared by Lewis Webster Jones (President, Rutgers University) at the request of the Special Committee to Study the Foreign Aid Program, March 1957, Washington, D.C.: US Government Printing Office, pp. 1 and 30.

8. Letter from C. Herter, Under Secretary of State, to Clarence Randall, President of the Foreign Economic Policy Council, 2 March 1957. *FRUS, 1955-1957*, vol. 8, p. 343.
9. Memorandum of a conversation, Department of State, 13 May 1957. Ibid, p. 342.
10. A few months later, the US Congress passed a bill creating the Development Loan Fund entrusted with offering long-term loans to the private as well as the public sector, repayable in local currency or in dollars. The DLF remained, nevertheless, dependent for its resources on budgetary credits voted annually by Congress.
11. Memorandum of a conversation, Department of State, 31 May 1957. *FRUS, 1955-1957*, vol. 8, pp. 344-8.
12. Letter from the Ambassador to India to F.P. Bartlett, Director of the Office of South Asian Affairs, 27 June 1957. Ibid, p. 348.
13. Nehru's notes on talks with Eisenhower, 17 and 18 December 1959. S. Gopal, *Jawaharlal Nehru: A Biography*, vol. 3, p. 104.
14. 'This victory of the Communists within a democratic, constitutional framework gives them an important foothold from which to expand in India, and enhances their respectability and prestige as a successful, parliamentary political party which may have a far-reaching effect on their future capabilities.' Operations Coordinating Board report, 3 July 1957. *FRUS, 1955-1957*, vol. 8, p. 356. Following this victory of the Communists, the State Department asked its Ambassador to evaluate the importance of the state of Kerala with regard to American interests.
15. Memorandum from the Secretary of State to the President, 4 November 1957. Ibid, p. 394.
16. Letter from the Deputy Under Secretary of State for Economic Affairs (D. Dillon) to C. Randall, 15 July 1957. *FRUS 1955-1957*, vol. 8, pp. 360-1. See also 'Recommendations for United States action to assist India in realizing its economic development objectives', 18 September 1957. Ibid., pp. 385-6.
17. *Economic Weekly*, 6 July 1957, p. 788. When compiling the figures for economic and technical aid to the countries of South Asia under the MSP between 1951 and 1957, India appeared to be the country which had benefited the most from US aid, with a total of \$ 402 million, followed by Pakistan (\$ 260 million), the countries of Indochina (\$ 229 million), the Philippines (\$ 160 million), Thailand (\$ 138 million), then in decreasing

order, Indonesia, Burma, Afghanistan, Ceylon, and Nepal. Figures supplied by C. Wolf, *Foreign Aid—Theory and Practice in Southern Asia*, p. 403.
18. Nehru to Vijayalakshmi Pandit, 17 September 1957. S. Gopal, *Jawaharlal Nehru: A Biography*, vol. 3, p. 13.
19. *Hindu*, 6 July 1957.
20. *Hindu*, 14 September 1957.
21. R.K. Hazari and S.D. Mehta, *Public International Development Financing in India*, p. 48.
22. *Hindu*, 13 December 1955.
23. *Hindu*, 15 September 1957.
24. *Hindustan Times*, 3 and 10 September 1957.
25. Memorandum of a conversation, Department of State, 25 September 1957. *FRUS, 1955-1957*, vol. 8, pp. 374-6.
26. Acting United Kingdom High Commissioner in India (W.A.W. Clark) to Secretary of State for Commonwealth Relations, 27 February 1958. *PRO*, FO 371 135947.
27. *Report of the Indian Industrial Delegation to the FICCI. On the tour in the USA, Canada, the UK, France & West Germany, September-November 1957*, FICCI Library, New Delhi, pp. 5-13.
28. Memorandum from the Director of the Office of South Asian Affairs (F. Bartlett) to the Assistant Secretary of State for Near East, South Asian and African Affairs (W. Rountree), 30 September 1957. *FRUS, 1955-1957*, vol. 8, p. 380.
29. Memorandum from the Secretary of State to the President, 4 November 1957. Ibid., p. 394.
30. Study prepared in the Embassy in India, 8 November 1957. Ibid., pp. 400-1.
31. Memorandum of a conference with the President, 12 November 1957. Ibid., pp. 405-6 and memorandum of a conversation, Department of State, 24 December 1957, p. 408. There was a question then of converting India's wheat loan repayments from a dollar to a rupee basis.
32. Dispatch from the British High Commissioner, Malcolm MacDonald, to the Secretary of State for Commonwealth Relations, 5 July 1958. *PRO*, FO 371 135949.
33. Memorandum of a conversation by Bartlett, 23 November 1957, Department of State, Secretary's memoranda of conversation, *FRUS, 1955-1957*, vol. 8, p. 405. The United States expected from Pakistan, as an important Muslim country, that it would exert a moderating influence on the exacerbated nationalism and the anti-West attitude of some Arab states. Considering the contribution of Pakistan during the Suez crisis as a positive one, they wanted this country, which supported the 'Eisenhower doctrine' of January 1957, to play an active role in the affairs of West Asia.
34. Memorandum from the Deputy Under Secretaries of State for Political Affairs (Murphy) and Economic Affairs (Dillon) and of the Assistant Secretary of State for Near Eastern, South Asian, and African Affairs (Rountree) to the Secretary of State, 16 October 1957. Ibid., p. 392. Amjad

Ali, the Pakistani Finance Minister, earlier Ambassador to the United States, had notified that he desired that the United States use its aid to India as a tool to bring about a resolution to these problems. Memorandum of conversation by Smith, Department of State, NEA/SOA/E files. Ibid., p. 392. See also memorandum of W. Rountree to the Secretary of State, 12 November 1957. Ibid., p. 402. An agreement was signed on 19 September 1960 by Nehru and Ayub Khan allocating the waters of the three eastern rivers (Ravi, Beas, Sutlej) to India and those of the western rivers (Indus, Jhelum, Chenab) to Pakistan. The mediation of the World Bank and the promise of credits for exploiting hydroelectric resources had played a crucial role in the signing of the agreement.

35. *Commerce*, 25 January 1958, p. 113.
36. J.F. Kennedy, 'Le Choix de l'Asie', *Le Monde Diplomatique*, May 1958, pp. 1 and 3. Eisenhower doubted the capacity of India to play the role of a counterweight *vis-à-vis* China, adding that 'if the US were actually to try to make India a counterweight to Communist China, the task would be so great that we would probably bankrupt ourselves in the process'. Memorandum of discussion at the 408th meeting of the National Security Council, 28 May 1959. *FRUS, 1958-1960*, vol. 15, p. 9.
37. John F. Kennedy, *The Strategy of Peace*, New York: Harper & Brothers, 1960, p. 157.
38. M. F. Millikan and W. W. Rostow, 'Foreign Aid: The Next Phase', *Foreign Affairs*, vol. 3, no. 3, April 1958, p. 433.
39. M. Friedman, 'Foreign Economic Aid : Means and Objectives', *Yale Review*, vol. 47, 1958, pp. 24-38. Quoted by J. Bhagwati and R.S. Eckhaus, *Foreign Aid (Selected Readings)*, Harmondsworth: Penguin, 1970, pp. 64-73. C. Wolf, 'Economic Aid Reconsidered', in G. Ranis (ed.), *The United States and the Developing Economies*, pp. 41-2. P.T. Bauer, *Indian Economic Policy and Development*, London: George Allen and Unwin, 1961, p. 136.
40. Planning Commission, *Appraisal and Prospects of the Second Five-Year Plan*, May 1958, pp. 5 and 23.
41. Planning Commission, *Second Five-Year Plan—Progress Report, 1959-1960*, March 1962, p. 3.
42. Ministry of Finance, Government of India, *External Assistance 1958*, p. 3.
43. Planning Commission, *Appraisal and Prospects of the Second Five-Year Plan*, p. 15.
44. Memorandum of a conversation, Department of State, 16 July 1958. *FRUS, 1958-1960*, vol. 15, p. 442.
45. *Hindu*, 31 August 1958.
46. 26 March 1958. J.L. Nehru, *Letters to Chief Ministers*, vol. 5, p. 29.
47. Planning Commission, *Second Five-Year Plan—Progress Report, 1958-59*, April 1960, pp. 1 and 24-5.
48. *Hindu*, 7 October 1958.
49. FICCI, *Report of the Goodwill Trade Mission, March-May 1959*, FICCI Library, Delhi, p. 28. S.S. Harrison, *India and the United States*, p. 145.
50. *Hindu*, 22 February 1959.

51. *Times of India*, 29 February 1960.
52. Planning Commission, *Third Five-Year Plan*, pp. 41 and 478-9.
53. *Economic Weekly*, 7 January 1961, p. 7. The Americans had to wait till 1965 before they got a chance to invest in this sector.
54. Planning Commission, *Second Five-Year Plan—Progress Report, 1959-60*, pp. 34-5.
55. 25 November 1959. *Rajya Sabha Debates*, vol. 27, no. 3, col. 304.
56. Statement by H. Alexander Smith, consultant to the Secretary of State, in the hearings before the Senate Committee on Foreign Relations on the Mutual Security Act of 1959, 20 May 1959. Quoted by R.K. Jain (ed.), *US-South Asian Relations*, vol. 1, p. 236.
57. *Economic Weekly*, 14 November 1959, p. 158.
58. Memorandum of a conversation, 10 December 1959. *FRUS, 1958-1960*, vol. 15, p. 523.
59. *Times of India*, 11 December 1959.
60. Telegram from E. Bunker to the Department of State, 23 April 1959. *FRUS, 1958-1960*, vol. 15, p. 490. An agreement had been signed in March 1956, by which the United States was to supply heavy water meant for the construction of a research reactor, known as CIRUS (Canadian Indian Reactor-United States). It was completed at Trombay in 1960 and was used to produce plutonium for the 'peaceful nuclear explosion' of 1974.
61. Most of the supplies of agricultural commodities came under Title I of PL-480. Title II enabled the US President to provide emergency assistance in meeting famine and other extraordinary relief requirements. Title III authorized the Commodity Credit Corporation to supply agricultural commodities to voluntary agencies for distribution abroad. It also provided for the possibility of barter agreements. Thus, in March 1959, an agreement was signed with India relating to the exchange of 450,000 tons of food grains against Indian manganese.
62. Planning Commission, *Third Five-Year Plan, A Draft Outline*, June 1960, p. 55.
63. *Asian Recorder*, vol. 6, no. 46, 12-18 November 1960, p. 3639.
64. *Le Monde*, 17 September 1960.

CHAPTER 12

The Consolidation of Bonds

THE SOVIET INTERVENTION in Hungary did not have any notable influence on the development of Indo-Soviet relations which remained cordial. It is true that some differences had emerged between the two countries, particularly when New Delhi expressed its concern over the abduction of Imre Nagy and when it co-sponsored a draft resolution urging the Hungarian government to accede to the UN Secretary General's request to permit observers to inquire into the allegations of forcible deportation of Hungarian nationals. Nehru even wrote to Bulganin to request that the Soviet Union accept this resolution, adopted on 21 November, and an invitation to Dag Hammarskjöld, the UN Secretary General, to visit Hungary. In response, the Soviets, through their Ambassador to India, gave Nehru to understand that their support on the question of Kashmir was not irrevocable.[1] This threat of blackmail was only a manifestation of temporary irritation. Moscow was more worried by the events in Hungary insofar as they had enhanced the prestige of the United States and raised Eisenhower's credibility as a defender of the rights of smaller nations against interference by larger powers.[2] Still, the Soviet leaders could take comfort in the fact that, while India remained critical of Soviet intervention in Hungary, it never displayed unfriendliness, and that it had refused to join in the Western resolutions at the UNO condemning the Soviet Union by name.

The expression of Soviet displeasure over India's position on the Hungarian crisis did not go beyond an abstention at the United Nations Security Council on 25 January after the Kashmir issue had again been brought up at the request of Pakistan. Even this vote may have reflected Moscow's wish not to distance itself from the Muslim countries, notably after the announcement on 5 January of the 'Eisenhower doctrine' proposing military and economic aid to interested West Asian countries. The USSR tried to put allay India's concerns when it used its veto power on 20 February against a resolution considering the demilitarization of Kashmir and the holding of a plebiscite in the disputed area with the help of UN forces. The Soviet delegation once again denounced the machinations of the West with a view to penetrating into a highly strategic region close to the Soviet republics of Central Asia. It also recalled that the elected Constituent Assembly of the state of Jammu and Kashmir had formally ratified, in February 1954, its accession to the Indian Union and that consequently, for the USSR, the Kashmir question had been settled by the Kashmiri people themselves.

The Soviets continued to praise the Indian government for its salutary role in international relations. For instance, on the occasion of the tenth anniversary of India's Independence, A. Diakov wrote an article entitled 'The Sixth Great Power', a title reflecting the intention of the Soviet Union to see India being admitted into the charmed circle of the world powers. The Soviet scholar stressed the economic progress achieved by India and praised Nehru's foreign policy for noteworthy its contribution to the promotion of peace and disarmament.[3] Convinced that it could take advantage of the opposing interests and policies of a non-aligned India which ran counter to those of the Western imperialist powers, the USSR sought the support of New Delhi in East-West disputes and championed the participation of India in international negotiations on problems relating to Asia and to disarmament. This was seen notably when West Asia faced another crisis after the dispatch of American troops to Lebanon and of British soldiers to Jordan in July 1958 following the bloody coup in Iraq which overthrew King Faisal and his pro-Western Prime Minister Nuri el-Said and brought General Kassem to power. On 19 July, Khrushchev invited not only Eisenhower, MacMillan, and de Gaulle to a summit conference to find a peaceful way out of the crisis in the Near and Middle East, but also Nehru. The latter gave his consent to the proposal, if the other leaders invited also favoured India's participation, but it was finally a meeting of the United Nations General Assembly which was called. Acknowledging the commitment of the Indian Prime Minister to the control and the destruction of nuclear arsenals, the Soviet Union supported, in June 1957, the participation of India in the disarmament commission which was to meet in London in August, but this was to no avail. A year later, and few months after Nehru had sent a message to the American and Soviet governments asking them to stop the nuclear arms race and testing, Khrushchev asked for the participation of India at the meeting of experts proposed by Eisenhower to call a halt to nuclear tests.

The Indian leaders were not insensitive to the Soviet action, which was in contrast to the lack of enthusiasm of the Western powers to see India intimately associated in the work of the Big Powers on important international issues. The chief of the Kremlin 'knows how to deal with us, neutral nations', Nehru once remarked, 'Khrushchev, by skillfulness or by conviction—but anyhow does it matter?—knows how to understand us, endeavour to respect us, manage to further the role that we have to play in the interest of mankind.' This attitude was not to be found among the Americans, who too often flaunted their scorn for the non-aligned countries.[4]

While the events in Hungary had no effect on the relations between India and the USSR, they nevertheless reinforced Nehru's aversion for the communist modes of operation. This perception was strengthened by the execution of Imre Nagy in June 1958 and the virulent and unexpected onslaught on Josip Broz Tito, who was castigated, among other things, for accepting US economic aid. Yugoslavia had to bear the postponement of the payment of Soviet loans promised in 1956 to Belgrade for the execution of its five year plan.[5] After the Hungarian crisis, these were new manifestations of a return to ideological sectarianism and an undermining of the principle of non-interference in the internal affairs of another country. After the decisions of the 20th Congress of the CPSU, Nehru had hoped that these were things of the past. In an article that the Prime Minister wrote in 1958, he remarked: 'Communism has definitely allied itself to the approach of violence. Even if it does not indulge normally in physical violence, its language is of violence, its thought is violent and it does not seek to change by persuasion or peaceful democratic pressures, but by coercion and indeed by destruction and extermination.'[6] This analysis undoubtedly prejudiced his attitude towards the communist government of E.M.S. Namboodiripad in Kerala, even though he refused to adopt a militant position as did some other members of his government and some among the leadership of the Congress party who were impatient to see it falling. The local Congress party had contributed a great deal to the deterioration in the political and social climate in the months that followed the coming into power of the Communists.

This confrontation led in July 1959 to the dismissal by the central government of Chief Minister, E.M.S. Namboodiripad, and the imposition of President's rule while awaiting fresh elections which ultimately the Congress won.

From the establishment of the communist government in Kerala to its dismissal, the Soviets proved that they did not intend to sacrifice their friendly relations with New Delhi by displaying unstinting support for the leadership of Namboodiripad. Significantly, the Soviet press had talked of the general elections in 1957 in a clearly less partisan tone than they had adopted on the eve of the earlier general elections in 1952. Subsequently, Moscow refrained from publicly expressing dissatisfaction despite the fact that a first-time democratically-elected communist government, thus validating the strategy of a peaceful transition towards socialism advanced during the 20th Congress, had to face attempts at destabilization mounted by the dominant national party.[7] When the Chief Minister of Kerala went to Moscow for the 21st Congress of the CPSU in January 1959, as a member of the CPI's delegation, he confided before his departure that he hoped to meet Khrushchev to see if it was possible that the aid being increasingly given to India could also benefit the development of Kerala, and to explore also the possibilities of bartering some of Kerala's products for Russian capital goods.[8] The Soviet leaders were not unaware that matters of aid and foreign trade fell ultimately within the competence of the central government and that they could hardly promise anything without risking the possibility of coming into conflict with New Delhi. As they had no intention of doing this, they remained non-committed as far as aid was concerned. It was just observed that the Soviets were buying more than likely required quantities of coir and cashew nuts from Kerala.[9] Less than two months after the fall of the communist government, an agreement on a credit of 1.5 billion roubles was signed between India and the Soviet Union. Once the Congress party returned to power in Kerala in early 1960, in spite of an increase in the communist share of the popular vote, the Eisenhower administration, on its part, conveyed its readiness to support developmental projects and encourage US investment and trade exchanges that would directly benefit Kerala and, hopefully, keep the Communists at bay.[10]

Political rapprochement continued to go hand in hand with the development of economic relations. At the time when the Soviet troops were ruthlessly crushing the popular uprising in Budapest, the Indian Minister for Production, K.C. Reddy, was in Moscow where he was discussing the prospects of Soviet assistance. At the end of his visit, it was announced that the USSR had offered a credit of 500 million roubles (Rs. 600 million) which the Indian government had accepted.[11] Twelve months passed before the agreement was signed, on 9 November 1957, determining which industrial projects in the public sector were to be funded with this credit. The financial aid for the purchase of Soviet equipment and for technical assistance concerned a number of realizations: a heavy machine-building plant at Ranchi (Bihar), a coal-mining machinery plant and an opthalmic glass project at Durgapur (West Bengal), a coal-mining project at Korba (Madhya Pradesh), and a thermal power station at Neyveli (Tamil Nadu).

The Soviets argued that by helping in the construction of a state industry they were contributing towards foiling the plans of neo-colonialists, restricting the role of local private entrepreneurship, and even modifying favourably the power equations between the social classes by swelling the ranks of the proletariat. M. Rubinstein argued that some measures such as the adoption of the somewhat vague notion of a 'socialistic pattern of society' and of a new industrial policy resolution in April 1956, aimed only at the development of a state capitalism and did not, strictly speaking, have a socialist character, representing at best only a stage in the path of a peaceful transition towards socialism. Nevertheless, he was of the view that these measures played, in the present situation, a progressive role by reinforcing the independence of India and by weakening the positions of imperialism as a whole.[12] This analysis of the economic policy followed by the Indian government was presented by Mikoyan to the Chinese during the 8th Congress of the Chinese Communist Party in September 1956. He declared there that the Marxists could not but 'regard positively' the growth of state capitalism in the newly decolonized countries, representing a transitional phase which would spare them 'the torments of capitalism'.[13]

The commercial intercourse between the two countries had also expanded. On 16 November 1958, a second five-year trade agreement was signed. The Indian rupee continued to serve as the currency for all payments between the two countries. The major change, apart from the inclusion of the most-favoured nation clause, was the adoption of the principle of a balanced trade based on a system of clearing of accounts. All Indian imports of Soviet goods and services were paid for in rupees, deposited in an account in the RBI and then utilized by the Soviets for settling the dues for their commercial transactions with India. Thereafter, the balance in this account would theoretically be nil and the possible convertibility of any surplus into pounds at the request of the Soviets was at the same time given up. This agreement did not meet with the unanimous approval of all leaders in the ruling circles. The Finance Minister, Morarji Desai, and senior officials of the ministries of External Affairs and Commerce, as well as the governor of the RBI did not approve of an agreement which made it, in principle, imperative for India to export to the Soviet Union as much as it imported from this country. India thus ran the risk of having to give up earning foreign exchange by diverting towards the USSR goods which would otherwise have been exported towards nations with which it traded in dollars or in pounds sterling. But Nehru, convinced of the political necessity of consolidating relations with the Soviet Union, intervened personally to overcome hesitations based either on petty trade considerations or on the fear of seeing the rupee accounts of the State Bank of the USSR in India used to finance propaganda activities.[14] Since the earlier agreement, in December 1953, the volume of trade between the two countries had increased substantially, even if it did still remain modest as compared to the total volume of foreign trade. Indian imports from the USSR had jumped from 0.1 to 2.5 per cent of the total imports. Indian exports to the Soviet Union had, at the same time, gone up from 0.2 to 2.5 per cent of the total exports.[15]

During the speech that he gave on 27 January 1959 at the inauguration of the 21st Congress of the CPSU, Khrushchev once again attacked the imperialists for having converted their economic relations with underdeveloped countries into a means of blackmail and extortion. According to him, the USSR, for its part, could take pride in the fact that it imposed no political or military conditions. Despite this, the Soviets did not claim that they were being philanthropic, but asserted they were giving aid simply on a fair commercial basis so as to make it possible for Third World countries to set up their own industries.[16] The following month, Rajendra Prasad, the Indian President, inaugurated the Bhilai steelworks, and a Soviet delegation, then on a visit to India, handed over to Nehru a letter from Khrushchev in which he offered all-round cooperation, and more specifically financial and technical assistance for the development of the pharmaceutical industry and the construction of an oil refinery factory in Barauni (Bihar).[17] A loan agreement was concluded on 29 May 1959 for the manufacture of antibiotics at Rishikesh (Uttar Pradesh) and of synthetic drugs in Hyderabad (Andhra Pradesh), as well as for the setting up of a surgical instruments plant in Madras.

The negotiations which led to this latter loan agreement tended once more to prove, as had already happened with the bargaining for the construction of steel plants, that the Soviet offer of assistance had led Western companies to re-examine their initial hesitation in participating in the development of the public sector. The government, desirous of developing state participation in the drug industry which till then had been largely in the hands of foreign enterprises, asked the Soviets in November 1955 to make proposals in this field. The following year, the Soviets offered credit for an overall programme of development integrating several projects. The Minister for Commerce and Industry then showed little interest in this programme. The study team that he sent to Moscow recommended on its return that the pharmaceutical industry should remain in private hands and that the cooperation of Western countries be sought for this purpose. The Soviets did not give up and in view of their insistence, the Indian government authorized a second team of specialists to make new proposals for a programme less ambitious than the original one.[18]

The Western companies began to get alarmed at the perseverance of the Soviets. A typical example is the case of the American pharmaceutical giant, Merck & Co. This firm had been in contact for some years with the Indian government for the production of drugs, notably used in the treatment of tuberculosis, but the hurdle to the negotiations lay in the government's preference to handle antibiotics in the public sector. A representative of Merck, testifying to the reasons which led his company to provide technical assistance to a government-owned company, Hindustan Antibiotics Limited, for the production of streptomycin and dihydrostreptomycin, acknowledged that a similar Soviet offer had affected the tempo of their deal with the Indian government. Merck & Co. signed the agreement with the Indian government in August 1958, at the time when the Soviet team of experts arrived in India. The Indian government also lent its support to a joint venture between Merck and Tata Sons

Private Ltd. for the construction of a chemical and pharmaceutical plant in the private sector.[19] This kind of bargaining also highlighted the desire among some Ministers to keep cooperation with the Communist bloc in the development of the country to the minimum and to opt for a Western alternative when one existed, even if it was more costly. At the time when, in end 1956, Soviet experts had proposed the establishment of a heavy machine-building plant to fabricate units for steel production, it was reported that the 'Big Three' of Nehru's Cabinet (Govind Ballabh Pant, the Home Minister, T.T. Krishnamachari, and Morarji Desai) suggested a plant half the recommended size for the feeling was notably that India should not commit itself too heavily with the Soviet Union.[20] Morarji Desai confided that he himself would not advocate the exclusion of Russian capital or trade exchanges, 'but he recognized that Russian assistance had strings and would far rather deal with those in whose way of life and method of dealing he had confidence'.[21]

In June 1959, an official industrial mission to Russia, led by Sardar Swaran Singh, the Minister for Steel, Mines, and Fuel, was the occasion for new talks on aid. The Soviet Union offered a credit of 1.5 billion roubles (Rs. 1.8 billion), the first one for Third Plan projects. This offer took shape on 12 September 1959 in an agreement relating to the expansion of five projects which had already benefited from Soviet aid (the Bhilai steel plant, the Neyveli and Korba thermal power stations, the heavy machine-building plant, and the coal-mining machinery plant) to which were added the grant of credits for a thermal power station at Singrauli (Uttar Pradesh), for a precision instruments project at Kota (Rajasthan), for a heavy electricals equipment plant, as well as for the exploration of gas and oil deposits and the installation of a refinery.

The financing for the last two projects was in the framework of the collaboration between Indians and Soviets in the development of the oil sector which had begun four years earlier and which aimed at freeing the country from its dependence on Western companies. In 1956, the indigenous oil production covered hardly a little more than 5 per cent of the needs of the country and it was controlled by Assam Oil Co., a subsidiary of the Burmah-Shell consortium. Imports were met by the three companies—two American (Stanvac-Esso and Caltex) and one British (Burmah-Shell)—with whom the government had entered into agreements for the construction of refineries. The refineries located near Bombay began to operate in 1955 and the one in Vishakhapatnam in 1957. As already mentioned, these companies received their supplies of crude from oil extracted from wells that the parent company possessed in the Middle East. They transported these in their own tankers before processing it in their refineries in India and then selling it through their own distribution networks. The monopoly that they enjoyed led to a brazen accumulation of enormous profits and royalties which Nehru wanted to bring to an end.[22] However, the various attempts of the government to get these companies to reduce their price remained unsuccessful and had little chance of being conclusive as long as a serious alternative had not been found. This became all the more urgent as the demand was constantly increasing and involved very costly imports at a time when the foreign exchange reserves were falling at an alarming rate. The Indian government was then trying, unsuccessfully, to explore with the British and American refinery companies and distributors a scheme under which it would import Soviet crude for use in the refineries as well as Soviet refined products for distribution. In 1959, India was said to have spent about a quarter of its foreign exchange earnings for imports of oil products or equipment. This percentage would definitely increase and become rapidly an unbearable burden if no effort was made to develop this industry indigenously.[23] The government also complained that these companies were not interested in searching for new deposits and were ill disposed to share their technical know-how and to train Indian personnel.

The industrial policy resolution of 1948 provided for the future development of the oil exploration within the ambit of the state and no concessions were to be granted to private oil companies. In March 1956, a team of Soviet experts, invited to assess the oil and gas deposits, had submitted an encouraging report. Following this, the government had shown a desire to go ahead as rapidly as possible with the search for deposits and the exploitation of mineral resources.[24] A little later, a state enterprise, the Oil and Natural Gas Commission (ONGC), was formed. In May 1956, two agreements were signed relating to the supply of drilling equipment and the deputing of Soviet engineers entrusted with the training of Indian personnel in the use of the equipment delivered. Later, in November, a new technical assistance agreement was concluded, providing for Soviet experts to assist India in its oil exploration programme.

The drilling operations conducted with Soviet collaboration led to

the detection, in 1958, of oil deposits in Cambay in Gujarat on the west coast. A large deposit was discovered in May 1960 at Ankleshwar, also in Gujarat. Again with Soviet assistance, new deposits were detected in the eastern part of Assam. These positive results were in contrast to the infructuous drilling of Stanvac which had obtained a concession for prospecting oil in West Bengal in the Ganges delta. As there was an urgent need also to increase the refining capacity of the country, a loan agreement was signed with the Soviets for the construction in the public sector of a refinery of a capacity of 2 to 2.5 billion tons in Barauni. It had been preceded in October 1958 by a technical and financial assistance agreement with Rumania for the setting up of a refinery with a production capacity of 750,000 tons at Nunmati in Assam. The crude oil for these refineries would be piped from the East Assam oilfield. To succeed in concluding these two agreements, K.D. Malaviya, who was an ardent defender of the public sector and of cooperation with the Soviets, had had to cold-shoulder a proposal of the Burmah Oil Co. to have one larger refinery, instead of two, for which a loan could be raised in London on condition that the refinery would be operated by the BOC until the loan was paid off. He also had to counter some reservations, those notably of T.T. Krishnamachari who had reminded the Minister of Mines and Oil that 'all patterns of loan assistance have to be vetted by Finance [Ministry] so that one agreement does not hurt the prospects of other agreements being entered into, though in different fields'.[25] This was a reference to the negative impact that such agreements might have on overall American aid, considering particularly the fact that American oil interests were powerful in the US Congress. In February 1961, a new loan agreement was signed with the Soviet Union for the construction of a third refinery in the public sector, this one at Koyali in Gujarat, along with a new credit given for the development of oil exploration, and for the exploitation of the deposits that had been discovered.

The Soviet cooperation enabled the government to recognize that the possibility existed of inviting foreign private companies to operate under conditions that were more palatable to the Indians. In the matter of exploration, it urged foreign companies to prospect while insisting on a state participation in the management, the capital, and the profits. Whereas Burmah-Shell agreed to negotiate on those lines a new concession in West Bengal, Stanvac was much more reluctant and discussions aborted for oil prospecting in Rajasthan.[26] As regards the exploitation of oil resources, Burmah-Shell surrendered in 1959 its exemption from import duties, followed soon thereafter by the two other Western companies, in the hope above all of being able to obtain in exchange the approval of the government for an increase in their refining capacity. The government was hesitant to do this as long as a redefinition of the terms of the refinery agreements signed a few years earlier had not been achieved. The oil companies agreed also to lower their prices a little bit. These concessions had probably much to do with the desire of the Soviets to make an entry in the world oil market. Following yet another visit of K.D. Malaviya to Moscow, it was announced in May 1960 that the USSR was offering to supply crude at a rate lower by 20 to 25 per cent than the one being charged by the Western companies. In view of this, an agreement was concluded on 16 June for the import of 1.5 million tons of Soviet crude, payable in rupees. In December, it had become 2.5 million tons. The Indian government, in order to save hard currency, asked the Western companies to process Soviet crude. They flatly refused, while recalling that one of the main clauses of the refinery agreement was the right to refine the oil of their choice only. Moreover, it was not in their business interest to facilitate the entry in the Indian market of a serious competitor whose motives were suspected to be basically political, and to enable it to benefit from installations for which the Soviets had incurred no cost on their erection. However, they offered reductions, ranging from 8 per cent to 11 per cent on the price of the crude imported from the Persian Gulf.[27] Fidel Castro's decision to seize, in July, the refineries of Standard, Texaco, and Royal Dutch/Shell, after the majors had also refused to handle Soviet crude, might have induced the Western companies to meet the Indians half-way. The Indian government was to sign an agreement in mid-July 1960, providing for the supply over four years by the Soviet Union of kerosene, diesel, and other petroleum products which were payable in rupees and to be sold through a public distribution company, the Indian Oil Company, set up in June 1959; the agreement was subsequently renewed.[28]

In its efforts to lead the Western companies to come to terms so that they effect a downward revision of the prices of petroleum products, the government had to indulge in some adaptation as the production and the refining capacities in the public sector and the imports of 'red' crude only partially met the increased demand which was becoming all the more pressing as the Sino-Indian war was contributing towards making it a crucial problem for the defence of the country. The Barauni refinery would start functioning only in 1964 and that of Koyali, also constructed with Soviet assistance, would start functioning in 1965. Western pressure, particularly from the World Bank, had also been exerted to convince the government to be more flexible in its oil policy. A few weeks before an important meeting of the Aid to India Club, B.K. Nehru went to New Delhi to apprise the government of the impression which persisted abroad that India had been rejecting offers of substantial private investment in the oil industry because of the desire to restrict all development to the public sector. It was seen as sheer obstinacy at a time when there was a shortage of foreign exchange.[29] The departure of K.D. Malaviya from the government in June 1963 removed yet another obstacle in the path of compromises with foreign private companies, which were finally authorized to increase their production capacities. These compromises apart, the government had succeeded in the early 1960s in weakening the dominant position of the Western companies in the oil industry, at every stage, from prospecting to marketing, and for that it had to be grateful to the Soviets. Thus, in April 1963, for the first time, an agreement signed with a foreign company for the construction of a refinery in Cochin provided for the American company Philips International to be a minority partner in a project in which the state was the main shareholder.

The visit of Voroshilov, Chairman of the praesidium of the Supreme Soviet, in January 1960, was followed by Khrushchev's second visit to India, from 11 to 16 February, at the head of a delegation which also included Andrei Gromyko, the Minister of Foreign Affairs. Khrushchev was then on his way to Indonesia, another country professing non-alignment and uneasy about China's intentions, where he assured Sukarno about the grant of a new credit of $ 250 million. The head of the Soviet government visited in India the two places symbolizing Soviet cooperation in industry and, to a much more modest extent, in agriculture: Bhilai and Suratgarh. The Soviet leaders rarely missed an opportunity to point out that the West would not be so considerate towards India, if there was no Russian assistance. Khrushchev thus declared at Bhilai that 'Westerners aid you because we aid you. If we give you one rouble they will give you two.'[30] Such comments, as also Khrushchev's attacks on the motives behind

Western aid and his attempts to dig up the anti-colonialist hatchet, were not generally to the liking of the Indians, who regarded them as crude and offensive since such comments reminded them of their dependence on the West and it did not fit in with India's interest in the de-escalation of East-West tensions.[31] The agreement on the expansion of the Bhilai steel plant, provided for by the Soviet loans granted in September 1959, was signed on 12 February 1960; it anticipated an increased output which from 1 million tons would jump to 2.5 million tons of steel ingots per year. Following the visit of Khrushchev, an Indian delegation led by Homi Bhabha went to the USSR in the summer of 1960 to discuss the terms of a collaboration on the use of atomic energy for peaceful purposes. This led to an agreement on 6 October 1961.

Khrushchev's idea in coming to New Delhi was more than anything else to 'neutralize' the success of Eisenhower's recent trip to India and to distance himself from the Chinese border activities. He was able to witness on his own the harm these had caused to the prestige of the Soviet Union, if only in the scant enthusiasm that his visit aroused. It had nothing in common with the triumphant welcome that had been given him four years earlier. The joint communiqué made a reference to his appreciation of the policy of non-alignment and it underlined the fact that 'at no time have their mutual relations rested on a firmer basis of friendship and understanding than now'.[32] This visit to India was charged with significance since it coincided with the tenth anniversary of the signing of the Sino-Soviet treaty of friendship and it revealed the deterioration of the relations between the Soviet and the Chinese leaders, one of their most important subjects of discord being precisely their differing perceptions of the Indian government. The head of the Kremlin had taken care to make no mention in public of the Sino-Indian dispute although he probably encouraged Nehru in private to achieve a negotiated settlement with China on the border problem. Just before this visit, and after some hesitation, Nehru accepted Zhou Enlai's demand for a summit meeting which took place in April 1960.

Since the 20th Congress of the CPSU, Beijing and Moscow had been following a confrontational path. Mao opposed the unrestrained criticism of Stalin and the diplomacy of détente toward the West; he also condemned any policy of appeasement towards capitalist powers and began to claim seniority and revolutionary legitimacy over the world communist movement. This position was reflected in the remarks made by the Chinese figurehead during the international conference of communist parties in November 1957. Without contesting the principle according to which monopolistic capitalism engendered war, Moscow felt that the socialist camp was now strong enough to dissuade any eventual aggressor, and peaceful coexistence was the only alternative to a conflict which could lead to cataclysmic consequences. Far from serving to reinforce imperialism, as Beijing claimed, peaceful coexistence would, according to Moscow, promote the expansion of socialism which would not fail to assert its superiority on the economic plane. For Mao Zedong, the Soviets were setting their foot on the dangerous path of compromise with imperialism and revisionism, sacrificing the cause of the world revolution and the struggle of the oppressed against bourgeois governments to the demands of its own security and economic progress.

Beyond the strictly ideological and rhetorical considerations, the Chinese leaders might have feared that détente between the two superpowers may compromise Chinese interests on issues such as the return of Formosa to the People's Republic of China, the admission of the PRC to the UNO, or may complicate China's hopes of becoming a nuclear power. In the Kremlin, Beijing's external initiatives were considered foolhardy. Growing radicalization of internal policies, such as the 'Great Leap Forward' and of the 'People's Commune', were also the subject of severe condemnation by Khrushchev during the 21st Congress of the CPSU in 1959. It was with some delay and to safeguard the image of a unity in the Communist bloc that Moscow had supported China during the renewed tension between it and the United States following a resumption of Chinese bombardments on Quemoy and Matsu in August 1958. Moreover, the Soviet leaders were less and less inclined to supply to China the arms that Beijing wanted. Thus, in June 1959, Moscow unilaterally scrapped a secret defense technology agreement, signed in October 1957, which provided for broad Soviet assistance in the development of nuclear warheads and delivery vehicles. But it was finally the worsening of the Sino-Indian border dispute during the summer of 1959 which brought into the limelight the serious differences of opinion between the two communist giants.

The armed clash between Indian and Chinese border guards occurred on 25 August 1959 at Longju, in the Subansari frontier division of the North East Frontier Agency (NEFA). This incident was followed, on 9 September 1959, by a *Tass* annoucement in which Soviet leaders expressed the confidence that, on one side, China with whom Moscow shared 'the unbreakable bonds of fraternal friendship based on the great principles of socialist internationalism', and, on the other side, India with whom friendly cooperation 'is successfully developing in keeping with the idea of peaceful co-existence', will peacefully settle the misunderstanding that has arisen.[33] The unexpectedly impartial tone of a communiqué in which the Soviets refused to make a choice between their 'Chinese brother' and their 'Indian friend' was music to Nehru' ears. The Chinese, on the other hand, had to admit that this was a clear rebuff and that, for the first time, the USSR was not automatically taking the side of a communist country in a dispute in which it came into conflict with a non-communist country. The apparent neutrality of the communiqué did not deceive the Chinese leadership, which considered it in fact as a *de facto* support for India.

The fresh outbreak of incidents was due partly to the dispatch of Indian reconnaissance patrols to the border areas, after they had discovered that the Chinese had constructed, in 1956-7, a road between Gartok (Tibet) and Yarkand (Xinjiang) passing through Aksai Chin, where India had till then shown no anxiety to make its presence felt. But over and above the urge felt by the Chinese to assert their territorial claims, the incidents seemed also to be the direct consequence of the desire of the Chinese to induce the Soviet leaders, and the latter understood this, to make a clear choice between a capitalist country led by a reactionary bourgeoisie, and a brotherly communist regime. The Chinese leadership made no effort to hide its irritation over what it saw as indulgence on the part of the Soviet leadership towards the Indian government. It saw proof of this in the attempts of the Soviets to promote India's candidature to international fora as a leader of the Afro-Asian countries while they were clearly less and less inclined to do this for China. For instance, the PRC had not been invited to take part in the different talks that Khrushchev proposed for settling the crisis in the Middle East during the summer of 1958, whereas India's participation was put forward. The Chinese leadership also did not view kindly the Soviet aid to India which could not but strengthen Nehru's government and do disservice to the communist cause. Beijing was not unaware of the fact that the United States attached importance to the competition taking place in the economic field between India and China, with, at the end of it all, a model of development that other Third World countries might be inspired to imitate. It felt, in this perspective, that Moscow, by helping India, was playing into the hands of the Americans. Now, three days after the *Tass* communiqué, Moscow granted a credit, already referred to, of 1.5 billion roubles to India.

Khrushchev had no intention of sacrificing India's good relations with the USSR on the altar of friendship with a communist country whose attitude more and more frequently gave occasion for disavowal rather than approval. It was undoubtedly the survival of non-alignment in India that was at stake when the Soviets were taking a position on the Sino-Indian border question. Moscow was not unaware of the fact that if it were to adopt a pro-Chinese attitude, it would become very difficult for Nehru to cope with the pressures from rightist bourgeois circles in favour of an alignment with the West. If India were to revise its neutralist foreign policy, the vast 'zone of peace' which brought together the socialist camp and those Asian and African states which were not part of a Western military alliance, would have suffer a serious reversal. Moreover, the Soviet leaders suspected that Beijing actually wanted New Delhi to drift towards the West in order to justify a return to the two-camp thesis, with the hope also of coming closer to a revolution in India.

Despite the Chinese explanations rejecting the responsibility for the border incidents on the Indians, Khrushchev did not seem to have any doubt that the instigator was Mao with the intention of torpedoing the process of détente on the eve of the Soviet leader's visit to the United States in mid-September. On his return from Washington, where he had concurred with President Eisenhower regarding the need for a reduction in international tension, heralding a new climate of cordiality in Soviet-American relations, Khrushchev went to Beijing for the celebration of the tenth anniversary of the People's Republic of China. This visit did not contribute towards clearing up the differences that had arisen between the two countries. If anything it was a worsening. Khrushchev's plea in favour of détente and his warning against any attempt at putting the resilience of the capitalist camp to the test, hardly enthused the Chinese leaders. The fact that the traditional communiqué in this kind of circumstance glorifying the indestructible Sino-Soviet friendship, was absent on this occasion, was significant of the extent of the rift prevailing over the analysis of the international situation. The issue of the Sino-Indian dispute had also been brought up when Chen Yi, the Minister of Foreign Affairs, had criticized the communiqué of *Tass* and declared that Nehru was an agent of American imperialism who had to be fought at any price if progressive forces were to be enabled to come to power in India. Khrushchev replied that he did not share this assessment of the Indian prime minister, feeling that while Nehru may indeed be a bourgeois politician, he remained nonetheless the most progressive leader in India outside the Communist party. Adding that his policy was steadfastly neutralist and anti-imperialist and that unlike Pakistan, India had signed no treaties with the Americans, he concluded by declaring that if Nehru came to be overthrown, more reactionary forces would take power. It was, therefore, not in the interest of the Communist bloc to alienate or to weaken his position, except at the risk of throwing India into the arms of the imperialist powers.[34]

On 21 October some Chinese soldiers opened fire on an Indian patrol in Ladakh, near Kongka Pass, resulting in the death of nine Indians and the capture of ten policemen. On 31 October 1959, in a speech before the Supreme Soviet, Khrushchev mentioned for the first time in public the border problem. He regretted the loss of lives during the recent skirmish and reiterated the desire to see the dispute settled peacefully to the mutual satisfaction of the two parties. On 6 February 1960, the central committee of the CPSU accused China, in a verbal notification to the central committee of the CPC, of 'narrow nationalist attitude' and declared that 'one cannot possibly seriously think that a state such as India, which is militarily and economically immeasurably weaker than China, would really launch a military attack on China and commit aggression against it'.[35]

While in India, there were an increasingly large number of people who wished that the government, in the face of a communist threat, should opt for a military alliance with the United States, Nehru remained on the contrary firm in his conviction that non-alignment should be strictly adhered to: First of all, because he felt that India would otherwise lose the position and prestige acquired precisely due to being non-aligned, and also its independence of action, while the United States seemed at last inclined to concede to non-alignment a certain merit. And then, an alliance with the West would lead the USSR to be more sympathetic to China's territorial claims even though this had not appeared to be its initial intention. In his public interventions on the subject of the recent skirmishes on the Sino-Indian border, Nehru unfailingly dissociated the USSR from China and treated the Soviet Union with consideration while avoiding any attack against communism in his criticisms: 'Chinese activities on our border have nothing to do with world strategy of communism or communism itself or Chinese communism. It has to do with Chinese expansionism.'[36] In end November, Nehru declared that there was no country in the world today more anxious for peace than the Soviet Union and that there was, on the other hand, probably no country which careless for peace than China.[37] This was a singular turnabout that the Prime Minister had to make in his attitude towards the two paramount communist powers. At the end of the 1940s and during the major part of the 1950s, Nehru had devoted a great deal of energy in slackening the ties between China and the Soviet Union and limiting China's dependence on the latter country by taking initiatives to bring the People's Republic of China out of its diplomatic isolation. From 1959, the positions were reversed and the Indian Prime Minister had come thereafter to aspire that the Soviet Union distance itself from China.

Much to the annoyance of the Chinese, the Soviets then did not in any way change the nature of their relations with India. This could be seen during Khrushchev's visit to India in February 1960, described earlier. A few months later, in June, during the 3rd Congress of the Rumanian Communist Party in Bucharest, there was an acrimonious exchange between Khrushchev and Marshal Peng Zhen, the mayor of Beijing, over their respective perceptions of the Indian government. The Chinese leader reproached the Soviet leader of strengthening the reactionary Indian government by giving it a large economic aid.[38] The Chinese leadership felt that the aid granted to countries led by the national bourgeoisie for the development of the public sector, far from guiding them on the non-capitalist path of development, only contributed in fact to the strengthening of a state capitalism which would in no way promote the transition towards socialism as long as the representatives of the proletariat had not acceded to power in the country. The Chinese could be all the more indignant as they themselves, having benefited from a substantial amount of aid in the early 1950s, found that no further credits were extended for their Second Five Year Plan (1958-62), although some technical assistance was still provided. Two agreements had been signed in August 1958 and in February 1959 for which the Soviet Union undertook to assist in the construction of 125 industrial projects, in addition to the 211 Soviet-aided projects being implemented or completed. But even this assistance was later refused to them when, in July 1960, Moscow decided to recall all its experts, causing disarray of China's largest economic projects and scientific research programmes.[39] And this at a time when China was facing enormous economic problems as a consequence of the failure of the 'Great Leap Forward' and of two consecutive years of inclement weather. Simultaneously, Moscow withdrew all its remaining military advisers and technicians. The affront suffered by the Chinese did not end there since the following month, the Soviet Union, just after the visits of Rajendra Prasad and of Morarji Desai to Moscow, offered an additional aid of 500 million roubles to India, coming in addition to the 1.5 billion roubles of the preceding year, taking the total Soviet involvement in the Third Plan to Rs. 2.4 billion.[40] Beijing may well have wondered whether the capacity of the USSR to increase its aid to India was not a result of the fact of the cessation of loans to China. The decision of the Soviets to terminate its assistance to the PRC came *in tandem* with Beijing's refusal to fall in line with the Soviet position a few months before the opening of the world conference of the 81 communist and workers parties in Moscow in November 1960. This conference, where the European communist leaders appealed to the Chinese not to break ranks, was the occasion for a fresh crossing of swords between Soviets and Chinese, with Deng Xiaoping explaining that the border provocation had been deliberately plotted by a desperate Indian government playing for time so as to delay its inevitable overthrow at the hands of the people.[41] It was even said that Nehru had no reason to solve the conflict with China since it brought more and more American aid.

For the benefit of underdeveloped countries, the final declaration adopted at the end of this conference put forward the concept of 'national democracy' for a state being at a transitory stage while treading on the 'non-capitalist path of development' leading to socialism. The state that this concept visualized was one which

> consistently upholds its political and economic independence, fights against imperialism and its military blocs, against foreign military bases on its territory; a state which fights against the new forms of colonialism and the penetration of imperialist capital; a state which rejects dictatorial and despotic methods of government; a state in which the people are ensured broad democratic rights and freedoms (freedom of speech, press, assembly, demonstrations, establishment of political parties and social organizations), the opportunity to work for the enactment of an agrarian reform and other

democratic economic and social changes, and for participation in shaping government policy.

There was nothing in this definition, noteworthy for the stress laid on external policy, which justified a radical new questioning of the confidence conceded by Moscow in the progressive governments of the Third World led by the national bourgeoisie.[42]

On 8 February 1961, negotiations were initiated in New Delhi between officials of the Indian government and a Soviet delegation, for the purpose of specifying the modalities for the utilization of the latest credit of 500 million roubles. An agreement was signed on 21 February 1961, following the arrival in India of A.N. Kosygin. The USSR promised to supply to India equipment and technical assistance for the Bhakra right bank hydroelectric power station, a coke washery, a refractories plant, as well as for the exploration, development, and oil production in Cambay, Ankleshwar, and in other areas. The Soviet Union was the biggest partner in building public sector industry which would otherwise have been seriously jeopardized considering the hesitation of the Western countries to participate in it.[43] By joining the countries giving aid to India, the USSR also brought in its train some of the countries of eastern Europe. Czechoslovakia and Poland granted credits during the Second Plan for the import of equipment meant for heavy industry. By the beginning of the Third Plan, the aid of the socialist camp covered between 7 and 8 of the 16 industrial projects in the public sector carried over from the Second Plan and 12 of the 22 new projects for which external credits had already been secured.[44]

Nehru's second visit to Moscow as Prime Minister was from 7 to 11 September 1961. He thanked the Soviet Union once again for its economic and technical assistance, confessing: 'We have become greedy and are looking forward to more help from you.'[45] While he rejoiced at the friendly nature of the relations between the two countries and although Khrushchev expressed the hope that a new stage was opening in the path of the strengthening of the Soviet-Indian bonds of friendship, the talks revealed some differences. Nehru was returning at that time from Belgrade where the first non-aligned conference had taken place, bringing together 25 nations which, according to him, were 'so non-aligned that they do not agree even among themselves'.[46] He had struggled hard to ensure that the traditional references to colonialism, imperialism, and racial discrimination were set aside to give place to the demands of disarmament. The USSR had just then resumed its nuclear tests (already in October 1958, the resumption by Moscow of nuclear tests, six months after having announced their suspension, had been received with coldness in India). In Moscow, Nehru consequently appealed for a halt to nuclear experiments irrespective of any global disarmament plan, but he was unable to convince Khrushchev to accept the Anglo-American offer to put an end immediately to atmospheric tests.[47] This was not at the time the only disagreement between Moscow and New Delhi. In the midst of the Berlin crisis, Nehru refused to conform to the Soviet position. On the volatile situation in Congo, he defended the presence of a United Nations peace-keeping force, which included an important Indian contingent, while Khrushchev asked for their withdrawal after the assassination of Lumumba. Nehru had also reiterated his confidence in the UN Secretary General, Dag Hammarskjöld, who Khrushchev accused of being a tool of the colonial powers and whose resignation he had demanded. He was then advocating the abolition of the post of Secretary General and its replacement by an executive body composed of a triumverate representing the Western camp, the socialist camp, and the non-aligned. Nehru, when invited, refused to join in this proposal. The French Ambassador in Moscow observed that 'the discretion that [Nehru] kept on certain topics of utmost importance for his Soviet interlocutor is all the more remarkable that Soviet sympathies represent for India the more effective, and possibly the only, protection against People's China's territorial covetousness.'[48] However, relations between India and the Soviet Union were sufficiently stable to withstand such differences. In end 1961, the *Times of India* emphasized the climate of confidence prevailing thereafter between the two countries:

> Since New Delhi's foreign policy is not ideologically determined, its friendly ties with the Soviet Union contain no element of hypocrisy or make-believe. It is a straightforward relationship unaffected by different and even inconsistent social and economic systems and uncomplicated by any desire to convert each other to a different point of view. . . . Not every aspect of Soviet policy regarding Berlin, disarmament or nuclear control is acceptable to New Delhi, but Moscow's recognition of the fact that any complete identity of views is unnecessary is most encouraging.

And to conclude that these bilateral relations could be invaluable to the extent that they persuade Moscow that the entire non-communist world was not imperialist and has not dedicated itself to the course of destroying the Soviet Union.[49]

Paradoxically, it was at the time when the policy of non-alignment was being subjected to the sharpest criticism it had known since Independence that Nehru was more than ever convinced of its soundness. Indeed, one of its merits had been to develop close relations with the USSR which politically were to make it possible to contain the Chinese threat and economically to receive additional aid directed towards sectors which had till then been disregarded by the Western creditor countries and which even led them to revise their own aid policy. When Mountbatten had tried to warn Nehru against the dangers of an ever-increasing dependence on Soviet assistance, the latter had pointed out that there was no question of spurning it and that as far as dependence was concerned, India's reliance on other countries was and would be far greater.[50]

NOTES

1. Telegram from Nehru to Bulganin, 22 November 1956, telegrams from the Indian Embassy in Moscow reporting a conversation with Khrushchev, 28 November, and from the Indian Ambassador, K.P.S. Menon, after an interview with Bulganin, 29 November 1956. S. Gopal, *Jawaharlal Nehru: A Biography*, vol. 2, pp. 296-7.
2. Note prepared by the Committee of Information, USSR, Ministry of Foreign Affairs on 'The Influence of Events in the Near East and in Hungary on the Attitudes of the 'Colombo Countries' toward England, the USA, and the Soviet Union', 28 December 1956. The Indian government is reported to have handed to Andrei A. Gromyko on 17 December 1956 a memorandum in which it was asserted that 'the events in Hungary shatter the belief of millions of people, who had begun to view the USSR as the defender of peace and rights of the weakest people'. Center for Storage of Contemporary Documentation (TsKhSD), Moscow. Cold War International History Project, Woodrow Wilson International Center for Scholars, *http//:cwihp.si.edu/cwihplib.nsf*
3. *New Times*, no. 32, 8 August 1957, pp. 14-15.
4. Nehru also added: 'If we have to take part in the Cold War to become friends of the United States, then what is the use of having friends? Khrushchev asks for nothing for that. I believe he is obviously quite happy with the attitude of the Cubans or the Guineans. But when the ground seems unfavourable to him, he does not insist, in any case not immediately!'

Remarks made during a conversation with Jean Daniel in New York, *L'Express*, 13 October 1960, p. 12.

5. As a country availing of Soviet aid, this last decision of Moscow did not go unnoticed in India. For instance, Nehru commented: 'If we do not get aid from a country, we have no business to blame it or to assume that we have a right to aid. But in the case of Yugoslavia, there appears to be another feature of this aid. There was an actual agreement for aid. The question therefore arises; not so much about refusal of aid but of a breach of an agreement between two countries.' J.L. Nehru, *Letters to Chief Ministers*, vol. 5, p. 56.
6. J.L. Nehru, 'The Basic Approach', *AICC Economic Weekly*, 15 August 1958, p. 4.
7. Sure enough, Nehru had the Soviet Ambassador reminded that there should be no interference in India's internal affairs. Nehru's note to the Secretary General, Ministry of External Affairs, 28 April 1957. S. Gopal, *Jawaharlal Nehru: A Biography*, vol. 3, p. 55.
8. *Eastern Economist*, 30 January 1959, p. 281. Constitutionally, the Indian states could not borrow directly from a foreign nation; on the other hand, they could draw the attention of the central government to a project for which they had the promise of a foreign country willing to take over its foreign exchange cost.
9. Conversation with Matthai. From W.H. Young, British Embassy in Moscow, to R.P. Heppel, South-East Asia Department, Foreign Office, 5 June 1959. *PRO*, FO 371 144187.
10. See, among other documents, a report prepared by the Operations Co-ordinating Board, 17 February 1960, *FRUS, 1958-1960*, vol. 15, p. 533.
11. *Hindu*, 17 November 1956.
12. Modeste Rubinstein, 'A Non-Capitalist Path for Underdevelope Countries', *New Times*, 5 July 1956, no. 28, pp. 4-6. At the time when th Soviets attempted to justify their aid to India by insisting on the positiv aspect of state capitalism in India, T.T. Krishnamachari, on a visit to th United States in early autumn 1957 to ask for aid, gave the assurance tha India was not thinking in terms of state capitalism since only 3 per cent o India's industry was state owned and that, over the next decade, the publi sector would perhaps expand to 10 per cent of the industrial sector. *Asia Recorder*, vol. 3, no. 45, 2-8 November 1957, p. 1719.
13. *Pravda*, 18 September 1956. Quoted by B. Sen Gupta, *The Fulcrum of Asia* p. 80.
14. Note from Nehru, 6 November 1958. S. Gopal, *Jawaharlal Nehru: A Biography*, vol. 3, p. 80. Some people averred that trade with the Sovie Union, far from representing a disadvantage in terms of foreign exchang was on the contrary an opportunity to have assured markets and stab prices for Indian exports of traditional products, thus making up for the inelasticity, for fluctuations in world prices and for protectionist measure See, for instance, the article by Manubhai Shah, 'Economics of Rupe Trade', *Eastern Economist*, 10 November 1967, pp. 852-6.

15. In comparison, imports from the United States represented, in 1957-8, 15 per cent of the total imports, while 21.2 per cent of the Indian exports went to the United States. Planning Commission, *Basic Statistics Relating to the Indian Economy 1950-51 to 1966-67*, pp. 114-15 and 124.
16. *Notes et Etudes Documentaires*, no. 2548, 12 June 1959, La Documentation Française, p. 10.
17. *Foreign Policy of India: Texts of Documents 1947-1959*, Lok Sabha Secretariat, pp. 363-4.
18. M. Kidron, *Foreign Capital in India*, pp.163-4.
19. S.S. Harrison, *India and the United States*, pp. 166-7.
20. *Economic Weekly*, 22 December 1956, p. 1492. These same three individuals also showed some reservations towards the development of the oil industry in the public sector with the assistance of the Soviets.
21. Record of a conversation between the Secretary of State for Commonwealth Relations and Morarji Desai in Montreal, 18 September 1958. *PRO*, FO 371 135948.
22. Nehru to Swaran Singh, 6 June 1957. S. Gopal, *Jawaharlal Nehru: A Biography*, vol. 3, p. 112.
23. *Economic Weekly*, 15 August 1959, p. 1124.
24. Already at Independence, the government had considered the question of carrying out an intensive oil-prospecting programme with the aid of up to date machinery and experts imported from America and the Soviet Union. In the light of the prohibitive rates charged by the Western companies for oil imported from the Middle East, there was also the question of contacting the Soviet authorities, through the Russian Trade Commissioner at Calcutta, to find out if and how imports of Soviet oil could be considered. *Eastern Economist*, 9 May 1947, p. 838.
25. T.T. Krishnamachari to K.D. Malaviya, 11 November 1957. H.N. Kaul, *K.D. Malaviya and the Evolution of India's Oil Policy*, p. 77.
26. Dispatch from the French Ambassador in India, J.P. Garnier, 18 May 1961. *AQO*, Asie-Océanie, 1956-1967, Inde, vol. 250.
27. Intervention of K.D. Malaviya, 11 August 1960, *Lok Sabha Debates (second series)*, vol. 44, no. 9, cols 2049-2052.
28. Harvey O'Connor, *World Crisis in Oil*, New York: Monthly Press Review, 1962, pp. 397-8. In fact, from 1965, practically all the imports of refined products, from the Soviet Union and elsewhere, were concentrated in the hands of the Indian Oil Company, which had negative repercussions on the profitability of the distribution network of the Western companies.
29. *Commerce*, 6 May 1961, p. 833. A mission of the World Bank to India in 1963 commented: 'Likewise, in the refining and distribution of oil, development should, so far as possible, be left in private hands, except to the extent that Government intervention may be needed to ensure an adequate measure of competition. Private oil companies have already invested large sums in refining, storage, and distribution, and there is no reason to doubt that they will be able, as part of their normal business, to finance the additional facilities required to meet the growth of demand.'

Capital, 3 January 1963, p. 23. Quoted by Biplab Dasgupta, *The Oil Industry in India*, London: Frank Cass & Co., 1971, p. 142.

30. *Statesman*, 15 February 1960.
31. Telegram to the Commonwealth Relations Office from Acting High Commissioner in New Delhi, 29 February 1960. *PRO*, FO 371 152546.
32. Indo-Soviet joint communiqué, 16 February 1960. R.K. Jain (ed.), *Soviet-South Asian Relations*, vol. 1, pp. 272-5.
33. Communiqué of Tass press agency, 9 September 1959. Ibid., p. 266. Already following the Tibetan insurrection in March 1959, the USSR, contrary to what had happened in 1950, did not want to join in the Chinese propagandist campaign unleashed against Nehru, who was accused of being influenced by the imperialist powers.
34. Strobe Talbott (ed.), *Khrushchev Remembers: The Last Testament*, p. 308.
35. 'The truth about how the leaders of the CPSU have allied themselves with India against China', *People's Daily*, 8 November 1963. R.K. Jain (ed.), *China-South Asian Relations, 1947-1980*, vol. 1, p. 304.
36. *Statesman*, 4 November 1959.
37. *Statesman*, 28 November 1959.
38. The Indian press noted that Beijing did not see eye to eye with Moscow on the latter's assistance to India. This led Ivan Alexandrovich Benediktov, the Soviet Ambassador, during Kosygin's visit to India in February 1961, to formally deny any differences existing between the Soviet Union and China in respect of extending Soviet technical and economic cooperation to India. *Hindu*, 27 February 1961.
39. John Gittings, *Survey of the Sino-Soviet Dispute*, London: Oxford University Press, 1968, pp. 130-3.
40. The *People's Daily* of 8 November 1963 attacked the Soviet leadership for having given or promised economic aid to India from 1955 to April 1963, totalling 5 billion rupees, 'the larger part being offered since the Indian reactionaries began their campaign against China'. R.K. Jain (ed.), *China-South Asian Relations, 1947-1980,* vol. 1, p. 306.
41. Edward Crankshaw, *The New Cold War, Moscow v. Peking*, Harmondsworth: Penguin, 1963, p. 127.
42. *New Times,* supplement to no. 50, December 1960, Statement of the Meeting of Representatives of the Communist and Workers' Parties, p. 11.
43. *Economic Weekly*, 28 April 1962, pp. 691-2.
44. M. Kidron, *Foreign Capital in India,* p. 160.
45. *Hindu*, 8 September 1961.
46. Memorandum of conversation, 7 November 1961. *FRUS, 1961-1963*, vol. 19, p. 135.
47. *Le Monde*, 8 September 1961.
48. Telegram from the French Ambassador in Moscow (M. Dejean), 12 September 1961. *AQO*, Asie-Océanie, 1956-1967, Inde, vol. 257.
49. *Times of India*, 20 December 1961.
50. Nehru to Mountbatten, 21 March 1959. S. Gopal, *Jawaharlal Nehru: A Biography*, vol. 3, p. 99.

PART IV

India at the Crossroads of Aid (1961-1966)

CHAPTER 13

The Iniquity of Promises

THE THIRD FIVE YEAR PLAN was made public in August 1961. While the Second Plan had been considered ambitious when it was published in 1956, the Third Plan was no less so. The Planning Commission announced in the plan document that the country proposed to accomplish in five years what had been achieved in the ten years of the First and the Second Plans during which the foundations for a rapid economic growth had been laid. The Third Plan period was to represent 'the first phase of a decade or more of intensive development leading to a self-reliant and self-generating economy', the dominant concept of this plan.[1] It provided for a 30 per cent increase in agricultural production, a 70 per cent increase in industrial production, and a 30 per cent increase in national income. These rates of increase bear comparison with those achieved during the Second Plan, of 16 per cent, 40 per cent, and 21.5 per cent respectively. To achieve these objectives it was necessary to make a large increase in public and private investments fixed at 104 billion rupees, i.e. an increase of a bit more than 50 per cent as compared to the Second Plan. Public sector investments amounted to Rs. 63 billion (total public outlay came to Rs. 75 billion, including Rs. 12 billion for the current expenditures) against Rs. 36.5 billion during the Second Plan, a sharp increase of 73 per cent.

While observing, in the light of the first two plans, and especially in the Second Plan, that the modest rate of growth of agriculture had been one of the main factors impeding the progress of the Indian economy, the planners decided to give the highest priority in the Third Plan to the agricultural sector. The sums meant for agriculture (including community development and irrigation) in public expenditure increased by about 80 per cent as compared to the amount actually allotted during the Second Plan: an increase higher than that of the expenditure meant for industry and minerals which rose by only 69 per cent.[2] The share of the agricultural sector increased by 3.5 per cent to represent almost 21 per cent of the planned public investment during the Third Plan. At the end of the Second Plan, the production of food grains had increased by 18 per cent, a figure lower than the 25 per cent considered desirable. The imports had clearly exceeded the 6 million tons initially anticipated to rise to 18 million tons, largely because of two mediocre harvests in 1957-8 and in 1959-60 and a more rapid population growth than foreseen. At the end of the Second Five Year Plan, India had a population of 438 million while the Second Plan's original estimate had forecast a population of 408 million in 1961.[3] Over the decade 1951-61, the population increased at the average rate of 2 per cent per year, as against 1.2 per cent during the 1941-51 decade. There was talk again not only of the need to achieve self-sufficiency in food grains by 1966, but also of a global growth of the agricultural sector, notably in the way of cash crops, so as to satisfy the local demand and to develop exports.

The second priority was the development of basic industry which would largely determine the speed with which the country could reach the day when the growth of the economy would become self-sustaining, meaning the day when India would succeed in producing capital goods enabling it to develop without being closely dependent on imports in this field, and be able to diversify its export products. Industry, with a planned share of 24 per cent, was, for the first time, the largest consumer of public investment. The stress laid on the responsibility of the state in the development of industry, as in that of the economy in general, was maintained. It was anticipated that investments in the public sector during the Third Plan would represent 61 per cent of the total investments as against 54 per cent made during the Second Plan and 46 per cent during the First Plan.[4]

To hope to achieve a 30 per cent rate of growth of national income at the end of the Third Plan, it was essential to attain a rate of investment of at least 14 per cent of the national income in 1966 as against only 11.5 per cent at the start of the plan. This meant that the rate of domestic savings (which during the Second Plan had grown by only 1.2 per cent) had to rise from 8.5 per cent to about 11.5 per cent by the end of the Third Plan. It still remained a substantial dependence on external assistance to close the gap between the investment rate and the savings rate.[5] Foreign aid became even more necessary in the face of the continuous increase in import of capital goods before the economy become more self-reliant. One could, therefore, not really expect a notable improvement in the foreign exchange reserves.

The amount of foreign aid utilized during the Second Five Year Plan had risen to Rs. 14.4 billion (of which Rs. 5.4 billion by way of imports of agricultural surpluses under the PL-480 and the PL-665), an amount much higher than the Rs. 8 billion originally planned. 60 per cent of the aid authorized, and 54 per cent of the aid utilized, had come from the United States alone, of which three-fourths had been in the form of deliveries of agricultural commodities. The loan component was now far greater than that of grants. Soviet aid accounted for 12.6 per cent of the aid given and 5.3 per cent of the aid utilized (the Soviet aid obtained during the last years of the Second Plan was explicitly meant for the implementation of projects which formed part of the Third Plan).[6]

Out of the Rs. 75 billion of expenditure in the public sector anticipated in the Third Plan, Rs. 22 billion, i.e. 29 per cent, were to be financed with external assistance. The share of this assistance, which was constantly increasing, had already gone from 10 per cent to 23 per cent of the financing of the public outlay between the First and the Second Plans. The overall needs in foreign exchange during the Third Plan were estimated to be Rs. 57.5 billion. It was anticipated that this amount would be covered by exports earnings assessed at Rs. 37 billion, and by a foreign aid component of Rs. 26 billion ($ 5.46 billion), this amount excluding the deliveries of agricultural commodities under the PL-480. Out of these Rs. 26 billion, Rs. 5.5 billion had to be subtracted by way of capital transactions, of which Rs. 4.5 billion went into the repayment of earlier loans falling due within the Third Plan period.[7] If to this was added the amount of Rs. 6 billion granted in a new PL-480 agreement signed in May 1960, the total came to Rs. 32 billion of foreign aid provided for during the Third Plan. This figure needs to be compared with the Rs. 14.35 billion of aid utilized during the Second Plan and the Rs. 2.28 billion of aid utilized during the First Plan. The aid expected during the Third Five Year Plan was practically double the entire aid utilized during the first two plans.

The Rs. 37 billion of income that the Planning Commission expected to derive from exports represented a significant increase if one considered the stagnation in exports during the 1950s, their value amounting to Rs. 31.1 billion during the First Plan and to

Rs. 31.4 billion during the Second Plan. The planners acknowledged that it was an ambitious objective and they counted on a favourable international trade environment and a determination on the part of government to adopt a set of measures providing incentives to export. There was no longer any question of hoping to make additional withdrawals from the foreign exchange reserves whose level had gone down by March 1961 to one-third of those of March 1956, i.e. they had decreased by Rs. 6 billion as against Rs. 2 billion anticipated in 1956. At the end of the Second Plan, the foreign exchange reserves were enough to pay for 3.3 months of imports as against for 14 months at the start of the plan. This continuous decline forced India to take recourse in August 1961 to a new loan from the IMF—the third since independence, coming after those obtained in 1948-9 and in 1956-7—of $ 250 million, of which $ 127.5 million were to be utilized for the repayment of the earlier IMF loan. The planners did not conceal the fact that the forecasts over the foreign exchange earnings had been evaluated at their maximum and those on expenditure had been reduced to the minimum and that consequently great care had to be taken in the matter of allocating foreign exchange.

The Planning Commission, while relying on the assurances of aid already given, entertained adequate hopes that the needs in foreign exchange for the Third Plan would be met. The Aid to India Club was now made up of six donor nations (United States, West Germany, Canada, United Kingdom, France, and Japan) and two financial institutions (IBRD and the International Development Association).[8] It had agreed, during the reconvened fourth meeting which took place from 31 May to 2 June 1961 in Washington, to give an aid of $ 2.225 billion (Rs. 10.6 billion) for the first two years of the plan, leaving a deficit to be bridged, with relation to the supposed needs of India in foreign exchange, of some $ 220 million. The sum of $ 1 billion would come from the United States which had insisted that the contribution of the other members of the India consortium put together should at least equal their own.[9] The United States' helpful approach, especially in exercising its influence on the other participants to raise their quantum of aid, was not lost on Nehru who thanked Kennedy for the generous assistance of the US notably ensuring that repayments in foreign exchange had been reduced to the minimum.[10] The Soviet Union, for its part, had already given loans of the extent of Rs. 2.38 billion for the implementation of projects provided for in the Third Plan. Other countries, namely, Czechoslovakia, Yugoslavia, Poland, and Switzerland had also advanced some credits amounting to Rs. 670 million. If to these was added the carry-over of total assistance available from the authorizations of the Second Plan, then assessed at Rs. 3.65 billion, the Planning Commission could, all said and done, feel rather optimistic, all the more so as the Aid to India Club, which more countries might possibly join, was to meet regularly to assess the progress of the Third Plan.[11]

The victory of John Fitzgerald Kennedy over Richard Nixon in the American presidential elections of November 1960 was welcomed with satisfaction in India where his attitude in favour of an ambitious policy of aid to underdeveloped countries, and to India particularly, was underlined. The Indians expected not only that Kennedy might take special interest in the development of their country but also that he might put an end to the legacy of Dulles and to the Cold War rhetoric. They did not have to wait long to obtain a confirmation of Kennedy's good intentions in the matter of aid. In the traditional State of the Union message, made by the President on 30 January 1961, he announced that he would ask 'the Congress the authority to establish a new and more effective program for assisting the economic, educational and social development of others countries and continents'.[12] The Indians could also count on the Harvard economist John Kenneth Galbraith, appointed US Ambassador to India, who was among those who were convinced that India was a crucial experimental ground for demonstrating the possibility for a parliamentary democracy of achieving rapid economic progress. In an article published in the journal *Foreign Affairs* in April 1961, Galbraith expressed the view that external resources would be all the better utilized if the receiving country was endowed with a set of criteria indispensable to development. And India was one of the rare underdeveloped countries where the requirements of development were present, namely 'a large literate minority and a highly educated élite, a considerable if still highly uneven measure of social justice, an effective administration and a fairly clear sense of direction. As a result, and despite the crushing problems imposed by tradition and population growth, India has been making a substantial measure of industrial progress.'[13]

B.K. Nehru was also actively trying to convince his interlocutors that India, unlike many other Third World countries, had reached a stage where it possessed all the elements indispensable for economic growth and that all it lacked was adequate capital. He suggested a more global solution to the problem of underdevelopment by appealing to the economic committee of the UN, asking that the developed countries pledge a 1 per cent tax on their net national income as aid to the Third World before a situation developed 'in which hope and energy would have given way to despair, bitterness and worse as a result of short-sighted and penny-pinching policies' and which would end up by being more costly in dollars and in human suffering.[14]

Kennedy made an appeal to the US Congress on 22 March 1961 in favour of a revision of the US aid programme so as to seize the historic opportunity to move in the coming decade 'more than half the people of the less developed nations into self-sustained economic growth, while the rest move substantially closer to the day when they, too, will no longer have to depend on outside assistance'. To enable the United States to be in a position to take up this challenge, Kennedy suggested the creation of a new mechanism bringing together the several confusing aid units that existed under a single agency which the authority to make five-year lending commitments. The loans would carry low or no rates of interest, repayable in dollars—more conducive to business-like relations and mutual respect—rather than in local currency. The necessity was thus referred to give special attention to the nations 'most willing and able to mobilize their own resources, make necessary social and economic reforms, engage in long-range planning, and make the other efforts necessary if these are to reach the stage of self-sustaining growth'.[15] This series of proposals, which had been asked for by those in charge of India's economy, was greeted as a step taken in the proper direction by the new American administration in Washington, D.C.

Kennedy occasionally took recourse to far more practical arguments to convince those who doubted the effectiveness of the American aid programmes because they felt that the results were disappointing as compared to the financial costs, and because they attributed to them a large responsibility for the balance of payments deficit. Proof of this is seen in the remarks he made during a press conference in Washington on 5 July 1962 that, when it comes to evaluate the rationality of US aid,

three facts should be kept in mind. Almost half of the money authorized in the foreign aid bill is for military assistance, or supporting funds for the defense of countries directly threatened by aggression or subversion. More than 80 per cent of the money committed to economic assistance is in the form of loans, not grants, and these loans will meet our aid criteria and be repaid in dollars. More than 80 per cent of the money appropriated for the foreign aid program will be spent here in the USA. on goods and services supplied by US businesses, and US workers, under new and tighter procedures which have been developed.[16]

Before he took up office, Kennedy had asked Max F. Millikan and Don D. Humphrey to make a study of the aid that the United States could give to India. The report, submitted in end December 1960, concluded that the Indians had greatly underestimated the amount of their foreign exchange needs for the Third Plan. They authors recommended to the Kennedy administration that it extend its unfailing support to India in the form of a multi-year commitment on the lines already approved for PL-480 food grains.[17] In March 1961, Averell Harriman, Kennedy's 'roving Ambassador', held talks with Nehru and with the Planning Commission. He confirmed the importance that the President attached to a proper perception of the Indian point of view on international matters and on its economic needs. Two months later, it was the turn of Vice President, Lyndon Johnson, to come to New Delhi to assure the Indian leaders of Kennedy's support for India's development plans. The joint communiqué published at the end of this visit gave considerable space to questions concerning aid and underlined the urgency of mounting a major attack on ignorance, poverty, and disease, whose conquest was 'the first step to the assurance of peace and freedom'.[18]

On the eve of a new meeting of the Aid to India Club at the end of May 1961, the *Economic Weekly* called the new American stand on aid 'heartening beyond expectations and reflects the radical change that has taken place in the US' policies after Kennedy replaced Eisenhower'. The credit that the new President enjoyed generally did not suffer too much from the Bay of Pigs escapade of April 1961. The same article in *Economic Weekly* considered that this expedition was too unlike the new US diplomacy to be anything but a regrettable and short-lived error.

The Cuban episode might, for the time being, spoil the good psychological effect of the changed US attitudes and policies toward aid to underdeveloped economies. But even on Cuba, US policy has to change. It is not possible to imagine that the new US administration can pursue a positive, purposive and imaginative policy with regard to aid to the other underdeveloped economies while maintaining its old reactionary line in Cuba and Latin America.[19]

As for Nehru, while he expressed his disapproval over the help given by the United States to the Cuban exiles who landed on the island, he restricted himself to pointing out that the invasion would constitute 'a bad precedent which, if followed elsewhere, would create international complications'.[20] He did not lose faith in Kennedy, all the more so as on other matters, such as the question of Congo or that of Laos, they shared an overall similarity of views.

In the first aid budget proposed to Congress by the new administration, for the fiscal year 1962, Kennedy had retained the total amount already requested by Eisenhower in his last proposed budget, i.e. $ 4 billion, with a slight shift in favour of economic assistance ($ 2.4 billion against $ 2.2 billion previously) as opposed to military assistance.[21] Whatever might be the good intentions of the American President, the Congress, whether dominated by Democrats, as was then the case, or by Republicans, always showed reluctance to delegate to the President some of its legislative prerogatives. It thus rejected Kennedy's plea for multi-year funding. On the other hand, the US Congress went along with Kennedy as regards his proposal for the setting up of a single body for managing the overall economic assistance programme. The revamping led to the establishment, in November 1961, of the Agency for International Development, incorporating the Technical Co-operation Mission, the DLF and the Food for Peace Programme. AID could give grants or loans repayable in dollars. The repayment was scheduled over forty years, including a grace period of ten years and it carried a rate of interest of 0.75 to 1 per cent (from 1964, this rate became, after the twelfth year of repayment, 2 to 2.5 per cent). The Indians had every reason to be satisfied with the amount of aid allotted by AID during its first year of operation since it peaked at $ 465 million. This was more than double the amount granted during the last year of the Eisenhower administration, which by itself already constituted a distinct increase since the creation of the DLF in 1957.

When handing over the reins to B.K. Nehru, the new Indian Ambassador in Washington, M.C. Chagla, made an assessment of the way the American attitude towards India had evolved. He rejoiced at the fact that India's economic policies were now receiving greater appreciation: 'There was a feeling here in the past that India was socialist, and socialism was equated with communism. Now there is understanding of the mixed public and private sector development we are pursuing.' Another noteworthy change was that neutralism, which had inspired distrust when he had taken over as Ambassador in 1958 was now respected to such a degree that, as he added, 'America now wants neutral states in Africa and South-East Asia', this being a reference to the 'neutralization' of Laos where the US government was keen to prevent a take-over by a communist-dominated regime.[22] The fear that by accepting Soviet aid, the Indian government was exposing itself to the influence of the USSR, had dissipated. George W. Ball, the Under Secretary for Economic Affairs, emphasized that India had a government and institutions that were sufficiently stable to be 'quite capable of absorbing resources from the Soviet Union without being subject to subversion or to endangering itself'. Henry R. Labouisse, the Director of the ICA, declared that acceptance of substantial Soviet aid by India was 'all to the good' and that he had no worry that through such aid the Soviet Union would obtain a place of primacy in India.[23]

The main hurdle in Indo-American relations still continued to be the military aid given to Pakistan. In August 1961, the delivery by the Americans of 12 F-104 Starfighter planes—a commitment made by the Eisenhower administration and known to the Indian government—put into the shade the $ 545 million that the United States had just pledged, during the recent meeting of the Aid to India Club, for the first year of the Third Plan. Galbraith subsequently noted, much to his consternation, that 'there were twelve times as many questions in the Indian Parliament about the planes as about the aid'.[24] Pakistan had also acquired Sidewinder missiles which India had earlier tried to obtain from the Americans in the spring of 1960, but with no success. At first Eisenhower had given his consent, but the State Department had subsequently pointed out that such a sale would be prejudicial to US relations with Pakistan. It suggested that the Indians ask the British to supply them with some equivalent equipment. Krishna Menon, Defense Minister since 1957, had greater success when, in May 1960, he asked for the urgent sale to India of C-119 transport planes to help in the deployment of troops near the border with China and for support road construction operation in that area.[25] Nehru tried hard to cool passions over the sale of F-104 planes to Pakistan and he declared in the Rajya Sabha in August 1961 that he was quite clear in his mind that in spite of this aid being given to Pakistan 'the fact remains that the present Government of the USA is not only friendly to us but more friendly than any Government in the last ten years or so'.[26]

The Pakistanis were the first to complain of a bias towards India. The government-controlled *Pakistan Times* of 11 June 1961 accused the Kennedy administration of seeking 'to widen the economic gap between two neighbours to such a degree that ultimately we may not be left with any other alternative but to accept India's leadership'.[27] The World Bank consortium had pledged only $ 350 million to Pakistan for the upcoming two-year period, as against more than 2 billion for India. The Pakistani government was still considering that the Americans have not used 'Nehru's imperative need for American assistance as an instrument to persuade him to be reasonable on the Kashmir problem, a solution to which is considered to be essential for the stability of and real progress in the area.'[28] This argument was reiterated by Ayub Khan during Vice President Johnson's visit to Pakistan in May and during the Pakistani President's conversation with Kennedy in the White House in July 1961. In a television interview broadcast on 10 July, on the eve of his arrival on US soil, the Pakistani President had expressed his growing apprehension about the proposed increased in US aid allocations to India and had warned that if India became more powerful, some of the smaller neighbouring countries might turn towards China for protection. On 13 July, talking to the National Press Club in Washington, Ayub Khan said that he had told Kennedy that any American decision to give arms aid to India would be a 'tremendous strain on Pakistan-American relations'.[29] In return Kennedy assured him that, at a time when India was showing an interest in the purchase of US aircraft, missiles, and electronic devices, the United States would not provide military assistance to India without prior consultation with Pakistan.

There was a new cordiality in Indo-American relations, seen for instance in the appreciation for India's moderating influence at the first non-aligned conference underscored by the admiration that Kennedy felt for the Indian Prime Minister. Nevertheless, Nehru's visit to the United States from 5 to 15 November 1961 was, in Kennedy's words, 'a disaster . . . the worst head-of-state visit I have had'. The American President reported that he had the sad impression of being faced with a man who was no longer the dynamic statesman he had once been and who now headed a country increasingly preoccupied with its own problems. Though Kennedy, while remaining convinced of the necessity of helping India develop economically, gave up hope that India could become in the next few years 'a great affirmative force in the world or even in South Asia'.[30] Kennedy had notably attempted, to obtain India's cooperation in finding an acceptable solution in South Vietnam, neither allowing communist penetration nor requiring US military deployment, but this had been in vain.[31] This disappointing meeting was followed by the controversy between New Delhi and Washington over the decision of the Indian government to free Goa, Daman, and Diu from the Portuguese yoke by military means. This decision was a foreseeable development considering the pressure building up within India to seize these territories and the need for the government, on the eve of the third general elections, to demonstrate force in the face of accusations of being lax about China's occupation of Indian-claimed territory. In August 1961, the Indian Parliament had passed a law sanctioning the integration of the small Portuguese enclaves of Dadra and Nagar Haveli into the Indian Union.

In spite of American pressure against any military action, the Indian armed forces, on 17 December 1961, moved in to take possession of the Portuguese colonies. It took them just twenty-four hours to put an end to four centuries of Portuguese domination. For several years, Nehru had hoped that the problem of this last vestige of colonialism in India would be settled peacefully, conscious that the use of force, however justifiable, would risk tarnishing the image of India which had built a good part of its prestige on the international scene precisely by becoming the indefatigable champion of the search for negotiated settlements. He had said no to Patel when the latter had suggested in 1950 that firm measures be taken—'a two hours' work'—to put an end to the Portuguese presence in Goa.[32] For a long time, the Indian government had counted on the Americans, hoping they would put pressure on their Portuguese ally to ensure that it abandon its possesions in India. Their expectation went unmet, for while Kennedy had let it be known that he considered these territories as colonies and not as Portuguese overseas provinces, the State Department was seen as dithering and not inclined to make Salazar see sense at the risk of compromising its relations with a NATO member accommodating important US facilities in the Azores. He had been able to make no other proposal to the Indian government than to enjoin it to attempt a hypothetical negotiated withdrawal and to vaguely promise to undertake an effort to help bring about a peaceful solution to the problem.

The vehemence of the American reaction to the Indian military operation—an unhoped-for opportunity for the United States to take its revenge for years of sermonizing by India against the use of force in international relations—aroused indignation in India where it was argued that this country was perfectly within its rights to put an end to an anachronism that had lasted far too long. On 18 December 1961, during an emergency meeting of the Security Council, the American representative, Adlai Stevenson, while touching on the matter of Portuguese colonialism, preferred to concentrate his attacks on the use of armed force by India to settle a dispute with another state not only in violation of the Charter of the United Nations but also in contradiction of India's own professions of faith and frequent declarations of exalted principles according to which no right end can be served by a wrong means, a rhetoric which India had till then repeatedly dinned into the ears of those at the UNO. Stevenson suggested an unequivocal condemnation of India if the United Nations was not to die as ignoble death as the League of Nations for not having condone, during its time, the use of force.[33] The same day, the United Kingdom, France, and Turkey co-sponsored, in the United Nations, a draft resolution that called for a cessation of hostilities, the withdrawal of Indian forces to positions prevailing before 17 December, and the resumption of negotiations between India and Portugal. This draft resolution was rejected on account of the veto by the Soviet delegate who supported, on the other hand, another resolution sponsored by the Afro-Asian countries rejecting the complaint of aggression submitted by Portugal and asking the latter country to cooperate with India to bring about the liquidation of its colonial possessions in India. Leonid Brezhnev, who was on an official visit to India when the Indian forces entered the Portuguese colonies, immediately approved of the decision of the Indian government while Khrushchev sent Nehru, on 20 December, a message of congratulations on the liberation of Goa, Daman, and Diu.

Following the criticism heard in the United States, the Indians feared that the aid promised by the latter might be in jeopardy. In spite of showing exasperation with India's policies, the US Secretary of State, Dean Rusk, attempted to adopt a reassuring tone by declaring on 7 January 1962, during a radio interview in America, that the United States had a basic interest in the economic and social development of India and that 'we have not abandoned that policy or that interest as a result of the Goa question. . . . We do have commitments to India's long-term development program, and I would expect that we would continue those commitments.'[34] The President, in spite of some resentment over the fact that Nehru did not take up the Goa issue with him the last November, gave a few days later the go-ahead for the pending assistance to India.[35] However, he did not rule out the possibility that the solution adopted by India to settle the question of Goa might have an adverse consequence on public opinion. Some Congressmen were tempted to put pre-conditions to this aid by demanding the payment by India of compensations to Portugal.[36] 'You are justified in asking that American action be considerate of the problems of Indian democracy', Kennedy wrote to Nehru, 'Similarly I think it is reasonable that American public opinion should be a subject of concern to you.'[37]

Some commentators in India could not help connecting cause and effect in the criticisms heard in the West regarding the military action in Goa and the fact that the meetings of the Aid to India Club, held in Washington on 29 and 30 January 1962, came to an end without the members reaching an agreement over the measures to bridge the gap in the foreign exchange deficit of around $ 220 million for the second year of the plan; the decision being put off to a subsequent meeting scheduled for May 1962. The *Times of India* even announced that it was India's friends in Washington who had suggested that the meeting of the AIC be postponed to give time for tempers to cool down.[38] It was at any rate an unwelcome postponement; the *Eastern Economist* reminded its readers that it was most vital that this deficit be made good, or at least reduced, from the viewpoint of budgeting and detailed planning of the projects to be taken in hand during the second year of the plan. The implementation of the projects requiring a substantial contribution of foreign exchange outlay risked having to be postponed to the third year of the plan.[39]

India was in for yet another disappointment when on 11 May the Senate Foreign Relations Committee declared that it was in favour of a reduction by 25 per cent in the amount of aid to India proposed by the Kennedy administration for the fiscal year 1963. No one doubted that the committee intended to show in this manner its displeasure at India's foreign policy. The liberation of Goa through the use of force was not then the only reason for dissatisfaction. Pakistan was eager to take advantage of the forcible taking of Goa; it questioned, on the one hand, the relevance of providing large scale economic aid which allowed India to divert resources to the purchase of arms, and requested, on the other hand, the Security Council to debate the Kashmir issue. The first proposition was dismissed by the Kennedy administration which considered that decrease in economic aid would be self-defeating as it would more surely translate into less economic development than into an *ipso facto* decrease in military purchases.[40] The latter proposition provided an opportunity for more heated exchanges in the United Nations, when the Kashmir problem was discussed from April to June 1962, between Krishna Menon, who had come to defend the Indian position, and the American delegation which once again complained about India's lack of goodwill towards facilitating the mediation of the United Nations with a view to organizing a plebiscite. To stave off a new debate on Kashmir in the UN, Kennedy had suggested in January that India and Pakistan accept the good offices of the President of the World Bank, Eugene Black, in evolving an amicable settlement in the wake of its successful facilitation on the distribution of the Indus waters. While finding a favourable reception from Ayub Khan, the suggestion was summarily rejected by Nehru under the oft-repeated preference for direct bilateral negotiations. A new draft resolution suggesting the services of the Secretary General of the United Nations owed its rejection on 22 June only to the opposition put up by the USSR. The Soviet veto was a foregone conclusion but Islamabad still expected to draw world attention to India's intransigence and to put pressure on New Delhi towards making concessions in eventual bilateral talks.

Those within Congress who opposed the government's aid policy to India accused it of a non-alignment that was more benevolent towards the USSR than towards the United States, backing up this claim by citing the way in which India had voted at the United Nations. Between 1958 and 1962, the years which had witnessed a distinct increase in American aid, India had more often shared the views of the Soviet Union than those of the United States. A study of India's voting record during this period to the United Nations General Assembly on 92 resolutions on which the United States and the USSR voted in direct opposition (i.e. ignoring abstentions by either country) showed that India had voted 38 times in agreement with the Soviets, 19 times in agreement with the Americans, had abstained 34 times, and on one occasion had not taken part in the voting.[41] The *Hindustan Times* noted that 'with Kennedy no longer strongly campaigning for India, the traditional forces in US politics—consisting of military tacticians, old-school diplomats and disappointed idealists—took the offensive'. Consequently, speeches in US Congress and in American newspapers were sharply critical of India.[42]

The announcement made in early May that talks had taken place between India and the Soviet Union for the purchase of MIG-21 fighter planes contributed to making the atmosphere around the programme of aid to India a little more unpleasant. Democrat Senator Symington went to the extent of asking for the suppression pure and simple of economic assistance since it helped India to build up its military capacity aimed essentially at Pakistan.[43] The Indian government felt that the acquisition of supersonic planes by its army was inevitable after the supply of F-104 Starfighter interceptors to Pakistan in replacement of the some of the older F-86 Sabrejet fighters. Galbraith pointed out to Nehru that an agreement on the sale of MIGs to India would put the Kennedy administration in a politically embarrassing position. The Congressional critics of the aid programme would immediately point out that, at a time when the United States was providing the bulk of India's economic assistance, the Indian government was turning more and more to the Soviet Union for its military equipment.[44] Mountbatten, who had in mind above all the continuance of his country as a privileged supplier of arms to India, also requested Nehru not to turn to the USSR for arms or aircraft for India was not in a position to do without US aid.[45] The Senate, while adopting the foreign aid authorization bill, asked that great attention should be given to those countries which 'do not as a result of US assistance deflect their own economic resources to military or propaganda efforts supported by the Soviet Union or Communist China directed against the United States or against any other countries receiving assistance under this act'. One senator illustrated this by citing India's example: 'If US aid to India is going to give the Indian Defense Minister, Mr. Krishna Menon, funds needed to buy Soviet MIGs to threaten Pakistan, then clearly US aid to India should be cut down at least by the amount of Indian purchases of Soviet weapons.'[46]

Nehru spoke his mind in the Rajya Sabha about the existence of threats of blackmail over aid, aimed at discouraging the government from purchasing Soviet MIGs:

It is patent that no independent country and certainly not India, can agree to the proposition that our purchases of aircraft or anything can be vetoed by any other country. . . . They have all agreed that we can buy where we like and what we like. Nevertheless they expressed their regret and sorrow that we should go and buy elsewhere, other than their own markets. And behind it all, although it is not said as a threat, behind it all is the question of aid. 'Aid will be given', they say, 'We shall try our best it will come' and so on. Nevertheless, as someone said, although there are no strings attached, something happens that is in its very nature, some kind of a threat, it may be a thin threat, but something which may have a certain psychological effect.[47]

The members of Parliament and the press supported the Indian government in its determination to refuse to give in to Anglo-American pressures on this matter, as also moreover on Goa and Kashmir. The *Times of India*, for instance, said: 'US aid to India has already been reduced and it would be realistic to assume that it may be reduced further. But there is no reason for alarm. There is nothing sacrosanct about the size of the Third Plan. What is and should be sacrosanct is our national sovereignty. After all man does not live by bread alone.'[48] On 23 June, Nehru, referring to Goa and Kashmir, deplored the fact that the United States and Britain were 'invariably against us in matters which concern us greatly and about which we feel passionately'. Galbraith noted in his journal on 26 June: 'President Kennedy is unhappy about the Indians. Nehru made a speech in Parliament suggesting that the West was invariably unfriendly on Kashmir (and not clearly confining his charge to this) and complaining of our pressure on MIG's. This reached the White House with resounding effect.'[49]

Far from falling in line with a press always ready to flare up every time the Americans were suspected of wanting to impose their will on the Indian government, the journal *Commerce* set itself apart once again by adopting a more balanced attitude, reminding the Indian leaders that with external resources standing at the nadir, exports running well below the targets, and with the capacity to borrow from the IMF already exhausted, it was not the moment for bravado. 'Our leaders, therefore, must be circumspect in what they say and do. It is not suggested that on issues like Kashmir they should be less than frank. But care must be taken to see that our foreign policy is not twisted in such a way as to give rise to the impression that India is leaning more and more to Russia.' Then, moving on to discuss the economic policy of the government, the journal felt that

> the powers that-be, as well as certain sections of the business community, have not been as realistic as they ought to be. There is too much of a dog-in-the-manger attitude and preoccupation with paper socialism. The result is that there is more bureaucracy than democracy, more planning and preaching, instead of production and distribution. This state of affairs is certainly not conducive to obtaining foreign aid on a scale the country needs and deserves.[50]

Despite the points of disagreement between the two countries which have just been mentioned, the Kennedy administration did not intend to go back on its support to India's economy and it succeeded in convincing the House of Representatives to approve the amount of aid proposed for India. Dean Rusk, the Secretary of State, declared that in spite of the MIG deal, it would be 'calamitous' if Kennedy were robbed of his authority to support the Indian development programme.[51] The State Department could always allege that the purchase of MIGs by India had its positive aspects too, for at a time when Sino-Indian relations were deteriorating, this would have the effect of further worsening the relations between Beijing and Moscow. The efforts of the Kennedy administration were not unfruitful since the Senate Foreign Relations Committee went back on its demand for a reduction in the amount of aid to be granted to India. In July, Congress authorized the totality of the aid proposed by the American government for India. This decision was welcomed with relative relief by those in charge of India's economy who were getting worried over the repercussions that the criticisms expressed in Congress might have on the other members of the India consortium. During its last meeting on 28 May in Washington, the AIC had not succeeded, any more than at the meeting of January, in coming to an agreement over the additional aid to be given to India during the second year of the Third Plan, the final decision being left to yet another meeting, this one scheduled for July in Washington.

The outcome of this meeting did not come up entirely to the expectations of the government. Out of the $ 1.15 billion asked for by India for the second year of the plan, the Aid to India Club offered only $ 1.07 billion, falling $ 80 million short.[52] Though the United States had indicated at the 1961 meeting that its contribution for the second year of the plan would be $ 500 million, they settled on $ 435 million after Congressional requirements mandated that the US contribution be proportionate to the contributions of the other member countries. The visit that Morarji Desai had just undertaken, from 2 to 22 July, to the United Kingdom, the Federal Republic of Germany, the Netherlands and Italy to mobilize their aid had not been a great success. The representatives of Austria and the Netherlands were to attend the India consortium as observers, whereas Belgium and Italy were to join it, raising the number of member countries to ten. The two largest aid-giving countries in Europe, Britain and West Germany had reduced their financial contribution by approximately half compared to the preceding year. The Indian government was grateful to the American representatives for having pleaded in favour of loans whose terms would contribute towards alleviating the burden of debt servicing. The average interest rate on the loans had been lowered from 4.3 per cent during the Second Plan to 3.2 per cent in 1961-2 and to 2.6 per cent in 1963-4. The lowering of the average rate of interest and the increase in the maturity of loans was attributed largely to a dynamic initiated by the soft terms of AID credits of forty years' maturity, until recently free of interest, and of those granted by the IDA.[53]

The results obtained in the economic field during the first year of the Third Plan were disquieting. National income increased by about 2.1 per cent, as against an average of 4 per cent during the Second Plan. The rate of growth in industrial output was only 6.8 per cent in 1961-2 as against 10.4 per cent in 1960-1. This was far less than the forecast of 14 per cent of annual average growth made in the text of the plan. The reason for this dismal figure could be found in the shortage in supply of raw materials, power and transport bottlenecks or again in a further decline in the foreign exchange reserves which put a check on imports. The foreign exchange reserves had declined during the year by Rs. 647 million as against only Rs. 486 million in 1960-1.[54] This led to new restrictions being imposed on imports in June 1962 and then, the subsequent month, to the signature of a stand-by agreement with the IMF for a credit of $ 100 million, repayable in three years and which could be utilized only during the coming twelve months. The postponement of the meeting of the AIC to July had left the government with no alternative but to contact the IMF. The sum of $ 25 million was immediately drawn to be able to settle payments for those imports most urgently required.

When Gulzarilal Nanda presented to the Lok Sabha, on 25 August 1962, a report on the progress of the plan, especially in the matter of foreign exchange resources, he announced that till then the total external assistance available for the Third Plan amounted to about Rs. 18.9 billion, of which Rs. 4.4 billion were for non-projects purposes. He further estimated that an additional Rs. 11 billion would be required till the end of the plan as there would inevitably be a carry-over of aid from the Third to the Fourth Plan of about Rs. 4 billion. Consequently, commitments for aid, as distinguished from payments estimated in the Third Plan at Rs. 26 billion, would have to be nearer Rs. 30 billion (excluding the PL-480 programme).[55]

Morarji Desai stated before the Lok Sabha on 21 November 1960: 'Over the entire period of the Third Plan, it is going to be a continuous and difficult quest for foreign exchange resources to match the external cost of projects included in the plan and to meet other commitments.'[56] And he had no idea then that India would have to bear the financial burden of two wars in the space of three years, whose first consequence would be the extension of India's dependence on foreign countries to the field of arms.

NOTES

1. Planning Commission, *Third Five-Year Plan*, p. 48.
2. Percentages calculated from the distribution of plan outlays in the public sector. Ibid., p. 58.
3. Planning Commission, *Towards a Self-Reliant Economy*, 1961, p. 14.
4. Planning Commission, *Third Five-Year Plan*, p. 32, *Towards a Self-Reliant Economy*, p. 82.
5. Planning Commission, *Third Five-Year Plan*, p. 51.
6. Ministry of Finance, Government of India, *External Assistance 1965-66*, Appendix II, pp. 168-71.
7. Planning Commission, *Third Five-Year Plan*, pp. 112-13.
8. The International Development Association came into existence in September 1960. The purpose of this financial institution, an affiliate of the IBRD, was to give loans whose terms would be more generous than those of the IBRD.
9. *Le Monde*, 4-5 June 1961.
10. Letter from Prime Minister Nehru to President Kennedy, 13 May 1961. *FRUS, 1961-1963*, vol. 19, pp. 39-40.
11. Planning Commission, *Third Five-Year Plan*, p. 115. Austria, Belgium, Italy,

and the Netherlands joined the AIC during its sixth meeting in Washington in July 1962.

12. Department of State, *American Foreign Policy, Current Documents—1961*, Washington, D.C.: Department of State Publication 7808, 1965, p. 17.
13. Galbraith argued that agricultural progress had been far less impressive since the basic requirements for advance were lacking: 'In the agricultural villages literacy is low; the social inequality is high and many know that, come what may, they will live on the bare margin of subsistence; village government is decayed and ineffective and only recently have efforts at rejuvenation been made; and the Indian village is hardly inclined to address itself purposefully to economic advance.' J.K. Galbraith, 'A Positive Approach to Economic Aid', *Foreign Affairs*, vol. 39, no. 3, April 1961, pp. 447-8.
14. H.R. Vohra, 'New Thinking on Aid', *Times of India*, 5 December 1960.
15. *Commerce*, 25 March 1961, p. 521.
16. *Commerce*, 14 July 1962, p. 55.
17. *Report of the Task Force on U.S. Policy with Respect to India*, 27 December 1960. Quoted by D.N. Prasad, *Food for Peace*, p. 85.
18. Indo-American Joint Communiqué, 19 May 1961. R.K. Jain (ed.), *US-South Asian Relations 1947-1982*, vol. 1, pp. 247-9.
19. *Economic Weekly*, 6 May 1961, p. 699.
20. See the declaration in the Rajya Sabha, 20 April 1961. J.L. Nehru, *India's Foreign Policy*, pp. 587-8.
21. *Eastern Economist*, 31 March 1961, p. 866.
22. *Dawn* (Karachi), 4 June 1961. The front page of *Dawn* this day also carried an interview given to the correspondent of the *New York Times* by Ayub Khan, in which he criticized the general trend of American policies as pursued in South Asia and trenchantly observed that the United States 'should be mindful of the fact, that, if our territory was violated, we would spend our time dealing with the enemy rather than putting the American weapons in cotton wool'. M.C. Chagla later disclosed that during a conversation with Kennedy on the eve of his return to India, the latter had expressed his desire that India assume greater responsibility for the security of the South-East Asian nations in the face of a threat from Communist China. If India agreed to accept her share of the burden, Kennedy, on his part, would guarantee the neutrality of the South-East Asian nations. Nehru did not show much interest in what might appear to be a sort of alliance of South-East Asian nations which would not fail to be looked upon by China as an anti-Chinese move deliberately aimed against its interests. M.C. Chagla, *Roses in December*, p. 290.
23. M.S. Venkataramani, 'Indo-US Relations', *Commerce* (annual number), December 1962, p. A 48.
24. Memorandum of conversation, 7 November 1961. *FRUS, 1961-1963*, vol. 19, p. 134.
25. Telegram from the Embassy in India to the Department of State, 5 May 1960. *FRUS, 1958-1960*, vol. 15, pp. 538-9. Memorandum by the Officer

in charge of India, Ceylon and Nepal Affairs (Fleck), 7 June 1960. Ibid., pp. 541-2.
26. *Hindustan Times*, 24 August 1961.
27. Quoted in *Statesman*, 12 June 1961.
28. Letter from the Ambassador to Pakistan (Rountree) to the Director of the Office of South Asian Affairs (Weil), 8 February 1961. *FRUS, 1961-1963*, vol. 19, p. 7.
29. *Asian Recorder*, vol. 7, no. 35, 27 August-2 September 1961, pp. 4131 and 4133.
30. Arthur M. Schlesinger, Jr., *A Thousand Days: John F. Kennedy in the White House*, Boston/Cambridge: Houghton Mifflin Co./The Riverside Press, 1965, p. 475.
31. Telegram from the French Ambassador to the USA, Hervé Alphand, 20 November 1961. *AQO*, Asie-Océanie, 1956-1967, Inde, vol. 250. See also, B.K. Nehru, *Nice Guys Finish Second*, p. 364. The Indians—India was chairman of the International Control Commission in Indochina—may have also suspected that those in the Kennedy administration in favour of a policy of reprisals against North Vietnam, with the dispatch of military equipment and troops, were getting the upper hand and that there was nothing much left to be done to deter them. See J.K. Galbraith, *A Life in Our Times*, London: A. Deutsch, 1981, pp. 470-1
32. K.P.S. Menon, *Many Worlds Revisited*, Bombay: Bharatiya Vidya Bhavan, 1981, p. 273.
33. Department of State, *American Foreign Policy, Current Documents—1961*, op. cit., pp. 956-60.
34. *Statesman*, 8 January 1962.
35. Memorandum from Robert W. Komer of the National Security Council Staff to the President's Special Assistant for National Security Affairs (Bundy), Washington, 12 January 1962. *FRUS, 1961-1963*, vol. 19, p. 190.
36. Telegram from the French Embassy in the USA, 22 December 1961. *AQO*, Asie-Océanie, 1956-1967, Inde, vol. 250.
37. Letter from Kennedy to Nehru, 18 January 1962. *FRUS, 1961-1963*, vol. 19, p. 198.
38. *Times of India*, 15 May 1962.
39. *Eastern Economist*, 9 February 1962, p. 440.
40. Memorandum of conversation, 27 April 1962. *FRUS, 1961-1963*, vol. 19, p. 237.
41. *Summary of India's voting record from 13th to 17th sessions of the General Assembly (1958-1962)*, Foreign Operations Assistance Appropriations for 1964, Hearings before a subcommittee of the committee on appropriations, House of Representatives, US Congress, 88th Congress, 2nd Session, pp. 238-45. Quoted by P.J. Eldridge, *The Politics of Foreign Aid in India*, pp. 203-4.
42. *Hindustan Times*, 10 July 1962.
43. Dispatch from the French Ambassador to the United States, H. Alphand, 15 May 1962. *AQO*, Asie-Océanie, 1956-1967, Inde, vol. 250.

44. *Times of India*, 13 May 1962.
45. Mountbatten to Nehru, 14 June 1962. S. Gopal, *Jawaharlal Nehru: A Biography*, vol. 3, p. 217.
46. *Times of India*, 9 June 1962.
47. 23 June 1962, *Rajya Sabha Debates*, vol. 39, no. 9, cols 1773-4.
48. *Times of India*, 27 June 1962.
49. *Times of India*, 24 June 1962. J.K. Galbraith, *Ambassador's Journal*, pp. 388-9.
50. *Commerce*, 14 July 1962, p. 53.
51. *Times of India*, 10 July 1962. The results of the third general elections in the spring of 1962 were quite close to what had been forecast by a National Intelligence Estimate of 25 October 1960 (*FRUS, 1958-1960*, vol. 15, pp. 569-70). Even though it was beginning to experience the consequences of a long stint in power, combined with the rise of factionalism, and had been able to gather only 46 per cent of the votes (as against 48 per cent in 1957), the Congress party had nevertheless secured almost three-fourths of the seats in the Lok Sabha. While the Communist Party remained the second largest party in India with 10 per cent of the votes and 29 seats, the size of its electorate had not really increased. The Praja Socialist Party had experienced a setback. In fact, the rightist parties had been the only ones, with some regional parties such as the DMK in Tamil Nadu and the Akali Dal in Punjab, which had made a distinct advance. The Swatantra Party, created in 1959 by some former right-wing leaders of the Congress, became the third largest party in India with 22 elected representatives, followed by the Jan Sangh.
52. *Eastern Economist*, 3 August 1962, p. 188.
53. Ministry of Finance, *Economic Survey—1964-65*, pp. 40-1.
54. Planning Commission, *Third Five-Year Plan—Progress Report, 1961-62*, pp. 1, 3 and 10.
55. *Lok Sabha Debates* (*third series*), vol. 7, no. 15, col. 3983.
56. *Asian Recorder*, vol. 6, no. 51, 17-23 December 1960, p. 3694.

CHAPTER 14

The Call to Arms

TILL THE EARLY 1960s, it had been India's firm policy to refuse military aid from any country, and it declared itself only ready to buy arms on purely commercial terms from wherever it wished.[1] Explaining why India had refused the offer of military aid from President Eisenhower in 1954, Nehru wrote: 'Even though we may get some temporary increase in our armed strength, we shall lose the essence of freedom and that spirit of self-reliance without which no free country can subsist for long.'[2] While the acceptance of military aid, inevitably alienating, was ruled out, the purchase of arms abroad, apart from involving a foreign exchange expenditure that was all the more burdensome as it was economically unproductive, was hardly more satisfactory since it created a bond of dependence for the servicing of the armaments bought. It was therefore desirable that the main needs of the army be assured by an indigenous arms industry. But that remained finally subordinate to the industrial and technological background. Nehru repeatedly stressed on the fact that the 'building up of our strength means certainly defense forces and the defense apparatus, but remember that defense means today industrial strength . . . the real strength, will come from rapid industrialization'.[3] As the industrialization of the country would in all likelihood take some time and since an aggression can always occur, the real difficulty was 'how to balance immediate danger with considerations of better security later on'.[4] Expenses on defense remained relatively modest over the fifties since they did not exceed 2 per cent of the GNP. The only military threat then really taken into account was the one that might come from Pakistan with whom India had already been at war in 1947-8. Consequently, with the delivery of armament by the United States to Pakistan, which notably included F-86 Sabre fighter planes and M-47/48 Patton tanks, following the signing between the two countries of a mutual assistance pact in May 1954, India undertook an effort at equipment and modernization. Apart from acquiring arms from abroad, a few agreements for collaboration and some others for manufacture under license were signed with foreign companies for local production which till then had rested largely on around fifteen technically outmoded ordinance factories which the government had inherited on Independence.

To meet the heavy armaments needs of a defense apparatus built up on the British model, a large number of whose high-ranking officers had received their training at Sandhurst, the government, in order to maintain continuity, had primarily turned towards the United Kingdom. Ranking second and third among the countries that supplied weapons to India were France and the United States. Between 1947 and 1962, the main acquisitions abroad for the Army were 210 Centurion tanks from England, 180 M-4 Sherman tanks from America, and 150 AMX-13 tanks from France. The Indian Air Force had been equipped with some British aircraft (182 Hawker Hunter fighters and 80 Canberra long-range bombers), some French Dassault fighter planes (110 Mystère IV and 104 Ouragan), and some American transport planes (55 Fairchild C-119 Packet). The Hindustan Aeronautics Limited at Bangalore produced under license 280 British De Havilland Vampire fighter planes during the 1950s and after 1960 some British Folland Gnats.[5] India had always settled its payments without making use of credits or taking recourse to payment by installments.

For a non-aligned country anxious not to be obliged to depend on a group of countries belonging to a single military bloc, it was almost surprising to note that India had for so long turned to the Western countries alone for its supplies of arms between 1947 and 1960. While the purchase of arms from the Soviet Union was inconceivable during the Stalin era, the new trend of Moscow's foreign policy after his death led Nehru to consider the possibility of making contacts with the Soviet autho rities right from the start of the year 1954 when the need for acquiring new aircraft became acute. He felt however that it was necessary 'to proceed very cautiously and let it be known privately that we are prepared to consider suitable offers provided they fit in with our requirements'.[6] By the end of the year, Nehru even saw some advantage to the purchase of Soviet aircraft since it would enable the IAF to have experience of a different type of aircraft even if one has to cope with servicing complications. It may also induced some profitable competition with the other potential sellers as had just happened with the steel plant project.[7] Just as the post-Stalin Soviet Union had displayed the desire not to leave it to the Western camp alone to dispense economic aid for development outside the Communist bloc, it was ready to contribute similarly towards reducing India's dependence on the West for its heavy armament. The majority of Indian decision-makers, both among civilians as well as in the military establishment, did not however seem to be prepared yet to consider offers of Soviet military equipment and still preferred to go to Britain to acquire the means to strengthen India's military potential. Consequently, in the months that followed the agreement between the United States and Pakistan, some Indian teams of military experts went to England to negotiate the procurement of Hunter fighters and of Canberra bomber planes.

Nevertheless, in June 1955, some senior IAF officers, invited for the first time to Moscow to a Soviet Air Force show, expressed some interest in Ilyushin-28 light bombers.[8] These Ilyushin had the advantage of being much less costly than the British Canberra, and would apparently be more rapidly available. When it was learnt in New Delhi that the Canberra could not be equipped with certain devices that were restricted to the NATO countries, this only increased the interest in the Ilyushin and anxiety grew in some Western circles. The British High Commissioner in India, Malcolm MacDonald, informed Nehru of Britain's concern over the purchase by India of Soviet military material.[9]

In early March 1956, it was the turn of the Prime Minister, Anthony Eden, to write to Nehru to inform him that he was ready to get the delivery of the Canberra to India accelerated and to make a special effort to get the price reduced to the minimum, while promising to get the approval of Washington that these Canberra be equipped with the protected devices sought by New Delhi.[10] But in exchange, New Delhi would have to give up the idea of buying Soviet aircraft.[11] At the same time, Dulles, who was passing through the Indian capital, bluntly brought up this matter with Nehru declaring, to quote his own words:

> Why do you do this? You can buy planes from the British. You can buy planes from us. I cannot see why you should buy planes from the Russians knowing that it would make it almost impossible for the United States to carry on its efforts to assist you materially in your second five year plan. That will be hard enough anyway, and this arms deal with Russia, I feel,

would make it impossible. I know you will not change your attitude because of foreign pressure and I do not mention the subject in that spirit. I do think that you ought to know what are the probable consequences and then you yourself can judge what is the best course for India.[12]

The Indian government had already abandoned the idea of purchasing for now Russian military equipment and the order was given to the British for the sale of Canberra bombers.[13] While the Indian government had largely been able to obtain satisfaction from the British side over its demands concerning these planes, it is also possible that it did not wish to antagonize further the United Kingdom and the United States which were already alarmed at the emerging political closeness between India and the USSR. The State Department recalled in July 1957 that it was important that India 'be given no cause to turn to the Communist bloc for military supplies. To date Indian has not purchased such supplies from the bloc, and this is one encouraging factor in US-Indian relations'. This comment figured in a report on the subject of the purchase of arms by India since the signature of the 1951 Indo-American military sales agreement. It was written that India had since then acquired a relatively small quantity (around $ 38 million) of US military goods and services. It was also specified that most of India's demands for arms had presented no problem from either the viewpoint of the national disclosure policy made for safeguarding information regarding certain types of military equipment or of preventing an undue imbalance of power in the subcontinent.[14]

The visit in January 1957 of the Soviet Defense Minister, Marshal Georgii Zhukov, at the head of a delegation of military experts from the three services, had led to renewed speculation over the acquisition of Soviet military equipment by India. While Nehru considered it necessary to make clear that there was nothing to prevent India from procuring aircraft from any country, including the Soviet Union,[15] the Indian government still seemed to consider such a possibility as inopportune, probably out of fear of providing a justification for an increase of American aid to Pakistan or again of jeopardizing the economic assistance from Washington and from London at a time when signs of a grave financial crisis were being seen on the horizon.[16] Nevertheless, contacts continued at between the Indian and Soviet military establishments. Unlike the Chief of Army Staff, General K.S. Thimayya, Krishna Menon was very much in favour of acquiring Soviet arms, notably because he considered that depending exclusively on NATO countries for military supplies was politically unsafe. Zhukov's visit was reciprocated by the visit of an Indian delegation led by Thimayya, in June-July 1957 and during which Soviet offers of military assistance was renewed. It was agreed on that occasion that a group of Indian officers would follow to undergo training in the Soviet Union.

It was not till three years later that India made up its mind to acquire for the first time Soviet military hardware. This decision was correlated to the deterioration of Sino-Indian relations, and to some extent to the sale of F-104 US fighters to Pakistan—the Indian government had been informed in May 1960—justifying that any possible Western recriminations be ignored. In the summer of 1960, the State Department was informed of the intention of the Indian government to buy around 10 Mi-4 helicopters preferred to the US Sikorsky S-62. India had then just received 29 C-119 transport planes. The visit to Moscow, in October 1960, of an Indian defense team, also led to the purchase of 24 Ilyushin-14 transport planes and 8 Antonov 12 cargo planes, notably to replace the old Dakotas. The Indian Ambassador, K.P.S. Menon, confided that 'the Russians had been more forthcoming than he had expected, given the fact that this equipment was needed for re-establishing Indian authority in the disputed areas bordering on China'.[17] These Soviet aircraft were to be able to fly at high altitudes and operate in the Himalayan border regions where they could be utilized to open links with the military outposts and assist in the border roads development programme. Additionally 8 An-12 and 16 Mi-4 helicopters were acquired in 1962.[18] The Soviet equipment had the advantage of being a great deal cheaper than comparable Western goods and payment could be made in rupees. The significance of this major reversal of India's traditional policy of procuring military hardware from Western sources was not lost to the Americans. 'The passage of time is now causing the British-trained, Western-oriented Indian officers to pass from the scene. Their replacements are not so pro-West and could easily be impressed by good, cheap Soviet equipment. The Soviets could accelerate the process by a careful choice of the military technicians who would be sent to India under the legitimate cover of supplying pilot training, technical training, and establishing aircraft manufacturing facilities under licensing agreement.' It was also considered that this would not have been possible without a seeming preference on the part of Krishna Menon for Soviet rather than

American sources of supply and the manipulations of senior officers assignments in favour of politically minded officers within the Indian Army and Air Force by the Defense Minister. The long-term implications were for all to see:

> Once the Soviets establish themselves in the eyes of the Indians as a dependable and economical source of aircraft, their opportunity to conclude other deals for military equipment would be enhanced, thereby increasing Indian dependence on the Soviet Union, fostering closer Indian-Soviet technical and military relations, and bringing about a diminution of Western influence in the Indian armed forces.

Since the US companies would find it very difficult to compete with the Soviet sale conditions, the Joint Chief of Staff recommended that the most productive way to counter Soviet moves seemed to be the early implementation of a programme of financial assistance in accelerating the expansion and development of the Indian aircraft and related military equipment industries.[19] An alternative proposed by the Department of Defense was for the US government to assume a part of the cost of supplying military equipment through long-term loans at low interest rates and accepting rupees in payment where necessary.[20]

For the Indian government, the fact that the Soviet Union offered to supply equipment used in particular for constructing roads in the northern region bordering China was in a sense a reflection of Moscow's neutrality. This was clear from the remarks made by Krishna Menon in February 1961 when he said: 'If it had been the intention of the Soviet Union to support China or to put it differently to weaken us in the dispute with China, she could have refused to sell this equipment to us.'[21] This must also have strengthened Nehru and Krishna Menon in their opinion that the Chinese would not take the risk of provoking an armed conflict with India. It may consequently have weighed on the decision taken in November 1961 to conduct an inadequately implemented 'forward policy' of setting up border posts where none existed.

The agreement in August 1962 on the delivery of 12 MIG-21 and their subsequent assembling under license in India represented a notable qualitative change as these were no longer planes meant to ensure functions of logistic support but supersonic fighters, with the inherent prospect of the acquisition of aircraft weapons and missile systems based on the Soviet pattern. This was the first time that the USSR was giving MIG-21 to a country outside the Communist bloc.

Even within it, China had received till then only some MIG-15 and MIG-19, models prior to the MIG-21. Talking to the press on 13 June 1962, Nehru justified the interest aroused in the MIG-21 by stressing the fact that, in the end, it was less the acquisition of the plane that mattered than the possibility of manufacturing it in India. In this perspective, the MIG offered the advantage of a plane that was technologically less complicated and sophisticated than the comparable Western aircraft and consequently relatively easier to manufacture.[22] Also, the price of the MIG was less than that of its potential competitors (the F-104 Starfighter, the British Mark II Lightning, or the French Mirage III) and, moreover, the transaction could be made in rupees which happened to be a not negligible factor at a time when the foreign exchange reserves were at their lowest. The prospective purchase of MIGs had been surrounded with intense diplomatic activity.

To Nehru's argument that if America or Britain were to offer aircraft at comparable terms, this would involve an element of subsidy running against the long-held Indian position on military procurement, the American Ambassador pointed out that acquiring Soviet armaments, of which no one knew the real cost, for rupees was *de facto* accepting a form of military aid, as much as food sales for rupees under PL-480 was economic aid. Indeed, Galbraith complained of a lack of sensitivity from Krishna Menon, and above all from Nehru, at a time when the United States were providing $ 500 million in economic aid and another $ 280 million in food grains. 'The Indians were saying in effect that this was insufficient so they must turn to the Soviets to equip their forces. This was callous of American public opinion and highly illogical to boot.'[23] He also stressed to the State Department that, apart from oft-repeated arguments on a long-term pro-Soviet tilt in military procurement and in the defense establishment, if New Delhi was to acquire MIG-21, the Soviets would emerge as 'the defender of India against dramatic border enemies' and 'this will be a source of gratitude and esteem outweighing power plants, steel mills or other economic aid'. Consequently, 'the movement of India toward the West during the past five years would be arrested and possibly reversed.'[24] Among the alternative proposals considered, American provision of F-104s was dismissed in view of the inevitable adverse reaction from Pakistan which may lead to a greater degree of 'independence' in foreign policy and compromise the special US facilities in this country, particularly the Peshawar air base from where the U-2 plane shot down by the Soviets on the eve of the Summit conference in Paris in May 1960, had taken off.[25]

An exchange of messages between Kennedy and the British Prime Minister, Harold Macmillan, took place in June and July in which were discussed counter offers. The French option of providing Mirage III was put aside since the French government was concerned that to sell for Indian rupees or on soft terms would have undesirable effects on French sales in other parts of the world. Macmillan stressed that it was as important to prevent the Russians from supplying an engine for the HF 24, an Indian fighter aircraft which was supposed to be ready in three or four years, than to propose the Mark II Lightning.[26] But he also pleaded financial inability to develop the alternative British Orpheus 12 engine or to sell fighter aircraft at a discounted price. In the end, Macmillan thought that the only factor which might bring the Indian to heel would be the fear of losing US economic support and that Kennedy should warn Nehru that buying Soviet armaments 'might prejudice the attitude of Congress so gravely as to endanger seriously India's future prospects of obtaining continuing aid on the present scale from the United States'.[27] While the latter point was taken up in a personal letter to Nehru, Kennedy approved a package in which the United States would share 50 per cent of the hard currency cost of 12 Lightning—one squadron—(it was even proposed later on to pay for three-quarters of the cost of one squadron and ancillary equipment), would finance 75 per cent of the further development cost of the Orpheus engine if the Indians showed an interest, and would offer to sell 9 C-130 transport planes for rupees.[28] If this proposal was to prove unsuccessful, it was at least expected that the whole question should be put in cold storage for several months as seemed to be the position defended in India by the President, Sarvepalli Radhakrishnan, and Morarji Desai.[29]

Despite representations made by Duncan Sandys, the UK Secretary of State for Commonwealth Relations, and Galbraith to the Indian government, hopes of dissuading New Delhi from acquiring some MIGs faded. While a delegation of the IAF went to England in mid-July 1962 to re-examine the offer of Lightning planes, this visit only resulted in reaffirming the choice of the MIG despite the fact that the British no longer ruled out the idea of the production of the Lightning under license in India. A few days later, a delegation from the Defense Ministry left for Moscow to negotiate terms for the purchase of 12 MIG-21 and the manufacture of this type of plane in India. By the end of July, Washington instructed its Ambassador that, if the MIG deal was all but settled, the United States should start disengaging from too vigorous an opposition so as 'to be in a position to observe its consequences in detached fashion, avoiding any implication that, as Ambassador [B.K.] Nehru implied, Indians were forced to decision by US pressure'. The Indians had heard the US arguments and the 'minimum immediate objective' of giving Menon's opponents a stick to beat him with if the MIG deal resulted in adverse consequences to Indian economic development was accomplished.[30]

While these transactions were taking place, Sino-Indian relations were deteriorating further. The agreement of 1954 which was coming to an end on 2 June 1962 had not been extended. Trying to regain some lost ground, India had decided to put out advanced patrols on the border. By the middle of 1962, in the Aksai Chin, 'forward posts of the two countries were interspersed like black and white pieces on a chessboard and some Indian posts were behind the Chinese line of occupation. Over thirty-seven posts had been set up in the North-East.'[31] On 8 September 1962, the Chinese People's Liberation Army surrounded an Indian army post on the northern side of the Namka-chu stream, below the disputed Thagla ridge at the Bhutan-Tibet-NEFA trijunction. Sustained firing only begun after order had been given on 22 September by the Ministry of Defense to evict the Chinese in the Kameng Frontier Division of NEFA. As the military situation grew worrisome, India requested, in early October, US assistance in arranging for the purchase of spare parts for C-119 transport planes in order to keep the airborne supply of forward positions going and of radio units for use in the border areas. On 4 October, the Indian Embassy in Washington requested that the United States divert two Canadian De Havilland-Caribou ordered for the Pentagon to the Indian Air Force for operation in mountainous territory. They were transferred to India in late October. On 20 October, China had launched a full-scale offensive both in the Eastern (NEFA) and in the Western (Ladakh) sectors. The Indians were largely unprepared for such an onslaught although, under pressure from Parliament, the government had opted for a firmer military policy of stopping or eventually pushing back the Chinese Communists. Nehru seemingly believed that China may try to push forward wherever possible but would refrain from undertaking any massive military moves which would necessarily involve the intervention of the superpowers.

By choosing 20 October as the date for sending troops against the Indian positions in the border areas, the Chinese leaders had probably intended to force the support of the Soviets. For, on this same day, in Washington, President Kennedy opted for a partial blockade around Cuba in response to the deployment of Soviet missiles in the island. A new trial of strength was starting between the two blocs. Two days later, Kennedy announced in public that all military equipment heading towards Cuba would be intercepted and he requested Khrushchev to withdraw the lethal weapons already installed in Cuba. For a whole week, the threat of a nuclear war hovered over the world. The missile crisis was sorted out when, on 28 October, Khrushchev announced the dismantling of the missile installations. In return, the Americans committed themselves not to invade the island.

The fickleness of the Soviet reaction to the Chinese military offensive against India was directly related to the evolution of the Cuban crisis. The attitude of Moscow was dictated during the missile crisis by the need to present at a critical moment a common front within the communist world. A few hours after the attack started, on 20 October, the Secretary General of the CPSU urged Nehru not to be carried away by emotion and to show a conciliatory attitude and to accept the Chinese proposals for negotiations without preconditions.[32] The *Pravda* of 25 October 1962 published an editorial entreating the Indians and the Chinese to stop their conflict which could only serve 'the interests not only of imperialism but also of certain reactionary circles inside India, most intimately associated with foreign capital and imperialist forces inimical to the Indian people'. Above all, it was the legality of the McMahon line that was denied and the Indians were advised to come to terms with Beijing on the basis of what were considered as constructive proposals made by the Chinese government for an immediate ceasefire (mutual withdrawal by both armed forces from the line of actual control to a distance of 20 km and a meeting between Zhou Enlai and Nehru at a suitable date). An agreement between the two countries, according to Moscow, would make it possible to 'strike a fresh blow at the intrigues of the aggressive quarters of the United States, that have recently embarked upon an extremely perilous venture spearheaded not only against Cuba and the socialist states but against all peace-loving forces in general'.[33] If the Indian government wanted to hear none of the Chinese proposals, Beijing was only partially satisfied with the Soviet attitude. While it lent support to the Chinese view on the border dispute, it did not really openly condemn the Indian regime as the Chinese leaders had expected the USSR would do.

While Nehru had not foreseen the Chinese offensive, he did believe against all the odds that the change in the Soviet position over the border conflict was nothing but circumstantial. In an interview given on 30 October to the CBS correspondent in New Delhi, he declared that the recent developments of the international situation had made it necessary for the Soviet Union 'not to fall out with China' and added that he did not think that this was 'a basic shift [in the Soviet Union's attitude] between us and China. . . . Now that I hope Cuba is out of the way, probably it is easier for them [Russia] to revert to their neutral attitude.'[34] It was the conviction that the divorce between Beijing and Moscow had almost reached a point of no return that was to lead Nehru to defend non-alignment, come hell or high water, in spite of the dependence of India on military aid from the United States.[35]

The Indian soldiers, trained mostly to fight in the plains, badly equipped, and ill-prepared for mountain warfare, were from the outset overwhelmed by the Chinese troops. While the Indian government turned to several Western countries to obtain arms, it was clear that it was the United States alone that was in a position to rapidly respond to India's needs. The State Department did not waste time in making publicly known that any request for military aid from India would be actively considered. On 22 October, Nehru, while talking to the BBC, held the fiction that arms supplies will be only on a cash sale basis even if it was clear that their foreign reserves position would force them to seek much easier terms. The next day, M.J. Desai, the Foreign Secretary, told Galbraith that the Indian government was soon going to turn formally to the Americans with a request for substantial assistance.[36] In response to Nehru's circular letter of 26 October asking all friendly heads of governments to support India's struggle directed to 'the elimination of deceit, dissimulation and force in international relations', Kennedy sent a personal message to Nehru, two days later, saying that the United States would stand by India in times of need. While regular contacts had already been established between the military attachés at the

American Embassy and the Indian Ministry of Defense over the nature of India's needs, Nehru communicated to Kennedy a request for military assistance on 29 October. The American Ambassador pleaded for acting tactfully:

> They [The Indians] do not want to break quickly with their past beliefs. Words like non-alignment still have great evocative power. Phrases like military blocs, military alliances, even Pentagon still have a bad sound. In particular a large influx of American military personnel however well-intentioned could have a most damaging effect.[37]

Kennedy's response was prompt. On 3 November, the first C-130 Hercules carrying infantry equipment and ammunition landed in Calcutta. This military assistance was granted under article 503 of the foreign aid bill of 1961 which authorized the President to deliver arms in case of emergency, from existing stockpiles, without having to seek the approval of Congress. From 12 to 14 November, informal US-UK talks were held in London to discuss the coordination of Indian demands for arms, the nature of the Chinese threat, and to assess the Indian needs and their effect on India-Pakistan relations. It was thought that any programme of assistance would have to be sufficient enough to allow the Indians to contain any further Chinese advances but also of limited scope so that they would not be in a position to try to re-conquer Chinese occupied areas without using half to two-thirds of the forces they had on the border with Pakistan. The idea was 'to combine a respectable amount of aid to the Indians with a continuation of pressure on them to improve their relations with Pakistan'. This last point was undoubtedly shared by Ayub Khan who pressed the US administration to use its influence to induce New Delhi to proceed to a settlement of the Kashmir dispute.[38] On the last day of the talks, American and British officials recommended the equipment of a force of about five badly needed mountain divisions and their supporting formations. Meanwhile, an exchange of diplomatic notes in Washington between B.K. Nehru and Phillips Talbot, Assistant Secretary of State for Near Eastern and South Asian Affairs, supplemented the March 1951 agreement on the sale of US military equipment to India, later amended by an agreement effected by an exchange of notes in 1958. The assistance was explicitly to lend support to the defense of India against 'the outright Chinese aggression' and the Indian government was to offer to return defense articles which were no longer needed to serve their original purpose. For the first time, New Delhi formally accepted in this agreement the principle of US inspections to observe the use of the defense articles provided. These controls had till then been considered incompatible with national sovereignty.[39] A US team, headed by Major General John E. Kelly, arrived in Delhi to set up a supply mission. In a letter to Kennedy, the American Ambassador commented, however, that the Indian Prime Minister was 'still playing down our role to protect the sensitivities of the Soviets and perhaps, more especially, to protect his own feelings'. He even conveyed to Nehru that 'this was something we couldn't take and have pictured the repercussions in the American press. We cannot decently help someone who is afraid to be seen in our company.'[40] There should, nevertheless, be no doubt that the United States stood 'on the edge of great opportunity here—reconciliation between India and Pakistan, security for the whole subcontinent, a decisive reversal for communism in its area of its greatest opportunity'. The situation required the striking of a delicate balance: 'We could lose the chance by not helping the Indians defend themselves according to their view of the Chinese danger. We could lose it by rushing in indiscriminately either with help or with unreal conditions.'[41]

The Indian government was keen to dispel any idea that a military alliance with the United States was on the cards. This would have dissuaded the Soviets from shifting towards an attitude of benevolent neutrality.[42] The Americans had some similar concerns and this explained also why they wanted to coordinate a response to Indian military demands with the United Kingdom. In Dean Rusk's words, 'the more we got in front the more we would push Moscow toward Beijing'.[43] What really then seemed to matter was less a public change of policy foregoing non-alignment than 'a change of emotional attitude' and also to develop a close and confidential relationship with the Indian defense authorities.[44] Nehru intended not to appear overtly dependent on the Western countries alone and he supported in principle the view that steps be taken, even if for the time being unsuccessful, to approach the Soviet authorities with the object of procuring arms. Consequently, T.N. Kaul, the recently appointed Indian envoy to the Soviet Union, met Khrushchev on 9 November to assess the Soviet position regarding the supply of military equipment. While the Soviet leader told him that he was in a predicament regarding the Sino-Indian conflict and that his government would provide arms to neither side, he assured him, on the other hand, that India had no greater and more sincere friend that the Soviet Union and that existing contracts regarding transport planes and their spare parts, as well as the training of the crew for these planes, would be fulfilled.[45] On 11 November, Nehru declared publicly that the Soviets would keep their promise regarding the delivery of MIG planes towards mid-December and the setting up of an assembly line for these planes in India. In saying so, Nehru had apparently spoken his mind rather than the truth since the Indian Ambassador had seemingly not taken up the 'MIG question' with Khrushchev. But the delivery of MIGs, even of just a few, was taking on a symbolic value, proving to those in India who could then have doubts about it, that non-alignment was not in vain. This is exactly what T.N. Kaul pointed out to Khrushchev when they met again on 24 November, to which the Soviet leader responded that he would keep his word.[46]

Quick to exploit the Soviet procrastination, politicians belonging to the parties favourably disposed towards the West, whether it be the Swatantra Party or the Praja Socialist Party, considered that non-alignment had outlived its time and should give place to a new friendship with the Western bloc. C. Rajagopalachari, the leader of the Swatantra Party, said he was convinced that the pursuit of a non-aligned policy had become suicidal and would only help the enemy. He, therefore, asked Nehru to draw a political conclusion from India's acceptance of the 'spontaneous and generous' Western arms aid.[47] Some Congress leaders also wondered whether non-alignment now had any meaning. It was after facing pressure from his own party that Nehru had to make up his mind to finally 'sacrifice' Krishna Menon since he was held largely responsible for the debacle and, furthermore, whose continuance in office could antagonize the Americans. Menon had already been 'downgraded' to the Ministry of Defense Productions after the outbreak of the war, and on 7 November he had to resign from the Indian Cabinet, much to Washington's relief. Nehru, in an interview to a US television channel in early November, declared that the essence of non-alignment was *stricto sensu* the refusal to join any military bloc and that on this point India's policy was so far unchanged.[48] This should, nevertheless, not prevent people from thinking that there could be some form of collaboration between India and the United States in the face of China's aggressive moves in Asia. Nehru later elaborated that there was 'no non-alignment vis-à-vis China'.[49]

After the relative lull that had followed the initial offensive of the

Chinese in end October, the fighting regained in intensity in mid-November with a new onrush of Chinese troops in the Eastern sector where they appeared to be henceforth in a position to rapidly occupy the whole of NEFA, and perhaps even to reach the Brahmaputra valley. The Indians faced an increasingly difficult military situation and they seemed to particularly fear bombardment of Calcutta and Delhi by the Chinese air force. This latter had not yet entered into action and the Indians, who could not match the strategic depth that the Chinese held thanks to their occupation of Tibet, had taken care not to provoke them in the skies. On 19 November, Nehru wrote two alarmist letters to Kennedy in which he described the situation as 'really desperate', emphasizing the fact that the Digboi oil fields in Assam were threatened and that 'unless something is done immediately to stem the tide the whole of Assam, Tripura, Manipur and Nagaland would also pass into Chinese hands'. It was said that the Chinese had also poised massive forces in the Chumbi valley between Sikkim and Bhutan, and the border areas in the states of Uttar Pradesh, Punjab, and Himachal Pradesh, as well as in Ladakh, seemed also threatened by the Chinese invasion. Therefore, he asked for the immediate dispatch of a minimum of 12 squadrons of supersonic all-weather fighters and the setting up of radar communications to be manned by American pilots and technicians in order to protect the Indian cities of the Ganges plain from Chinese air attacks. He also wanted the United States to send planes flown by American personnel to assist the IAF in air battles with the Chinese over Indian areas in case air action over Tibet by IAF planes manned by Indian personnel against Chinese communication lines, supplies, and troop concentration may lead to counter air action by the Chinese. He requested finally the dispatch of two squadrons of B-47 bombers to enable India to neutralize Chinese bases and airfields. To this end, Indian pilots and technicians would be sent immediately for training in the United States. Any delay in the assistance reaching India would, according to Nehru, result in nothing short of a catastrophe. Kennedy was so taken aback by requests 'far reaching in the extreme' that he was not 'convinced that Nehru's appreciation of the situation was entirely sound', notably because the Americans did not think that the Chinese intended to launch a large-scale invasion of India.[50] Dean Rusk pointed out that Nehru's message amounted 'to a request for an active and practically speaking unlimited military partnership between the United States and India. . . . This involves for us the most far-reaching political and strategic issues and we are not at all convinced that Indians are prepared to face the situation in the same terms.' For Rusk, India was implicitly asking the United States to get closely embroiled in a war with China and this could be contemplated only if India agreed to fulfil certain minimum conditions which would enable her to make a full contribution to her own defense. These conditions included the need for India to come to terms with Pakistan over Kashmir, to gain the active support of the Commonwealth, to report the situation to the United Nations, and to drum up support from other countries in the area.[51] As for Galbraith, he observed that non-alignment was 'far out of date; the Indians are pleading for military association'.[52]

Non-alignment may have been given a quiet burial if India had been forced into a prolonged war against China. This was not to be and on 21 November, while, as a stopgap measure, the US Department of Defense had decided to dispatch 12 C-130 aircraft, along with spares for the C-119 planes owned by the IAF, and whereas a US aircraft carrier was on its way to the Bay of Bengal, China imposed a unilateral cease fire followed ten days later by a withdrawal of its troops to 20 km on its own side of the actual line of control between China and India on 7 November 1959 in the Eastern sector and on the first day of the war in the Western sector. Beijing felt it preferable to stop the combats and to show magnanimity by a withdrawal of its troops while enabling it at the same time to conserve its territorial acquisition in the region that mattered most to it, i.e. Aksai Chin, since each further day of conflict strengthened the military collaboration between India and the United States and would present logistical problems. The Soviet unwillingness to support the Chinese, not only militarily but in fuel and other things, was also, according to Krishna Menon, one of the main factors behind the Chinese withdrawal.[53]

The Chinese government had achieved several objectives. By humiliating India, it had weakened non-alignment and had given a serious blow to New Delhi's prestige among the Afro-Asian countries. Most of them, Nasser and Tito being among the rare exceptions, took care not to openly condemn China. The only real intervention of the non-aligned countries in the Sino-Indian dispute came from six nations (Burma, Cambodia, Ceylon, Egypt, Ghana, and Indonesia) which met in Colombo from 10 to 12 December

1962 to make a set of proposals for a negotiated settlement of the border dispute. The PRC considered that it had proved that it was the undisputed leader of the Third World countries and that it alone could champion their interests in the face of American imperialism. Beijing prided itself at having unmasked the real affinities of the national bourgeoisie in power in India. A communiqué of the New China News Agency asserted that Nehru could no longer make use of non-alignment to conceal the fact that it has sold itself to the United States. Nehru's government, firstly by accepting economic aid and then military aid from the United States, 'holding dollars in one hand and American arms in the other in order to attack China, has in fact entered into an alliance with the United States, even without having signed a treaty'.[54] Months later, in a letter to Kennedy, Nehru commented that the Chinese aim was not acquisition of territory but

> to force on India a political settlement which will involve India re-orienting its policies to suit the pattern of Chinese global policies. Failing this, China would like to put all possible pressures on the Indian Government and cause internal disintegration as China regards India as the main obstacle in its plans of domination over Asia.[55]

The Soviet Union was also blamed for having betrayed the socialist camp and for having failed in its internationalist duty, for by supporting the reactionary Indians, Moscow had demonstrated its collusion with American imperialism. This was corroborated by the fact that on 12 December 1962, before the Supreme Soviet, Khrushchev, while giving credit to the Chinese for having ordered a unilateral cease fire and a withdrawal of their troops, declared that, in the first place, they would have done better by not moving from the positions on which these troops stood initially. Furthermore, he did not consider that India would have wanted to start a war with China. On 15 December, the Indian Ambassador received from the Soviet leader the assurance of political and material support.[56] Therefore, during the Congress at Berlin of the Socialist Unity Party of Germany, the Chinese delegate declared that while the Indian government was supported by imperialists, it was regrettable that it was supported also by some so-called Marxist-Leninists, who had disregarded the facts and reversed the rights and wrongs from end to end as regards the Sino-Indian border issue. He went on to say that such an attitude had nothing in common with Marxism-Leninism nor with proletarian internationalism.[57] According to Beijing, only

Moscow's support still enabled the Indian government to maintain the illusion of non-alignment. The Soviet leaders, for their part, underlined the incoherence of the Chinese discourse when, moreover, the PRC did not hesitate to get closer to reactionary regimes in Asia and Africa, including even some countries belonging to Western military alliances. It was, in particular, the development of friendly relations between China and Pakistan that were being thus targeted. Beijing would have indeed run the risk of losing its newly found friendliness with Islamabad in re-engaging India militarily and thereby forcing the rapprochement between India and Pakistan that the Western countries were demanding.

As the Indian government considered that a new Chinese attack was still possible in the near future, the matter of a tacit air defense pact was again raised with the Americans. The Indians made a proposal according to which they would look after the ground installations and would commit their tactical aircraft into active combat, while the Americans would undertake the defense of the cities. Galbraith pleaded with the President in favour of this arrangement of air defense as 'a long-run foundation for a political association of the first importance'.[58] As it happened, the State Department was more inclined to leave the initiative for an arrangement of this type to the Commonwealth. Paradoxically, while at the end of the 1940s it had sought to make India a military ally against the expansionist danger of Communist China, the State Department now balked at the idea of furthering the possibilities of a military collaboration with India. The Americans had to keep in mind the reactions of their ally, Pakistan. The latter obviously made no secret about its disapproval of all that could in the least bit resemble a programme of American military aid, coming as it would, to add to the deliveries of Soviet arms to India. This would enable New Delhi to significantly alter the ratio of military strength between the two countries and directly increase the danger to the security of Pakistan. Islamabad was not convinced by the assurances given by Washington and New Delhi that these arms were meant only to contain the Chinese threat, and it even raised the possibility of withdrawing, by way of retaliation, from SEATO and CENTO.

The Pakistani cause had its champions within the State Department and the Pentagon, and especially within the intelligence community, who did not wish to lose the strategic advantages that military cooperation with Islamabad offered, nor giving good reasons to Pakistani leaders to get closer to China. In May 1962, it had been announced that the two countries would conduct negotiations on a border settlement to cover the frontier between Xinjiang and the Pakistani-held segment of Kashmir, and substantive Sino-Pakistani talks begun in Beijing on 12 October 1962. If Ayub Khan was reminded that the alliance ties were for the express purpose of meeting the communist threat, the onus was also on India to reassure the American people that it had taken every possible step to pre-empt the possibility of Pakistan breaking its Western ties or conspiring with Beijing against India, otherwise the US ability to help India would be 'severely circumscribed'.[59] The American officials had no alternative but to undertake a balancing increase in their military assistance to Pakistan, or preferably to make an effort to convince both Indians and Pakistanis to meet and negotiate a lasting solution to the question of Kashmir. It was understood that New Delhi would have to make certain concessions beyond the actual cease fire line. This last point was raised during the visit of Averell Harriman, the Assistant Secretary of State for Far Eastern Affairs, in New Delhi, where he arrived on 22 November at the head of a high-level delegation, including several senior army and air force officers, that had come to make an assessment of India's military needs.[60] Harriman and, more insistently, Duncan Sandys, who led a parallel British mission, made a series of to and fro journeys between New Delhi and Rawalpindi, and eventually succeeded in convincing Nehru to conduct bilateral ministerial talks 'on Kashmir and other related matters' in end December. The State Department had instructed the Embassy in India to ensure, at its discretion, that the relationship between the US capacity to help and the resolution of the Kashmir dispute should be widely understood among the key political leaders both at the centre and in the states and 'similar missionary work should be carried out among senior officers of the Indian military establishment'. President Radhakrishnan might also be called upon to urge Nehru to make necessary concessions to reach an agreement.[61] Implicit in this was the understanding that these talks would relate to a territorial division of the Vale of Kashmir and to the demarcation of an international boundary running through this area, with the hope that the two parties would ultimately agree on a joint defense of the subcontinent. The negotiations ran into rough weather from the very first day. On the eve of the first round of ministerial talks, which took place in Rawalpindi (27-29 December), Pakistan had signed with China an agreement in principle on the demarcation of the Himalayan border between the two countries. For Indians, it was a deliberate affront.

In early December, Kennedy approved the recommendations of the National Security Council subcommittee on South Asia for a military aid programme covering the next two-three months, with a ceiling of $ 60 million, exclusive of air defense, but including $ 22.8 million already committed.[62] The UK and other Commonwealth countries were expected to match this amount. The Joint Chiefs of Staff, reviewing the Harriman report, considered that the American air commitment in the mid-term period (till the end of 1963) should be limited to the provision of three fixed radars in the Bihar-Assam area and, on a longer-term basis, of three mobile radars and the retrofit of three squadrons of Indian aircraft with Sidewinder missiles. The United Kingdom, Canada, and Australia were supposed to provide for command and control communications, and fighter modernization, including air-to-air missiles, for three fighter squadrons, together with training support and operational assistance.[63] This matter was discussed when Kennedy and Macmillan met at Nassau in the Bahamas on 20 December 1962. The outcome of this meeting failed to meet the expectations of the Indian government. The two statesmen had indeed agreed that they would give emergency arms aid to India to convert six existing divisions into mountain divisions with appropriate supporting units, to make available reasonable airlift assistance and to make existing combat aircraft effective. The assistance was to be extended on a grant or rupee sale basis. But the Indian proposal for a comprehensive air defense assistance was received with scant enthusiasm, notably because it was considered the most important card to persuade the Indians to reach a Kashmir settlement. This fell far short of Galbraith's grand design for India. He commented that 'a great opportunity to bring India into much closer working association with the Western community . . . had been largely dulled over' when Indians seemed at last ready to cooperate with the United States on the political and the military plane with a view to containing China in the rest of Asia.[64] For the *Times of India*, it was an indication that the relaxation of tension between the two superpowers was not conducive to the granting of massive US military aid to India: 'Emergency aid has been and will probably continue to be available when required, but anything more would threaten to destroy the delicate balance of interests between the Soviet Union and the United States that is being gradually achieved.'[65] Should India make a significant tilt towards the Western camp, this balance would be upset, to be followed by the tightening of bonds between the two giants of communism. Indeed, Dean Rusk conceded that it was not in the interests of the United States to 'compromise' Indian non-alignment, 'lest we promote a Soviet-Chinese rapprochement which would greatly up our bill'.[66]

Eager not to be 'pushed around' again by China in case hostilities should resume once the snows has melted and the mountain passes reopened, Nehru was eager to move ahead with an arrangement on air defense and conveyed, in a letter sent to Kennedy on 29 December, that the visit of a joint US/Commonwealth air defense team would be definitely welcomed. The mission, soon followed by a defense production team, arrived in India about one month later. As the weeks passed and the danger of an immediate resumption of hostilities with China receded whereas national pride re-asserted itself, the Indian proponents of non-alignment raised their heads. To reassure them, Nehru denied that there was any plan of an Anglo-American 'air umbrella' *per se* and gave the assurance that no foreign air force would be stationed and no foreign air bases established in India. At the same time, he announced that the air strips and ground equipment were going to be improved so as to make it possible, in times of emergency, for friendly countries to help India more effectively.[67] The US/Commonwealth air defense mission estimated that a measure of security from Chinese air attacks could be provided to the Calcutta and New Delhi areas by two or three Western fighter squadrons using US-UK mobile radars. It had the advantage of strengthening India at a minimum cost, both in financial terms and regarding the relations of the West with Pakistan. The defense production team mapped out a programme to meet the combat needs of the 'Nassau six mountain divisions'.

The British side, eager not to give reasons to Pakistan for pulling out of the Western alliances, was more sanguine than Kennedy about making additional military aid to non-aligned India conditional to serious progress on the Kashmir issue. The US President was convince that military aid to India should only be partly conditioned on the course of Indo-Pakistan relations. He wrote to Macmillan: 'I am still persuaded that adding to Indian confidence vis-à-vis the Chinese is more likely to help promote a Kashmir settlement than to make the Indians more intransigent. It appears to us that Nehru is unlikely to settle Kashmir with too obvious a gun at his back.'[68] It was, nevertheless, clear that his ability to secure from the Congress the massive—but yet to be clearly defined—aid that India wanted, on top of an already staggering economic assistance, would be compromised without evidence of India's own seriousness of purpose on a Kashmir settlement. There was to be a relationship between the progress made on the Kashmir issue and the pace and quantity of the military assistance.

Before the fifth round of ministerial talks between India and Pakistan, to be held in Karachi in April 1963 (which proved to be unsuccessful), Galbraith proposed that the US should strike a 'crude bazaar level' political bargain with Nehru.[69] The deal was that the US would give substantial support on machinery, equipment, and raw material for the development of India's defense industry, backup support on air, and negotiate a sizeable programme of long-term aid in exchange for a clear indication that India would make a substantial concession in the Valley and offer guarantees on the rivers. If Pakistan decided not to respond to a suitable Indian offer, the US would go ahead with military aid to India. If a Kashmir settlement was arrived at, the US would additionally provide India with high-performance fighters, pilot training, and probably transport planes. Such a proposal did not find favour with Dean Rusk since the open-ended military commitment to India, even before a settlement was reached, would only serve the purpose of infuriating Pakistan and negate any chance of agreement.[70] In any case, Nehru was getting more and more restive over the linkage between Kashmir and the problem of arms aid. Dean Rusk conceded, on the eve of a visit to the subcontinent in early May to promote the idea of a mediation, that the combination of the Chinese withdrawal, the Pakistani exploitation of the Indian difficulties with the Chinese, and America's own strategic interests in the subcontinent did limit the US leverage with the Indians on the Kashmir issue.[71] It soon became evident that the issue was really one of how large US assistance would be if the Kashmir talks failed. The offer of long-range military assistance ensued from the need to maintain a degree of Indian military strength on the border with China and to strengthen the political relationship in a concrete manner without losing sight of the long-term geopolitical significance of India as the only non-communist country in Asia capable of becoming a counterpoise to Communist China. There was also always the risk that abandoning the Indians would drive them towards the USSR or even encourage them to patch things up with China. Kennedy was of the view that Pakistan and the United Kingdom should not be allowed to hold off US aid indefinitely merely because of the Karachi's quarrel with New Delhi and of the British fears of offending China which may lead to reprisals against Hong Kong. His analysis was driven by Cold War objectives and his priority was to build up India's military strength as a bulwark against Communist China. To Macmillan, Kennedy wrote that it would be a mistake to let the Indians conclude that there was little prospect of any further military help in the absence of a Kashmir settlement while 'Indian support is so essential to a satisfactory non-nuclear balance of power in Asia that we don't want to risk unduly any Indian backsliding from their new determination to counter the Chinese communist threat.'[72] The real challenge was to strike a fine balance between giving to India enough so as not to lose it and not too much so as not to alienate Pakistan. What was immediately at stake for Washington was the deployment, in case of a Chinese attack, of three Commonwealth/American squadrons for use in the air defense of the Delhi and Calcutta areas, the installation of radar and communication facilities, and the conduct of peacetime air defense exercises with the IAF in India. The British were obviously reluctant since an 'air umbrella plan', without being part and parcel of a joint defense of the subcontinent, implied too far-reaching commitments, especially at a time when India's favourable frame of mind towards the Kashmir dispute and on the subject of 'non-alignment' in the wake of the Chinese invasion was melting away.[73]

The Soviet leadership, for its part, anxious to prevent any pro-Western tilt by India, gave assurance to the Secretary General in the Ministry of External Affairs, Ratan Kumar Nehru, who went to the Russian capital in January 1963, that they would, apart from expanding their economic cooperation, consider the request which he made for defense equipment and defense production aid.[74] Moscow did not express any major objection to the Western military assistance to India as long as it did not take the form of a permanent military presence on Indian soil. In return, R.K. Nehru conveyed to his Soviet interlocutors that the watershed principle of non-alignment would be maintained. In early February 1963, the first four MIG 21 arrived in Bombay at the time when the Anglo-

American air defense mission was in India. In April, the government was able to give the information, after compromising between the recommendations of an expert committee headed by J.R.D. Tata and Biju Patnaik's wishes, that the airframes for the MIGs were to be manufactured near Nasik in Maharashtra and the engines at Koraput in Orissa. It was reported in July that the Soviets had privately informed the Indian government that the USSR would be ready to offer substantial military equipment, in particular surface-to-air missiles. The publicity generated over the offer, just before crucial discussions were held in Moscow to set Sino-Soviet relations right, was pinned on US intelligence services.[75]

T.T. Krishnamachari, in his new avatar as Minister for Economic and Defense Coordination, flew in May 1963 to Great Britain and the United States for talks on India's immediate and long-term defense needs with President Kennedy and a wide range of officials from the Department of State, the Pentagon, the National Security Council, the Treasury, the AID, as well as with members of Congress. In this endeavour, he had been preceded in March by Biju Patnaik, the high-profile Chief Minister of Orissa and a one-time aspirant to Krishna Menon's chair in the Defense Ministry, who was sent as a personal emissary of Nehru to hold discussions with the Pentagon and the Department of State. He was soon followed by Bhoothalingam, the Secretary of the Ministry for Economic and Defense Coordination, who led a team of defense experts to Washington in the third week of April to prepare the ground for his Minister's visit. During a press conference in Washington on 22 May, T.T. Krishnamachari revealed that he had asked assistance roughly to double the strength of the army over the next three years, to create manufacturing capacity, and to build radio communications, airfields, and the like in two phases over the same period. To this he added that India's request for aircraft included transport planes (C-130s), fighter-bombers, bombers, and supersonic fighter planes. He justified the request for the latter by explaining that they were needed to intercept Chinese planes because of the difficulties of an early-warning radar system in the sub-Himalayan and Himalayan regions. Finally, he mentioned the possibility of regular exchanges of views in future on India's military problems and strategy between his country, the Commonwealth, and the United States.[76] India's expectations—$ 1.6 billion in aid over three years (this came down subsequently to $ 1.3 billion)—were considered unrealistic at a time when the United States was only ready to consider as militarily realistic only $ 300 million, offered in partnership with the United Kingdom.[77] The Americans, during the T.T. Krishnamachari mission, remained elusive regarding the Indian bid for large-scale aid, especially substantial hardware (three supersonic squadrons) to build up the Indian Air Force, and found rather utopian the doubling of the land forces. The United States favoured a limited programme tailored in conformity with their appraisal of the Chinese capabilities and would, therefore, stick to the air defense plan mentioned above, along with additional transport and communication support for the IAF, road construction assistance, and training for the Army and the Air Force. They were also ready to consider what they could do toward providing equipment for Indian divisions and defense production aid. Nevertheless, it was not deemed advisable to build up too much of an indigenous production base since it would make India less dependent on the United States and would be deeply resented by Pakistan. The supply of F-104Gs to India was not on the US agenda; the only planes that the United States agreed to supply that year to India were some additional C-119 transport planes, and that too as replacements for the Hercules C-130 that had been lent in November 1962.

In early June, it was the turn of the Indian President Radhakrishnan to visit the United States and to express India's anxiety to develop its military potential. He held views that were hardly gandhian in nature: 'military weakness is a temptation; military strength may prove a deterrent'.[78] As any sizeable aid to India necessitated the consent of Congress, this could hardly be considered at the time. First of all because a fresh Chinese offensive did not seem on the cards and, at worst, the United States could always respond with a one-time emergency aid whose magnitude would depend on the force of the Chinese attack. Then, it was certain that the failure of the negotiations between India and Pakistan after six meetings held between 27 December 1962 and 16 May 1963 did act as a deterrent to Congressional approval of military assistance. On 2 March 1963, a border agreement was signed by Chen Yi and Zulfikar Ali Bhutto, the Chinese and Pakistani Ministers of Foreign Affairs. This agreement, signed a little before the fourth Indo-Pakistani meeting held at Calcutta on 9-12 March, was to remove any hope of New Delhi and Islamabad coming to an understanding. Undoubtedly, the Pakistani government intended to make good use of the threat of a Sino-Pakistani front. This, added to the Anglo-American pressure, was aimed at forcing New Delhi to come to an agreement on Kashmir. But, as W.W. Rostow, who had been sent by Kennedy to the subcontinent in early April in his capacity as chairman of the policy planning council at the State Department, to assess the prospects for an accommodation between India and Pakistan, rightly observed: 'Indian minds run into a real block in surrendering any substantial part of the Vale; and Pakistani minds run into an even greater block in ceding once and for all any part of the Vale to India.'[79]

The failure of the negotiations between India and Pakistan strengthened those who, in the US government and Congress, considered that the careful attention paid to India had only resulted in compromising the alliance with Pakistan to please a non-aligned State, without even lessening the risks of confrontation between the two countries. In August, a new joint US-UK mediation proposal was dismissed by the Indian Prime Minister who argued that such effort would be a fruitless exercise as long as Pakistan is determined to achieve a settlement entirely upon its own terms. It prompted Kennedy to remind Nehru that the setback to mediation would inevitably have an adverse impact on the Administration efforts to fight back the mounting resistance in the Congress against aid programmes which seem destined to aggravate disputes between two nations.[80] If some American officials were to consider Nehru as the real stumbling block to a Kashmir settlement, some were also exasperated by Ayub Khan oft-repeated request not to give the Indians more means to threaten his country. A doubtful Kennedy asserted once that 'what Ayub was really worried about was that he was losing the capability to attack India successfully or at least to get his way vis-à-vis India'.[81]

When Kennedy and Macmillan met at Birch Grove (Sussex) in end June 1963, they promised to carry on with some military assistance to India but refrained from backing the grandiose modernization plans of the Indian military chiefs. To counter the latest Soviet offer of arms to India, including surface-to-air missiles, it was decided to finalize quickly a proposal for air training exercises. In this regard, in July 1963, a tripartite agreement to strengthen India's defense against possible future air attacks from Communist China was clinched. It provided for the supply of two mobile radar installations, with related communication equipment, to be located in the Delhi and Calcutta areas (to be subsequently replaced by fixed radar installations), the training of Indian technicians in the use of these installations, and the participation of elements of the US Air Force and the Royal Air Force in joint training exercises with the IAF. The agreement did not involve any firm commitment on the part of the Western participants to come to India's assistance in the event of a renewed Chinese attack. Some in India considered that this agreement constituted nothing but a palliative to alleviate the refusal to supply supersonic planes and anti-aircraft missiles, and it was all the less satisfactory as is went contrary to the spirit of non-alignment. Thus, the editorialist of the *Times of India* wrote:

> It needs to be precisely understood that the agreement is not simply a training programme or the generous gift of an elaborate radar system but an understanding whereby in certain conditions Western air aid will materialize and for which the radar installations are to be provided. This is nothing less than a military pact which can be justified only if it can be shown that there is no alternative and that a drastic modification of the non-aligned policy is in Indian interest.[82]

Nehru side-stepped these criticisms, but also chose to downplay the first exercise which took place in November when the weather conditions for flying over the high Himalayan ranges were more favourable. A second exercise was provisionally fixed for April 1964.

On the other hand, Nehru had to concede defeat during the same summer of 1963, when his government was accused once again of compromising the policy of non-alignment, this time by authorizing the Voice of America to broadcast its programmes for South-East Asia from the state radio broadcasting corporation. This decision was another fallout of the Sino-Indian conflict of the preceding autumn. In November 1962, the Indian government considered it an urgent matter to counter the Chinese propaganda being disseminated in South-East Asia by Radio Peking. It had then made inquiries concerning the possibility of acquiring a high-power transmitter (1,000 KW) and had come to the conclusion that only the VOA could supply a medium-wave transmitter rapidly and at no cost. The latter accepted to do so in March 1963 but on certain conditions. The most important condition, ratified by the agreement signed on 9 July 1963, stipulated that the government-owned All India Radio would allow the VOA to get daily three hours of the broadcasting time for its own programmes over a five-year period. There was also to be no programme in Urdu or Bengali, languages spoken in East

Pakistan. Many in the press and certain politicians castigated this agreement. The *Times of India* recalled that the VOA broadcasts have

> never pretended to be anything other than blatant propaganda of a kind with which no country can be associated without attracting the charge of intentionally serving the policies of the United States. . . . It is incredible that an agreement so obviously and outrageously damaging to everything that has been understood to constitute non-alignment should have been negotiated without, it would seem, the slightest apprehensions of political involvement. . . . The plain irrefutable fact is that non-alignment and Indian interests in South-East Asia will be seriously affected by this latest folly.[83]

Nehru was forced to declare on 17 July that the agreement signed would be re-examined with the American authorities. After intermittent negotiations in the months that followed, it was announced in March 1964 that the deal was off. The Soviet Union immediately informed India that it was ready to supply two medium-wave transmitters of 500 KW and an agreement was signed to this effect in October 1965. These were not the only decisions taken by Nehru dictated by the now near-obsessive fear of a renewed Chinese offensive, after having for long underestimated the seriousness of this threat.

Nehru was once again put on the mat for not having opposed the planned visit of the Seventh Fleet, normally operating in the China Sea, in the Indian Ocean, and about which the US General Maxwell Taylor, the Chairman of the Joint Chiefs of Staff, had come to talk to him on 17 December 1963. The official aim was to fill up a strategic vacuum in the Indian Ocean with the dispatch of US warships which would conduct periodic patrols, and eventual calls at Indian ports to deter any bellicose moves by the Chinese in the region. Such a presence would also have a stabilizing influence in South Asia not only regarding the Chinese threat but also in possibly pacifying the Pakistani leadership which was crying wolf over India's supposedly aggressive intentions fed by US military assistance. Once again, an editorial in the *Times of India* considered that

> the quibble over United States' right to operate outside India's territorial waters completely ignores the truth that the Seventh Fleet is to be used as [a] political weapon in support of what Washington considers is or will be in the interests of South-East Asia. This is something which it is inconceivable New Delhi would have silently accepted before the October-November crisis of 1962. . . . It is still not too late for Mr. Nehru to

undertake the second thoughts for which he is so well-known and which, incidentally, saved the country from the humiliation of Voice of America. One possible interpretation of New Delhi's indeterminate attitude is that it wishes to avoid anything that might jeopardize American economic and military aid, including the supersonic aircraft which Washington has refused, on which the Indian Air Force has seemingly set its heart.[84]

The *Economic Weekly* felt that, by his behaviour the Prime Minister, whose leadership was then being increasingly questioned, was contravening a certain number of principles which had led India in the past to oppose the existence of military bases, the spread of nuclear arms into the region, and the extension of the Cold War into the subcontinent. Nehru's refusal to protest against the projected entry of the nuclear-armed Seventh Fleet into the Indian Ocean apparently marked 'the beginning of a foreign policy of non-involvement. Reactions will be subdued in future. There will be no eloquent espousals of Afro-Asian causes. Even the tense borders with Pakistan and China will be left "disengaged" to await a future settlement. All attention will "focus" on economic development.'[85]

It was learnt later that Nehru had granted facilities to U-2 spy planes monitoring military activities in Xinjiang and Tibet to land and refuel in India.These CIA-supervised missions were operated from a military base at Charbatia in Orissa with the connivance of the state Chief Minister, Biju Patnaik.[86] During the latter's visit to the United States in March 1963, discussions were held over signals intelligence operations. This visit was also linked to the establishment in Chakrata (north-east of Mussoorie) of a commando training school composed of elements coming from Tibet, Ladakh, and the eastern border region put under the orders of Indian officers assisted by American advisers. The commandos were to serve in a secret unit whose aim was to help Tibetan guerillas fighting from the Mustang region of Nepal and in Kham.[87] In 1964, the Indian government secretly endorsed an American proposal aimed at installing a remotely-operated telemetry intelligence device with nuclear power-pack atop Nanda Devi with the object of securing information about Chinese nuclear and missile tests. A first expedition, in October 1965, failed because of bad weather conditions and an avalanche carried away the device. The operation was successfully conducted on a nearby peak in the spring of 1967 but weather hazards hampered the proper functioning of the sensor and it was finally returned to the Americans in 1968. By 1969, two new devices trained on China had been installed, one in Leh (Ladakh), and the other in the Arunachal mountains.[88] On the eve of Indira Gandhi's visit to Washington, in early November 1971, a US report assessing the bilateral relations mentioned the existence of 'a small, significant and clandestine intelligence cooperation program which is of great importance to India in monitoring Chinese military and other activities in Tibet and Chinese and Soviet nuclear testing. These intelligence programs are of at least equal importance to us.'[89]

Chester Bowles, who had once again become America's Ambassador to India after the departure of Galbraith in July 1963, reported that Nehru, whom he had met in the autumn of 1963 to talk to him about a prospective long-term military assistance, had conveyed that he was ready in return to negotiate an agreement with Pakistan to fix a ceiling on their respective military expenditures, and also to cooperate in the political arena with the United States to arrive at a peaceful solution ensuring the independence of South Vietnam, Laos, and other countries of the region endangered by Chinese expansionist designs. This was something he had until then been very reluctant to do.[90] On 13 November, a few days before Kennedy's assassination, Bowles met the President to propose a trade off over a five-year US military commitment—at $ 75 million or so per year—in exchange for a tacit understanding that the government of India would comply with a force ceiling implicitly to placate Pakistan, would limit its purchases from the USSR, would avoid major diversions of foreign exchange to defense expenditure, and would take a more active role in the US grand strategy against China.[91] Bowles's proposal was well received—even if found somewhat on the higher side—within the State and the Defense Departments, and orders for the preparation of a five-year military assistance programme for India in the $ 50–$ 60 million annual range were given, provided also that the Indians produce a firm five-year military plan. The American valuation of a reasonable amount of Soviet military aid would be based on the quantities and types of Soviet aid accepted, the effects on the security of US equipment, the extent to which Soviet assistance required the introduction of Soviet technicians, and the overall degree of dependence on the Soviets.[92] The report submitted by Maxwell Taylor to the Secretary of Defense, McNamara, following his visit to the subcontinent, took up similar recommendations which ran concurrently with a parallel long-term military programme with Pakistan. Regarding India, the stakes were high considering the declining health of Nehru. It was assumed that 'the post-Nehru leadership could be far more pro-US than Nehru'.[93] Lyndon Johnson, who did not share the sense of personal involvement of Kennedy in favour of India, while broadly agreeing to proceed along these lines, called for caution and dismissed any aid figures subject to a better reading on Congressional attitudes and commitments from the prospective recipients of long-term military aid. In particular, India was to hold foreign exchange diversions from development to defense to a reasonable level, lest the United States end up 'indirectly helping finance an excessive defense effort via aid which we provide for quite another purpose'. For their part, the Pakistanis were reminded that MAP help should be 'appropriately linked to satisfactory performance with respect to its alliance obligations and to our intelligence facilities'.[94] The rapprochement between Rawalpindi and Beijing did not fail to irritate Washington. For instance, following an air agreement on civil aviation in August 1963 whereby Pakistan International Airlines became the first non-communist airline to serve China with regular international flights, the State Department, protesting against this 'violation of the solidarity of the free world', had held up a loan of $ 4.3 million meant for the modernization of Dhaka airport in East Pakistan. The Pakistani leadership was told to give assurances that it would limit its relationship with Beijing and would pursue policies which would not be adverse to American interests.

Pakistan continued to display hostility towards closer Indo-US relations and it was certainly to prevent any moves in this direction that it decided to refer the Kashmir issue to the Security Council in February 1964, apparently without prior consultations with the United States, in the wake of further integration moves into the Indian Union (some crucial provisions of India's Constitution—including Article 356 relating to President's Rule—were additionally extended to Kashmir) and the demonstrations over the theft in Srinagar of a relic of the Prophet Muhammad. Not content with reminding the US government that nothing would stop India in its move to integrate Kashmir unless it threatened to stop aid, the more the Pakistani leadership could distract New Delhi from Beijing, the more they could disturb the Indo-US rapprochement. In doing so, Pakistan was also to remind India of its dependence on Soviet support and the importance of maintaining non-alignment.

The United States found itself at the receiving end and had to bear the indignation of Indian official and public circles. It was assumed that the Pakistani decision to go again to the UN could not have been taken without the certainty that the Johnson administration was more favourable to Rawalpindi than the previous one. The impression gaining ground was that India had been denied the close relations it wanted with Washington, and the fact that substantial assistance was not forthcoming was proof of this. As Chester Bowles noted:

> In India, President Kennedy was looked upon as [a] special friend who was author of Indian resolution in Congress, who had frequently spoken in behalf of Indian aid, and who had singled out India as great experiment in democracy. With [the] loss of this friend, Indians now believe [that] we favor Pakistan in its disagreement with India and discount India's importance.[95]

The Indian reading was somewhat unfair since the US government still did intend to go forward on a long-term military assistance programme and to give aid on a grant basis with possibly some dollar military sales on favourable terms under an export promotion programme. The emphasis was again laid on the need for the Indian government not to go overboard and work out an austere minimum five year plan for its defense against the Chinese threat which would not jeopardize its developmental projects. The State Department was anxious not to provide military assistance to meet legitimate Indian needs just to see additional hard currency given for economic development diverted from it. At the same time, it was worrying to observe that Moscow had made up for the time lost due to its initial ambiguous response to India's war with China and was now wooing, rather successfully, the Indian military establishment. The situation called for introspection since millions of dollars in military aid had been given to Pakistan for a military alliance directed against communism—and not just to protect it against India—whereas its leadership was increasingly interacting with China when the latter was squeezing the United States in South-East Asia.[96] Furthermore, Pakistan had got much more per capita aid than India. 'We can and should protect Pakistan against India, but we cannot permit our ties—or our taste for Ayub against Nehru—to stand in the way of a strong Indian policy. This would permit the tail to wag the dog, which is just what Pakistanis are trying to do', commented Robert Komer of the National Security Council.[97] Now it was also acknowledged that if the United States had trouble getting over a 'painful transition of disengaging from the out and out pro-Pak policy of the 1950s, and shifting to one more consonant with our real strategic interests', the Indian slate was by no means clean either considering the VOA fiasco, the failure of Bokaro's plant and New Delhi's tediously slow handling of its military programme.[98] Doubts in India were clearly on the rise regarding the American ability to antagonize the Pakistanis or even to restrain them if they should cause trouble alone or in association with the Chinese, and consequently the possibility of relying increasingly on Soviet military supplies gained ground. To pursue different options in the economic field had paid dividends and it was tempting to do the same in the area of military procurement.

The Americans were conscious of the need to regain some of the lost post-war momentum. The time had come to encourage the emerging leadership around Shastri, Nehru's heir apparent, and to 'minimize the risk of a swing back toward Menonism'.[99] The immediate US concern was indeed to try to pre-empt, in some measure, the Soviet SAM and MIG offers. An air package offer was put together, involving mainly 72 surplus F-6As interceptors. This aircraft had the advantage of not being as sophisticated as the F-104s—which would assuage the feelings of the Pakistanis—but good enough to face the Chinese air threat. Alternatively, the Indians could get two squadrons of F-5As, but not till 1965-7. The United States, along with the United Kingdom, could also try to find an engine to power at supersonic speed India's homegrown HF-24 fighter supposed to become available in 1967 at the earliest. The US government was obviously keen not to introduce a radical alteration of the balance of power in the subcontinent. This reserve was fought against by Chester Bowles, who reminded his countrymen that delayed decisions regarding US military assistance to India was leaving the field open to the Soviet Union, increasingly freed of its inhibitions *vis-à-vis* China, and the chances to develop a close working partnership in the military field, similar to the one which had developed over a period of time regarding India's economic development, were now fading. The Chinese bogey was still the best bet and it was thus considered urgent not to minimize the Chinese threat at this time, particularly after having spent years in persuading India that China was an aggressive and dangerous power. Furthermore, any other approach:

> would only play into the hands of Communists, Menonites and Hindu extremists who are following precisely this same line in effort to substitute Pakistan for China as India's number one enemy. Our approach should be

to play up evil intent of Chinese and then distinguish between the intent on one hand and capacity on the other of Chinese to bring their strength to bear.[100]

Yeshwantrao Balwantrao Chavan, who had replaced Krishna Menon as Defense Minister, went to the United States in May 1964 to ascertain, notably with his American counterpart, Robert McNamara, the extent of military assistance that the Americans were ready to give. Some weeks earlier, Chavan, in a speech in Parliament, had tried to relativize the importance of the military assistance given till then by the West.[101] In Washington, he presented the broad outlines of a $ 12 billion (Rs. 56.7 billion) five year plan (April 1964-March 1969) concerning the expansion and the modernization of the army. The plan provided for the creation of a well-equipped army with the strength of 825,000 men, a 45-squadron Air Force (including a programme of re-equipment and replacement of the older aircraft such as Vampires, Mystères, and Toofanis by more modern aircraft) with the latest radar and communications facilities, a phased programme of modernization of the Navy, an adequate network of border roads and supply lines, and the establishment of a proper defense productive base to meet most of the requirements of the armed forces. It was assessed that the total amount of foreign exchange for the defense plan would come to about three times the normal allocations which were made to defense from India's export earnings. Hence, the urgent necessity to secure assistance from friendly countries to ensure that India's economic progress was not unduly affected. The Minister of Defense seemed resolutely optimistic and hopeful that the American government would not fail to be generous at a time when his country was engaged in an unprecedented effort to build up its defense potential to meet aggression from an untrustworthy neighbour, 'an effort to save democracy and democratic values in that sensitive part of the world'.[102] As it turned out, the discussions focused on the size of the five-year defense plan. It initially called for foreign exchange outlays amounting to $ 1.91 billion, including aircraft procurement. The Americans were keen to see a reduction in the overall defense expenditure to $ 10,500 million (Rs. 50 billion) and the foreign exchange component to be cut down to a maximum of $ 1.43 billion (Rs. 6.82 billion), averaging $ 286 million annually and preferably moving towards the $ 1.3 billion (Rs. 6.5 billion) level. This amount included all identifiable offshore acquisitions, including US, UK, and

Soviet assistance as well as those from India's own foreign exchange. The possibility of providing Indians with $ 50 million in military credit sales for fiscal year 1965 (on top of $ 50 million military grant aid assistance) was considered, as well as the offer of supersonic F-104s, advocated by Bowles but opposed by the Pentagon, since it was an almost foregone conclusion that the Indians would not buy the aid package of subsonic F-6A Skyray plus help on the HF-24 designed to limit MIGs to acceptable numbers. If India did not renege on the MIG-21 production line, the credit would at least go to the Americans for having been forthcoming and shown that they did not consider the Indians as 'second-class citizens' *vis-à-vis* Pakistanis.[103]

Before he could even meet Lyndon Johnson. Chavan's talks in Washington were cut short by Nehru's death on 27 May 1964. However, even before Lal Bahadur Shastri was sworn in as Prime Minister on 9 June, a memorandum of understanding was concluded between Bowles and Chavan on 6 June, much to the dismay of the Pakistanis who feared that the previous three-to-one military balance on which they counted heavily might be seriously altered. The MoU held, in fact, more promises than actual commitments and it did not include any jet offer designed to pre-empt the Indian MIG deal with Moscow, nor was any financial commitment, partly precluded by the upcoming US presidential election in the autumn, made beyond the fiscal year 1965. In return for a ceiling on rupee defense expenditure and Indian military procurement abroad, India could nevertheless expect that US assistance would be forthcoming throughout the five-year defense plan. In concrete terms, India had been assured of an immediate credit of $ 10 million for the purchase of defense articles and services. A grant aid of $ 50 million under MAP and sales on credit terms of the same amount, repayable over ten years at 3 per cent, would be given for the fiscal year 1965 to ensure the continued support, on the one hand, for the Indian mountain divisions, the air defense communication equipment, the transport aircraft support, and the road-building equipment for the Border Roads Organization, and, on the other hand, for the modernization of plant and equipment in ordnance factories and for the setting up of new units of production as, for instance, an artillery shell plant at Ambajhari.[104]

The Indian delegation had met with a certain number of refusals while in the United States. On the question of the supply of vessels for replacing the overaged ships or the acquisition of submarines (the US supplied in 1964 one submarine to Pakistan), it was recommended that the matter be first discussed with the British government considering the fact that the Indian fleet was till then equipped almost solely with British equipment. And above all, the negotiations on the delivery of three squadrons of F-104s, which was the primary item on Chavan's shopping list, was still in a state of deadlock. The United States stuck to the proposed air defense package of selling or granting to India three squadrons of (72) F-6As and helping to develop the HF-24 into an operational Mach 2 interceptor. Only if the HF-24 did not work out, would the US provide 36 F-104Gs, or eventually F-5, in a few years; all this was based only on the condition that India would drop its plan for obtaining MIG-21s beyond rounding out a single squadron of no more than 24 aircraft.[105] The agreement signed in August 1962 for the production of MIGs in India did not cover all aspects of the manufacturing programme since what really mattered at the time was to speed up deliveries of the supersonic planes. Also, there was still to negotiate a series of supplementary arrangements for the supply of major assemblies, sub-assemblies, and raw materials from the Soviet Union for the production of initial batches of MIG-21s. Bowles was still trying hard to convince Washington of the need to prevent the Indians to turn to the Soviets for military hardware denied by the Americans, explaining that

> if the Soviet Union is prepared to put nearly one billion dollars worth of military aid into a confused situation such as Indonesia or into a relatively limited one such as the United Arab Republic, it would be foolhardy for the United States or Pakistan to assume that Khrushchev will refuse to invest equally sizeable amounts of semi-obsolescent military equipment in India in order to strengthen his political position in the one country in Asia which has the capacity to provide a significant counterweight to Communist China.[106]

The expected Pakistani protests were to be taken care of by pointing out that the US review of India's five year plan had resulted both in a substantial reduction in Indian plans and also in an increased concentration of the build up to respond to the communist threat. If ever the Indians were to get F-104s, the Pakistanis would also be offered additional F-104s.

The debate on the nature of the defense air package to India soon became irrelevant since the MIG deal was to hold good. The final decision seems to have been made personally by Nehru in April 1964 'in face of some differences of opinion with the government of India'.[107] Commitment for production facilities made some two years earlier was reasserted during Mikoyan's brief visit to New Delhi (20-21 June 1964) on his way to Indonesia. US officials in New Delhi, nevertheless, entertained a slender hope that the Indians might back away from the MIG-21 agreement. In January 1965, Chavan let it be known to Ambassador Bowles that India could indeed not afford the F-104Gs and raised the possibility of procuring between three and six squadrons of F-5As over two or three years. Besides, US experts could help technically and financially in developing the Indian-produced HF-24 Mark I, putting the Mark II version off indefinitely.[108]

Official circles in Moscow had been preoccupied with the growing influence that the pro-Western rightist forces seemed to be exerting on Indian policy. They saw proof of this in the joint exercises conducted by the Indian, the American, and the British air forces in the autumn of 1963, in the tentative agreement with the VOA, or again in the departure of Krishna Menon from the government and then of K.D. Malaviya in June 1963, both these Ministers representing the left wing of the Congress in the government.[109] Clearly annoyed with the air defense dealings with the United States, Moscow offered to supply India with missiles, radar equipment, and transport planes. In early July 1963, the Chief of Air Staff, A.M. Engineer, went to Moscow at the invitation of the Commander-in-Chief of the Soviet Air Force, Marshal Konstantin A. Vershinin. A few days later, a delegation of senior civil and army personnel led by S. Bhoothalingam arrived in Moscow to negotiate the purchase of military equipment. This visit was charged with significance since it took place at a time when Sino-Soviet talks were being held in the Soviet capital which were to set the seal on the divorce between the two countries and set further aside Moscow's hesitations regarding large-scale arms sales to India. The negotiations conducted in this year led to the supply of additional Mi-4 helicopters and An-12 transport planes, as well as K-13 'Atoll' air-to-air missiles meant to arm the MIG-21.

The death of Nehru caused further anxiety in Moscow over the intensity of India's determination to pursue the policy of non-alignment. The Soviet Ambassador, Benediktov, was said to have been preoccupied by the pro-Western frame of mind of most of the army officers and to have feared that, after Nehru's departure, the United States may try to encourage reliable military elements to play a more active role in the political life of the nation.[110] Mikoyan was entrusted with the task of meeting the new Prime Minister, Lal Bahadur Shastri, in June 1964 to get confirmation that there would be no change in India's foreign policy and in the pursuit of its cooperation with the USSR. He also held talks on this occasion with Chavan, who had just returned from Washington. On 28 August, the latter arrived in Moscow in the hope of getting from the Soviets what had been refused to him by the Americans. The Soviet Defense Minister, Marshal Rodion Y. Malinovsky, who had visited Delhi in December 1963, assured him that his country would continue to help India, adding: 'what is important is that you should preserve your independence and non-alignment'.[111] If the IAF had been till then the only recipient of Soviet assistance, 'an unexpected result of the Soviet authorities' offer to meet India's defense requirements was the perceptible change in the attitude of our army and navy top brass towards Soviet-made equipment and armaments', commented the private secretary to the Defense Minister, R.D. Pradhan.[112] An agreement over substantial new Soviet military assistance was signed on 11 September 1964, the day the Indian President, Dr S. Radhakrishnan, arrived in Moscow on a state visit to reassert the excellence of the bilateral relations and their common mistrust of China, and two days after the Indian Defense Minister had a very positive meeting with the Chairman of the USSR Council, Khrushchev.[113] Chavan gave details of the agreement in a communication to Parliament ten days later.[114] He specified that the Soviet government had now agreed to provide plant and machinery to facilitate the early establishment of the MIG complex and factories in addition to the 12 MIG-21s provided for in the August 1962 agreement (by then only six had been delivered). The order had been placed for the supply of 38 additional planes of an improved version. The Soviet authorities also agreed to supply some 93 amphibious PT-76 tanks to replace the old British Sherman—giving the Soviets their first foothold in the Indian Army—and some 20 additional Mi-4 helicopters as well as SA-2 surface-to-air missiles meant to protect the large Indian cities. The purchase of all this equipment involved also the training of several hundred Indian personnel in the USSR. The Soviet military loan was to be repaid in rupees over the next ten years at a 2 per cent interest rate. As usual, the rupees were to be used by the Soviet Union to import Indian goods under the existing trade agreement and to service its local expenditure. One could also argue that the purchases from the Soviet Union had the advantage of not coming directly under the foreign exchange ceiling insisted upon by the Americans.

Chavan clarified on this occasion that there was nothing that came in the way of Soviet military aid being utilized against China. While Chavan considered it necessary to give a public assurance that the government had not 'the slightest intention of playing military assistance from one country against military assistance from another', one may well doubt his words. For instance, the Defense Minister gave the impression in particular of wanting to kindle the interest of the British to prevent the Soviet Union from supplanting their hold over supplies to the Indian Navy. The United Kingdom, after much hesitation linked notably to the fact that there was no immediate Chinese naval threat and that it would be difficult to justify such an action to Pakistan, had just agreed to provide financial assistance towards the renovation of the Mazagaon docks in Bombay and the subsequent construction of three Leander class frigates under license. In Moscow, Chavan had been offered four submarines and some modern frigates on attractive terms. Nevertheless, Prime Minister Shastri, before making any commitment to the USSR, advised his Defense Minister to go to London to find out from the new Labour government the final word of the British on the acquisition of naval craft. A note of the British Foreign Office, prior to Y.B. Chavan's November visit, stressed that 'we do not wish to see any increase or further consolidation of the Soviet presence in India and particularly in the Indian Navy'. This would result 'in increasing Soviet influence in India and over the Indian government with a consequent weakening of the Western position. Furthermore, although there is no danger of a Communist takeover in India in the foreseeable future, a growing military dependence on the Soviet Union will inevitably strengthen local Communist forces.' Faced with tough Soviet competition and financial constraints, the British even asked the Americans whether they would be able to help by making an offer which would encourage the Indians to continue to rely upon the West for naval assistance.[115] Eventually, Chavan's visit drew a blank. India was refused the advanced Dagger class frigates which the Indian Navy wanted and was instead offered the older Leander frigates, and the acquisition of the Oberon type submarine also fell through. With no assurance of UK assistance, India finally signed an agreement in early September 1965 with the Soviets for the sale of Petya class frigates as well as landing crafts and patrol boats.

These agreements on the sale of naval craft to the Indian Navy were the first to be concluded after the removal of Khrushchev on 15 October 1964 which almost coincided with China's first nuclear explosion. On learning of his dismissal, which had caused people in New Delhi to speculate about the future of Indo-Soviet relations, the Indian government hastened to reaffirm that it valued its relationship with the Soviet Union and 'looked forward with confidence that these friendly ties will continue and grow stronger under the new leadership'.[116] When Indira Gandhi, the new Minister for Information and Broadcasting and whose first trip to the USSR dated back to 1953, went through Moscow on her way back to Delhi, a few days after Khrushchev's dismissal, Alexei Kosygin, the head of the government, told her that the latter had not been blamed for his policy of aid and friendship towards India, and promised that this policy would be continued.[117] In this matter, Moscow also directed the first deputy chairman of the praesidium of the Supreme Soviet to break journey in Delhi to explain to India's former Ambassador to the Soviet Union, President Radhakrishnan, that nothing had changed in Indo-Soviet relations.[118] When Shastri came to the Soviet capital on 12 May 1965, shortly after his visit to the USA had been postponed, he immediately thanked them for the aid given to India, adding that it was no exaggeration to say that India's ability to pursue a policy of non-alignment had 'to a large measure, been due to the understanding and support with which your government has regarded this policy'.[119] India once again used the Soviet card to thwart China when plans were being made for a second Afro-Asian conference, to be held in Algiers in 1965 (the conference was finally postponed *sine die*). India insisted, with Moscow's encouragement, on the participation of the USSR, which had been absent at the Bandung conference, while Beijing opposed this move.

In 1954, the Indian government had warned the Americans that they would not be able to prevent the Pakistanis from using against India the armour and equipment that they were supplying to India's traditional enemy. This forewarning proved to be correct in April 1965 when an exchange of fire between the Indian and Pakistani border police in the Rann of Kutch, a salt marsh in the Gujarat-

Sindh border area, escalated into an eyeball-to-eyeball confrontation between the two regular armies. Ultimately, a *de facto* cease fire was secured on 29 April 1965 with the good offices of the United Kingdom, and on 30 June, India and Pakistan signed an agreement providing for arbitration regarding the conflicting claims of territorial jurisdiction which formally ended the fighting. But this confrontation had a significant impact on Indo-American relations. Pakistan's use of US-supplied tanks to pound Indian positions was seen as a reminder of the insecurity resulting from the US-Pakistan security agreements of the 1950s, whereas India had to comply in 1962 with stricter conditions imposed on the utilization of American military equipment (i.e. only against Communist China).[120] Just a month before, Averell Harriman, Under Secretary of State for Political Affairs, on a visit to India to explain the US position on Vietnam, had appreciatively reported that there was 'quite a new attitude towards the United States and the world situation reflected by Indian officials as well as the press'. There were only limited disagreements over India's belief in the Soviet Union's good intentions or the fear that American policies towards Hanoi may bring Moscow and Beijing together again. But all together,

> I almost felt I was in a different country. With one exception [this was Swaran Singh who had become Minister of External Affairs in July 1964], discussions with Indian Ministers and officials were relaxed and frank with full agreement on such matters as aggressive intents of Red China, need to prevent Reds' take-over in South Vietnam and South-East Asia, willingness to consider objectively our policies and work with us for common objectives in other areas of the world. They show greater confidence in their ability to solve India's economic problems with increased production in agriculture and industry and have greater understanding of need to develop private sector by both domestic and foreign investment, although not yet taking all necessary actions.[121]

When Harriman was in Delhi, Ayub Khan was in Beijing on a state visit, accompanied by Foreign Minister Z.A. Bhutto who was by now perceived by the Americans as the subcontinental successor to Krishna Menon for his ability to antagonize the United States. The State Department was getting exasperated by Pakistan's flirtation with China and was of the opinion that it was high time to shake the Pakistani confidence that continued US economic and military support should be taken for granted, irrespective of the government's international posturing. In other words, 'Pakistan is being a lot more friendly to Beijing than to Washington, despite the fact that we still pay all the bills.'[122]

The fighting in the Rann of Kutch came on the heels of the unexpected postponement of the visits by Ayub Khan and, consequently, by Shastri to Washington which had been planned respectively for 26-27 April and 2-3 June. The argument put forward was that such visits would jeopardize the passage of foreign assistance legislation by the US Congress, given notably the differences regarding Pakistan's flirtation with China and the pressing and very sensitive Vietnamese problem—more so in the case of Pakistan which had been given highly preferential treatment over a far bigger India in per capita aid allocation. There were also the depressing tensions between the two countries as the flare-up in the Rann of Kutch had proved. The unilateral postponement of Shastri's visit at short notice was bitterly resented in New Delhi and it was thought disgraceful since it treated on an equal footing both Ayub Khan, who was cooperating with the Chinese, and the Indian Prime Minister, who was opposing them. Shastri was no doubt personally hurt by this postponement and in a letter to President Johnson he suggested that the latter should consider a cessation of the air strikes against North Vietnam prior to negotiations. To this suggestion, the US President responded that one had to keep in mind that 'the Chinese Communist-supported aggression in Vietnam poses the same kind of threat to Free World interests as Communist China's attack on India in 1962'.[123] Johnson was sensitive to any criticism of US policy in Vietnam and was deeply irritated by 'the way the Indians seemed compelled to comment so often on Vietnam'. He might have had in mind a reference made to a bombing halt in the joint communiqué issued at the end of Shastri's visit to the Soviet Union in May 1965, wherein the responsibilities of Hanoi regarding infiltration into South Vietnam found no mention. This kind of undesirable comment had, furthermore, the inconvenient result of antagonizing a pernickety US Congress after the US government had made known its willingness to contribute $ 435 million to the AIC for the forthcoming year. The US Congress increasingly questioned the soundness of aid appropriations to India and Pakistan when little leverage and effectiveness seemed to result from these countries, whereas they both showed a lack of consideration for American interests and susceptibilities.[124] It appeared that Johnson, who was more sensitive than his predecessor to the opinion of Congressmen and Senators, was also determined to take a long hard look at India and Pakistan and ensure that they should be held more accountable for the assistance which they received even if that meant delaying it. On 9 June, he ordered a review of economic aid to both countries. This reappraisal was to encompass economic aid as well as the MAP. Confronted with the facts that roughly $ 70 million of military assistance for India still remained undelivered, whereas $ 50 million had been planned for the forthcoming fiscal year, Johnson argued that everything military should be held in abeyance for both India and Pakistan.[125] The aid given to India and Pakistan, according to Dean Rusk, amounted to one-third of the total aid given by the Americans and that the total aid given to India till then substantially exceeded half the total given under the Marshall Plan, bringing about the feeling that no more American money should be given to India and Pakistan, countries whose sole objectives seemed to prepare to fight each other and not to cooperate in dealing with their very grave social and economic problems.[126]

American assurances that they would not permit Pakistan to aggressively use MAP-supplied military equipment against India was put to the test for the second time. This happened when massive infiltration of armed groups trained in Pakistan across the cease fire line into Indian held-Kashmir during the month of August escalated into open warfare from 1 September 1965 when the Pakistan army launched a major thrust in the southern part of the state. Pakistan's dramatic decision to undertake a provocative action *vis-à-vis* India may have been influenced by their determination to derail what seemed a US policy favouring India over Pakistan and to do it quickly before the military balance tilted too heavily in India's favour. A telegram from the US Embassy Office in Rawalpindi stressed that the Pakistanis

> by and large remain suspicious that US plans for them to play second fiddle to India in containment of Communist China on this flank. They are increasingly convinced we will not use our growing leverage on India (resulting from increased Indian economic dependence on the US) to induce Kashmir settlement which would solve whole problem of sub-continental solidarity. With US consortium pledge to India already made they consider that we are blind both to India's military trafficking with Soviet Russia and to India's abysmally poor economic performance. They consider that either of these circumstances should result in India's getting short shrift from the US instead of—as they see it—far better treatment than Pakistan.[127]

The infiltration started after the two-month postponement of the pledging session of the Aid-to-Pakistan Consortium which was supposed to be held on 27 July (the Pakistan consortium meeting scheduled for 23 September was again postponed to a later date). The Pakistani leadership may also have thought that in reactivating the Kashmir dispute, through a presumably popular rebellion in the Indian-held part of the state, they would force upon India a mediation by the Western powers, especially after the Rann of Kutch episode.

The twenty-two-day-long conflict ended on 22 September with the acceptance by India and Pakistan of Security Council resolution 211 adopted two days before, which demanded a cease fire and a withdrawal of all armed personnel back to the position held by them before 5 August 1965, and also allowing the Security Council to consider the steps that could be taken to assist towards a settlement of the political problem underlying the conflict. Earlier, the US Secretary of State had made it known on 8 September that his country had suspended military assistance shipments to India and Pakistan and, subsequently, all licenses for commercial shipments of military items. This decision was taken four days after the unanimous adoption by the United Nations Security Council of a first resolution calling for an immediate cease fire, which remained ineffective, and two days after Indian forces launched a large-scale offensive across the border in the vicinity of Lahore. It also occurred two days after Ayub Khan, invoking the US-Pakistan agreement of 1959, delivered a formal request to the American government for assistance against what he called an Indian aggression.

The immediate worry for the United States government was not to let the situation in the subcontinent get out of hand and lead to the collapse of one or both countries or to the outbreak of large-scale communal chaos which would in the end benefit Chinese Communist ambitions. Washington also assured New Delhi that other countries in the NATO, SEATO, and CENTO pacts had been advised not to supply US-origin arms to Pakistan. For India, this meant first of all that the delivery of American military equipment anticipated for the first year (1964-5) of the five year defense plan was suspended.[128] The US decision to cut off military aid was *de facto* more damaging for Pakistan but still the Indian government, deeming itself the victim of an aggression, took offence at being treated on the same basis as Pakistan, the aggressor. New Delhi considered this decision to be all the more unjust as there was no comparison between the tens of millions of dollars of mainly non-lethal equipment which it had received from the United States and the one billion dollars plus worth of military aid granted to Pakistan, embracing all three services, and of which a good part was in the form of fighter planes and Patton tanks which had been utilized in the fighting. Chavan recalled that the US aid 'was to enable India to defend itself against the Chinese threat, which still continues'.[129] An official from the US Defense Department confirmed that only 4 per cent of the military assistance supplied by the United States to India to meet the Chinese threat was regarded as lethal.[130] Inequity of treatment was also set forth by Bhutto but with a different conclusion: how could Pakistan, which had become almost totally dependent on US supply sources over the years, keep its defense machine going while facing an adversary relying on varied sources of foreign arms and a larger domestic armaments industry?[131] This charge of inequity was reinforced by the fact that the United States were willy-nilly continuing the supply of food which was then India's prime requirement (see next chapter) whereas they had cut off supplies to meet Pakistan's primary need.

India was also worried during the conflict that China may enter the fray and had looked for a formal warning from the United States that in such a case they would not remain passive. Beijing wasted no time in taking advantage of the situation to criticize what it saw as the Indo-American-Soviet collusion while recalling that

> it is not just today that the Soviet leaders and US imperialism treat the Indian reactionaries as their darling child. Kennedy, Khrushchev and Nehru became partners in a company. Two of the three founders are dead and the third has fallen from power. But their successors are trying to keep their failing concern going. . . . It was the encouragement, support and assistance of the revisionist leadership and US imperialism that emboldened the Indian reactionaries to launch armed aggression against China a few years ago. It is precisely their encouragement, support and assistance that has emboldened the Indian reactionaries to unleash armed aggression against Pakistan now.[132]

On 8 September, the Chinese government went beyond giving verbal support to Pakistani actions to protest against violations of China's territory and sovereignty by Indian troops and alleged that military works on the Tibetan side of the Sikkim-China border and on the border itself had been constructed. On 13 September, Dean Rusk warned China to keep out of the India-Pakistan war. Moscow also advised 'other countries' not to interfere. As China issued, on 16 September, a three-day ultimatum to India regarding the alleged military structures on Chinese territory, the Indian government asked if the United States would be willing to authorize US personnel to initiate secret contingency planning with Indian military planners. The reply to this query was a flat refusal, Washington considering that it would create ambiguity about the US position in the conflict with Pakistan.[133] Ultimately, Beijing's threatening noises stopped, with Pakistan accepting the UN Security Council resolution of 20 September demanding an immediate cease fire.

At the time that the suspension was ordered, India had received, since the autumn of 1962, around $ 130 million of military aid from the United States, of which more than three-quarters had been in the form of grants.[134] Still, the ratio of US assistance was ten to one in favour of Pakistan over India, the aid received by Pakistan between 1954 and 1965 amounted to over $ 630 million worth of direct grant assistance, to which must be added over $ 670 million in concessional sales and defense support.[135]

The suspension of the supply of military equipment by the West left India with no choice but to turn to the USSR for the pursuit of its defense programme—and Pakistan turned to China which was notably to provide MIG-19 and T-59 tanks.[136] India appreciated that the Soviet Union did not suspend arms shipments during the war.[137] A high-powered team led by H.C. Sarin, Special Secretary, Defense Production, was sent to the Soviet Union to hold discussions regarding the swifter implementation of previous contracts and concerning the acquisition of additional military equipment (T-55 tanks, 130-mm field guns, SA-2 missiles, An-12, Mi-4, as well as three submarines and the direct purchase of MIG-21). During a meeting with Bowles in mid-1966, the Army Chief, General J.N. Chaudhuri, argued that India had really turned to the USSR in August 1964 when it became clear that they could not secure the military equipment they wanted from the United States. He observed that only $ 140 million was made available by US and Western sources whereas $ 396 million had been anticipated in the first three years of the 1964 agreement. He suggested that the difference of $ 256 million was roughly comparable to the amount that India had since committed for equipment from the USSR.[138] Whatever the exact figures, it did not take long, since India first started to obtain

Soviet military equipment in 1960, for the Soviet Union to emerge as the largest supplier of arms to India, outstripping the United Kingdom. This trend was to have long-term implications if one considers that military aid, on account of the training of personnel and military advisers abroad or again keeping in mind the continuous need for spare parts and ammunition, creates durable links between the supplier and the purchaser. The search for Soviet support in the face of Chinese aggression, the reluctance of the West to sell to India the arms that it sought, and the possibility of paying in rupees at a time when the country was grappling with balance of payments problems, all these factors had enabled the Soviet Union to acquire this position. India had no illusions that US military assistance, if ever restarted, would remain hostage to predictable US policy complications with Pakistan.[139] The American government seemed prepared to make the best of it. As long as these deliveries helped in averting a Chinese threat, the interests of Moscow and Washington converged. Moreover, in this way Washington's relations with Pakistan were prevented from deteriorating. As for India, the extension of foreign aid to the military field had constituted yet another encounter with *realpolitik*. It is pertinent to recall that in August 1962 Nehru had reasserted that the advantage drawn from the 'few crores that we may save if we got those military equipment as a gift would be far outbalanced by the tremendous loss in prestige, in position and even in sympathy, that we may have from the rest of the world'.[140]

NOTES

1. The Pakistani leaders recalled that the distinction between commercial supplies and military aid was blurred if credits made in the name of economic assistance released funds to purchase military equipment. Concurring with this view, Selig S. Harrison felt, in 1959, that while India had refused all military aid from the United States, the $ 1.7 billion of US economic assistance ($ 1.05 billion of it in loans) that it had received had 'made possible—in the name of countering US aid to Pakistan—some $ 500 million in Indian military spending which would have been insupportable without US aid'. 'India, Pakistan and the United States (Part I)', *New Republic*, 10 August 1959, p. 10. Nehru challenged this kind of insinuation by arguing that the 'aid that we get from any country abroad, normally

speaking, is for a particular purpose and if not one purpose, a group of purposes according to our planning: it is all tied up . . . we get it mostly for the foreign exchange element for the capital goods that come in. In fact that aid does not release any of our domestic resources and in fact we have to spend domestic resources to make good that aid for a project.' If aid for a project failed to come, explained Nehru, it was the project itself that would have to be given up. 'Foreign aid does not lead to any release of our domestic resources for military or like purposes because any project that we take up is a drain on our domestic resources.' 17 August 1961. *Lok Sabha Debates (second series)*, vol. 56, no. 8, cols. 2770-1.

2. 1 February 1954. J.L. Nehru, *Letters to Chief Ministers*, vol. 3, p. 491.
3. 22 December 1959. *Lok Sabha Debates (second series)*, vol. 37, no. 27, col. 6726.
4. *Amrita Bazar Patrika*, 22 March 1956.
5. SIPRI (Stockholm International Peace Research Institute), *Arms Trade Register—The Arms Trade with the Third World*, Stockholm: Almqvist & Wiksell International, 1975, pp. 33-7.
6. Note to the Ministry of Defense Organization, 21 February 1954. J.L. Nehru, *Selected Works of Jawaharlal Nehru (second series)*, vol. 25, p. 296.
7. Note to the Commonwealth Secretary, 12 November 1954. J.N. Nehru, *Selected Works of Jawaharlal Nehru (second series)*, vol. 27, pp. 493-4.
8. Y. D. Gundevia, *Outside the Archives*, p. 347.
9. Note on Nehru's talk with MacDonald, 26 November 1955. J.L. Nehru, *Selected Works of Jawaharlal Nehru (second series)*, vol. 31, p. 239. The then Indian Defense Minister, K.N. Katju, felt also that the acquisition of Soviet bombers could raise some questions over India's professed non-alignment. K.N. Katju to Nehru, 29 November 1955. S. Gopal, *Jawaharlal Nehru: A Biography*, vol. 2, p. 252.
10. The United States replied favourably to a request from the British to equip the Canberras meant for India with certain specialized bombing equipment and radar systems, subject to some protective measures, in the hope of forestalling the purchase by India of 60 Soviet light bombers. *Progress Report of the Operations Coordinating Board*, Department of State, 30 March 1956. *FRUS, 1955-1957*, vol. 8, p. 5.
11. Eden to Nehru, 8 March 1956. S. Gopal, *Jawaharlal Nehru. A Biography*, vol. 2, p. 274.
12. Telegram from Secretary of State to the Department of State, 11 March 1956. *FRUS, 1955-1957*, vol. 8, p. 310.
13. Record by the United Kingdom Commissioner (MacDonald) of a conversation between Nehru, Mountbatten, R. Pillai, and himself, 17 March 1956. *PRO*, FO 371 123587.
14. *Operations Coordinating Board Report*, Department of State, 3 July 1957. *FRUS, 1955-1957*, vol. 8, p. 358.
15. Intervention in the Lok Sabha. *Hindu*, 31 May 1957.

16. Marshal Zhukov was also said to have made some blunders in his interaction with the military establishment when he clumsily dwelt upon the reminders of the British legacy of the Indian army (drills, music, room names in military schools, etc.). Zhukov's ironic comments did not go down well with the officers who had valiantly served the British. Dispatch of Henri Dumont, Consul-General in Bombay, to the French Ambassador following conversations with K.S. Thimayya, 23 March 1957. *AQO*, Asie-Océanie, 1956-1967, Inde, vol. 222.
17. From Moscow, the British Ambassador, Sir F. Roberts, to the Foreign Office, 4 November 1960. *PRO*, FO 371 152548.
18. The British had been anxious to prevent Indians from buying Russian helicopters, also needed for military defense against the Chinese, since this may give Soviet technicians access to sensitive locations. Unable to offer suitable helicopters within the time scale required, they were even resigned to the possibility of the Indians meeting some of their requirements from France or from America. Note from the Ministry of Aviation (Geoffrey Rippon) to the Secretary of State for Commonwealth Relations, 18 August 1960. *PRO*, FO 371 152548.
19. Memorandum from the Joint Chiefs of Staff to the Secretary of Defense (Gates), 15 November 1960. *FRUS, 1958-1960*, vol. 15, pp. 575-8.
20. Letter from the Deputy Secretary of Defense (Roswell L. Gilpatric) to the Under Secretary of State (Bowles), 12 June 1961. *FRUS, 1961-1963*, vol. 19, pp. 57-8. The US Department of Defense reported that certain senior members of the Indian military had made 'informal and unsolicited approaches' with specific proposals for circumventing what they considered to be the negative policies of Krishna Menon towards the purchase of US equipment. Letter from the Deputy Secretary of Defense to the Under Secretary of State (Bowles), 13 September 1961. Ibid., p. 97
21. *Statesman*, 26 February 1961. On 8 October 1962, a Chinese leader informed the Soviet Ambassador in Beijing that the fact that Soviet-made helicopters and transport planes were being used by India for air-dropping and transporting military supplies in the Sino-Indian border areas was making a bad impression on their border guards, and that he considered it his internationalist duty to inform the Soviet side of the situation. The Chinese later accused the Soviet leaders of having begun to supply military aid to India right from 1960, after 'the Indian reactionaries had started their armed provocations against China'. 'The truth about how the leaders of the C.P.S.U. have allied themselves with India against China', *People's Daily*, 8 November 1963. R.K. Jain (ed.), *China-South Asian Relations, 1947-1980*, vol. 1, pp. 305-6.
22. J.L. Nehru, *Press Conferences—1962*, pp. 29-30.
23. Telegram from the Embassy in India to the Department of State, 8 May 1962. *FRUS, 1961-1963*, vol. 19, p. 241.
24. Telegram from the Embassy in India to the Department of State, 18 May 1962. Ibid., p. 249.

25. Special National Intelligence Estimate, 6 June 1962. Ibid., p. 263. The original agreement governing the establishment of a facility at Peshawar was concluded on 18 July 1959 and was to remain in force for a period of ten years.
26. The government of India had decided in 1956 to build their own supersonic fighter, known as HF 24. The prototype, designed by a German team, was flown for the first time in 1961. It was then fitted with an early-type Bristol Orpheus engine just powerful enough to enable it to achieve supersonic flight. The project ran into difficulties when it became apparent that the Orpheus 12 engine was not likely to undergo further development after the NATO requirement for this engine disappeared. Although Bristol Siddeleys were prepared to continue the development of the engine in India, they would do so at Indian expense. This proved unacceptable to the Indians, who then began to consider seriously a Russian engine for the HF 24.
27. Message from Harold Macmillan to Kennedy, 13 June 1962. *PRO*, FO 371 164881.
28. Memorandum of conversation, 14 June 1962. *FRUS, 1961-1963*, vol. 19, p. 269.
29. Message from Harold Macmillan to Kennedy, 19 June 1962. *PRO*, FO 371 164881.
30. Telegram from the Department of State to the Embassy in India, 27 July 1962, *FRUS, 1961-1963*, vol. 19, pp. 314-15. Galbraith was still doubtful in early August whether the MIG deal would go through, thinking that 'the Soviets will be reluctant to arouse Chinese passions at a time when they are pressing the Chinese and Indians to stop playing war with their elbows on the northern border'. Letter from the Ambassador to India to President Kennedy, 6 August 1962. Ibid., pp. 320-1.
31. R.D. Pradhan, *Debacle to Revival—Y.B. Chavan as Defense Minister, 1962-1965*, p. 5.
32. Khrushchev to Nehru, 20 October 1962. S. Gopal, *Jawaharlal Nehru: A Biography*, vol. 3, p. 222.
33. *Pravda*, 25 October 1962. R. K. Jain (ed.), *Soviet-South Asian Relations 1947-1978*, vol. 1, pp. 302-3. The article in the *Pravda* did not please the secretariat of the CPI which feared that 'in all probability [it] will inaugurate a new period of anti-Soviet hysteria in India'. The General Secretary of the CPI, E.M.S. Namboodiripad, in a conversation with the Soviet Ambassador, pleaded with Moscow to influence China to cease military actions 'without damage to the prestige of India and of Nehru himself'. Diary of I.A. Benediktov, 26 October 1962. Archive of Foreign Policy of the Russian Federation, f. 090, op. 24, d. 6, p. 80, l, pp. 134-9. Cold War International History Project, Woodrow Wilson International Center for Scholars, *http:/cwihp.si.edu/cwihplib.nsf*
34. *Hindu*, 1 November 1962. It was learnt later that Sino-Soviet relations had once again deteriorated following disturbances which had broken out in the spring of 1962 in the border province of Xinjiang. There was then an exodus of Kazhak Muslims towards the USSR. The Soviet consulate in

Xinjiang was closed in July 1962 and the Chinese accused the Soviets of having fomented the unrest.

35. Not many then shared Nehru's analysis. Y.B. Chavan, who had just been nominated Defense Minister, expressed the view in a public meeting in Pune on 14 November that 'Russia would ultimately be on the side of China.' Nehru strongly advised him to show more restraint in his statements. R.D. Pradhan, *Debacle to Revival*, p. 40.
36. J. K. Galbraith, *Ambassador's Journal*, p. 431.
37. Telegram from the Embassy in India to the Department of State, 1 November 1962. *FRUS, 1961-1963*, vol. 19, p. 362.
38. Memorandum from the President's Deputy Special Assistant for National Security Affairs (Kaysen) to President Kennedy, 16 November 1962. Telegram from the Embassy in Pakistan (McConaughy) to the Department of State, 27 October 1962. Ibid., p. 385 and p. 355. The Pakistani President had been complaining that the US government had decided to give arms aid to India without prior consultation with him and that this decision was communicated to India before it was communicated to Pakistan, contrary to a firm oral pledge said to have been made by Kennedy to Ayub Khan in the course of his July 1961 official visit to the US. Mohammad Ayub Khan, *Friends Not Masters*, Karachi: Oxford University Press, 1967, p. 145.
39. Indo-American military assistance agreement, 14 November 1962. R.K. Jain (ed.), *US-South Asian Relations*, vol. 1, pp. 262-3.
40. Letter from Galbraith to Kennedy, 13 November 1962. *FRUS, 1961-1963*, vol. 19, p. 382.
41. Telegram from the Embassy in India, 17 November 1962. Ibid., p. 389.
42. Galbraith's meeting with Nehru, 29 October and with T.N. Kaul, 31 October 1962. J.K. Galbraith, *Ambassador's Journal*, p. 445 and p. 452.
43. Memorandum for the record: Presidential meeting on the Sino-Indian conflict, 19 November 1962. *FRUS, 1961-1963*, vol. 19, p. 396.
44. Record of Anglo-American meeting on the Sino-Indian conflict, 12 November 1962. *PRO*, FO 371 164929.
45. T. N. Kaul's telegram to Nehru, 9 November 1962. S. Gopal, *Jawaharlal Nehru: A Biography*, vol. 3, p. 226.
46. Telegrams of the French Ambassador to Moscow (Dejean), dated 20 and 30 November 1962. *AQO*, Asie-Océanie, 1956-1967, Inde, vol. 258.
47. *Hindu*, 17 November 1962.
48. *Hindustan Times*, 10 November 1962. N. Raghavan Pillai, former Secretary General of the Ministry of External Affairs, expressed the view that the acceptance of military assistance during a defensive war cannot prejudice the position of a non-aligned country as long as it stands short of entering into a military alliance. It would then make it obligatory for a member country to judge an international issue as a member of a group rather than as an independent nation. He gave the example of Tito who, when Stalin turned his wrath on Yugoslavia, had accepted military assistance from the United States, but this step had not prevented Yugoslavia from remaining a communist country. *Eastern Economist*, 31 December 1962, p. 1232.

49. *Hindustan Times*, 6 December 1962.
50. Telegrams from Washington (Sir D. Ormsby Gore) to Foreign Office, 20 November 1962. *PRO*, FO 371 164880.
51. Telegram from the Department of State to the Embassy in India, 20 November 1962. *FRUS, 1961-1963*, vol. 19, pp. 400-1.
52. Ibid. J.K. Galbraith, *Ambassador's Journal*, p. 486.
53. M. Brecher, *India and World Politics*, p. 169.
54. *Le Monde*, 13 November 1962.
55. Letter from Nehru to Kennedy, 11 August 1963. *FRUS, 1961-1963*, vol. 19, p. 634. This partly echoed what Mao Zedong said, during an acrimonious discussion with Khrushchev in October 1959, about 'our struggle to pull Nehru to our side'. Vladislav M. Zubok, 'The Khrushchev-Mao Conversations, 31 July-3 August 1958 and 2 October 1959'. Cold War International History Project, Woodrow Wilson International Center for Scholars, *http://cwihp.si.edu/cwihplib.nsf*
56. T. N. Kaul, *Diplomacy in Peace and War*, pp. 127 and 131.
57. *Le Monde*, 20-1 January 1963.
58. J. K. Galbraith, *Ambassador's Journal*, p. 504 and letter from Galbraith to Kennedy, 6 December 1962, Ibid., p. 513.
59. Telegram from the Department of State to the Embassy in India, 18 November 1962. *FRUS, 1961-1963*, vol. 19, p. 390.
60. Telegram from the Embassy in India to the Department of State, 30 November 1962. Ibid., pp. 416-17.
61. Telegram from the Department of State to the Embassy in India, 8 December 1962. Ibid., pp. 424-5.
62. Telegram from the Department of State to the Embassy in India, 8 December 1962. Ibid, p. 428.
63. Memorandum from the Joint Chiefs of Staff to the Secretary of Defense McNamara, 14 December 1962. Ibid., p. 433.
64. J. K. Galbraith, *Ambassador's Journal*, pp. 522-3. In a letter to Macmillan, dated 5 December 1962, Kennedy had proposed that the US would provide the radar and other ground equipment necessary while the UK and some of the Commonwealth countries would accept the commitment to send an appropriate number of fighter squadrons to India in the event of renewed Chinese aggression. *FRUS, 1961-1963*, vol. 19, p. 420.
65. *Times of India*, 5 February 1963.
66. Memorandum for the record: President's meeting on India, 17 May 1963. *FRUS, 1961-1963*, vol. 19, p. 593.
67. 21 February 1963. *Lok Sabha Debates* (*third series*), vol. 13, no. 4, col. 545.
68. Message from Kennedy to Macmillan, 22 January 1963. *PRO*, FO 371 170644.
69. For an account of the Indo-Pakistani bilateral talks on Kashmir, see Sir Morrice James, *Pakistan Chronicle*, pp. 89-102.
70. Memorandum from Secretary of State to President Kennedy, 31 March 1963. *FRUS, 1961-1963*, vol. 19, p. 530.

71. Memorandum from Secretary of State to President Kennedy, 25 April 1963. Ibid., p. 557.
72. Message from Kennedy to Macmillan, 13 May 1963. *PRO*, FO 371 170644.
73. Message from Macmillan to Kennedy, 15 May 1963. Ibid. The British ultimately agreed to occasional visits to India by two fighter squadron, one American and one British, with the radar and ground equipment provided by the US.
74. Dispatch from the French Ambassador in India, J.P. Garnier, 31 January 1963. *AQO*, Asie-Océanie, 1956-1967, Inde, vol. 258.
75. Telegram from J.P. Garnier, French Ambassador in India, 2 July 1963. Ibid.
76. *Asian Recorder*, vol. 9, no. 6, 25 June-1 July 1963, p. 5267.
77. Memorandum for the record: The President's views on India as expressed at 25 April meeting, 26 April 1963. *FRUS, 1961-1963*, vol. 19, p. 566.
78. *Hindustan Times*, 7 June 1963.
79. Memorandum from the Department of State Counsellor and Chairman of the Policy Planning Council (Rostow) to President Kennedy, 8 April 1963. *FRUS, 1961-1963*, vol. 19, pp. 538-9.
80. Message from Kennedy to Nehru, 15 August 1963. Ibid., p. 640.
81. Memorandum for the record: Meeting with the President on Pakistan, 12 August 1963. Ibid., p. 638.
82. *Times of India*, 21 August 1963.
83. *Times of India*, 17 July 1963.
84. *Times of India*, 21 December 1963.
85. *Economic Weekly*, 21 December 1963, pp. 2060-1, and 11 January 1964, p. 44.
86. *The Times*, 22 May 1978. Quoted by S. Gopal, *Jawaharlal Nehru: A Biography*, vol. 3, p. 254. See also D.K. Palit, *War in High Himalaya*, p. 361.
87. Telegram of the French Ambassador in India, J.P. Garnier, 1 August 1963. *AQO*, Asie-Océanie, 1956-1967, Inde, vol. 251. See also R.D. Pradhan, *Debacle to Revival*, pp. 66-7.
88. Declaration of Morarji Desai, then Indian Prime Minister, 17 April 1978. *Lok Sabha Debates (sixth series)*, vol. 13, no. 38, cols. 307-17. See also M.S. Kohli and Kenneth Conboy, *Spies in the Himalayas*, Delhi: HarperCollins, 2003.
89. Memorandum from Secretary Rogers to President Nixon, 28 October 1971. F.S. Aijazuddin (ed.), *The White House & Pakistan: Secret Declassified Documents, 1969-1974*, Karachi: Oxford University Press, 2002, p. 325.
90. C. Bowles, *Promises to Keep*, p. 476.
91. Memorandum from Robert W. Komer of the National Security Council Staff to the Deputy Assistant Secretary of Defense for International Security Affairs (Bundy), 14 November 1963. *FRUS, 1961-1963*, vol. 19, pp. 690-1.
92. Telegram from the Department of State to the Embassy in India, 23 December 1963. Ibid., p. 727.
93. Memorandum from Robert Komer of the National Security Council Staff to President Johnson, 21 January 1964. *FRUS, 1964-1968*, vol. 25, p. 15.

94. National Security Action memorandum no. 279, 8 February 1964. Ibid., pp. 26-7.
95. Telegram from the Embassy in India to the Department of State, 20 February 1964, Ibid., p. 35.
96. The US Ambassador to Pakistan, McConaughy reported, after the recent Zhou Enlai's visit to Pakistan, that Ayub Khan wanted to play the role of a honest broker in establishing more effective communication between the United States and China. Telegram from Karachi dated 5 March 1964. Ibid., p. 49.
97. Memorandum from Robert Komer to President Johnson, 26 February 1964. Ibid., pp. 45-6.
98. Letter from the President's Special Assistant for National Security Affairs (Bundy) to the Ambassador in India (Bowles), 9 March 1964. Ibid., p. 51.
99. Memorandum from Robert Komer to President Johnson, 2 April 1964. Ibid., p. 76.
100. Telegram from the Embassy in India (Bowles) to the Department of State, 20 April 1964. Ibid., p. 86.
101. Y.B. Chavan noted that some money had remained unspent in the defense budget because the effort at establishing new factories was married to the possibility of getting aid from other countries and this has not been very forthcoming. Moreover, the army equipment and ammunition promised for the 'Nassau six mountain divisions' amounted to Rs. 300 million which came to only 15 per cent of the actual cost of the equipment needed estimated at nearly Rs. 2 billion. 23 March 1964. *Lok Sabha Debates (third series)*, vol. 28, no. 32, cols. 6940 and 6946.
102. Statement by Y. B. Chavan at the National Press Club, Washington, D.C. 21 May 1964. R.K. Jain (ed.), *US-South Asian Relations*, vol. 1, p. 299.
103. Memorandum from Robert Komer of the National Security Council Staff to the President's Special Assistant for National Security Affairs (Bundy) 21 May and 27 May 1964. Memorandum of conversation, 22 May 1964 *FRUS, 1964-1968*, vol. 25, pp. 102-10.
104. Report of Y. B. Chavan in Parliament on his visits to the United States and to the Soviet Union, 21 September 1964. *Times of India*, 22 September 1964.
105. Letter from Secretary of State (Rusk) to Secretary of Defense (McNamara), 17 June 1964. *FRUS, 1964-1968*, vol. 25, p. 127. In his response, McNamara wanted to limit the number of F-104G eventually offered to India, primarily on a credit sales basis, to a total of 24 aircraft In order to maintain a balance between the high performance aircraft of India and Pakistan, the latter should be offered 12 additional F-104 through grant aid, bringing Pakistan's total of F-104 aircraft to 24 Furthermore, he wished to limit the acquisition of MIG-21 by India to a dozen aircraft. Letter from Secretary of Defense to Secretary of State 2 July 1964. Ibid., p. 131.
106. New Delhi telegram 143, 16 July 1964, FOI document. Quoted by H.B Schaffer, *Chester Bowles: New Dealer in the Cold War*, p. 263.

107. Telegram from the Embassy in India to the Department of State, 27 August 1964. *FRUS, 1964-1968*, vol. 25, p. 150. The MIG-21 became the backbone of the IAF for four decades, equipping 21 out of 35 combat squadrons at one time.
108. Telegram from the Embassy in India to the Department of State, 29 January 1965. Ibid., pp. 184-5.
109. In July 1963, Nehru had delegated his daughter to Moscow to assure Khrushchev that the tripartite air defense agreement did not involve putting non-alignment in jeopardy. The government retreat on the agreement with the VOA, then the departure from the government in September of Morarji Desai and of S.K. Patil, two men known to be rightists, following the 'Kamaraj Plan', was hailed in the Soviet Union. However, anxiety remained over what would happen after Nehru. An article in *New Times*, analyzing the AICC meeting of November 1963 and the annual session of the Congress in January 1964 at Bhubaneswar, noted that the equations of power within the leadership of the party were evolving in favour of the conservatives and the supporters of capitalism in India. V. Pavlov and I. Redko, 'Débats au CNI', *Temps Nouveaux*, no. 5, 5 February 1964, pp. 7-9.
110. Telegram from J.P. Garnier, French Ambassador to India, 1 May 1964. *AQO*, Asie-Océanie, 1956-1967, Inde, vol. 259.
111. *Times of India*, 1 September 1964.
112. R.D. Pradhan, *Debacle to Revival*, p. 212.
113. Record of Radhakrishnan's talks with Khrushchev, 11, 12 and 18 September 1964. S. Gopal, *Radhakrishnan : A Biography*, pp. 333-4.
114. Chester Bowles's advice to the Indian leadership on 'the advisability of keeping publicity regarding whatever agreements may be reached with the USSR to an absolute minimum, and, if at all possible, of spreading these agreements over a period of several months in order to cushion the public impact here and in the United States' had been of little avail. Letter from the Ambassador to India (Bowles) to the President's Special Assistant for National Security Affairs (Bundy), 18 July 1964. *FRUS, 1964-1968*, vol. 25, p. 140. Before Chavan's visit, Washington officials did not seem overly worried by the purchases of Soviet arms: 'So long as we demonstrate responsiveness and steady support for principal Indian requirements in military field, we do not see Soviet aid, including that in the military field, as seriously threatening over the long term our present basic level of influence in India or India's capability to maintain its independence and integrity.' Joint State/Defense telegram, 24 July 1964. Ibid., p. 142.
115. Foreign Office minute (E. Bolland), 3 November 1964. *PRO*, FO371 175904 / FO 371 175907.
116. *Times of India*, 17 October 1964.
117. *Times of India*, 31 October 1964. Indira Gandhi, *My Truth*, Delhi: Vision Books, 1981, p. 105.
118. Note of foreign secretary on Radhakrishnan's talk with I.G. Ignatov, 7 November 1964. S. Gopal, *Radhakrishnan: A Biography*, pp. 334-5.

119. *Hindu*, 13 May 1965.
120. In a telegram from the US Embassy in Pakistan, it was recalled that US assistance had significantly enhanced the military capacities of Pakistan since 'five and one-half of its seven and one-half divisions are MAP supported'. This was also true of India, it was argued with an obvious bias, for 'US military aid and US assistance in defense production area serve indirectly if not directly to upgrade appreciably India's ability to sustain operations like Rann of Kutch engagements'. To the Department of State, 27 April 1965. *FRUS, 1964-1968*, p. 236.
121. Telegram from the Embassy in the Philippines to the Department of State, 7 March 1965. Ibid., pp. 197-8.
122. Memorandum from Robert Komer of the National Security Council Staff to President Johnson, 2 April 1965. Ibid., p. 202.
123. Letter from Prime Minister Shastri to President Johnson, 23 May 1965. Ibid., p. 264. Letter from President Johnson to Prime Minister Shastri, 5 June 1965. Ibid., p. 270.
124. Memorandum for the record: President's talk with Ambassador B.K. Nehru, 13 July 1965. Ibid., pp. 301-2.
125. Memorandum from Robert Komer to President Johnson, 9 July 1965. Ibid., p. 296.
126. Rusk added that if India was to purchase Soviet submarines, it would add another element to the feeling of resentment. From Patrick Dean, British Embassy in Washington to Paul Gore-Booth, Foreign Office, 22 July 1965. *PRO*, FO 371 180968.
127. Telegram from the Embassy Office in Pakistan to the Department of State, 30 July 1965. *FRUS, 1964-1968*, vol. 25, p. 320. This was the time when the United States started considering to develop alternate intelligence facilities in case they had to renounce to those in Peshawar.
128. It happened that few days earlier, on 19 August, Chester Bowles had sent a memorandum to Johnson in which he argued that the United States should not repeat the mistake made in the wake of 1962 border war when the United States had the historic opportunity to become India's main source of military aid. He strongly favoured the continuation of the five-year $ 50 million grant and $ 50 million sales assistance support programme for India. The United States should not also shy away from providing to India the weapons it needed for its defense, including the F-5 fighters. Johnson's first reaction was not very forthcoming. Ibid., pp. 338-9.
129. 8 November 1965. *Lok Sabha Debates* (*third series*), vol. 47, no. 4, col. 772.
130. Economic and Military Aid, meeting in the State Department, 10 June 1966. *PRO*, FO 371 186961.
131. Telegram from the Embassy Office in Pakistan to the Department of State, 10 September 1965. *FRUS, 1964-1968*, vol. 25, p. 385.
132. *People's Daily*, 5 September 1965. Quoted by H. Ray, *Sino-Soviet Conflict Over India*, p. 118.

133. Telegram from the Embassy in India to the Department of State, 18 September 1965. *FRUS, 1964-1968*, vol. 25, pp. 405-6.
134. United States Agency for International Development (USAID), Delhi (see table on p. 406).
135. Stephen P. Cohen, *The Pakistan Army*, Karachi: Oxford University Press, 1992, p. 138.
136. To prevent an overwhelming dependence, in February 1966, Johnson authorized a more flexible policy to permit some commercial sales and MAP credit sales of non-lethal military on a case-by-case basis subject to continued satisfactory moves toward peace in the subcontinent. But it stopped short of permitting a resumption of grant aid and sale of lethal items.
137. In fact, India, worried about Indonesia's intentions during the conflict, made official request to the Soviet Union to cut off spare parts, ammunition and other supplies to Jakarta. Telegram from the Embassy in India to the Department of State, 11 September 1965. *FRUS, 1964-1968*, vol. 25, p. 390. Pakistan's Air Marshal Asghar Khan went to Indonesia during the conflict, looking for the loan of two submarines and four missile boats from the Navy, together with fighters from the Indonesian Air Force.
138. Telegram from the Embassy in India to the Department of State, 15 June 1966. *FRUS, 1964-1968*, vol. 25, p. 683. A British document estimated that the gross value of agreements regarding the sale of Soviet arms signed up to August 1965 was of the order of £ 150 million and, since September 1965, amounted to at least £ 100 million. In comparison, it was said that deliveries under US grant aid from 1962 to 1964 of £ 44 million worth of military equipment had virtually been completed at the time of the India-Pakistan war, but no more than £ 26 million of the £ 72 million 1964 to 1966 commitment had been delivered by September 1965. Brief on defense aspects of military aid to India and Pakistan, Report by the Defense Intelligence Staff, 6 June 1966. *PRO*, FO 371 186966
139. In April 1967, the United States were to officially announce their decision to end their military assistance programmes to India and Pakistan and also to renounce to sell lethal weapons on a cash basis. Nevertheless, and to New Delhi's dismay, restrictions over the supply of spare parts required for previously supplied lethal equipment could be considered on a case by case basis. Requests for non-lethal equipment to be supplied on a commercial basis or through MAP credit sales, for which the embargo had already been lifted in March 1966, would continue to be entertained.
140. 22 August 1962. *Rajya Sabha Debates*, vol. 40, no. 12, col. 2991.

CHAPTER 15

The Pitfalls of Dependence

THE WAR WITH China in autumn 1962 led to a 34 per cent increase in the defense budget for the current financial year 1962-3. From the budget figure of Rs. 3.76 billion, it jumped to Rs. 5.05 billion. The budgetary provision for defense further increased by 72 per cent in 1963-4, going up to Rs. 8.67 billion.[1] The defense expenditure thus crossed from 1.9 per cent of the GNP in 1961 to 3.6 per cent in 1964.[2] This was an unwelcome additional financial cost after the disappointing economic results noted at the end of the first year of the Third Plan. Yet the conflict with the Chinese communist enemy and the supplementary burden imposed on India did not arouse, in the face of the ever-increasing need for aid, any particular feelings of generosity among the Western credit-lending countries. The *Times of India* of 7 March 1963 commented: 'We have come a long, long, way from the days of 1951 when we shyly sought a wheat loan (declining a wheat gift) to now when our appetite for assistance of all kinds, including military, has truly assumed oceanic proportions.'

In May 1963, the Indian government sent a mission to the United States and to other countries of the aid consortium to inform them of the urgency and the magnitude of the aid required. When the eighth meeting of the AIC concluded in Washington on 7 August, \$1.052 billion was finally promised for the third year of the plan. This amount was less than the \$ 1.295 billion obtained for the first year of the Plan and the \$ 1.07 billion for the second year. This was less than the Indian bid of \$ 1.25 billion but this was a significant improvement on the figure of \$ 915 million arrived at when the meeting opened in Paris in early June. The tendency towards stagnation or levelling off of the aid granted by the AIC was confirmed the following year with an even slightly smaller amount of aid: \$ 1.028 billion. On the positive side, the terms of aid had improved. About two-fifths of the total aid pledged in Washington was to be non-project assistance while just over half the aid was in the form of grants or long-term loans at nominal rates of interest. Considering the growing importance of foreign aid in the development process, the Indian government decided, in June 1963, to set up a committee under the chairmanship of Professor V.K.R.V. Rao, entrusted with examining the procedures for the negotiation, allocation, and disbursement of external assistance and with suggesting measures in the light of such examination to ensure speedier and more efficient utilization of available assistance in keeping with the priorities of the plan.[3]

The mid-term appraisal that the Planning Commission published in November 1963 made an initial gloomy assessment of the Third Plan. At the end of the first two years of the plan, the national income had increased by only 5 per cent. It was illusory to believe in the possibility of achieving a 30 per cent growth during the overall plan period. No notable improvement in the balance of payments position had taken place and the foreign exchange reserves were under pressure. It was, moreover, acknowledged that the total foreign exchange commitments to be entered into during the Third Plan period for projects and programmes in the public and private sectors would be considerably larger than the sum of Rs. 20.3 billion mentioned in the plan.[4] The *Economic Weekly* felt that India would need Rs. 40 to 45 billion (including PL-480) of foreign aid. It pointed out that 'the poor economic performance, [India's] inability to defend herself against China and the utter abandon with which she has gone about asking for all types of aid has sullied the image of India, and strengthened the hands of those, especially in the United States, who are hostile to India'.[5] Recalling that at the time of the formulation of the Third Plan, it was decided that the economy should reach a reasonable degree of self-reliance by the Fifth Plan, the planners, faced with an unhealthy reliance on foreign aid, sought to do the impossible while hoping that 'the projects that we take in hand from now on are designed primarily to strengthen the balance of payments by increasing exports and replacing imports without at the same time involving an excessively large foreign exchange component'.[6]

The foreign exchange crisis deteriorated further. The very slight increase in the foreign exchange reserves in 1963-4, following a large increase in exports, comparable to the one that occurred in 1951-2 at the time of the 'Korean boom', and a better allocation of aid, was a passing phase. Right from the following year, the rate of growth in exports earnings declined whereas imports were higher on account of food grains, fertilizers, and defense, and the situation concerning the debt servicing worsened. All these factors contributed towards bringing the level of the foreign exchange reserves, down from Rs. 1.88 billion in March 1964 to Rs. 1.16 billion in March 1965, to their lowest level since Independence. These could simply cover payments for two months of imports. The situation even necessitated the transfer of gold from government reserves to the RBI to fulfil the statutory obligation of having to maintain a minimum of Rs. 2 billion of reserves in the form of gold and foreign securities. The only consolation was that the national income in 1964-5 had increased by 7.6 per cent, a growth distinctly higher than that achieved during the first years of the plan. The Finance Minister, T.T. Krishnamachari, was forced, on 17 February, to call for 'the strictest fiscal and monetary discipline'. He announced a series of pre-budget financial measures to curb inflation and to improve the balance of payments position. It was decided to increase the Bank rate from 5 per cent to 6 per cent, to levy a regulatory customs duty of 10 per cent *ad valorem* on all imports except food grains and a few other goods (fertilizers, pesticides, etc.), and to make an urgent request to the IMF for a stand-by credit 'to the maximum extent possible'.[7] These measures were also intended to mollify the IMF and the AIC whose members were beginning to despair of the chronic deficit in foreign exchange in India. The IMF approved, in March 1965, a new line of credit of $ 200 million for the coming twelve months, notably to enable India to make repayments for the loans granted earlier by this agency, which were to rise to $ 175 million between March 1965 and March 1966.

In the same month, the Indian Finance Secretary, Bhoothalingam, went to Paris to take part in an AIC meeting. He had come to ask for $ 1.25 billion of aid (20 per cent more than the amount granted the earlier year) and a greater amount of aid not tied to any particular project. Non-project aid had constituted 35 per cent of the aid given by the AIC in 1963-4 and 49 per cent in 1964-5, which had made it possible to improve its utilization. The Indians hoped to obtain henceforth 60 per cent of non-project aid intended to be used to finance the imports required for the maintenance of the Indian economy. The third request that Bhoothalingam submitted was the transition to a pluriannual assistance to synchronize with the five year plan.[8] Once again, a new meeting had to be awaited, which took place in Washington in April, before the amount of aid to be granted for 1965-6 could be decided upon. The aid consortium agreed in Washington to renew the amount granted the preceding year, two-thirds of which would be in the form of grants and loans at low rates of interest and would be reimbursable over 25 years or more. India had obtained a total of Rs. 26.06 billion from the AIC for the overall period of the Third Plan, a figure that compared favourably with the Rs. 26 billion of foreign assistance (outside of PL-480) that had been anticipated at the beginning of the plan.

As India's dependence on foreign aid kept growing, it became more and more difficult for its leaders to oppose the demands, at least those of an economic nature, of the donor states. This was all the more so as the use of the American and Soviet aid was more complementary than competitive. The time when the Soviet Union would do almost anything to woo India with attractive aid offers was coming to an end. As the USSR now had a virtual 'monopoly' over assistance in the development of heavy industry in the public sector, it intended hereafter to fix conditions to its offers of co-operation. The discussions over the Bokaro steel project illustrated this shift in attitude. It had been contemplated during the Third Five Year Plan to double the production capacity of the three steel mills

CONSORTIUM AID TO INDIA DURING THE THIRD FIVE YEAR PLAN
(*millions of dollars*)

	1961-2	1962-3	1963-4	1964-5	1965-6	*total*
Austria	-	5	7	1	5	18
Belgium	-	10	10	-	4	24
Canada	28	33	31	41	41	174
France	15	45	20	20	20	120
Germany (Fed. Rep.)	225	139	99	95	86	644
Italy	-	53	45	36	36	170
Japan	50	55	65	60	60	290
Netherlands	-	11	11	11	11	44
United Kingdom	182	84	84	84	84	518
United States	545	435	435	435	435	2,285
IBRD + IDA	250	200	245	245	245	1,185
TOTAL	1,295	1,070	1,052	1,028	1,027	5,472
(*millions of rupees*)	6,167	5,095	5,010	4,896	4,890	26,058

Source: Ministry of Finance, Government of India, *External Assistance 1965-66*, pp. 157-8.

established in the public sector (Bhilai, Rourkela, and Durgapur) so as to produce 6 million tons of ingots by 1966. The government had, moreover, decided to set up a fourth major steel plant in the public sector at Bokaro in the state of Bihar with an initial capacity of 1 million tons. To that production level was to be added a 3 million tons capacity in private plants.[9]

In a note prepared in 1961, the Planning Commission expressed optimism regarding the possibility of securing a loan from the new US Agency for International Development to cover the foreign exchange required for the realization of the Bokaro steel plant. The Americans, aware of the prestige acquired by the Soviet Union with the erection of the Bhilai steel plant, had already communicated that they would be interested in the execution of a large-scale project. During the initial contacts, at the end of the 1950s, the idea that found favour with the Eisenhower administration, and apparently also secured the support of some Ministers belonging to the right wing of the Congress party, was that an agreement be evolved for a private joint venture, supplemented by a generous share of public aid. Although this would have been contrary to the industrial policy resolution of 1956, the Indian government appeared inclined to show some pragmatism, all the more so as in the thick of the financial crisis it was becoming essential to reduce steel imports as quickly as possible. The negotiations, however, stumbled over irreconciliable differences and the Indian government finally abandoned the idea of implementing the Bokaro project in the private sector. With the Democrats taking over in Washington from a Republican administration, it was expected that they would show more flexibility in the aid policy, and it revived the hope of a US funding. This impression was quickly reinforced by some remarks made by Galbraith in New Delhi when he indicated that the fact of the steelworks being in the public sector should not constitute an obstacle to American aid.

The Planning Commission reckoned on the United States being satisfied with offering India a credit to cover the purchase of equipment from American suppliers and the services of some American steel experts, leaving the main designing and the construction of the steelworks to Indian consultants and contractors. The Planning Commission had not contended with the desire of the Americans to contribute to an exemplary technical achievement which would symbolize America's economic assistance to India's development far better than the assistance broken up over several less visible projects had done till then. In reality, the Americans, feeling that they had already made a major concession by possibly joining an industrial project in the public sector, not only wanted to take charge of the designing and the construction of the steelworks but, considering the lack of confidence that they had in Hindustan Steel Limited, they also wanted to control the management of the steel plant during the first few years after it came into operation.

The American mistrust of the qualification of the Indians was made clear when, in May 1962, the AID announced that a team of the US Steel Corporation would be sent to India to conduct a feasibility study. Meanwhile, the Ministry of Industry had already asked the private Indian consultancy firm Dastur & Co., which had conducted a preliminary study, to make a detailed report on the steel project. The same month, the Union Minister for Steel, Chidambaram Subramaniam, hinting at the possibility of turning to the Soviet Union, declared for the benefit of the Americans that Bokaro would see the light of day whatever might be the American response, for India was not 'without friends in the world with ability, capacity and willingness to extend help'.[10] The report of the US Steel Corporation, published in March 1963, proposed that the management of the plant should be entrusted to an American team for a period of ten years, at the end of which the rated capacity of 4 million tons would be set rolling. The maximum number of American technicians who would work on the site would be 670 during this period, whereas a note of the Planning Commission provided for only 30 to 40 top-ranking foreign technicians to man the key posts at Bokaro for a limited period of time.[11]

The disagreements over the distribution of tasks between Indians and Americans and over the management of the factory, as brought out in this report, did not directly cause the Indian government to decide to give up the idea of American assistance. The Ministry of Industry was apparently ready to show some flexibility to keep the Americans satisfied. The cause in reality was the report of the commission led by General Lucius Clay, whose appointment had been decided by Kennedy in December 1962. This commission was entrusted with the task of re-examining the military and economic assistance programmes so as to determine whether 'their scope and distribution was contributing to the optimum security of the United States and the economic and political stability of the free world'. The report, published in March 1963, much more than the discussions in Congress revolving around the viability of the project or the decision of the Indian government to go back on the agreement with the VOA, was to strike a fatal blow to the American financing of the Bokaro project. The report, replete with liberal dogma, reaffirmed that American aid should help create economic units which utilize not only limited governmental resources wisely but also mobilize the great potential and range of private efforts. Henceforth,

> the United States should not aid a foreign government in projects establishing government-owned industrial and commercial enterprises which compete with existing private endeavours. . . . Countries which would take this route should realize that while the United States will not intervene in their affairs to impose its own economic system, they too lack the right to intervene in our national pocket book for aid to enterprises which only increase their costs to government and the foreign assistance burden they are asking us to carry.[12]

For Galbraith, it was like going back to the policies of the Eisenhower administration: 'These were a grievous failure. Nothing substantial was done to advance private investment; and they talked about it enough to cause everyone to suppose our concern was to sustain capitalism rather than help the Indians.'[13]

After the decision taken by the AID on 27 April 1963 to indefinitely postpone its response to the grant of a $ 512 million loan (the amount required in foreign exchange for the implementation of the steel plant, according to the US Steel Corporation report), even *Commerce* considered as excessive the zeal with which some in the United States insisted that the Bokaro steel plant should be in the private sector. The journal raised the following questions:

> Was American aid withheld from several European countries because of their widespread nationalization measures? These measures, primarily affecting industrial undertakings, sprang at least as much from political and ideological as from economic considerations in countries, such as the United Kingdom, France, Netherlands, Norway, Austria and Italy. By giving massive aid to them, the United States were not only assisting general economic recovery but also strengthening the public enterprise sector in the process. Why should they now quail from the prospect of aiding public sector industries in the developing countries where the need for public investment is any day greater than in the advanced industrialized countries?

That did not mean, added the author, that the United States should entirely ignore the dangers of planning on socialist lines, but it should at least keep in mind the fact 'that a mixed economy like India's, which generally provides, except in the field of oil, the fullest scope for private enterprise to grow, as well as to benefit from public investment, is on the right track'.[14]

On 8 May 1963, during a press conference, to address the effect that the Clay Commission report might have on the Bokaro project, President Kennedy declared unambiguously that he was in favour of American assistance. He attacked those who wanted to make it the subject of a controversy in the name of an ideological rigidity which totally ignored India's needs: 'I think we ought to do it. Now, the Congress may have other views, but I think it would be a great mistake not to build it. India needs that steel.'[15] No heed was given to the President. Alluding to a recommendation of the Clay Commission advocating tight Congress control over aid appropriations, Senator William S. Broomfield, introduced in August 1963, an amendment to the aid bill requiring the US Congress to examine thoroughly all funding for a single project in excess of $ 100 million. The vote on this amendment meant for the Indian government a further postponement of the decision of the United States on the assistance to the steel plant project. The prevailing feeling in the US Congress was that the results of the foreign aid programmes had not met expectations as compared to the large sums involved, and this came at a time when the US balance of payments deficit was itself worsening. Kennedy, who encountered numerous difficulties in ensuring the adoption of the aid budget proposed by his administration, reminded Congress that 'the relative burden of our assistance programs has been steadily reduced from some 2 per cent of our national product at the beginning of the Marshall Plan to seven-tenths of 1 per cent today—from 11.5 per cent of the Federal budget in 1949 to 4 per cent today'.[16] In line with the overall stagnation of the foreign aid budget, the amount of aid to India was never to regain the level it had reached during the first year of the Kennedy administration. The average trend over the period of the Johnson administration was one towards decline, although the amount of aid never fell below that of 1960.

New Delhi was anxious not to make Bokaro a subject of controversy that would risk souring Indo-American relations at a time when India badly needed US military assistance in the face of a threat from China. Hence, Nehru wrote, in end August 1963, to Kennedy to inform him that India was withdrawing its request for assistance from the United States.[17] The indecision of the Americans had already led to great delays and it was now doubtful whether the work could begin before 1966, while the steel plant had originally been planned to start production before the end of the Third Plan. Kennedy, in turn, assured Nehru that whatever the ups and downs in the relations between the two countries, the United States would remain committed to India's development and security.[18] With the possibility of American funding having come to an end, the Indian government had no other option but to turn to the Soviets. The Indians had considered the possibility of not having to depend upon any single source to obtain the various kinds of equipment it required, but no country could really match the credit terms granted by the USSR. A few days after the beginning of the Sino-Indian war and at the time when K.D. Malaviya was in Moscow, the Soviet authorities, far from showing a diminishing interest in strengthening India's industrial sinews, indicated that they would cooperate in expediting India's plans to develop the strategic oil, coal, and power industries, whatever the Chinese views might be on the matter.[19] After a visit to the USSR from 18 to 26 January 1963, R.K. Nehru announced at a press conference that Moscow agreed to take up with the Indian government the possibility of collaborating in the setting up of 15 Third Plan projects, involving a foreign exchange outlay of about Rs. 540 million. Moreover, the Soviet leaders had assured New Delhi in advance of their support for the Fourth Plan and had promised to diversify their imports of Indian goods to include industrial products.[20] In the months that followed, several economic and technical assistance agreements were signed, such as the one signed on 25 May concerning the expansion of the Barauni and Koyali refineries and the undertaking to construct a precision instruments factory in Kerala, financed from earlier unutilized credits.

In June 1963, Manubhai Shah, the Minister for Foreign Trade, went to Moscow to sign a new trade agreement, the third one, covering the period 1964-8; this agreement provided for doubling the value of trade by 1966. In 1965-6, Indian exports to the USSR constituted 11.5 per cent of the total exports (as against only 0.2 per cent in 1953-4 at the time of the first trade agreement), which made the Soviet Union India's third largest client after the United States (18.3 per cent) and Great Britain (18.1 per cent). The imports of Soviet products constituted for the year 1965-6 5.9 per cent of the total imports (0.1 per cent in 1953-4), which placed them just behind the imports from the United States (37.7 per cent) and from Great Britain (10.7 per cent).[21] The total volume of Indo-Soviet trade had multiplied almost hundred times between 1953-4 and 1965-6. Imports and exports over this entire period balanced each other out almost exactly. The aid had contributed to a large part in the expansion of bilateral trade since Soviet imports from India were in principle to be equal to Soviet assistance plus exports on a commercial basis. Soviet development credits utilized by India over the Second and Third Plans accounted for 82.4 per cent and 66.1 per cent of imports from the Soviet Union respectively.[22]

The American government did not really mind the economic links between India and the Soviet Union. For instance, Averell Harriman reminded those who wanted to terminate American aid unless India broke with the Soviet Union, that it would be 'a stupid thing to do. . . . It is in our interests for the Soviet Union to continue giving assistance to India. . . . We want to avoid anything that would bring the two [Moscow and Beijing] together. For that reason I suggest we make no attempt to interfere with India's foreign policy in relation to Russia.'[23] On 1 May 1964, C. Subramaniam announced in the Lok Sabha that the Soviet Union had offered financial and technical assistance required for the whole project rather than for sections as was originally planned. The fact that New Delhi had waited for several months after the withdrawal of its request for US assistance before accepting the Soviet offer could be seen as an exercise in damage control *vis-à-vis* the US Congress. In July 1964, an Indian delegation went to Moscow for talks with the Soviets. The following month, technical discussions opened in New Delhi between representatives of the two governments. The Soviets immediately obtained what had initially been refused to the Americans: control over the designing and the construction of the steelworks without any interference from Dastur & Co., the Indian consultants which had already submitted a detailed project report. This caused the *Economic Weekly* to comment that 'the refusal to associate Indians with the design and engineering of Bokaro when a considerable amount of creditable preliminary work had already been done on it puts the two Great Powers on par as far as distrust of Indian skills is concerned'.[24] Just the day before, Shastri had inaugurated the Sharavathi hydroelectric power station in India's southern state of Mysore, one of the largest in South Asia, set up with American credit. On 25 January 1965, India signed an agreement for financial and technical collaboration with the USSR. The Soviet government extended a credit of up to 200 million roubles for meeting the foreign exchange cost of the plant. The agreement obviously anticipated criticism from political and economic circles for it mentioned that the Soviets would try to encourage the 'maximum participation' on the part of Indians both in the construction as well as in the supply of equipment that could be produced locally, particularly from the factories that had been set up with Soviet assistance (for instance, the heavy machine-building plant at Ranchi). Soviet experts prepared a detailed project report which left Dastur & Co. with a subsidiary role in the setting up of the Bokaro steel plant. This development was interpreted as a disguised snub to the Indian consultancy firm, a precedent that American companies, often severely criticized for not associating Indians to a sufficient degree with the technical management of their projects, may well avail of in the future.[25]

In December 1965, Tiazpromexport, the Soviet consultant, submitted the detailed project report, which was accepted on 29 March 1966 by the Indian government, not without the latter being accused of having botched up their critical evaluation and especially for having minimized the potential for a significant reduction in the overall cost. Some eyebrows were raised at the estimate of Rs. 7.7 billion, assessed by the Soviets, for the construction of a steel mill to produce 4 million tons. When the US Steel Corporation had given a figure of Rs. 6.6 billion for an even output in 1963, the cost was rated too high. Similarly, Dastur & Co.'s proposal was Rs. 5.6 billion and the consultant agency expressed the opinion, although without much success, that a cost reduction on the Soviet estimate of Rs. 1 billion was possible. Critical appraisals from the business community also emphasized the high per ton production cost which would ensure that Bokaro steel was not internationally competitive.[26] In fact, in defense of the Indian negotiators, it must be admitted that, for lack of an alternative foreign aid proposal, they had little choice but to comply with the requirements of the Soviets, and therefore leave to them the designing of the steel plant and the total control over the construction in exchange for the supply of equipment. Its management, however, was left to the Indians. It is likely that considerations of a political nature, such as the growing dependence of India on the Soviet Union for its military supplies, or more generally the need to retain the support of the USSR, had also compelled the Indian negotiators to be particularly accommodating.

A few days before the visit of the Indian Prime Minister to Moscow, scheduled from 12 to 19 May 1965, Asoka Mehta, the deputy chairman of the Planning Commission, went there with Mahalanobis with the intention of asking for about Rs. 6 billion of aid for the Fourth Plan. The expansion of oil exploration, coal mining, and the Bhilai steel plant were among the topics discussed. During the visit of Lal Bahadur Shastri, Kosygin promised that the amount of Soviet aid for the coming Fourth Plan would be twice the amount given for the Third Plan.[27] In the joint communiqué published at the end of Shastri's visit to the USSR, the Soviet leaders reiterated their willingness to continue economic and technical cooperation with India in the industrial sector and announced that specialists would be sent to study on the spot the projects likely to be the subject of new cooperation agreements. The Soviets showed some reluctance to commit to projects on an *ad hoc* basis because they suspected that India was using 'their commitments only to extract more favourable terms from the West'.[28] These issues figured prominently in the talks that the Finance Minister, T.T. Krishnamachari, had in Moscow in November 1965. If no specific commitment regarding Soviet assistance to the Fourth Plan was finalized, at least one Indian request was taken into consideration when it was revealed in the new trade agreement, signed on 7 January 1966, that equipment needed to operate the plants built with Soviet assistance—somewhat similar to the Western aid for maintenance imports—would be obtained on terms close to those granted for the loans. The trade agreement, extending the former one by two years, again provided for doubling the value of trade between 1965 and 1970, from Rs. 1.5 billion to Rs. 3 billion, and anticipated that more than 40 per cent of India's exports would be manufactured items, including garments, leather and jute goods. However, from an ideological point of view, the Soviets displayed a distinct disenchantment with the capacity of the Indian government to pursue a non-capitalist path of development. It is true that the closeness to the West which followed the Sino-Indian war and the increased dependence on aid from the United States and from the World Bank were exploited by the conservative elements within the Congress party to check the programme for the socialization of the economy. An article in *New Times* in August 1965 on the evolution of the Congress party after the death of Nehru noted that 'the reactionaries have grown more active than ever, bent on further strengthening their position at people's expense. In this they have been helped by the division and disunity among the democratic forces, including the split in India's communist movement.'[29] India was not among the 'revolutionary democracies' which in 1964 included the non-communist Third World countries moving towards socialism such as Egypt, Algeria, Ghana, and Burma. However, as we have just seen, there was, in principle, no question of going back on the matter of aid to India.

The dominant position held by the Soviet Union regarding the development of heavy industry in the public sector went hand in hand with the US dominance in the area of food assistance. The first three years of the plan were marked by a stagnation in the production of food grains, following which their import jumped from 3.6 million tons in 1962 to 6.3 million tons in 1964, of which about 5.25 million tons were imported under the PL-480 programme.[30] Indeed, receipts under PL-480 assistance formed 40 per cent of the total external assistance during the financial year 1964-5 and 38 per cent during the subsequent year.[31] Far from decreasing, as might have been expected after agricultural development and self-reliance had been given the highest priority in the Third Plan, India's dependence on the PL-480 programme did not cease to grow. When the implementation of the agreement signed in May 1960 was reviewed in May 1963, the Minister of Food and Agriculture contemplated its renewal once the current agreement expired in June 1964. In June 1963, S.K. Patil was entrusted with taking up with the US Ministry of Agriculture the possibility of concluding a new four-year agreement relating to around 10 million tons of food grains. This question was again raised in April 1964 during the visit to India of Orville Freeman, US Secretary of Agriculture. S.K. Patil, who meanwhile had become Minister for Railways, took advantage of another visit to the United States in July to once again talk to the Americans about the urgency of arriving at a pluriannual agreement. His efforts were not crowned with success for while a new PL-480-Title I agreement was indeed signed on 30 September 1964, its duration was restricted to the fiscal year 1965. However, the volume of food grains supplied remained large: 4 million tons of wheat, 300,000 tons of rice, and 75,000 tons of vegetable oil. It was reported that imports expected to be made during 1964-5 under PL-480 constituted 20 per cent of the American wheat production and 15 per cent of the rice production.[32] It was crucial to reach an agreement since riots had broken out in several places in India following the increase in the price of food grains. Further, worsened by hoarding and speculation, the price had increased by almost 50 per cent between March 1963 and September 1964.[33]

By taking care not to make any but short-term commitments on sales of agricultural commodities, the American government intended to make the Indians aware of the fact that they could not always count on American surpluses, all the more so as the measures taken in the United States to reduce these surpluses began to bear fruit. Several studies conducted in the United States which compared demographic growth with the growth of food production tended to emphasize that a Malthusian crisis would be inevitable in the Third World countries if nothing was done to rapidly improve their agricultural yields. The Ford and the Rockfeller foundations and the AID mission in Delhi had been pressing for a higher food grain output through minimum price support programmes for farmers, higher production and availability of fertilizers, more intensive irrigation, and the development and distribution of high-yielding varieties of wheat and rice. This was the message that Freeman communicated to his Indian counterparts by insisting on the urgency of substantially increasing investments in agriculture, particularly in the manufacture of chemical fertilizers or pesticides and by offering to the farmers easy access to these products. Chester Bowles disclosed in September 1964 that in response to an official Indian request, a consortium of American companies was being formed to assist in providing the technical skill, foreign exchange, and management planning to build at least five new plants, each with an annual capacity of 200,000 tons of nitrogenous fertilizers.[34] The threat to political stability that could result from these repeated food grains deficits also caused some anxiety in Washington. A memorandum meant for the Secretary of Agriculture brought up this question, setting out that

> the food crisis, the political crisis and the development crisis (which is first of all a long-run food crisis) are serious and inseparable. . . . An awkward result was that the middle ground in the political spectrum was fast disappearing as the various political factions polarized on the Right and on the Left. Also US efforts to alleviate the food crisis could be thwarted if the country did not hold together and if Shastri was to be replaced by a Left of center group.[35]

In early 1965, a CIA report also mentioned the probable political repercussions of Indian food shortages. It was feared that the chances of victory of the ruling Congress party in the upcoming state and national elections in 1967 might be jeopardized, and there was a distinct possibility that two decades of political stability might come to an end. It might produce a formal shift in power from the centre to the provincial and local governments and 'the Communists —both the Beijing and Moscow-oriented wings—would be quick to try to exploit any general decline in India's political stability and order'.[36]

The record harvest of 88 million tons in 1964-5 (10 per cent higher than in 1963-4), did not suffice to compensate for the mediocre levels of production of the preceding years. What is more, the worst had yet to come. The south-west monsoon brought too little rain to save the autumn crops and the persistent drought seriously endangered the spring crops. Thus, agricultural production declined by 19 per cent in 1965-6. The imports of food grains in 1965 attained the unprecedented level of 7.5 million tons which was even surpassed the following year with 10.4 million tons (80 per cent of these food grains were American). With government stocks reduced to the bare minimum, the slightest slowing down of imports, as happened during a strike by American dockers in early 1965, brought the threat of famine looming large on the horizon. To bring out the magnitude of the problem, B.R. Bhagat, the Minister of Planning, pointed out that imports of wheat in 1964, most of it under the PL-480 programme, were nearly twice as large as the marketable surpluses from indigenous production. This meant that nearly two-thirds of the supply in the urban areas came from imported wheat.[37] In the face of this unprecedented crisis, when the agreement on the sale of agricultural commodities signed in September 1964 expired on 30 June 1965, the Indian government requested for a new two-year 16 million ton deal on PL-480 assistance, which was at first cut down by the US government to a one-year 7 million ton deal. The gravity of the situation had not escaped the attention of McGeorge Bundy, Special Assistant to the President for National Security Affairs, who wrote to Johnson on 28 June 1965 that

> if we do not make some interim arrangement for shipments of wheat within that time-frame [in the next week or two], there may well be a real problem of food shortage in India which the Indians could successfully blame on us. That could bring us a lot of violent and quite unnecessary criticism, and

might even give the Soviets a chance to make emergency deliveries and make us look foolish.[38]

It was also recalled that if the United States did not come through, India would have to use its own scarce foreign exchange to buy wheat elsewhere and, in this case, American aid dollars would be indirectly subsidizing Indian wheat purchases to help out someone else's balance of payments.[39] With the distribution arrangements on the verge of a breakdown and the prospect of hoardings leading to higher prices if shipments were to be interrupted, Shastri wrote to Johnson on 9 July to press him to intervene personally to expedite the negotiations of a new agreement; Shastri also asked Johnshon if he would discuss with the Finance Minister, T.T. Krishnamachari, the draft of the Fourth Five Year Plan when the latter visited Washington in September.[40]

But Lyndon Johnson had decided that in the context of a review of US economic aid—so that the United States could get more leverage for their money, both in terms of more effective self-help and political purposes—he would keep India on a leash. To force New Delhi to undertake the revision of its agricultural policy, the United States opted for a 'ship-to-mouth' policy on food shipments, limiting the duration and size of PL-480 agreements and mandated frequent reviews of Indian progress in adopting and carrying out self-help reform measures in food and agriculture policy as a condition for further deliveries. Ultimately, no less than four agreements under the PL-480 programme were to be signed during the second semester of 1965, the first one covering a sixty-day period and the following ones for only one month: on 26 July 1965 for the sale of 1 million tons of wheat, on 29 September and on 4 November for 500,000 tons of wheat, and on 10 December for the despatch of 1.5 million tons of wheat and millet. In the midst of the India-Pakistan war, Chester Bowles warned that the United States should not give the Indians further reason for exasperation: 'our unique ability to assist in easing food shortages will do much to improve our political position here which has been severely damaged by use of US planes and tanks by Pakistan'.[41] Bowles's pleas for a 15-month agreement went unheard and Johnson was not prepared to 'send about 35 million a month in giveaway food to India'. 'There is no reason why they can't pay for their wheat if they can pay for munitions', argued the US President: 'Napoleon said an army fights on its belly, and I don't know if we got an obligation the rest of our lives just to ship them 10 per cent of what they eat. And not without even having agreement or discussions, or tying in any alliance, or to be sure of serving our national interests.' Even the Soviet bogey did not play since 'it might be a good thing if Russia did a little of it for a while'.[42] Not letting himself be taken in by Johnson's unyielding attitude, Bowles insisted that the domestic situation would be fraught with danger if PL-480 shipments were to stop, or be curtailed, or be delayed since the US would not remain unscathed if 'image in world press as well as in India of United States government loaded with wheat putting squeeze on 40 million Indian slum dwellers in order to bring pressure to bear on Indian government which is faced with potential two-front war (while shipment continue to Pakistan) would be profoundly harmful; Communists will have a field day'.[43] In his memoirs, Johnson justified his uncompromising attitude in these words:

> What we called the 'short tether' policy was profoundly unpopular among India's leaders, especially the staunch advocates of industrialization. It was hardly more popular with those in our own government who considered aid to India essential to the survival of that country and to its continued existence as a democracy. I stood almost alone, with only a few concurring advisers, in this fight to slow the pace of US assistance, to persuade the Indians to do more for themselves, and to induce other nations to lend a helping hand. This was one of the most difficult and lonely struggled of my Presidency.[44]

Also when Johnson approved, at the end of October, a new extension of the food shipments for an additional thirty days, he made clear that the United States must continue to use all the leverage at its disposal to ensure that the Indian government put its food house in order. He referred to a report he had received from John A. Schnittker, Under Secretary for Agriculture, in which the latter pointed out that the Indian government had failed to meet its food production goals. It was expected from the Indian government that it would increase the resources allocated to agriculture in the Fourth Plan. American observers continued to feel that New Delhi, and notably the Finance Minister and the Planning Commission, had not learnt the required lessons from the shortage of food grains in 1963 and 1964 and considered that the priority officially given to agriculture was only on paper. Schnittker also made a biased assessment of the production of chemical fertilizers in India which was

> one of plants planned but never built, of plants which were built but did not function properly; of a negative attitude toward outside capital; of an

unwillingness to provide the incentives required for profitable foreign private investment . . . India's cultivators are asking for two-three times as much fertilizer as is available. To meet these demands and her own food needs, India must turn to private foreign investment to do the job.[45]

On the occasion of a session of the Food and Agriculture Organization held in Rome, a new agricultural strategy was defined during the meeting held on 25 November 1965, between Orville Freeman and the reform-minded C. Subramaniam who, as Minister of Food and Agriculture, shared most of the American views on this politically explosive issue. The two came quickly to an agreement which was kept as a close secret to prevent the opposition in India from using it to accuse the government of yielding to US pressure. Under the agreement, investments in agriculture during the coming year (1966-7) would be increased by at least 40 per cent above the current year. As far as the whole Fourth Five Year Plan was concerned, there would be Rs. 24 billion or more than double the investment level during the Third Plan. The highest priority given to the agricultural programme would also apply to the allocation of foreign exchange estimated at $ 2 billion. Fertilizer consumption targets for the next five years, as also a food aid phase-out schedule, were laid down.[46] On 7 December 1965, Subramaniam made a public pronouncement on the new agricultural policy in Parliament. The Indian government intended to do everything in its power to achieve self-reliance, fixed this time for 1971, and would adopt for this purpose a strategy encouraging the farmers on the most productive land to adopt modern agricultural methods based on the large-scale use of chemical fertilizers, the selection of new high-yielding varieties of seeds, an intensive irrigation system, and better access to credit for cultivators. Encouragement was given to foreign private investment in the manufacture and distribution of fertilizers. Every foreign company setting up a fertilizer factory before 31 March 1967 would have the right to price and market their product during the first seven years of operation, the only conditions being that the Indian partner, whether it be the government or a private enterprise, would control the majority of equity and that the Indian government would reserve to itself the right to buy 30 per cent of the annual production at negotiated prices so as to ensure a fair distribution across the country.

In the face of the worst drought in recent history, an American expert estimated that the shortfall in production would run as high as 20 million tons, instead of 10-12 million tons, and that some degree of famine or starvation seemed inevitable.[47] In order to fend off accusations of insensitivity now that the Indian government had committed itself to agricultural reforms, Johnson announced on 9 December, on the eve of Ayub Khan's visit to the United States, a two-month extension of the PL-480-Title I programme and the early shipment of an additional 1.5 million tons of wheat to India (the Indian government would have preferred to receive an extension under Title II since the freight cost was entirely borne by the United States). He also announced a $ 50 million loan for the import of fertilizers urgently needed for the crops which would be planted during the coming summer. Johnson and Subramaniam discussed the food crisis and further PL-480 requirements for the 1966 calendar year—assessed at 10 million tons of wheat and 1 million tons of sorghum—when the Indian official went to Washington a few days later to prepare the ground for Shastri's projected visit at the beginning of February 1966. Subramaniam also pressed for a release of assistance already committed by the USA under the 1965 AIC pledge. Freeman argued that the pressure on the Indian government should not be relaxed. He recommended that when the American government resumed negotiations for economic assistance, 'it will be made perfectly clear privately that assistance will be geared to the Indian performance in meeting their agricultural commitments and targets'.[48] Besides, the Johnson administration encouraged the Indians to approach other wheat-producing countries such as Canada and Australia. The nerve-racking policy of signing short-term agreements, which was generating a lot of resentment in India, was pursued till the time that India began to surmount its food crisis thanks to an unprecedented harvest of 96 million tons during the year 1967-8, which marked the start of the 'Green Revolution'.

People in India had come to believe that economic reasons were not the only grounds for the allocation of food grains on a monthly basis. Reflecting this opinion, the *Times of India* of 4 October 1965 felt that

> the US administration which has so much wheat to spare would not have decided to go through the wearisome process of contracting for the supply of small quantities of wheat every month unless it had some political purpose in doing so. The only purpose in the present circumstances can be the achievement of a settlement in Kashmir in accord with the American policy.

Chester Bowles did his utmost to persuade the Shastri government that the American reluctance to negotiate a long-term PL-480 agreement was not an effort to bring political pressure to bear on India, but he had to concede that this line of argument had few buyers in India. He shared some of the Indians' perplexity since Subramaniam has adopted 'just about every suggestion we have made in the sixteen months he has had the job' and, he is 'by all odds the ablest Minister in the cabinet, vigorously pro-American and with great amount of courage. In the last two weeks he has performed valiantly answering attacks of left wing element who have charged that we have been using PL-480 food as political lever.'[49] The Indians were entitled to think that food aid would be more readily forthcoming if they were publicly supportive of the increasing US military involvement in Indochina. In a telegram to Bowles, Dean Rusk himself admitted that India, as a great Asian country alert to the threat of China's expansionism, should give more support to the efforts made by the United States and others to thwart Chinese ambitions in Vietnam. Rusk wrote: 'We recognize the government of India's difficulties, particularly with the Soviet Union, in taking strong public position on this and that privately it does not wish to see an American pull out of Southeast Asia. But we consider that India's position and actions to date fall considerably short of what is possible.'[50]

The US Ambassador warned that the consequences of a new surge in nationalistic fervour in the wake of the war with Pakistan might, in fact, lead to a hardening of the Indian position on Kashmir, a rapid decline in American influence, and an accelerating shift towards the USSR. While everyone in India agreed that being dependent on food from abroad was dangerous and also detrimental to national dignity, Subramaniam, intervening in the Lok Sabha on 12 November 1965, warned against an irresponsible 'go it alone' mood:

> It is not merely PL-480, it is not merely American aid but international cooperation and assistance from the various friendly countries would be absolutely necessary to tide over this crisis. Therefore, at this critical juncture if we go about and say in a huff 'no, we do not want aid', it will be committing not only a political suicide as far as the party is concerned but others may take advantage of it and create sufficient difficulties for the Government, for the party and ultimately for the country.

He concluded that 'if anybody says that in the coming years we are going to go alone without any aid whatsoever, he is living in a fool's paradise'.[51]

A document of the Planning Commission concerning the Fourth Five Year Plan (1966-71), published in September 1965, relied on the availability of an aggregate amount of Rs. 40 billion of net external assistance. While this projected figure was substantially larger than the amount of Rs. 26 billion planned during the Third Plan, the requirements of net assistance after allowing for interest payments and repayments of capital (the debt servicing obligations were estimated at Rs. 13.5 billion) were not very much larger as compared to the Third Plan. The net external assistance required to finance new projects (Rs. 24.5 billion) and for maintenance imports not covered by exports (Rs. 2 billion) came to Rs. 26.5 billion, i.e. in fact, a modest increase, as compared to Rs. 21 billion for the Third Plan, calling for savings on project imports and greater use of components, machinery, and equipment manufactured in the country.[52]

After the India-Pakistan war, the United States decided to keep both countries short of aid until assurances were forthcoming that there would be no diversion of development resources to military ends, that military disengagement would go forward, and that, in Pakistan's case, cooperation with China would be reduced. While authorizing shipments in accordance with past agreements, the stoppage of new economic aid loans and grants, even under that year's pledge to India, drew protests. The American argument that economic aid should not be wasted in fighting its enemy irritated the Indians more than it convinced them, argued the *Amrita Bazar Patrika*, for what it revealed more than anything else was that economic aid had been withheld by 'the world's strongest democracy when Indian democracy was under a severe assault mounted by a theocratic dictatorship'.[53] The Johnson administration made it known that the resumption of economic aid would be conditional to assurances that economic development in the subcontinent was not again to be disrupted by resource-wasting tensions between India and Pakistan and that reforms should be implemented. Not only had the agricultural sector stagnated, but industrial projects were also considered slow and inefficient, with the emphasis being placed on capacity rather than on production. As a result, India had been out-performed by other countries, notably Pakistan, Korea, and Taiwan. Consequently, the United States government had for some time told New Delhi that unless better results could be shown, India could not expect America to continue their massive economic aid.[54] Johnson wanted to have personal talks with the Indian Prime Minister to convey that their relations must be a two-way street before he was prepared to consider granting further aid of any kind along well-defined lines.

As Indian industry suffered as the result of the lack of raw materials, components, and spare parts, the US government was only willing to let the Vice President, Hubert Humphrey, during his visit to India in February 1966, announce the release of a $ 100 million programme loan under stiff conditions: India would have to match this amount, to use the money for reviving existing capacity, to undertake not to start new projects, to certify that it would not siphon off too much for defense, and that it would reopen the dialogue on economic reforms with the World Bank.[55] US assistance had become so critical that Indira Gandhi's visit to Washington in March 1966 centred on it.[56] Here again, Bowles warned against a too obvious arm-twisting by the Americans at a time when Indira Gandhi 'has emerged as a politically competent, liberal-minded democratic leader who appears to recognize the Communist-Left as her primary domestic enemy and who understands the crucial importance of the US in providing the support required to make India economically self-sufficient and politically viable'. This was indeed not without political risk in an election year, and Bowles recommended that 'as the political temperature rises we must be careful not to expose Mrs Gandhi to the leftist charge that her policies are directed by the US Government in Washington and administered by the US Embassy in Delhi'.[57] The American aid was to resume only in mid-June 1966, several months after the Tashkent Declaration and after the announcement by the Indian government, on 6 June, of the devaluation of the rupee by 57.5 per cent (the official rate increasing from Rs. 4.76 to Rs. 7.50 per US dollar) and of other decisions such as the relaxation of import controls and various internal bureaucratic controls to enable investment decisions to be taken on economic criteria (the devaluation was to ensure that imports would not be over-competitive with domestic products). This set of measures to liberalize the tightly controlled ways in which the Indians managed their economy and to move the country to a more pragmatic, market-oriented system had been in principle accepted during the visit of Indira Gandhi to the United States and had been insisted upon by the World Bank—a high-level mission had visited India in 1965—as a precondition to the granting of all fresh credits. B.K. Nehru recalled that when he met George Woods, head of the World Bank, and Pierre Paul Schweitzer, Director of the IMF, in December 1965, he had been told in polite but unambiguous terms that if there was to be no devaluation, there would be no money for the Fourth Plan.[58] There was a tacit understanding that the economic reforms had a cost which would require substantial AIC financial support, but also that if India did not liberalize to American taste, it just will not 'get the dough'. The highly sensitive political decision to devalue the rupee had the support of C. Subramaniam, Sachin Chaudhuri, the new Finance Minister, and the Minister of Planning, Asoka Mehta, who had discussed the details of the economic policy changes with the IBRD and with US officials in April-May 1966. The devaluation had been somehow facilitated by the resignation from the Cabinet of T.T. Krishnamachari, a determined opponent of such a measure. On 17 July 1965, while rumours over the devaluation of the rupee were already spreading, Krishnamachari had appeared on an unscheduled radio broadcast to declare that this measure would not help in any way to solve the immediate problem of making ends meet, although it might serve as 'an opiate'.[59]

The decision by the United States to suspend economic and military aid to India and Pakistan on acount of the war left the field open for the Soviets to launch a peace offensive. On 4 September 1965, Kosygin sent separate letters to Shastri and Ayub Khan pleading for the cessation of military operations and calling for the withdrawal of troops to positions behind the cease fire line established by agreement between India and Pakistan in July 1949. Moreover, the USSR was ready to offer its good offices to negotiate for a peaceful settlement of India-Pakistan differences. However, this step led to no immediate results. Similarly, the visits of the United Nations Secretary General, U Thant, to New Delhi and to Rawalpindi between 9 and 15 September. Kosygin, in a second message, on 18 September, to Shastri and Ayub Khan offered them an opportunity to meet on Soviet soil to establish direct contacts with the aim of bringing about improved relations between the two countries. The Soviet leaders may then have wished to avoid at all costs a situation involving a Chinese attack on India and consequently an American intervention in support of the latter. The Soviet mediation offer survived the cease fire, and by mid-November it had been formally accepted by the two parties and it was decided to have a round table meeting at Tashkent.

The Indian government was hardly in a position to refuse Kosygin's offer of mediation, which had already been endorsed by Washington, even though it implied a relative readjustment of the Soviet policy in the subcontinent which did not fail to cause the Indians some anxiety. The Indian Ambassador to Moscow, T.N. Kaul, even wondered if the Soviet offer of its 'good offices' did not mean a more balanced policy of military supplies to India and Pakistan. The Soviets assured him that there was no such intention for 'India was a bigger country, her needs were greater, she was not a member of a military alliance and had to be prepared to defend her territory against the Chinese threat'.[60] Moscow also noted that by seeking an improvement in its relations with Pakistan, the Soviets would make it possible to undercut both the Chinese and the American influences in the region and this would also serve India's interests.

The Pakistanis assented to the Soviet proposal, confirming the recent development of warmer relations between Moscow and Rawalpindi, preceded, as in the case of India a few years earlier, by the development of economic relations. In January 1961, Zulfikar Ali Bhutto, Minister for Fuel, Power and Natural Resources, announced, on his return from a visit to Moscow, that the Soviet Union had renewed an offer, already formulated in 1958, for assistance in oil exploration which Pakistan had accepted this time. For the first time, a $ 30 million loan agreement was signed on 4 March 1961 in this regard.[61] But more than anything else, on the political plane, the USSR moved towards a less partisan attitude over the Kashmir issue. When Kosygin had come to New Delhi to attend Nehru's funerals, he suggested to the interim Prime Minister, G.L. Nanda, a greater autonomy for Kashmir. Mikoyan, in June 1964, declared to Shastri that it was time to settle the thorny dispute. The USSR took care not to take sides over the confrontation that had occurred in the Rann of Kutch in April 1965. In the same month, for the first time, a Pakistani head of state went on an official visit to the USSR. Moscow justified this policy, saying it was due to the fact that Pakistan was now taking a more independent stand on international problems. It had thus been noted that Rawalpindi was seeking to distance itself from the American policy in Vietnam, that it now supported the entry of the PRC to the United Nations, and had adopted a more passive role within SEATO and CENTO. Proof of this change was seen in the way the Americans showed their displeasure by postponing economic aid commitments.[62]

US diplomacy was willing to let Moscow attempt to solve the intractable Kashmir issue and seek to reduce tensions in the subcontinent. Already, during the September conflict, the United States chose not to engage in exerting direct pressure on either country but instead to place primary reliance on mediation by the United Nations. The conflict seemed to provide persuasive evidence that both countries were too concerned with their mutual antagonism to play a major constructive role in helping the United States achieve its principal foreign policy objectives. To Chester Bowles, who tried to convince him that India could still be an indigenous Asian counterweight to China, Johnson replied that it seemed very unlikely 'unless India regards it as part of its own responsibility to work actively towards the normalization of its relations with Pakistan', otherwise 'far too much of India's diplomatic energies and military resources will be focussed on the Pakistani problem'.[63] The Johnson administration had its hands full with the US involvement in Vietnam and, in fact, Averell Harriman came to India on the eve of the Tashkent conference to ask Shastri to urge Kosygin to get Hanoi to the negotiating table. Also, Johnson told Ayub Khan, when they both met in Washington in December 1965, that the United States welcomed the Soviet mediation offer and wished it well. Any successful mediation on the part of the Soviets, who had the advantage of coming relatively fresh to the dispute, would almost inevitably involve concessions by India and, according to the State Department, would help 'in cooling down somewhat the increasingly warm Indo-Soviet relations'. The Soviet involvement would relieve the United States of 'some of the burden of being the court of appeal in Indo-Pakistani disputes, thus permitting us to devote our energies, in part at least, to more constructive pursuits'.[64] It might also undercut Chinese interference in South Asian affairs. In case the conference failed, the Soviets would have shown the world that they were no better than the Americans in ensuring peace in the subcontinent.

The meeting between Ayub Khan and Shastri in Tashkent from 4 to 10 January led to a declaration in which India and Pakistan agreed that all armed personnel should be withdrawn not later than 25 February 1966 to the positions they had held prior to 5 August

1965. The two parties also promised to exert all efforts to create good-neighbourly relations in accordance with the United Nations Charter. They also reaffirmed their obligations under the Charter to reject the use of force and to settle their disputes through peaceful means. Shastri did not obtain formal safeguards against Pakistani infiltration into Kashmir whereas Ayub Khan did not get a self-executing arrangement for the settlement of the Kashmir dispute. Kosygin's efforts at conciliation greatly contributed to such a solution after the negotiations had been on the verge of a breakdown. Unfortunately, this declaration ensured only a limited peace in the subcontinent for in 1971 the third India-Pakistan war broke out. The Tashkent conference had, nevertheless, been at the time an image-enhancing success for the Soviet Union as a peacemaker in Asia, even if Moscow did not succeed in seriously weakening the links between Pakistan and the United States nor the links between Rawalpindi and Beijing.[65] Yet it was the first time that two non-communist states had accepted a communist state as their mediator. For the Americans, on the other hand, this conference underlined their ineffectiveness in bridging a gap between the two countries of the Third World which had benefited the most from US assistance. Over the past 15 years, the United States had provided, according to an estimate, about $ 3 billion in economic aid to India and about $ 2.1 billion to Pakistan. It had also shipped PL-480 grains worth some $ 3 billion to India and $1.1 billion to Pakistan.[66] India had become a hostage to multiple dependence, witnessed by the recurrent visits by Ministers and officials to Washington and Moscow in search of assistance. It had to do its share of soul searching. In a letter to Lyndon Johnson, in May 1966, Indira Gandhi reminded the aid-giving countries that they may find it difficult to mobilize funds to help developing countries, but she noted, 'What is not so easily or widely appreciated is the reluctance and sometimes even resentment with which aid is accepted by the recipient. Ever since my return, I have been asked searching questions in Parliament and by the Press to discover whether I have been pressurized by you or the World Bank to do things against our better judgment.' But every cloud has a silver lining: 'I do not mind this. Indeed, I welcome it because in part the questioning reflects the spirit of self-respect and dignity which survives in our people in spite of the many problems of poverty. This is a source of strength to me'.[67] The Indians indeed realized to the accompaniment of much pain that they had crossed the threshold of dependence on a particular type of aid, beyond which the recipient was at the mercy of the donor country and the conditions that it might choose to lay down for granting its aid.

NOTES

1. Planning Commission, *Third Five-Year Plan, Mid-Term Appraisal*, p. 32.
2. SIPRI, *World Armaments and Disarmament: SIPRI Yearbook 1977*, London, 1977, pp. 230-1.
3. See *Report of the Committee on Utilisation of External Assistance*, Ministry of Finance, Department of Economic Affairs, Government of India.
4. Planning Commission, *Third Five-Year Plan, Mid-Term Appraisal*, p. 50.
5. *Economic Weekly*, 10 August 1963, p. 1350.
6. Planning Commission, *Third Five-Year Plan, Mid-Term Appraisal*, p. 51.
7. *Asian Recorder*, vol. 11, no. 10, 5-11 March 1965, pp. 6333-4.
8. *Le Monde*, 21-22 March 1965.
9. Planning Commission, *Towards a Self-Reliant Economy*, p. 223.
10. *Eastern Economist*, 25 May 1962, p. 1255.
11. P. Desai, *The Bokaro Steel Plant*, pp. 24 and 33.
12. *The Clay Committee Report*, pp. 5-6. Quoted by J.P. Stillman, *Foreign Aid, Ideology and Bureaucratic Politics: The Bokaro Steel Mill and Indian-American Relations*, p. 184.
13. J.K. Galbraith, *Ambassador's Journal*, p. 544. In 1963, the American investments in the private sector constituted only 15 per cent of the outstanding foreign business investments, far behind the British capital invested which represented 60 per cent of the total. Table VII.41 'Foreign Investment in India', *Statistical Outline of Indian Economy*, p. 146.
14. *Commerce*, 4 May 1963, p. 770.
15. Declaration of Kennedy on 8 May 1953. R.K. Jain (ed.), *US-South Asian Relations 1947-1982*, vol. 1, p. 273.
16. Kennedy's Message to Congress, 2 April 1963. Department of State, *American Foreign Policy—Current Documents, 1963*, Washington, D.C.: US Government Printing Office, 1967, p. 1167.
17. Nehru to Kennedy, 28 August 1963. S. Gopal, *Jawaharlal Nehru: A Biography*, vol. 3, p. 254. C. Subramaniam, the Minister of Steel and Heavy Engineering, wrote that, as the negotiations with the Americans were stalemated, he had wanted to switch over to the USSR for assistance but Morarji Desai insisted that the matter should be pursued with the Americans in the hope that they might in the end be convinced to help put up the Bokaro plant in the public sector. C. Subramaniam, *Hand of Destiny, vol. 2: The Green Revolution*, p. 34.
18. Kennedy to Nehru, 5 September 1963. S. Gopal, *Jawaharlal Nehru: A Biography*, vol. 3, p. 254.

19. *Times of India*, 3 November 1962.
20. *Times of India*, 29 January 1963.
21. Planning Commission, *Basic Statistics Relating to the Indian Economy, 1950-51 to 1966-67*, pp. 114-15 and 124.
22. S. Mehrotra, *India and the Soviet Union, Trade and Technology Transfer*, p. 15.
23. *Hindu*, 20 April 1963.
24. *Economic Weekly*, 17 October 1964, p. 1674.
25. *Le Monde*, 27 January 1965.
26. Dispatch from the French Ambassador of France to India, Jean Daridan, 5 January 1966 and 30 March 1966. *AQO*, Asie-Océanie, 1956-1967, Inde, vol. 260. One of the criticisms related to the needlessly large number of Soviet technicians employed to supervise the construction of the steel plant, whereas Indian engineers possessed the required qualifications.
27. *Hindu*, 8, 12, and 15 May 1965.
28. *Economic and Political Weekly*, 22 May 1965, p. 836.
29. P. Nikolsky, 'Nehru's Party without Nehru', *New Times*, no. 32, 11 August 1965, p. 16. In 1964, some members of the CPI, who did not share the unconditional support given by the leadership of the party to the Soviet line, founded the CPI (Marxist), closer to the Chinese theses.
30. 20 April 1965. *Lok Sabha Debates* (*third series*), vol. 42, no. 41, col. 9965.
31. B.M. Bhatia, *India's Food Problem and Policy since Independence*, p. 152.
32. 1 December 1964. *Lok Sabha Debates* (*third series*), vol. 36, no. 12, col. 2627.
33. *Economic Weekly*, 31 October 1964, p. 1733.
34. *Eastern Economist*, 18 September 1964, p. 520. At the end of the year, the Indian government entered into negotiations with the American company Bechtel on a project associating it with the Indian government for the construction of five fertilizer factories. While the principle of a majority share by the state was conceded by Bechtel, the American company insisted on complete technical and managerial control during construction, and also on assuming sole responsibility for the laying down of the price policies, marketing, and distribution. Finally, the agreement fell through after T.T. Krishnamachari vetoed it, feeling that the terms of this agreement were prejudicial to India's economic independence. F. Frankel, *India's Political Economy*, pp. 267-8.
35. Memorandum from Under-Secretary (John A. Schnittker) to the Secretary of Agriculture, 21 November 1964. Office of the Secretary of Agriculture, 1964, Box 90, File RG. 16 Foreign Relations 3, National Archives and Records Center, Washington. Quoted by M.B. Wallerstein, *Food for War—Food for Peace*, p. 133.
36. Central Intelligence Agency, 'India's Food Shortages: Causes and Consequences', 19 February 1965. National Security Files: India, Box 1, File: India memos & misc., vol. 4, Lyndon Johnson Library, Austin, Texas. Ibid., p. 133.
37. B.R. Bhagat, 'Meaning of Self-Reliance', *Yojana*, 24 October 1965, pp. 2-3.

38. Memorandum from the President's Special Assistant for National Security Affairs (Bundy) to President Johnson, 30 June 1965. *FRUS, 1964-1968*, vol. 25, p. 286.
39. Memorandum from Robert Komer of the National Security Council Staff to the President's Special Assistant for National Security (Bundy), 2 July 1965. Ibid., pp. 288-9.
40. Johnson Library, National Security File, Special Head of State Correspondence File, India, 15/4/65-28/2/66. Ibid., p. 301.
41. Telegram from the Embassy in India to the Department of State, 9 September 1965. Ibid., p. 379.
42. Johnson Library, recordings and transcripts, recording of telephone conversation between Johnson and Ambassador Goldberg. 18 September 1965. Ibid., p. 408. In another telephone conversation with Freeman, on 2 February 1966, Johnson reaffirmed that he did not want to have anything to do with the business of 'the Communists [which] might help you a little, therefore I've got to give you everything I've got'. Ibid., p. 554.
43. Telegram from the Ambassador to India to Robert Komer of the National Security Council Staff, 21 September 1965. Ibid., p. 420.
44. Lyndon Baines Johnson, *The Vantage Point*, Delhi: Vikas, 1972, p. 225. W. W. Rostow recalled that 'Johnson mobilized in those years a fifth of the American wheat crop for India, and some 600 ships, in the largest maritime assemblage since the Allied Forces crossed the English Channel on D-Day. For a period of two years, more than 60 million Indians were sustained entirely by American food shipments.' W.W. Rostow, *Eisenhower, Kennedy and Foreign Aid*, p. 177.
45. Memorandum from J.A. Schnittker to the President, 23 October 1965. Johnson Library, National Security Files, Country File, India, vol. 4, memos & miscellaneous. Quoted by M.B. Wallerstein, *Food for War—Food for Peace*, pp. 150-1.
46. Telegram from the Embassy in Italy to the Department of State, 26 November 1965. *FRUS, 1964-1968*, vol. 25, pp. 476-9.
47. Memorandum from the President's Deputy Special Assistant for National Security Affairs (Komer) to President Johnson, 6 December 1965. Ibid., pp. 484-5.
48. Memorandum from Secretary of Agriculture to President Johnson, 1 December 1965. Ibid., p. 482. On 4 February, the White House announced the authorization for an extension of the PL-480 agreement with India to provide an additional 2 million tons of wheat and 1 million tons of sorghum.
49. Telegram from the Embassy in India to the Department of State, 15 November 1965. Ibid., p. 467.
50. Telegram from the Department of State to the Embassy in India, 10 November 1965. Ibid., p. 462.
51. *Lok Sabha Debates* (*third series*), vol. 47, no. 7, cols 1722-3.
52. Planning Commission, *Fourth Five-Year Plan—Resources, Outlays and Programmes*, p. 25. In view of the deterioration of the economic situation and uncertainties regarding the financial resources available, this draft plan

was abandoned in favour of three successive annual plans; the Fourth Five Year Plan finally began only in 1969.

53. *Amrita Bazar Patrika*, 19 November 1965.
54. Economic and Military Aid, meeting in the State Department, 10 June 1966. *PRO*, FO 371 186961.
55. Memorandum from the President's Deputy Special Assistant for National Security Affairs (Komer) to President Johnson, 1 February 1966. *FRUS, 1964-1968*, vol. 25, p. 552.
56. About this visit, R.W. Komer wrote to the President that 'we finally have the Indians where you've wanted them ever since last April—with the slate wiped clean of previous commitments and India coming to us asking for a new relationship on the terms we want'. Memorandum from the President's Deputy Special Assistant for National Security Affairs (Komer) to President Johnson, 27 March 1966. Ibid., p. 593.
57. Letter from the Ambassador to India (Bowles) to President Johnson, 5 May 1966. Ibid., p. 642.
58. B.K. Nehru, *Nice Guys Finish Second*, p. 447.
59. *Asian Recorder*, vol. 11, no. 32, 6-12 August 1965, p. 6595.
60. T.N. Kaul, *Diplomacy in Peace and War*, p. 160.
61. Ministry of Finance, Government of Pakistan, *Pakistan Economic Survey, 1966-67*, Rawalpindi, 1967, p. 217.
62. Economic aid to Pakistan was resumed, as was aid to India, on 15 June 1966. A coincidence or otherwise, it was a few days after the resignation of Z.A. Bhutto, the instigator of the policy of friendship with the communist camp. While the United States did not at the time appreciate Sino-Pakistan friendship, they later took advantage of it by utilizing Pakistan as a mediator to further pursue their policy of getting closer to China which led Kissinger to pass through Islamabad on his way to his secret mission to Beijing in July 1971.
63. Letter from President Johnson to Chester Bowles, 20 May 1966. *FRUS, 1964-1968*, vol. 25, p. 652.
64. 'Moscow Considers its Further Diplomatic Course in India-Pakistan Crisis', Research Memorandum from the US Department of State, Director of Intelligence and Research, 5 October 1965. *PRO*, FO 371 180964.
65. When, in May 1966, Benediktov, the Soviet Ambassador, asked the British High Commissioner his opinion on the current state of Indo-Pakistan relations, the latter expressed surprise since his country was not part of the Tashkent dialogue. To which Benediktov answered that Tashkent was by now a dead letter. From T.J. O'Brien to V.C. Martin, South Asia Department, CRO, 16 May 1966. *PRO*, FO 371 186952.
66. Special National Intelligence Estimate, 7 December 1965. *FRUS, 1964-1968*, vol. 25, p. 488. Another estimate set US total economic assistance at $ 6,77 billion between 1946 and 1966 (See table on p. 405).
67. Letter from Prime Minister Indira Gandhi to President Johnson, 12 May 1966. Ibid., p. 647.

CHAPTER 16

Aid: An Appraisal

DESPITE A HIGHER level of expenditure than initially anticipated, most of the objectives fixed at the start of the Third Plan were not achieved. The national income increased on an average by only 2.2 per cent annually as against the expected rate of 6 per cent. During the year 1965-6, with the effects of the India-Pakistan war added to the drought, the national income even fell by 4.2 per cent. Agricultural production during the first four years of the plan increased on an average by 2.6 per cent, a rate distinctly lower than the annual rate of growth of 4 per cent noted during the 1951-61 decade. Industrial production also declined as compared to the objective set, growing by only 5.7 per cent per year on an average between 1961 and 1966, as against the anticipated 14 per cent.

To assess the growing importance acquired by aid in the funding of the development process, one has only to note that the amount of aid utilized during the Third Plan was more than double the amount used during the Second Plan. During the first three five year plans,

PUBLIC SECTOR OUTLAY AND FINANCIAL RESOURCES

(in billions of rupees)

	Public sector outlay	Domestic savings	Deficit financing	External resources
First Plan (1951-6)	19.60	14.39 (73.4 %)	3.33 (17 %)	1.88 (9.6 %)
Second Plan (1956-61)	46.00	25.62 (55.7 %)	9.48 (20.6%)	10.90 (23.7 %)
Third Plan (1961-6)	86.31	50.26 (58.2 %)	11.50 (13.3 %)	24.55 (28.5 %)

Source: Statistical Outline of the Indian Economy, Table XV.85, p. 254.

the share of aid in the financing of public expenditure had increased three times more quickly than the total of this expenditure. Also significant was the noteworthy increase in the rate of utilization of the aid authorized. As a corollary, the external debt servicing increased rapidly: Rs. 238 million during the First Plan, Rs. 1.194 billion during the Second Plan, and Rs. 5.426 billion during the Third Plan.[1] The ratio of external debt servicing to export earnings went up from 0.8 per cent during the First Plan to 3.9 per cent during the Second Plan, and 14.5 per cent during the Third Plan. Net inflow of foreign aid financed 37 per cent of commodity imports during the Third Plan compared to 27 per cent of these during the earlier plan.[2]

The aid given by the countries and the international organizations that were members of the AIC put together came to nine-tenths of all the aid utilized between 1 April 1961 and 31 March 1966, the share of the socialist camp not exceeding 8 per cent. American grants and loans alone represented 58.3 per cent of the total aid utilized (44.4 per cent of the aid authorized) over the same period, of which half was in the framework of the PL-480 programme, as against 7.4 per cent for Soviet aid.[3]

An examination of American and Soviet assistance over the first three five year plans, reveals that the American grants and loans constituted 52 per cent of all the authorized aid as against 8.4 per cent for Soviet aid. In terms of absolute value, the former was more than six times the latter. An even larger difference emerges if one were to evaluate the aid in terms of the aid actually utilized: aid from the United States represented 57.9 per cent as against 6.4 per cent for the Soviet aid. It should also be emphasized that a part of the World Bank assistance came from funds contributed by the United States to this international organization. Five sources supplied 87 per cent of all the foreign aid granted between 1951 and 1966. The Soviet Union ranked third, coming behind the United States and the World Bank (12.6 per cent), but before West Germany (7.7 per cent) and Great Britain (6.2 per cent). These last two countries came before the Soviet Union as concerns the percentage of the aid utilized. The aid contributed by the entire Communist bloc represented one-tenth of all the authorized aid and 7 per cent of the aid utilized.

A more detailed study of the utilization of American and Soviet aid to India reveals some interesting facts.[4] What needs to be noted first of all is the importance of the sales of agricultural commodities

External Assistance During the First Three Five Year Plans
From 1 April 1951 to 31 March 1966

(in millions of rupees)

	Authorizations	Utilizations
Australia	256.7	196.7
Austria	84.9	47.0
Belgium	114.2	48.9
Canada	2,224.3	1,616.1
Czechoslovakia	635.0	130.1
Denmark	24.1	6.0
Federal Republic of Germany	4,499.6	3,473.3
France	571.3	209.8
Italy	813.2	116.5
Japan	1,653.7	1,047.1
Netherlands	219.0	95.1
New Zealand	42.8	38.5
Norway	51.3	51.3
Poland	413.0	113.4
Sweden	58.6	25.8
Switzerland	245.1	60.4
United Kingdom	3,664.3	2,935.3
United States	30,297.2	25,884.6
Wheat Loan, 1951	903.1	903.1
PL 665	318.7	318.7
PL-480	15,636.3	13,684.5
Technical Cooperation Agreement	1,895.0	1,851.5
Agency for International Development	6,793.3	4,981.3
Export-Import Bank	1,950.6	1,622.6
Development Loan Fund	2,426.1	2,242.3
President's Asian Eco. Development Fund	87.5	84.5
Third Country Currency Assistance	27.8	27.8
US Banks	258.8	168.3
USSR	4,892.7	2,870.4
Yugoslavia	214.3	97.1
Ford Foundation	208.5	180.0
IBRD	4,628.1	3,799.7
IDA	2,785.5	2,006.3
UN Special Fund	84.9	18.3
Total	58,628.3	45,067.7

Source: Ministry of Finance, Government of India, *External Assistance, 1965-66*, pp. 168-71.

in American aid, which represented more than half (54 per cent) of the total American loans and grants made to India. Then, it is observed that around one-fifth of the American aid utilized took the form of grants (in view of the fact that about one-fourth of the counterpart funds of the PL-480 programme were given as grants to the Indian government) while the grant component in Soviet aid was only 1 per cent.

While in the mid-1950s, the terms of Soviet loans (repayable in rupees in 12 years with the rate of interest being 2.5 per cent) appeared particularly attractive at a time when the proportion of grants in American aid declined, these terms, ten years later, were less noteworthy or remarkable. Almost 65 per cent of the American loans used (mainly those from the PL-480 and PL-665 programmes) were repayable in rupees. The PL-480 loans had a maturity of 40 years with a rate of interest which, after having been fixed at 3.5 per cent to 5 per cent for the first credits, came down to 1 per cent in the early 1960s. These terms were again repeated in the AID loans, which, however, remained repayable in dollars. This trend in the terms of American loans was brought about at least as much by the necessity of keeping in mind the solvency of the recipient country as by the desire to match the terms offered by the Soviet Union. None of the lending institutions except the Export-Import Bank credits (about 6 per cent of American aid) imposed requirements that were close to commercial conditions. The Eximbank loans were repayable in dollars over a period of 7 to 14 years with a rate of interest of 5.25 per cent to 6 per cent.

These factors emphasize the relatively modest scale of Soviet aid as compared to that of the United States. Hence, the extent of prominence given in India to the assistance from Moscow rests on factors other than simply the quantum of aid given. It was related to the priority given by the Indian government from the mid-1950s, to the development, with state funding, of key sectors of the economy considered as guaranteeing the independence of the country, such as basic industries or oil. It was this that the United States balked at, as we have seen in the case of the Bokaro steel plant. The contribution to the development of heavy industry and energy is seen in the sector-wise distribution of the contracts placed for purchase of equipment financed by Soviet credits: 54 per cent of the loans were meant for the steel industry, 16.9 per cent for oil and gas projects, 12.6 per cent for power projects, 11.5 per cent for different types of heavy machinery plants (building, electrical, and coal mining equipment), 2.2 per cent for drug projects, and 2 per cent for coal projects.[5]

American aid to the public sector took the form mainly of contributions to the expenditure for infrastructure, hydroelectric projects, and thermal stations. This is seen notably in the distribution of the 64 loans granted by the DLF and the AID between June 1958 and January 1966, as well as by the placement of the PL-480 counterpart funds allocated to the Indian government. In 1958, P.C. Mahalanobis regretted that Western countries had till then refrained from promoting the industrialization of the underdeveloped countries in any significant way.[6] But this proved less true subsequently.[7] As a study of the DLF and the AID loans shows, the American contribution to the development of the private industrial sector was significant, particularly in the form of maintenance imports. However, by giving preference to the development of the private sector, the Americans were accused of 'enriching capitalists' while the Soviets were hailed for constructing factories 'belonging to the people'.

The greater dispersal of US loans and the substantial share that aid untied to projects came to assume may explain to a large extent the distinctly higher rate of utilization of American aid over the entire length of the three five year plans, as compared to the Soviet aid which was tied both to the project and to the source. These were 82 per cent for American aid as against 58 per cent for Soviet aid. Leaving aside the specific circumstances that led to the aid agreement for the Bokaro steel plant, the slow utilization of Soviet aid can also explain why no new lines of credit were granted during the Third Plan (all the Soviet aid agreements, except the earlier agreement, on the construction of the Bhilai steel plant, had been signed between November 1957 and February 1961).

India had drawn wide benefits from the aid granted by the two superpowers. It was the foremost among the non-communist countries of the Third World to have obtained economic aid from the Soviet Union from 1953 till March 1966, followed by Egypt, Afghanistan, Indonesia, and Algeria. These five countries received almost 70 per cent of the total amount of Soviet loans. As regards the American loans and grants coming from AID and predecessor agencies between 1948 and June 1965, India was surpassed only by South Korea and it was ahead of a number of countries that were US allies. This would tend to demonstrate apparently that, on the whole,

LARGEST THIRD WORLD RECIPIENT OF SOVIET LOANS
BETWEEN 1953 AND MARCH 1966

	(*in millions of dollars*)
India	1,018.5
Egypt	824.5
Afghanistan	488.2
Indonesia	374.2
Algeria	228.0
Syria	225.5
Iraq	180.5
Argentina	130.0
Ghana	102.4
Ethiopia	100.0
Pakistan	72.5
Guinea	68.0
Mali	55.6
Somalia	52.2
Burma	45.8

Source: Kurt Muller, *The Foreign Aid Programs of the Soviet Bloc and Communist China: An Analysis*, p. 219.[8]

LARGEST THIRD WORLD RECIPIENT OF AID FROM AID
AND PREDECESSOR AGENCIES BETWEEN JULY 1947 AND JUNE 1965

	(*in millions of dollars*)
South Korea	2,503.2
India	2,485.6
South Vietnam	2,084.5
Pakistan	1,730.0
Turkey	1,608.0
Taiwan	1,375.1
Indochina (till 1954)	825.6
Brazil	633.6
Iran	596.9
Israel	503.9
Chile	436.5
Laos	414.9
Jordan	393.9
Thailand	365.6
Morocco	289.5

Source: Agency for International Development, *The AID Story,* Washington, D.C., US Government Printing Office, 1966, p. 36, p. 42, p. 48, p. 54.

India had gained more in terms of aid by following a policy of non-alignment than it would have had by aligning itself with the United States. But this observation was rejected by B.K. Nehru who argued during an interview granted to an American television network in

May 1962, that it was wrong to assume that the non-aligned make the best of both possible worlds: 'We get aid from Eastern world and Western world but we get less aid per capita on combined basis from both sides than your allies—all of your allies—get from one source.'[9] This argument needs to be kept in mind although the number of inhabitants of a country and the rate of growth of its population are not foremost factors that determine the quantity of aid allocated. It is probable that India would have received a larger amount of aid from the United States if it had given up non-alignment. That this increase would have been much greater is less certain. On the other hand, there appears to be no doubt that the development programmes of the Indian government and, more than anything else, the development of industry in the public sector would have been affected.

NOTES

1. Ministry of Finance, Government of India, *Economic Survey 1971-72*, p. 156.
2. Ministry of Finance, Government of India, *Economic Survey 1966-67*, p. 50. The approximately Rs. 45 billion of foreign aid utilized during the first three five year plans to cover imports represented an amount around six times higher than the Rs. 7.3 billion drawn—for the same purpose—from the foreign exchange reserves during the same period.
3. The rupees accumulated by the United States in an account in the Reserve Bank of India as a result of funds generated from the repayment of development loans and, above all, PL-480 proceeds, and which were not given as grants or loans to the Indian government for the execution of projects mutually agreed upon, gave rise to controversy. Some people suspected that a part of these large funds were used by the CIA to finance various political organizations. Lyndon Johnson, during Indira Gandhi's visit to the United States in March 1966, suggested that a part of this capital be utilized for the creation of an Indo-American Educational Foundation headed by an Indo-American Trust. The idea of a bi-national cultural foundation, which had been first mooted by Chester Bowles in March 1964, faced strong opposition in India from all parts of the political and academic spectrum. In the forefront were the Communists who saw in the proposed plan 'a gigantic instrument of massive American penetration into cultural life, above all, the sphere of moulding the ideology and political outlook of adolescent youth'. The Congress rulers were accused of having accepted the proposal for a foundation as 'part of the price they have been compelled

to pay for their economic dependence on US imperialism'. *Asian Recorder*, vol. 12, no. 28, 9-15 July 1966, p. 7174. The Indian government, faced with the accusation of allowing the Americans having a powerful voice in controlling India's education policy, stalled this proposal.

4. Ministry of Finance, Government of India, *Economic Survey, 1967-68*, pp. A-70–A-73.
5. Based on Ministry of Finance, Government of India, *External Assistance 1966-67*, pp. 103-4.
6. Speaking on the general outlooks of the West and the East, Mahalanobis did not mince his words: 'Western aid, primarily military in nature, is usually welcomed by being given to small groups of persons who happen to be in power often against popular will; and thus serves to preserve reactionary social and political conditions and hamper industrialization in countries receiving such aid. The aid from the USSR and China, on the other hand, is being increasingly sought by and given to groups who are more eager for economic progress and, therefore, tend to have greater popular support behind them.' Remarks made in Austria in September 1958. P.C. Mahalanobis, *Talks on Planning*, Calcutta/Bombay: Indian Statistical Institute/Asia Publishing House, 1961, p. 133.
7. See Ministry of Finance, *External Assistance, 1966-67*, pp. 126-46.
8. While the figures of Soviet aid to these countries may vary slightly from source to source, the classification and the order of magnitude remain practically the same.
9. *Rajya Sabha Debates*, vol. 39, no. 6, 20 June 1962, col. 890.

Conclusion

STARTING FROM the postulate that aid is not disinterested generosity, we have attempted to show, on the one hand, the nature of the objectives that guided the United States and the Soviet Union in their policies of aid to India, and, on the other hand, to determine whether India's decision to seek foreign aid may have led it to significantly alter some of its politicies, at the bidding of a donor state. In response to the first question, at least one thing is clear. Both the United States and the Soviet Union gave aid less as a result of a wide identity of political and economic views or ideological affinities than in order to prevent India, acknowledged as a leading non-aligned country and also recognized for its geopolitical importance, from falling into the sphere of influence of the enemy camp, either as the result of economic contingency or because of a military threat. The primary policy determinant was defensive even if India could also have been promoted as a model of economic development or as an exemplar of peaceful co-existence.

The US government expressed its disapproval of non-alignment or India's repprochement with the Soviet Union and showed some irritation at Indian denunciations of America's policy in Asia. However, US displeasure against India was also tempered by considerations of political expediency; for instance, when Indian actions served US interests by contributing towards a deterioration of relations between Moscow and Beijing. The United States often communicated its discontentment, sometimes through the intervention of the World Bank or the IMF, *vis-à-vis* the economic policy of the Indian government which was considered to be opposed to the precepts of liberalism as indicated by the decision to accord state control over the economy, the priority given to the development of the public sector, and the obstacles to the entry of foreign capital. The Americans also felt that the Indians did not show enough gratitude for the aid given to them which was quantitatively far greater than the aid from any other country, and they castigated India for its leniency *vis-à-vis* the USSR. Yet these differences never caused a disruption in the flow of American aid to India for these were eclipsed by one imperative. In the context of the Cold War, the Americans fully appreciated the importance of a Third World parliamentary democracy opposed to communist totalitarianism. Given India's singular importance as a pluralist regime and a geo-strategic pivot, it was essential to ensure its political stability and economic viability. As a consequence, the Indians had tended to take American aid for granted, notably taking advantage of the situation by opting for decisions which deliberately they knew would in all probability incur the criticism of the US Congress, if not the administration of the day.

The Soviet Union, from the time that it acknowledged the credibility of non-alignment, particularly after the advent of *Panchsheela* and subsequent to India's refusal to collaborate with Washington's strategic designs, opted for a policy of aid to India with three objectives. The first aim was to assure the Indian government of its support, and thus to prevent India's dependence for its development programme exclusively on Western aid, as the latter might become, especially in times of crisis, conditional on political alignment. The second goal was the desire of the USSR to claim its place as an acknowledged Asiatic power by forging closer relations with non-communist Asian states. It decided to this end that establishing close relations with India would show the way to the others. The third objective arose out of the second, and emerged out of the rivalry between the two largest communist powers to woo the Third World. The Soviets aimed at making India a power that would counterpoise China in Asia. Moscow's decision to grant military aid to New Delhi was based on the desire to preclude the possibility of India being forced into aligning with the West in order to safeguard its security threatened by Chinese hegemonic aspirations. While Moscow gave many arguments, hardly convincing in terms of communist orthodoxy, to justify its aid by holding forth on the progressive nature of the economic policy of the Indian government, the primary intention of the Soviet leaders was to neutralize American and Chinese influences in the region. They were even ready to overlook the interests of the Communist Party of India to further their own foreign policy objectives.

A comparison of the reactions aroused in India by the American and the Soviet aid policies is instructive. With the exception of the negotiations that preceded the agreement on the Bokaro steel mill,

Soviet aid policies did not give rise to any strong public debate. But in the case of the American aid, Indians reacted much more vigorously. The Americans were frequently criticized for instrumentalizing aid to exert pressure on the Indian government; this hostility was based on numerous political disagreements resulting from the US containment policy *vis-à-vis* communism based on military alliances that New Delhi had vehemently denounced as this had enabled Pakistan to find favour with Washington and to strengthen itself militarily. Lyndon Johnson's arm-twisting techniques when he linked food supplies to a review of India's economic priorities did also generate a lot of resentment.

On the other hand, Soviet aid came with broad political convergence with India. This is seen most clearly in the decision of the Soviet Union to support the foreign and economic policies of the Indian government. Thus, the USSR provided aid to the development of public sector undertakings, which were perceived as a guarantee of national independence, but which the United States refused to subsidize. One of the consequences of this development was the emergence of pressure groups interested in fostering Indo-Soviet relations within ministries where till then had seen only pro-West lobbies. Soon New Delhi came to appreciate to a far greater degree the advantages drawn from privileged relations with the USSR than the possibility of acquiring larger aid from the United States.

India's official stand was that it preferred to give up aid, whatever be the consequences, rather than make concessions that would compromise its national interest. Nevertheless, the Indian government sometimes had to come to terms with the creditor country. For, instance, when exports of strategic minerals could have on influence on US assistance. In many cases, the need to obtain foreign aid was only one of the elements, sometimes a crucial one, which led the Indian government to take certain decisions. It is tempting to interpret what may seem as muted criticism of the USSR, when one would have expected a more resolute opposition, by referring to the advantages flowing from Soviet support to India's development plans. But it is also possible that India equally appreciated the backing of the Soviet Union *vis-à-vis* Pakistan or China. Similarly the consent given by the Indian government, after the Sino-Indian war, to American military operations in the region. This was due as much to the fear of a new confrontation with China as the desire to have the United States contribute to the modernization plan of the

Indian army. While the necessity for the resumption of American aid, suspended at the time of the India-Pakistan war, had weighed heavily in the decision to devalue the rupee in June 1966, it should also be remembered that devaluation had its supporters within the Indian government too.

Although India's foreign policy was based on the refusal to recognize the logic of blocs, the Indian government did not hesitate to take advantage of the East-West confrontation to mobilize aid from both superpowers, implying that if assistance was lacking or taking too long to come, it might rely for support on the opposite camp. This ability of India to obtain aid from both superpowers, from the mid-1950s, constituted a remarkable trump card in the face of a growing dependence on foreign aid. Apart from a few accommodations India did not allow itself to be dictated to on its fundamentals and continued to pursue its policy goals without unduly jeopardizing its national development.

Appendices

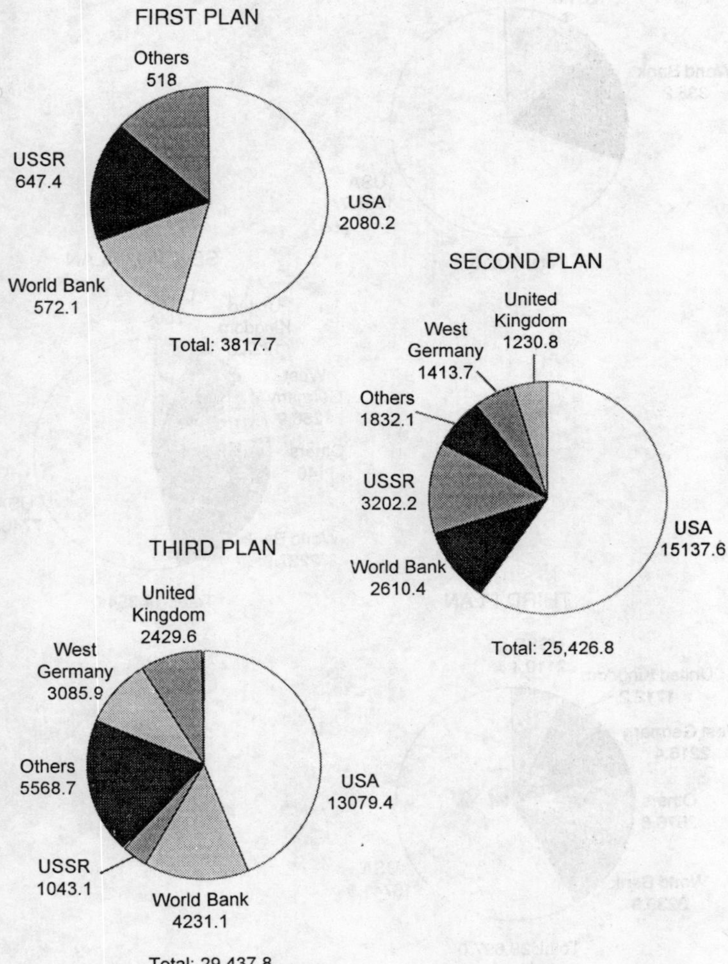

Source: Ministry of Finance, Government of India, *External Assistance 1965-66*, Appendix II, pp. 168-71.

FIGURE 1: AID AUTHORIZATION DURING THE FIRST THREE FIVE YEAR PLANS (in million of rupees)

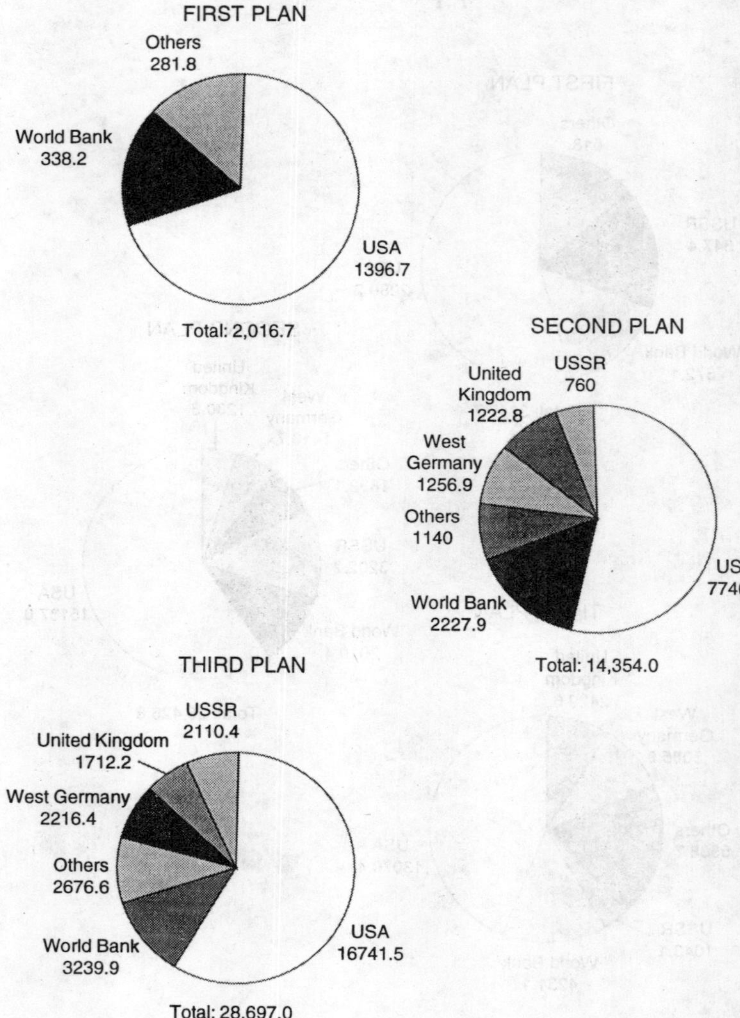

Source : Ministry of Finance, Government of India, *External Assistance 1965-66*, Appendix II, pp. 168-72.

FIGURE 2: AID UTILIZATION DURING THE FIRST THREE FIVE YEAR PLANS
(in million of rupees)

American Aid to India, 1946-66

(*US Fiscal Years —$ millions*)

Programme	US Overseas Loans And Grants —Net Obligations And Loan Authorizations											
	Post-war Relief Period	Marshall Plan Period	Mutual Security Act Period				Foreign Assistance Period					
	1946-8	1949-52	1953-7	1958	1959	1960	1961	1962	1963	1964	1965	1966
AID and predecessor agencies—total	-	57.3	342.5	89.8	137.0	194.5	200.8	465.5	397.2	336.5	264.6	308.9
Loans	-	-	130.0	75.0	120.0	171.3	180.1	445.9	392.3	330.6	255.8	299.4
Grants	-	57.3	212.5	14.8	17.0	23.3	20.7	19.6	4.9	5.9	8.8	9.5
Food For Peace—Total	-	0.6	357.9	65.0	229.0	517.7	311.8	271.5	272.0	290.0	415.2	595.4
Title I—(Total Sales Agreements)	(-)	(-)	(349.8)	(50.0)	(237.9)	(584.1)	(328.2)	(274.1)	(288.6)	(287.8)	(426.7)	(685.6)
Less: (Planned for US Uses)	(-)	(-)	(74.3)	(5.6)	(28.3)	(78.5)	(35.1)	(28.8)	(30.2)	(30.2)	(42.7)	(137.1)
Title I—Planned For Loans And Grants	-	-	275.5	44.4	209.6	505.6	293.1	245.3	258.4	257.6	384.0	548.5
Grants for Economic Development	-	-	54.1	-	37.5	253.6	140.0	101.0	101.0	101.0	-	-
Loans to Private Industry	-	-	-	12.4	58.8	29.1	16.4	12.2	14.5	14.5	42.7	34.3
Loans to Governments	-	-	221.4	32.1	113.4	222.9	136.7	132.0	142.9	142.1	341.4	514.2
Title I – Third Country Assistance	-	-	-	4.0	-	2.1	-	-	-	-	-	-
Title II – Emergency Relief and Economic Development	-	-	4.9	-	-	-	0.3	3.4	-	7.9	3.4	20.9
Title III – Voluntary Relief Agencies	-	0.6	77.5	17.6	19.4	10.0	18.4	22.8	13.6	24.5	27.8	26.0
Export-import Bank Long-term Loans	-	-	-	151.8	-	13.6	79.5	25.7	35.6	57.2	38.2	-
Other US Economic Programmes	39.9	190.8	-	-	-	-	-	0.4	1.0	1.7	3.2	8.9
Total Economic	39.9	248.7	700.4	307.6	366.0	725.9	592.1	763.1	705.8	685.4	721.2	913.1
Loans	39.9	190.2	351.4	271.3	292.2	436.9	412.7	615.8	585.3	544.4	678.1	847.9
Grants	-	58.5	349.0	36.4	73.9	289.0	179.4	147.2	120.5	141.0	43.2	65.3

(contd.)

American Aid to India, 1946-66 (contd.)

(US Fiscal Years —$ millions)

Programme	US Overseas Loans And Grants —Net Obligations And Loan Authorizations											
	Post-war Relief Period	Marshall Plan Period	Mutual Security Act Period				Foreign Assistance Period					
	1946-8	1949-52	1953-7	1958	1959	1960	1961	1962	1963	1964	1965	1966
Military Assistance	-	-	-	-	-	-	-	-	-	-	114.8	7.1
Credit Sales	-	-	-	-	-	-	-	-	-	-	27.7	-
Grants	-	-	-	-	-	-	-	-	-	-	87.1	7.1
Transfers From Excess Stocks	-	-	-	-	-	-	-	-	-	-	7.4	-
Total Military Programmes	-	-	-	-	-	-	-	-	-	-	122.2	7.1

Notes: - Excludes $20.0 million loan in FY 1958 financed by Asian Economic Development Fund.
- Includes the utilization during FY 1946 of $ 29.2 million of lend-lease silver credits.

Source: USAID (United States Agency for International Development), New Delhi.

Abbreviations

AQO	:	Archives du Quai d'Orsay
AIC	:	Aid to India Club
AICC	:	All India Congress Committee
AID	:	Agency for International Development
CPI	:	Communist Party of India
CPC	:	Communist Party of China
CPSU	:	Communist Party of the Soviet Union
DLF	:	Development Loan Fund
ECA	:	Economic Cooperation Administration
ECAFE	:	Economic Commission for Asia and the Far East
FICCI	:	Federation of Indian Chambers of Commerce and Industry
FRUS	:	Foreign Relations of the United States
IBRD	:	International Bank for Reconstruction and Development
IAF	:	Indian Air Force
ICA	:	International Cooperation Administration
IDA	:	International Development Association
IMF	:	International Monetary Fund
INC	:	Indian National Congress
MAP	:	Military Assistance Programme
MEA	:	Ministry of External Affairs
MSP	:	Mutual Security Programme
NEFA	:	North East Frontier Agency
NDC	:	National Development Council
PRC	:	People's Republic of China
PRO	:	Public Record Office
RBI	:	Reserve Bank of India
UK	:	United Kingdom
UNGA	:	United Nations General Assembly
UNRRA	:	United Nations Relief and Rehabilitation Administration
VOA	:	Voice of America

Bibliography

PRIMARY SOURCES

Archival Documents

Archives Du Quai D'orsay, Ministère des Affaires Etrangères, Paris
Asie-Océanie, 1947-1955, Inde
Asie-Océanie, 1956-1967, Inde
Nations-Unies et Organisations Internationales, 1945-1959
Nations-Unies et Organisations Internationales, 1960-1965
British Public Record Office, Kew Gardens, London
Record of the Foreign and Commonwealth Relations Office, FO 371
Department of State, *Foreign Relations of the United States*, Washington, D.C. Department of State Publication, US Government Printing Office:
1941, vol. 3, British Commonwealth, Near East and Africa, 1959.
1942, vol. 1, General, British Commonwealth, Far East, 1960.
1943, vol. 4, Near East and Africa, 1964.
1944, vol. 5, Near East, South Asia and Africa, Far East, 1965.
1945, vol. 6, British Commonwealth, Far East, 1969.
1946, vol. 5, British Commonwealth, Western and Central Europe, 1969.
1947, vol. 3, British Commonwealth, Europe, 1972.
1948, vol. 5, Near East, South Asia and Africa, part 1, 1975.
1949, vol. 6, Near East, South Asia and Africa, 1977.
1950, vol. 1, National Security Affairs, Foreign Economic Policy, 1977.
1950, vol. 5, Near East, South Asia and Africa, 1978.
1951, vol. 1, National Security Affairs, Foreign Economic Policy, 1979.
1951, vol. 6, Africa and South Asia, part 2, 1977.
1952-1954, vol. 11, Africa and South Asia, part 2, 1983.
1955-1957, vol. 8, South Asia, 1987.
1958-1960, vol. 15, South and Southeast Asia, 1992.
1961-1963, vol. 19, South Asia, 1996.
1964-1968, vol. 25, South Asia, 2000.
Cold War International History Project, Woodrow International Center for Scholars *http//:cwihp.si.edu/cwihplib.nsf*

COLLECTION OF DOCUMENTS

Bright, Jagat S. (ed.), *Important Speeches of Jawaharlal Nehru: From 1922 to 1945*, Lahore: The Indian Printing Works, 1945.

Das, Durga (ed.), *Sardar Patel's Correspondence 1945-1950*, vol. 10, Ahmedabad: Navajivan Publishing House, 1974.

Foreign Policy of India: Texts of Documents, 1947-1959, Delhi: Lok Sabha Secretariat, December 1959.

INC (Indian National Congress), *Resolutions on Economic Policy, Programme and Allied Matters (1924-1969)*, Delhi: All India Congress Committee, 1969.

Jain, Rajendra K. (ed.), *US-South Asian Relations, 1947-1982*, vol. 1 (Kashmir Question 1947-1964 and India 1947-1982), Delhi: Radiant Publishers, 1983.

Jain, Rajendra K. (ed.), *Soviet-South Asian Relations, 1947-1978*, vol. 1 (Kashmir Question 1952-1964, Kutch Conflict, Indo-Pak War of 1965, Bangladesh Crisis and Indo-Pak War of 1971, India), Delhi: Radiant Publishers, 1978.

Ministry of Finance, Department of Economic Affairs, Government of India, *External Assistance during the First Five-Year Plan*, Delhi: Government of India Press, 1956.

Ministry of Finance, Department of Economic Affairs, Government of India, *External Assistance* (annual publication from 1958 onwards).

Ministry of Finance, Department of Economic Affairs, Government of India, *Report of the Committee on Utilisation of External Assistance*, Delhi, 1964.

Ministry of Finance, Department of Economic Affairs, Government of India, *Economic Survey* (annual publication).

Nehru, Jawaharlal, *India's Foreign Policy, Selected Speeches, September 1946-April 1961*, Delhi: The Publications Division, Ministry of Information and Broadcasting, GOI, 1961.

Nehru, Jawaharlal, *Letters to Chief Ministers, 1947-1964*, Delhi: Oxford University Press:
vol. 1 (1947-1949), 1985.
vol. 2 (1950-1952), 1986.
vol. 3 (1952-1954), 1987.
vol. 4 (1954-1957), 1988.
vol. 5 (1958-1964), 1989.

Nehru, Jawaharlal, *Press Conferences 1951, 1952, 1953, 1954, 1962*, Delhi: Information Service of India.

Nehru, Jawaharlal, *The Unity of India* (*Collected Writings, 1937-1940*), London: Lindsay Drummond, 1941.

Jawaharlal Nehru's Speeches, Delhi: Publications Division, Ministry of Information and Broadcasting, GOI:

vol. 1 (September 1946–May 1949), 1949
vol. 2 (August 1949–February 1953), 1954.
vol. 3 (March 1953–August 1951), 1953.
vol. 4 (September 1957–April 1963), 1964
vol. 5 (March 1963–May 1964), 1968.

Selected Works of Jawaharlal Nehru, Delhi: Orient Longman:
vol. 10 (15 July 1939–3 March 1940), 1977.
vol. 11 (4 March 1940–3 December 1941), 1978.
vol. 12 (4 December 1941–8 August 1942), 1979.
vol. 13 (9 August 1942–15 June 1945), 1980.
vol. 14 (15 June 1945–18 February 1946), 1981.
vol. 15 (19 February 1946–1 September 1946), 1982.

Selected Works of Jawaharlal Nehru (*second series*), Delhi: Jawaharlal Nehru Memorial Fund:
vol. 1 (2 September 1946–31 January 1947), 1984.
vol. 2 (1 February 1947–31 May 1947), 1984.
vol. 3 (1 June 1947–15 August 1947), 1985.
vol. 4 (15 August 1947–31 December 1947), 1986.
vol. 5 (1 January 1948–6 April 1948), 1987.
vol. 6 (7 April 1948–30 June 1948), 1987.
vol. 7 (1 July 1948–5 October 1948), 1988.
vol. 8 (6 October 1948–19 December 1948), 1989.
vol. 9 (20 December 1948–15 February 1949), 1990.
vol. 10 (16 February 1949–30 April 1949), 1990.
vol. 11 (1 May1949–20 June 1949), 1991.
vol. 12 (21 June 1949–15 August 1949), 1991.
vol. 13 (16 August 1949–14 November 1949), 1992.
vol. 14 part 1 (15 November 1949–8 April 1950), 1992.
vol. 14 part 2 (8 April–31 July 1950), 1993.
vol. 15 part 1 (1 August–25 October 1950), 1993.
vol. 15 part 2 (26 October 1950–28 February 1951), 1993.
vol. 16 part 1 (1 March–30 June 1951), 1994.
vol. 16 part 2 (1 July–31 October 1951), 1994.
vol. 17 (1 November 1951–31 March 1952), 1995.
vol. 18 (1 April 1952–15 July 1952), 1996.
vol. 19 (16 July 1952–18 October 1952), 1996.
vol. 20 (19 October 1952–31 December 1952), 1997.
vol. 21 (1 January 1953–31 March 1953), 1997.
vol. 22 (1 April 1953–30 June 1953), 1998.
vol. 23 (1 July 1953–30 September 1953), 1998.
vol. 24 (1 October 1953–31 January 1954), 1999.
vol. 25 (1 February 1954–31 May 1954), 1999.
vol. 26 (1 June 1954–30 September 1954), 2000.
vol. 27 (1 October 1954–31 January 1955), 2000.

vol. 28 (1 February 1955–31 May 1955), 2001.
vol. 29 (1 June –31 August 1955), 2001.
vol. 30 (1 September–17 November 1955), 2002.
vol. 31 (18 November 1955–31 January 1956), 2002.

Planning Commission, Government of India, *First Five-Year Plan*, Delhi: Publications Divisions, Ministry of Information and Broadcasting, repr. 1991 [1953].

Planning Commission, Government of India, *Review of the First Five-Year Plan*, Delhi: Government of India Press, 1957.

Planning Commission, Government of India, *Second Five-Year Plan*, Delhi: GOI Press, repr. 1991 [1956].

Planning Commission, Government of India, *Appraisal and Prospects of the Second Five-Year Plan*, Delhi: GOI Press, May 1958.

Planning Commission, Government of India, *Third Five-Year Plan*, Delhi: GOI Press, 1961.

Planning Commission, Government of India, *Third Five-Year Plan, Mid-Term Appraisal*, Delhi: GOI Press, November 1963.

Planning Commission, Government of India, *Fourth Five-Year Plan. Resources, Outlays and Programmes*, Delhi: GOI Press, September 1965.

Planning Commission, Statistics and Surveys Division, Government of India, *Basic Statistics Relating to the Indian Economy. 1950-51 to 1966-67*, Delhi: GOI Press, December 1968.

Planning Commission, Statistics and Surveys Division, Government of India, *Basic Statistics Relating to the Indian Economy. 1950-51 to 1970-71*, Delhi, GOI Press, December 1972.

Reserve Bank of India, *India's Balance of Payments, 1948-49 to 1961-62*, Bombay: Reserve Bank of India, 1963.

Constituent Assembly (Legislative) Debates.

Lok Sabha Debates.

Parliamentary Debates.

Rajya Sabha Debates.

MEMOIRS AND AUTOBIOGRAPHIES

Bhoothalingam, Subramanya, *Reflections on an Era: Memoirs of a Civil Servant*, Delhi: Affiliated East-West Press, 1993.

Bowles, Chester, *Ambassador's Report*, New York: Harper & Brothers, 1954.

Bowles, Chester, *A View from New Delhi*, Delhi: Allied Publishers, 1969.

Bowles, Chester, *Promises to Keep*, Delhi: B.I. Publications, 1972.

Chagla, M.C., *Roses in December*, Bombay: Bharatiya Vidya Bhavan, 1973.

Deshmukh, C.D, *The Course of My Life*, Delhi: Orient Longman, 1974.

Dutt, Subimal, *With Nehru in the Foreign Office*, Calcutta: Minerva Associates, 1977.

Eisenhower, Dwight D., *The White House Years, vol. 2: Waging Peace 1956-1961*, New York: Doubleday, 1965.

Galbraith, John Kenneth, *Ambassador's Journal*, London: Hamish Hamilton, 1969.

Gundevia, Y.D., *Outside the Archives*, Hyderabad: Sangam Books, 1984.

James, Morrice, *Pakistan Chronicle*, London: Hurst, 1992.

Kaul, T.N., *Diplomacy in Peace and War*, Delhi: Vikas Publishing House, 1979.

Kaul T.N., *Reminiscences—Discreet and Indiscreet,* Delhi: Lancers Publishers, 1982.

Talbott, Strobe (ed.), *Khrushchev Remembers. The Last Testament*, Boston: Little, Brown & Co., 1974.

McGhee, George, *Envoy to the Middle World*, New York: Harper & Row, 1969.

Menon, K.P.S., *The Flying Troika*, Bombay: Oxford University Press, 1963.

Nehru, B.K., *Nice Guys Finish Second*, Delhi: Viking, 1997.

Nehru, Jawaharlal, *Soviet Russia*, Bombay: Chetana, repr. 1949 [1929].

Nehru, Jawaharlal, *Glimpses of World History*, Delhi: Oxford University Press, 1982 [first published in two vols. 1934-5].

Nehru, Jawaharlal, *The Discovery of India*, Delhi: Oxford University Press, 1981 [1946].

Palit, D.K., *War in High Himalaya, the Indian Army in Crisis, 1962*, Delhi: Lancer International, 1991.

Pradhan, R.D., *Debacle to Revival, Y.B. Chavan as Defence Minister 1962-1965*, Delhi: Orient Longman, 1998.

Reid, Escott, *Envoy to Nehru*, Delhi: Oxford University Press, 1981.

Subramaniam, C., *Hand of Destiny, vol. 2: The Green Revolution*, Bombay, Bharatiya Vidya Bhavan, 1995.

NEWSPAPERS AND MAGAZINES

A.I.C.C. Economic Weekly (Delhi)
Amrita Bazar Patrika (Calcutta)
Asian Recorder (Delhi)
Commerce (Bombay)
Eastern Economist (Delhi)
Economic Weekly (Bombay, *The Economic and Political Weekly* from 1965 onwards)
Hindu (Madras)
Hindustan Times (Delhi)
Le Monde (Paris)
New Times (Moscow)
New York Times (New York)
Statesman (Delhi)
Times of India (Bombay)

SECONDARY SOURCES

BOOKS

Agrawal, A.N., *Industrial Problems of India*, Delhi: Ranjit, 1956 [3rd ed.].

Agarwal, Sushila, *Super Powers and the Third World*, Jaipur: Aalekh, 1985.

Akbar, M.J., *Nehru: The Making of India*, London: Viking, 1988.

Appadorai, A., *The Domestic Roots of India's Foreign Policy, 1947-1972*, Delhi: Oxford University Press, 1981.

Appadorai, A. and M.S. Rajan, *India's Foreign Policy and Relations*, Delhi: South Asian Publishers, 1985.

Arora, U.K. and A. Appadorai, *India in World Affairs, 1957-1958*, Delhi: Sterling, 1975.

Balachandran, G., *The Reserve Bank of India 1951-1967*, Delhi: Oxford University Press, 1998.

Barnds, William J., *India, Pakistan and the Great Powers*, London: Pall Mall Press.

Bauer, P.T., *Indian Economic Policy and Development*, London: George Allen & Unwin, 1961.

Berliner, Joseph S., *Soviet Economic Aid*, New York: Frederick A. Praeger, 1958.

Bettelheim, Charles, *L'Inde Indépendante*, Paris: Armand Colin, 1962.

Bhagwati, Jagdish and Padma Desai, *India. Planning for Industrialization: Industrialization and Trade Policies since 1951*, Delhi: Oxford University Press, 1970.

Bhatia, B.M., *India's Food Problem & Policy since Independence*, Bombay: Somaiya, 1970.

Bhatia, H.L., *Does Foreign Aid Help?*, Delhi: Allied Publishers, 1981.

Brecher, Michael, *Nehru. A Political Biography*, London: Oxford University Press, 1959.

Brecher, Michael, *India and World Politics: Krishna Menon's View of the World*, London: Oxford University Press, 1968.

Burke, S.M., and Lawrence Ziring, *Pakistan's Foreign Policy: An Historical Analysis*, Karachi: Oxford University Press, 1990 [2nd ed.].

Carter, James R., *The Net Cost of Soviet Foreign Aid*, New York: Frederick A. Praeger, 1969.

Chakravarty, Sukhamoy, *Development Planning. The Indian Experience*, Delhi: Oxford University Press, 1987.

Chandrasekhar, S., *American Aid and India's Economic Development*, New York: Frederick A. Praeger, 1965.

Chaturshreni, Ved Vati, *Indo-US Relations*, Delhi: National Publishing House, 1980.

Clarkson, Stephen, *L'Analyse Soviétique des Problèmes Indiens du Sous-Développement, 1955-1964*, Paris: Mouton, 1970.

Dagli, Vadilal (ed.), *Two Decades of Indo-US Relations*, Bombay: Vora & Co., 1969.

Dagli, Vadilal (ed.), *Indo-Soviet Economic Relations*, Bombay: Vora & Co., 1971.

Desai, Padma, *The Bokaro Steel Plant: A Case Study of Soviet Economic Assistance*, Amsterdam: North Holland Publishing Co., 1972..

Donaldson, Robert H., *Soviet Policy toward India. Ideology and Strategy*, Cambridge: Harvard University Press, 1974.

Duroselle, Jean-Baptiste, *Histoire Diplomatique de 1919 à nos Jours*, Paris: Dalloz, 1978 [7th ed.].

Eldridge, P. J., *The Politics of Foreign Aid in India*, Delhi: Vikas, 1969.

Feis, Herbert, *Foreign Aid and Foreign Policy*, London: Macmillan & Co., 1964.

Frankel, Francine, *India's Political Economy, 1947-1977*, Delhi: Oxford University Press, 1984 [1st ed. 1978].

Fontaine, André, *Histoire de la Guerre Froide, vol. 1: De la Révolution d'Octobre à la Guerre de Corée (1917-1950)*, Paris: Fayard, 1966.

Fontaine, André, *Histoire de la Guerre Froide, vol. 2. De la Guerre de Corée à la Crise des Alliances (1950-1967)*, Paris: Fayard, 1967.

Gill, Sucha Singh, *Political Economy of Indo-Soviet Relations, 1947-1980*, Delhi: Rajesh Publications, 1983.

Goldman, Marshall I., *Soviet Foreign Aid*, New York: Frederick A. Praeger, 1967.

Gopal, Sarvepalli, *Jawaharlal Nehru: A Biography, vol. 1: 1889-1947*, Delhi: Oxford Uuniversity Press, 1976.

Gopal, Sarvepalli, *Jawaharlal Nehru: A Biography, vol. 2: 1947-1956*, Delhi: Oxford University Press, 1979.

Gopal, Sarvepalli, *Jawaharlal Nehru: A Biography, vol. 3: 1956-1964*, Delhi: Oxford University Press, 1984.

Gopal, Sarvepalli, *Radhakrishnan: A Biography*, Delhi: Oxford University Press, 1989.

Gregory, Theodore, *India on the Eve of the Third Five Year Plan*, Calcutta: The Associated Chambers of Commerce, 1961.

Grover, Verinder (ed.), *USA and India's Foreign Policy*, Delhi: Deep & Deep, 1992.

Grover, Verinder (ed.), *USSR and India's Foreign Policy*, Delhi: Deep & Deep, 1992.

Gupta, Surendra K., *Stalin's Policy towards India, 1946-1953*, Delhi: South Asian Publishers, 1988.

Hanson, A.H, *The Process of Planning*, London: Oxford University Press, 1966.

Harrison, Selig S, *India and the United States*, New York: The Macmillan Co., 1961.

Hartmann, Horst, *Political Parties in India*, Meerut: Meenakshi Prakashan, 1982.

Hazari, R.K. and S.D. Mehta, *Public International Development Financing in India*, Bombay: Asian Studies Press, 1968.

Hess, R., *America Encounters India, 1941-1947*, Baltimore: The John Hopkins Press, 1971.

Hoffman, Steven A., *India and the China Crisis*, Delhi: Oxford University Press, 1990.

Imam, Zafar, *Ideology and Reality in Soviet Policy in Asia*, Delhi: Kalyani, 1975.

Indian-American Relations, Proceedings of the India-America Conference held in New Delhi in December 1949, Delhi: Oxford University Press, 1950.

Jain, B.M., *India and the United States, 1961-1963*, Delhi: Radiant, 1987.

Johansen, Robert C., *The National Interest and the Human Interest—An Analysis of US Foreign Policy,* Princeton: Princeton University Press, 1980.

Joshi, Nirmala, *Foundations of Indo-Soviet Relations*, Delhi: Radiant, 1975.

Karunakaran, K.P., *India in World Affairs, August 1947–January 1950*, London: Oxford University Press, 1952.

Karunakaran, K.P., *India in World Affairs, February 1950–December 1953*, Calcutta: Oxford University Press, 1958.

Kaul, Hriday Nath, *K. D. Malaviya and the Evolution of India's Oil Policy*, Delhi: Allied Publishers, 1991.

Kaushik, Devendra, *Soviet Relations with India and Pakistan*, Delhi: Vikas, 1974.

Kavic, Lorne, *India's Quest for Security: Defence Policies, 1947-1965*, Berkeley: University of California Press, 1967.

Kidron, Michael, *Foreign Investments in India*, London: Oxford University Press, 1965.

Kidwai, Saleem, *Indo-Soviet Relations*, Delhi: Rima, 1985.

Kothari, Rajni, *Politics in India*, Delhi: Orient Longman, 1985 [1st ed. 1970].

Krupadanam, B.J.B., *Food Diplomacy—A Case Study: Indo-US Relations*, Delhi: Lancers Books, 1985.

Kulkarni, Maya, *Indo-Soviet Political Relations*, Bombay: Vora & Co., 1968.

Kulkarni, V.G. (compiled by), *Statistical Outline of Indian Economy*, Bombay: Vora & Co., 1968.

Kunhi Krishnan, T.V., *The Unfriendly Friends—India and America*, Delhi: Indian Book Co., 1974.

Kux, Dennis, *Estranged Democracies. India and the United States, 1941-1991*, Delhi: Sage Publications, 1993.

Lewis, John P., *Quiet Crisis in India*, Washington: The Brookings Institution, 1962.

Little, I.M.D. and J.M. Clifford, *International Aid*, London: George Allen & Unwin, 1965.

Longer, V., *The Defence and Foreign Policies of India*, Delhi: Sterling, 1988.

Mahajan, Harpeet, *Arms Transfer to India, Pakistan and the Third World*, Delhi: Young Asia, 1982.

Mahalanobis, P.C., *The Approach of Operational Research to Planning in India*, Bombay: Asia Publishing House, 1963.

Mahmud, Farhat, *A History of US-Pakistan Relations*, Lahore: Vanguard, 1991.

Mahmud Ali, S., *Cold War in the High Himalayas —The USA, China and South Asia in the 1950s*, Richmond: Curzon Press, 1999.

Mason, Edward S., *Foreign Aid and Foreign Policy*, New York: Harper & Row, 1964.

Mehrotra, Santosh, *India and Soviet Union: Trade and Technology Transfer,* Delhi: Oxford University Press, 1991.

Mehta, Vinod, *Soviet Union and India's Industrial Development*, Delhi: Manas, 1975.

Mende, Tibor, *De l'Aide à la Recolonisation*, Paris: Points Seuil, 1979 [1st ed. 1972].

Merrill, Dennis, *Bread and the Ballot—The United States and India's Economic Development, 1947-1963*, Chapel Hill and London: The University of North Carolina Press, 1990.

Mishra, Sudhakanta, *The Role of Foreign Capital in Under-Developed Economies*, Allahabad: Kitab Mahal, 1967.

Montgomery, John D., *Foreign Aid in International Politics*, Delhi: Allied Publishers, 1969.

Mudumbai, Srinivas C., *United States Foreign Policy towards India, 1947-1954,* Delhi: Manohar, 1980.

Mukherji, Sadhan, *India's Economic Relations with USA and USSR*, Delhi: Sterling, 1978.

Muller, Kurt, *The Foreign Aid Programs of the Soviet Bloc and Communist China. An Analysis*, New York: Walker & Co., 1967.

Naik, J.A., *Soviet Policy towards India*, Delhi: Vikas, 1970.

Natarajan, L., *American Shadow over India*, Bombay: People's Publishing House, 1952.

NCAER (National Council of Applied Economic Research), *Development without Aid*, Delhi: NCAER, 1966.

Nehru, Jawaharlal, *Inside America*, Delhi: Malhotra, 1950.

Nehru, Jawaharlal, *Visit to America*, New York: The John Day Co., 1950.

Patel, I.G., *Foreign Aid*, Delhi: Allied Publishers, 1968.

Patwardhan, M.S., *Oil and Other Multinationals in India,* Bombay: Popular Prakashan, 1986.

Pavlov, V.I., *India. Economic Freedom versus Imperialism*, Delhi: People's Publishing House, 1963.

Pouchepadass, Jacques, *L'Inde au XXe Siècle,* Paris: Presses Universitaires de France, 1975.

Prasad, Devki Nandan, *Food for Peace—The Story of US Food Assistance to India*, Bombay: Asia Publishing House, 1980.

Rajan, M.S., *India in World Affairs, 1954-1956*, London: Asia Publishing House, 1964.

Rangnekar, D.K., *Poverty and Capital Development in India*, London: Oxford University Press, 1958.

Ranis, Gustav (ed.), *The United States and the Developing Economies*, New York: W.W. Norton & Co., 1964.

Rao, V.K.R.V. and Dharm Narain, *Foreign Aid and India's Economic Development*, Delhi: Asia Publishing House, 1963.

Ray, Hemen, *Indo-Soviet Relations, 1955-1971*, Bombay: Jaico, 1973.

Ray, S.S., *The Red Star and the Lotus*, Delhi: Konark Publishers, 1990.

Remnek, Richard B., *Soviet Policy Towards India*, Delhi: Oxford & IBH Publishing Co., 1975.

Rosinger, Lawrence K., *India and the United States: Political and Economic Relations*, New York: The Macmillan Co., 1950.

Rostow, Walt Whitman, *Eisenhower, Kennedy and Foreign Aid*, Austin: University of Texas Press, 1985.

Rubinstein, Alvin Z., *The Soviets in International Organizations*, Princeton: Princeton University Press, 1964.

Sahai, Jitendra, *Dollar in India*, Delhi: National Publishing House, 1982.

Schaffer, Howard B., *Chester Bowles—New Dealer in the Cold War*, Delhi: Prentice-Hall of India, 1994.

Sengupta, Bhabani, *The Fulcrum of Asia—Relations among China, India, Pakistan and the USSR*, Delhi: Konark, 1988.

Sharma, R.K., *Foreign Aid to India*, Delhi: Marwah, 1977.

Sharma, R.K. (ed.), *Indo-Soviet Cooperation and India's Economic Development*, Delhi: Allied Publishers, 1982.

Singh, S.P., *Political Dimensions of India-USSR Relations*, Delhi: Allied Publishers.

Shirokov, G.K., *Industrialisation of India*, Delhi: People's Publishing House, 1980.

Simha, S.L.N. (prepared by), *History of the Reserve Bank of India (1935-51),* Bombay: Reserve Bank of India, 1970.

Singh, L.P., *India's Foreign Policy. The Shastri Period*, Delhi: Uppal, 1980.

Srivastava, C.P., *Lal Bahadur Shastri: A Life of Truth in Politics*, Delhi: Oxford University Press, 1995.

Stanislaus, M. Sebastian, *Soviet Economic Aid to India*, Delhi: N.V. Publications, 1975.

Stein, Arthur, *India and the Soviet Union*, Chicago: University of Chicago Press, 1969.

Stillman, J. Peter, *Foreign Aid, Ideology and Bureaucratic Politics: The Bokaro Steel Mill and Indian-American Relations*, University of Columbia, Ph.D., 1975.

Taneja, S.K., *India and International Monetary Management*, Delhi: Sterling, 1976.

Tansky, Leo, *US and USSR Aid to Developing Countries*, New York: Frederick A. Praeger, 1967.

Tewari, Madan Mohan, *External Resources and Economic Development in India* (*with Special Reference to US Aid*), Delhi: B.R. Publishing Corporation, 1982.

Venkataramani, M.S., *Bengal Famine of 1943: The American Response*, Delhi: Vikas, 1973.

Venkataramani, M.S. and B.K. Shrivastava, *Quit India: The American Response to the 1942 Struggle*, Delhi: Vikas Publishing House, 1979.

Wallerstein, Mitchel B., *Food for War—Food for Peace: United States Food Aid in a Global Context,* Cambridge: The MIT Press, 1980.

Walters, Robert S., *American and Soviet Aid*, University of Pittsburgh Press, 1970.

Wolf, Charles, *Foreign Aid—Theory and Practice in Southern Asia*, Princeton: Princeton University Press, 1960.

Zins, Max Jean, *Histoire Politique de l'Inde Indépendante*, Paris: Presses Universitaires de France, 1992.

ARTICLES

Achutan, Nisha Sahai, 'Soviet Arms Transfer Policy in South Asia, 1955-1981', *IDSA Journal*, vol. 19, no. 3, January-March 1987, pp. 409-588.

Balasubramanyan, V., 'President Truman's "Point Four", *India Quarterly*, vol. 6, no. 1, January-March 1950, pp. 67-84.

Bowles, Chester. 'America and Russia in India', *Foreign Affairs*, July 1971, vol. 49, no. 4, pp. 636-51.

Brecher, Michael, 'India's Decisions on the Voice of America: A Study in Resolution', *Asian Survey*, vol. 14, no. 7, July 1974, pp. 637-50.

Brodkin, E.I., 'United States Aid to India and Pakistan: The Attitude of the Fifties', *International Affairs*, vol. 43, no. 4, October 1967, pp. 664-77.

Chari, P.R, 'Indo-Soviet Military Cooperation : A Review', *Asian Survey*, vol. 19, no. 3, March 1979, pp. 230-44.

Cohen, Stephen P., 'US Weapons & South Asia—A Policy Analysis', *Pacific Affairs*, vol. 49, no. 1, Spring 1976, pp. 49-69.

Feis, Herbert, 'Political Aspects of Foreign Loans', *Foreign Affairs*, vol. 23, no. 4, July 1945, pp. 609-19.

Galbraith, J.K., 'A Positive Approach to Economic Aid', *Foreign Affairs*, vol. 39, no. 3, April 1961, pp. 444-57.

Ganguly, Shivaji, 'US Military Assistance to India, 1962-1963: A Study in Decision-Making', *India Quarterly*, vol. 28., no. 3, July-September 1972, pp. 216-26.

'Government Foreign Debt', *Tata Quarterly*, vol. 21, no. 1, January 1966, pp. 1-19.

Graham, Ian C.C., 'The Indo-Soviet Mig Deal & Its International Repercussions', *Asian Survey*, vol. 4, no. 5, May 1964, pp. 823-32.

Harrison, Selig S., 'India, Pakistan and the United States', *New Republic*, 10 August, 1959 (pp. 10-17), 24 August, 1959 (pp. 20-5), 7 September, 1959 (pp. 11-17).

Harrison, Selig S., 'Troubled India and Her Neighbours', *Foreign Affairs*, vol. 43, no. 2, January 1965, pp. 312-30.

Hasan, Zubeida, 'Soviet Arms Aid to India and Pakistan', *Pakistan Horizon*, vol. 21, no. 4, 1968, pp. 344-55.

Ilchman, Warren F., 'A Political Economy of Foreign Aid: The Case of India', *Asian Survey*, vol. 7, no. 10, October 1967, pp. 667-88.

Kapur, Ashok, 'Indo-Soviet Military Relations: Dependency, Inter-Dependency and Uncertainties', *India Quarterly*, vol. 33, no. 3, July-September 1977, pp. 263-80.

Lokanathan, P.S., 'The Bombay Plan', *Foreign Affairs*, vol. 23, no. 4, July 1945, pp. 680-6.

Lokanathan, P.S., 'Indo-American Economic Relations', *India Quarterly*, vol. 2, no. 1, January 1946, pp. 11-17.

Loomba, Joanne F., 'US Aid to India, 1951-1967: A Study in Decision-Making', *India Quarterly*, vol. 28, no. 4, October-December 1972, pp. 304-31.

Maheshwari, B., 'Bokaro: The Politics of American Aid', *International Studies*, vol. 10, July 1968–April 1969, pp. 162-80.

Millikan, M.F. and W.W. Rostow, 'Foreign Aid: The Next Phase', *Foreign Affairs*, vol. 36, no. 3, April 1958, pp. 418-36.

Mukherjee, Aditya, 'The Controversy over India's Sterling Balances, 1939-1947', *Studies in History*, vol. 6, no. 2, n.s., 1990, pp. 229-51.

'The Soviet Connection', *Seminar*, 265, September 1981, pp. 9-47.

Venkataramani, M.S., 'The US Senate Committee on Foreign Relations and India 1958-1959', *India Quarterly*, vol. 16, no. 1, January-March 1960, pp. 51-61.

Venkataramani, M.S., 'The Soviet Union and the Indian Food Crisis of 1946', *International Studies*, vol. 4, no. 4, April 1963, pp. 395-403.

Zins, Max Jean, 'British Perceptions of India's External Policy, 1947-1953', *International Studies*, vol. 24, no. 1, January-March 1987, pp. 25-44.

Index